# THE ART OF

# PUBLIC
# SPEAKING

# THE ART OF
# PUBLIC
# SPEAKING

Dale Carnegie

J. Berg Esenwein

**FALL RIVER PRESS**

New York

## FALL RIVER PRESS

New York

An Imprint of Sterling Publishing Co., Inc.
1166 Avenue of the Americas
New York, NY 10036

*The Art of Public Speaking* originally published in 1915.
This 2019 edition published by Fall River Press.

ISBN 978-1-4351-6952-4

Distributed in Canada by Sterling Publishing Co., Inc.
c/o Canadian Manda Group, 664 Annette Street
Toronto, Ontario M6S 2C8, Canada
Distributed in the United Kingdom by GMC Distribution Services
Castle Place, 166 High Street, Lewes, East Sussex BN7 1XU, England
Distributed in Australia by NewSouth Books
University of New South Wales, Sydney, NSW 2052, Australia

For information about custom editions, special sales, and premium and
corporate purchases, please contact Sterling Special Sales at 800-805-5489
or specialsales@sterlingpublishing.com.

Manufactured in the United States of America

6 8 10 9 7 5

sterlingpublishing.com

Cover design by David Ter-Avanesyan

# *Dedication*

TO

## F. ARTHUR METCALF

FELLOW-WORKER AND FRIEND

# Table of Contents

# Things to Think of First

## A Foreword

The efficiency of a book is like that of a man, in one important respect: its attitude toward its subject is the first source of its power. A book may be full of good ideas well expressed, but if its writer views his subject from the wrong angle even his excellent advice may prove to be ineffective.

This book stands or falls by its authors' attitude toward its subject. If the best way to teach oneself or others to speak effectively in public is to fill the mind with rules, and to set up fixed standards for the interpretation of thought, the utterance of language, the making of gestures, and all the rest, then this book will be limited in value to such stray ideas throughout its pages as may prove helpful to the reader—as an effort to enforce a group of principles it must be reckoned a failure, because it is then untrue.

It is of some importance, therefore, to those who take up this volume with open mind that they should see clearly at the out-start what is the thought that at once underlies and is builded through this structure. In plain words it is this:

Training in public speaking is not a matter of externals—primarily; it is not a matter of imitation—fundamentally; it is not a matter of conformity to standards—at all. Public speaking is public utterance, public issuance, of the man himself; therefore the first thing both in time and in importance is that the man should be and think and feel things that are worthy of being given forth. Unless there be something of value within, no tricks of training can ever make of the talker anything more than a machine—albeit a highly perfected machine—for the delivery of other men's goods. So self-development is fundamental in our plan.

The second principle lies close to the first: The man must enthrone his will to rule over his thought, his feelings, and all his physical powers, so that the outer self may give perfect, unhampered expression to the inner. It is futile, we assert, to lay down systems of rules for voice culture, intonation, gesture, and what not, unless these two principles of having something to say and making the will sovereign have at least begun to make themselves felt in the life.

The third principle will, we surmise, arouse no dispute: No one can learn *how* to speak who does not first speak as best he can. That may seem like a vicious circle in statement, but it will bear examination.

Many teachers have begun with the *how*. Vain effort! It is an ancient truism that we learn to do by doing. The first thing for the beginner in public speaking is to speak—not to study voice and gesture and the rest. Once he has spoken he can improve himself by self-observation or according to the criticisms of those who hear.

But how shall he be able to criticise himself? Simply by finding out three things: What are the qualities which by common consent go to make up an effective speaker; by what means at least some of these qualities may be acquired; and what wrong habits of speech in himself work against his acquiring and using the qualities which he finds to be good.

Experience, then, is not only the best teacher, but the first and the last. But experience must be a dual thing—the experience of others must be used to supplement, correct and justify our own experience; in this way we shall become our own best critics only after we have trained ourselves in self-knowledge, the knowledge of what other minds think, and in the ability to judge ourselves by the standards we have come to believe are right. "If I ought," said Kant, "I can."

An examination of the contents of this volume will show how consistently these articles of faith have been declared, expounded, and illustrated. The student is urged to begin to speak at once of what he knows. Then he is given simple suggestions for self-control, with gradually increasing emphasis upon the power of the inner man over the outer. Next, the way to the rich storehouses of material is pointed out. And finally, all the while he is urged to speak, *speak*, *SPEAK* as he is applying to his own methods, in his own *personal* way, the principles he has gathered from his own experience and observation and the recorded experiences of others.

So now at the very first let it be as clear as light that methods are secondary matters; that the full mind, the warm heart, the dominant will are primary—and not only primary but paramount; for unless it be a full being that uses the methods it will be like dressing a wooden image in the clothes of a man.

J. Berg Esenwein
Narberth, PA
January 1, 1915

# CHAPTER I

# *Acquiring Confidence*
# *Before an Audience*

There is a strange sensation often experienced in the presence of an
audience. It may proceed from the gaze of the many eyes that turn
upon the speaker, especially if he permits himself to steadily return
that gaze. Most speakers have been conscious of this in a nameless
thrill, a real something, pervading the atmosphere, tangible, evanescent,
indescribable. All writers have borne testimony to the power of a
speaker's eye in impressing an audience. This influence which we are now
considering is the reverse of that picture—the power *their* eyes may exert
upon him, especially before he begins to speak: after the inward fires of
oratory are fanned into flame the eyes of the audience lose all terror.

—William Pittenger, *Extempore Speech*

Students of public speaking continually ask, "How can I overcome self-
consciousness and the fear that paralyzes me before an audience?"

Did you ever notice in looking from a train window that some horses feed near the track
and never even pause to look up at the thundering cars, while just ahead at the next railroad
crossing a farmer's wife will be nervously trying to quiet her scared horse as the train goes by?

How would you cure a horse that is afraid of cars—graze him in a back-woods lot
where he would never see steam-engines or automobiles, or drive or pasture him where
he would frequently see the machines?

Apply horse-sense to ridding yourself of self-consciousness and fear: face an audience as frequently as you can, and you will soon stop shying. You can never attain freedom from stage-fright by reading a treatise. A book may give you excellent suggestions
on how best to conduct yourself in the water, but sooner or later you must get wet,
perhaps even strangle and be "half scared to death." There are a great many "wetless"
bathing suits worn at the seashore, but no one ever learns to swim in them. To plunge
is the only way.

Practise, *practise*, PRACTISE in speaking before an audience will tend to remove all
fear of audiences, just as practise in swimming will lead to confidence and facility in the
water. You must learn to speak by speaking.

The Apostle Paul tells us that every man must work out his own salvation. All we can do here is to offer you suggestions as to how best to prepare for your plunge. The real plunge no one can take for you. A doctor may prescribe, but *you* must take the medicine.

Do not be disheartened if at first you suffer from stage-fright. Dan Patch was more susceptible to suffering than a superannuated dray horse would be. It never hurts a fool to appear before an audience, for his capacity is not a capacity for feeling. A blow that would kill a civilized man soon heals on a savage. The higher we go in the scale of life, the greater is the capacity for suffering.

For one reason or another, some master-speakers never entirely overcome stage-fright, but it will pay you to spare no pains to conquer it. Daniel Webster failed in his first appearance and had to take his seat without finishing his speech because he was nervous. Gladstone was often troubled with self-consciousness in the beginning of an address. Beecher was always perturbed before talking in public.

Blacksmiths sometimes twist a rope tight around the nose of a horse, and by thus inflicting a little pain they distract his attention from the shoeing process. One way to get air out of a glass is to pour in water.

## Be Absorbed by Your Subject

Apply the blacksmith's homely principle when you are speaking. If you feel deeply about your subject you will be able to think of little else. Concentration is a process of distraction from less important matters. It is too late to think about the cut of your coat when once you are upon the platform, so centre your interest on what you are about to say—fill your mind with your speech-material and, like the infilling water in the glass, it will drive out your unsubstantial fears.

Self-consciousness is undue consciousness of self, and, for the purpose of delivery, self is secondary to your subject, not only in the opinion of the audience, but, if you are wise, in your own. To hold any other view is to regard yourself as an exhibit instead of as a messenger with a message worth delivering. Do you remember Elbert Hubbard's tremendous little tract, "A Message to Garcia"? The youth subordinated himself to the message he bore. So must you, by all the determination you can muster. It is sheer egotism to fill your mind with thoughts of self when a greater thing is there—*TRUTH*. Say this to yourself sternly, and shame your self-consciousness into quiescence. If the theater caught fire you could rush to the stage and shout directions to the audience without any self-consciousness, for the importance of what you were saying would drive all fear-thoughts out of your mind.

Far worse than self-consciousness through fear of doing poorly is self-consciousness through assumption of doing well. The first sign of greatness is when a man does not attempt to look and act great. Before you can call yourself a man at all, Kipling assures us, you must "not look too good nor talk too wise."

Nothing advertises itself so thoroughly as conceit. One may be so full of self as to be empty. Voltaire said, "We must conceal self-love." But that can not be done. You know this to be true, for you have recognized overweening self-love in others. If you have it, others are seeing it in you. There are things in this world bigger than self, and in working for them self will be forgotten, or—what is better—remembered only so as to help us win toward higher things.

## Have Something to Say

The trouble with many speakers is that they go before an audience with their minds a blank. It is no wonder that nature, abhorring a vacuum, fills them with the nearest thing handy, which generally happens to be, "I wonder if I am doing this right! How does my hair look? I know I shall fail." Their prophetic souls are sure to be right.

It is not enough to be absorbed by your subject—to acquire self-confidence you must have something in which to be confident. If you go before an audience without any preparation, or previous knowledge of your subject, you ought to be self-conscious— you ought to be ashamed to steal the time of your audience. Prepare yourself. Know what you are going to talk about, and, in general, how you are going to say it. Have the first few sentences worked out completely so that you may not be troubled in the beginning to find words. Know your subject better than your hearers know it, and you have nothing to fear.

## After Preparing for Success, Expect It

Let your bearing be modestly confident, but most of all be modestly confident within. Over-confidence is bad, but to tolerate premonitions of failure is worse, for a bold man may win attention by his very bearing, while a rabbit-hearted coward invites disaster.

Humility is not the personal discount that we must offer in the presence of others—against this old interpretation there has been a most healthy modern reaction. True humility any man who thoroughly knows himself must feel; but it is not a humility that assumes a worm-like meekness; it is rather a strong, vibrant prayer for greater power for service—a prayer that Uriah Heep could never have uttered.

Washington Irving once introduced Charles Dickens at a dinner given in the latter's honor. In the middle of his speech Irving hesitated, became embarrassed, and sat down awkwardly. Turning to a friend beside him he remarked, "There, I told you I would fail, and I did."

If you believe you will fail, there is no hope for you. You will.

Rid yourself of this I-am-a-poor-worm-in-the-dust idea. You are a god, with infinite capabilities. "All things are ready if the mind be so." The eagle looks the cloudless sun in the face.

## Assume Mastery Over Your Audience

In public speech, as in electricity, there is a positive and a negative force. Either you or your audience are going to possess the positive factor. If you assume it you can almost invariably make it yours. If you assume the negative you are sure to be negative. Assuming a virtue or a vice vitalizes it. Summon all your power of self-direction, and remember that though your audience is infinitely more important than you, the truth is more important than both of you, because it is eternal. If your mind falters in its leadership the sword will drop from your hands. Your assumption of being able to instruct or lead or inspire a multitude or even a small group of people may appall you as being colossal impudence—as indeed it may be; but having once essayed to speak, be courageous. BE courageous—it lies within you to be what you will. MAKE yourself be calm and confident.

Reflect that your audience will not hurt you. If Beecher in Liverpool had spoken behind a wire screen he would have invited the audience to throw the over-ripe missiles with which they were loaded; but he was a man, confronted his hostile hearers fearlessly—and won them.

In facing your audience, pause a moment and look them over—a hundred chances to one they want you to succeed, for what man is so foolish as to spend his time, perhaps his money, in the hope that you will waste his investment by talking dully?

## Concluding Hints

Do not make haste to begin—haste shows lack of control.

Do not apologize. It ought not to be necessary; and if it is, it will not help. Go straight ahead.

Take a deep breath, relax, and begin in a quiet conversational tone as though you were speaking to one large friend. You will not find it half so bad as you imagined; really, it is like taking a cold plunge: after you are in, the water is fine. In fact, having spoken a few times you will even anticipate the plunge with exhilaration. To stand before an audience and make them think your thoughts after you is one of the greatest pleasures you can ever know. Instead of fearing it, you ought to be as anxious as the fox hounds straining at their leashes, or the race horses tugging at their reins.

So cast out fear, for fear is cowardly—when it is not mastered. The bravest know fear, but they do not yield to it. Face your audience pluckily—if your knees quake, *MAKE* them stop. In your audience lies some victory for you and the cause you represent. Go win it. Suppose Charles Martell had been afraid to hammer the Saracen at Tours; suppose Columbus had feared to venture out into the unknown West; suppose our forefathers had been too timid to oppose the tyranny of George the Third; suppose that any man who ever did anything worth while had been a coward! The world owes its progress to the men who have dared, and you must dare to speak the effective word that is in your heart to speak—for often it requires courage to utter a single sentence. But remember that men erect no monuments and weave no laurels for those who fear to do what they can.

Is all this unsympathetic, do you say?

Man, what you need is not sympathy, but a push. No one doubts that temperament and nerves and illness and even praiseworthy modesty may, singly or combined, cause the speaker's cheek to blanch before an audience, but neither can any one doubt that coddling will magnify this weakness. The victory lies in a fearless frame of mind. Prof. Walter Dill Scott says: "Success or failure in business is caused more by mental attitude even than by mental capacity." Banish the fear-attitude; acquire the confident attitude. And remember that the only way to acquire it is—*to acquire it*.

In this foundation chapter we have tried to strike the tone of much that is to follow. Many of these ideas will be amplified and enforced in a more specific way; but through all these chapters on an art which Mr. Gladstone believed to be more powerful than the public press, the note of *justifiable self-confidence* must sound again and again.

## QUESTIONS AND EXERCISES

1. What is the cause of self-consciousness?

2. Why are animals free from it?

3. What is your observation regarding self-consciousness in children?

4. Why are you free from it under the stress of unusual excitement?

5. How does moderate excitement affect you?

6. What are the two fundamental requisites for the acquiring of self-confidence? Which is the more important?

7. What effect does confidence on the part of the speaker have on the audience?

8. Write out a two-minute speech on "Confidence and Cowardice."

9. What effect do habits of thought have on confidence? In this connection read the chapter on "Right Thinking and Personality."

10. Write out very briefly any experience you may have had involving the teachings of this chapter.

11. Give a three-minute talk on "Stage-Fright," including a (kindly) imitation of two or more victims.

# CHAPTER II

## *The Sin of Monotony*

> One day Ennui was born from Uniformity.
>
> —MOTTE

OUR ENGLISH HAS CHANGED WITH THE YEARS SO THAT MANY WORDS NOW CONnote more than they did originally. This is true of the word monotonous. From "having but one tone," it has come to mean more broadly, "lack of variation."

The monotonous speaker not only drones along in the same volume and pitch of tone but uses always the same emphasis, the same speed, the same thoughts—or dispenses with thought altogether.

Monotony, the cardinal and most common sin of the public speaker, is not a transgression—it is rather a sin of omission, for it consists in living up to the confession of the Prayer Book: "We have left undone those things we ought to have done."

Emerson says, "The virtue of art lies in detachment, in sequestering one object from the embarrassing variety." That is just what the monotonous speaker fails to do—he does *not* detach one thought or phrase from another, they are all expressed in the same manner.

To tell you that your speech is monotonous may mean very little to you, so let us look at the nature—and the curse—of monotony in other spheres of life, then we shall appreciate more fully how it will blight an otherwise good speech.

If the Victrola in the adjoining apartment grinds out just three selections over and over again, it is pretty safe to assume that your neighbor has no other records. If a speaker uses only a few of his powers, it points very plainly to the fact that the rest of his powers are not developed. Monotony reveals our limitations.

In its effect on its victim, monotony is actually deadly—it will drive the bloom from the cheek and the lustre from the eye as quickly as sin, and often leads to viciousness. The worst punishment that human ingenuity has ever been able to invent is extreme monotony—solitary confinement. Lay a marble on the table and do nothing eighteen hours of the day but change that marble from one point to another and back again, and you will go insane if you continue long enough.

So this thing that shortens life, and is used as the most cruel of punishments in our prisons, is the thing that will destroy all the life and force of a speech. Avoid it as you would shun a deadly dull bore. The "idle rich" can have half-a-dozen homes, command all the varieties of foods gathered from the four corners of the earth, and sail for Africa or

Alaska at their pleasure; but the poverty-stricken man must walk or take a street car—he does not have the choice of yacht, auto, or special train. He must spend the most of his life in labor and be content with the staples of the food-market. Monotony is poverty, whether in speech or in life. Strive to increase the variety of your speech as the business man labors to augment his wealth.

Bird-songs, forest glens, and mountains are not monotonous—it is the long rows of brown-stone fronts and the miles of paved streets that are so terribly same. Nature in her wealth gives us endless variety; man with his limitations is often monotonous. Get back to nature in your methods of speech-making.

The power of variety lies in its pleasure-giving quality. The great truths of the world have often been couched in fascinating stories—"Les Miserables," for instance. If you wish to teach or influence men, you must please them, first or last. Strike the same note on the piano over and over again. This will give you some idea of the displeasing, jarring effect monotony has on the ear. The dictionary defines "monotonous" as being synonymous with "wearisome." That is putting it mildly. It is maddening. The department-store prince does not disgust the public by playing only the one tune, "Come Buy My Wares!" He gives recitals on a $125,000 organ, and the pleased people naturally slip into a buying mood.

## How to Conquer Monotony

We obviate monotony in dress by replenishing our wardrobes. We avoid monotony in speech by multiplying our powers of speech. We multiply our powers of speech by increasing our tools.

The carpenter has special implements with which to construct the several parts of a building. The organist has certain keys and stops which he manipulates to produce his harmonies and effects. In like manner the speaker has certain instruments and tools at his command by which he builds his argument, plays on the feelings, and guides the beliefs of his audience. To give you a conception of these instruments, and practical help in learning to use them, are the purposes of the immediately following chapters.

Why did not the Children of Israel whirl through the desert in limousines, and why did not Noah have moving-picture entertainments and talking machines on the Ark? The laws that enable us to operate an automobile, produce moving-pictures, or music on the Victrola, would have worked just as well then as they do today. It was ignorance of law that for ages deprived humanity of our modern conveniences. Many speakers still use ox-cart methods in their speech instead of employing automobile or overland-express methods. They are ignorant of laws that make for efficiency in speaking. Just to the extent that you regard and use the laws that we are about to examine and learn how to use will you have efficiency and force in your speaking; and just to the extent that you disregard them will your speaking be feeble and ineffective. We cannot impress too thoroughly upon you the necessity for a real working mastery of these principles. They are the very foundations of successful speaking. "Get your principles right," said Napoleon, "and the rest is a matter of detail."

It is useless to shoe a dead horse, and all the sound principles in Christendom will never make a live speech out of a dead one. So let it be understood that public speaking is not a matter of mastering a few dead rules; the most important law of public speech is the necessity for truth, force, feeling, and life. Forget all else, but not this.

When you have mastered the mechanics of speech outlined in the next few chapters you will no longer be troubled with monotony. The complete knowledge of these principles and the ability to apply them will give you great variety in your powers of expression. But they cannot be mastered and applied by thinking or reading about them—you must practise, *practise*, *PRACTISE*. If no one else will listen to you, listen to yourself—you must always be your own best critic, and the severest one of all.

The technical principles that we lay down in the following chapters are not arbitrary creations of our own. They are all founded on the practices that good speakers and actors adopt—either naturally and unconsciously or under instruction—in getting their effects.

It is useless to warn the student that he must be natural. To be natural may be to be monotonous. The little strawberry up in the arctics with a few tiny seeds and an acid tang is a natural berry, but it is not to be compared with the improved variety that we enjoy here. The dwarfed oak on the rocky hillside is natural, but a poor thing compared with the beautiful tree found in the rich, moist bottom lands. Be natural—but improve your natural gifts until you have approached the ideal, for we must strive after idealized nature, in fruit, tree, and speech.

## QUESTIONS AND EXERCISES

1. What are the causes of monotony?
2. Cite some instances in nature.
3. Cite instances in man's daily life.
4. Describe some of the effects of monotony in both cases.
5. Read aloud some speech without paying particular attention to its meaning or force.
6. Now repeat it after you have thoroughly assimilated its matter and spirit. What difference do you notice in its rendition?
7. Why is monotony one of the worst as well as one of the most common faults of speakers?

# CHAPTER III

# Efficiency Through Emphasis and Subordination

In a word, the principle of emphasis . . . is followed best, not by
remembering particular rules, but by being full of a particular feeling.

—C. S. BALDWIN, *Writing and Speaking*

THE GUN THAT SCATTERS TOO MUCH DOES NOT BAG THE BIRDS. THE SAME PRINCI-
ple applies to speech. The speaker that fires his force and emphasis at random into
a sentence will not get results. Not every word is of special importance—therefore only
certain words demand emphasis.

You say MassaCHUsetts and MinneAPolis, you do not emphasize each syllable alike,
but hit the accented syllable with force and hurry over the unimportant ones. Now why
do you not apply this principle in speaking a sentence? To some extent you do, in ordinary speech; but do you in public discourse? It is there that monotony caused by lack of
emphasis is so painfully apparent.

So far as emphasis is concerned, you may consider the average sentence as just one big
word, with the important word as the accented syllable. Note the following:

"Destiny is not a matter of chance. It is a matter of choice."

You might as well say *MASS-A-CHU-SETTS*, emphasizing every syllable equally, as to
lay equal stress on each word in the foregoing sentences.

Speak it aloud and see. Of course you will want to emphasize *destiny*, for it is the principal idea in your declaration, and you will put some emphasis on *not*, else your hearers
may think you are affirming that destiny *is* a matter of chance. By all means you must
emphasize *chance*, for it is one of the two big ideas in the statement.

Another reason why *chance* takes emphasis is that it is contrasted with *choice* in the next
sentence. Obviously, the author has contrasted these ideas purposely, so that they might be
more emphatic, and here we see that contrast is one of the very first devices to gain emphasis.

As a public speaker you can assist this emphasis of contrast with your voice. If you say,
"My horse is not *black*," what color immediately comes into mind? White, naturally, for
that is the opposite of black. If you wish to bring out the thought that destiny is a matter
of choice, you can do so more effectively by first saying that *"DESTINY is NOT a matter
of CHANCE."* Is not the color of the horse impressed upon us more emphatically when

you say, "My horse is *NOT BLACK*. He is *WHITE*" than it would be by hearing you assert merely that your horse is white?

In the second sentence of the statement there is only one important word—*choice*. It is the one word that positively defines the quality of the subject being discussed, and the author of those lines desired to bring it out emphatically, as he has shown by contrasting it with another idea. These lines, then, would read like this:

"*DESTINY* is *NOT* a matter of *CHANCE*. It is a matter of *CHOICE*." Now read this over, striking the words in capitals with a great deal of force.

In almost every sentence there are a few *MOUNTAIN PEAK WORDS* that represent the big, important ideas. When you pick up the evening paper you can tell at a glance which are the important news articles. Thanks to the editor, he does not tell about a "hold up" in Hong Kong in the same sized type as he uses to report the death of five firemen in your home city. Size of type is his device to show emphasis in bold relief. He brings out sometimes even in red headlines the striking news of the day.

It would be a boon to speech-making if speakers would conserve the attention of their audiences in the same way and emphasize only the words representing the important ideas. The average speaker will deliver the foregoing line on destiny with about the same amount of emphasis on each word. Instead of saying, "It is a matter of *CHOICE*," he will deliver it, "It is a matter of choice," or "*IT IS A MATTER OF CHOICE*"—both equally bad.

Charles Dana, the famous editor of *The New York Sun*, told one of his reporters that if he went up the street and saw a dog bite a man, to pay no attention to it. *The Sun* could not afford to waste the time and attention of its readers on such unimportant happenings. "But," said Mr. Dana, "if you see a man bite a dog, hurry back to the office and write the story." Of course that is news; that is unusual.

Now the speaker who says "*IT IS A MATTER OF CHOICE*" is putting too much emphasis upon things that are of no more importance to metropolitan readers than a dog bite, and when he fails to emphasize "choice" he is like the reporter who "passes up" the man's biting a dog. The ideal speaker makes his big words stand out like mountain peaks; his unimportant words are submerged like stream-beds. His big thoughts stand like huge oaks; his ideas of no especial value are merely like the grass around the tree.

From all this we may deduce this important principle: *EMPHASIS* is a matter of *CONTRAST* and *COMPARISON*.

Recently the *New York American* featured an editorial by Arthur Brisbane. Note the following, printed in the same type as given here.

> We do not know what the President THOUGHT when he got that message, or what the elephant thinks when he sees the mouse, but we do know what the President DID.

The words *THOUGHT* and *DID* immediately catch the reader's attention because they are different from the others, not especially because they are larger. If all the rest of the words in this sentence were made ten times as large as they are, and *DID* and *THOUGHT* were kept at their present size, they would still be emphatic, because different.

Take the following from Robert Chambers' novel, "The Business of Life." The words *you, had, would,* are all emphatic, because they have been made different.

He looked at her in angry astonishment.

"Well, what do *you* call it if it isn't cowardice—to slink off and marry a defenseless girl like that!"

"Did you expect me to give you a chance to destroy me and poison Jacqueline's mind? If I *had* been guilty of the thing with which you charge me, what I have done *would* have been cowardly. Otherwise, it is justified."

A Fifth Avenue bus would attract attention up at Minisink Ford, New York, while one of the ox teams that frequently pass there would attract attention on Fifth Avenue. To make a word emphatic, deliver it differently from the manner in which the words surrounding it are delivered. If you have been talking loudly, utter the emphatic word in a concentrated whisper—and you have intense emphasis. If you have been going fast, go very slow on the emphatic word. If you have been talking on a low pitch, jump to a high one on the emphatic word. If you have been talking on a high pitch, take a low one on your emphatic ideas. Read the chapters on "Inflection," "Feeling," "Pause," "Change of Pitch," "Change of Pace." Each of these will explain in detail how to get emphasis through the use of a certain principle.

In this chapter, however, we are considering only one form of emphasis: that of applying force to the important word and subordinating the unimportant words. Do not forget: this is one of the main methods that you must continually employ in getting your effects.

Let us not confound loudness with emphasis. To yell is not a sign of earnestness, intelligence, or feeling. The kind of force that we want applied to the emphatic word is not entirely physical. True, the emphatic word may be spoken more loudly, or it may be spoken more softly, but the *real* quality desired is intensity, earnestness. It must come from within, outward.

Last night a speaker said: "The curse of this country is not a lack of education. It's politics." He emphasized *curse, lack, education, politics.* The other words were hurried over and thus given no comparative importance at all. The word *politics* was flamed out with great feeling as he slapped his hands together indignantly. His emphasis was both correct and powerful. He concentrated all our attention on the words that meant something, instead of holding it up on such words as *of this, a, of, It's.*

What would you think of a guide who agreed to show New York to a stranger and then took up his time by visiting Chinese laundries and boot-blacking "parlors" on the side streets? There is only one excuse for a speaker's asking the attention of his audience: He must have either truth or entertainment for them. If he wearies their attention with trifles they will have neither vivacity nor desire left when he reaches words of Wall-Street and skyscraper importance. You do not dwell on these small words in your everyday conversation, because you are not a conversational bore. Apply the correct method of everyday speech to the platform. As we have noted elsewhere, public speaking is very much like conversation enlarged.

Sometimes, for big emphasis, it is advisable to lay stress on every single syllable in a word, as *absolutely* in the following sentence:

I ab-so-lute-ly refuse to grant your demand.

Now and then this principle should be applied to an emphatic sentence by stressing each word. It is a good device for exciting special attention, and it furnishes a pleasing variety. Patrick Henry's notable climax could be delivered in that manner very effectively: "Give—me—liberty—or—give—me—death." The italicized part of the following might also be delivered with this every-word emphasis. Of course, there are many ways of delivering it; this is only one of several good interpretations that might be chosen.

> Knowing the price we must pay, the sacrifice we must make, the burdens we must carry, the assaults we must endure—knowing full well the cost—yet we enlist, and we enlist for the war. For we know the justice of our cause, and *we know, too, its certain triumph.*
>
> —From "Pass Prosperity Around," by ALBERT J. BEVERIDGE, *before the Chicago National Convention of the Progressive Party*

Strongly emphasizing a single word has a tendency to suggest its antithesis. Notice how the meaning changes by merely putting the emphasis on different words in the following sentence. The parenthetical expressions would really not be needed to supplement the emphatic words.

> *I* intended to buy a house this Spring (even if you did not).
> I *INTENDED* to buy a house this Spring (but something prevented).
> I intended to *BUY* a house this Spring (instead of renting as heretofore).
> I intended to buy a *HOUSE* this Spring (and not an automobile).
> I intended to buy a house *THIS* Spring (instead of next Spring).
> I intended to buy a house this *SPRING* (instead of in the Autumn).

When a great battle is reported in the papers, they do not keep emphasizing the same facts over and over again. They try to get new information, or a "new slant." The news that takes an important place in the morning edition will be relegated to a small space in the late afternoon edition. We are interested in new ideas and new facts. This principle has a very important bearing in determining your emphasis. Do not emphasize the same idea over and over again unless you desire to lay extra stress on it; Senator Thurston desired to put the maximum amount of emphasis on "force" in his speech on page 32. Note how force is emphasized repeatedly. As a general rule, however, the new idea, the "new slant," whether in a newspaper report of a battle or a speaker's enunciation of his ideas, is emphatic.

In the following selection, "larger" is emphatic, for it is the new idea. All men have eyes, but this man asks for a *LARGER* eye.

This man with the larger eye says he will discover, not rivers or safety appliances for aeroplanes, but *NEW STARS* and *SUNS*. "New stars and suns" are hardly as emphatic as the word "larger." Why? Because we expect an astronomer to discover heavenly bodies rather than cooking recipes. The words, "Republic needs" in the next sentence, are emphatic; they introduce a new and important idea. Republics have always needed men, but the author says they need *NEW* men. "New" is emphatic because it introduces a new idea. In like manner, "soil," "grain," "tools," are also emphatic.

The most emphatic words are italicized in this selection. Are there any others you would emphasize? Why?

> The old astronomer said, "Give me a *larger* eye, and I will discover *new stars* and *suns*." That is what the *republic needs* today—*new men*—men who are *wise* toward the *soil*, toward the *grains*, toward the *tools*. If God would only raise up for the people two or three men like *Watt*, *Fulton* and *McCormick*, they would be *worth more* to the *State* than that *treasure box* named *California* or *Mexico*. And the *real supremacy* of man is based upon his *capacity* for *education*. Man is *unique* in the *length* of his *childhood*, which means the *period* of *plasticity* and *education*. The childhood of a *moth*, the distance that stands between the hatching of the *robin* and its *maturity*, represent a *few hours* or a *few weeks*, but *twenty years* for growth stands between *man's* cradle and his citizenship. This protracted childhood makes it possible to hand over to the boy all the *accumulated stores achieved* by *races* and *civilizations* through *thousands* of *years*.
>
> —Anonymous

You must understand that there are no steel-riveted rules of emphasis. It is not always possible to designate which word must, and which must not be emphasized. One speaker will put one interpretation on a speech, another speaker will use different emphasis to bring out a different interpretation. No one can say that one interpretation is right and the other wrong. This principle must be borne in mind in all our marked exercises. Here your own intelligence must guide—and greatly to your profit.

## QUESTIONS AND EXERCISES

1. What is emphasis?

2. Describe one method of destroying monotony of thought-presentation.

3. What relation does this have to the use of the voice?

4. Which words should be emphasized, which subordinated, in a sentence?

5. Read the selections on pages 31–34, devoting special attention to emphasizing the important words or phrases and subordinating the unimportant ones. Read again, changing emphasis slightly. What is the effect?

6. Read some sentence repeatedly, emphasizing a different word each time, and show how the meaning is changed, as is done on page 14.

7. What is the effect of a lack of emphasis?

8. Read the selections on pages 18–19 and 30, emphasizing every word. What is the effect on the emphasis?

**9.** When is it permissible to emphasize every single word in a sentence?

**10.** Note the emphasis and subordination in some conversation or speech you have heard. Were they well made? Why? Can you suggest any improvement?

**11.** From a newspaper or a magazine, clip a report of an address, or a biographical eulogy. Mark the passage for emphasis and bring it with you to class.

**12.** In the following passage, would you make any changes in the author's markings for emphasis? Where? Why? Bear in mind that not all words marked require the same *degree* of emphasis—*in a wide variety of emphasis, and in nice shading of the gradations, lie the excellence of emphatic speech.*

> I would call him *Napoleon*, but Napoleon made his way to empire over *broken oaths* and through a *sea of blood*. This man *never* broke his word. "No Retaliation" was his great motto and the rule of his life; and the last words uttered to his son in France were these: "My boy, you will one day go back to Santo Domingo; *forget* that *France murdered* your *father*." I would call him *Cromwell*, but Cromwell was *only* a *soldier*, and the state he founded *went down* with him into his grave. I would call him *Washington*, but the great Virginian *held slaves*. This man *risked* his *empire* rather than *permit* the slave-trade in the *humblest village* of his dominions.
>
> You think me a fanatic to-night, for you read history, *not* with your *eyes*, but with your *prejudices*. But fifty years hence, when *Truth* gets a hearing, the Muse of History will put *Phocion* for the *Greek*, and *Brutus* for the *Roman*, *Hampden* for *England*, *Lafayette* for *France*, choose *Washington* as the bright, consummate flower of our *earlier* civilization, and *John Brown* the ripe fruit of our *noonday*, then, dipping her pen in the sunlight, will write in the clear blue, above them all, the name of the *soldier*, the *statesman*, the *martyr*, TOUSSAINT L'OUVERTURE.
>
> —WENDELL PHILLIPS, *Toussaint l'Ouverture*

Practise on the following selections for emphasis: Beecher's "Abraham Lincoln," page 48; Lincoln's "Dedication of Gettysburg Cemetery," page 31; Seward's "Irrepressible Conflict," page 42; and Bryan's "Prince of Peace," page 287.

# CHAPTER IV

# Efficiency Through Change of Pitch

Speech is simply a modified form of singing: the principal difference
being in the fact that in singing the vowel sounds are prolonged and
the intervals are short, whereas in speech the words are uttered in what
may be called "staccato" tones, the vowels not being specially prolonged
and the intervals between the words being more distinct. The fact that
in singing we have a larger range of tones does not properly distinguish
it from ordinary speech. In speech we have likewise a variation of tones,
and even in ordinary conversation there is a difference of from three
to six semi-tones, as I have found in my investigations, and in some
persons the range is as high as one octave.

—WILLIAM SCHEPPEGRELL, *Popular Science Monthly*

BY PITCH, AS EVERYONE KNOWS, WE MEAN THE RELATIVE POSITION OF A VOCAL
tone—as, high, medium, low, or any variation between. In public speech we apply it
not only to a single utterance, as an exclamation or a monosyllable (Oh! or the) but to any
group of syllables, words, and even sentences that may be spoken in a single tone. This
distinction it is important to keep in mind, for the efficient speaker not only changes the
pitch of successive syllables (see Chapter VII, "Efficiency Through Inflection"), but gives
a different pitch to different parts, or word-groups, of successive sentences. It is this phase
of the subject which we are considering in this chapter.

## Every Change in the Thought Demands a Change in the Voice-Pitch

Whether the speaker follows the rule consciously, unconsciously, or subconsciously, this
is the logical basis upon which all good voice variation is made, yet this law is violated
more often than any other by *public* speakers. A criminal may disregard a law of the state
without detection and punishment, but the speaker who violates this regulation suffers
its penalty at once in his loss of effectiveness, while his innocent hearers must endure the
monotony—for monotony is not only a sin of the perpetrator, as we have shown, but a
plague on the victims as well.

Change of pitch is a stumbling block for almost all beginners, and for many experienced speakers also. This is especially true when the words of the speech have been
memorized.

If you wish to hear how pitch-monotony sounds, strike the same note on the piano over and over again. You have in your speaking voice a range of pitch from high to low, with a great many shades between the extremes. With all these notes available there is no excuse for offending the ears and taste of your audience by continually using the one note. True, the reiteration of the same tone in music—as in pedal point on an organ composition—may be made the foundation of beauty, for the harmony weaving about that one basic tone produces a consistent, insistent quality not felt in pure variety of chord sequences. In like manner the intoning voice in a ritual may—though it rarely does—possess a solemn beauty. But the public speaker should shun the monotone as he would a pestilence.

## Continual Change of Pitch Is Nature's Highest Method

In our search for the principles of efficiency we must continually go back to nature. Listen—really listen—to the birds sing. Which of these feathered tribes are most pleasing in their vocal efforts: those whose voices, though sweet, have little or no range, or those that, like the canary, the lark, and the nightingale, not only possess a considerable range but utter their notes in continual variety of combinations? Even a sweet-toned chirp, when reiterated without change, may grow maddening to the enforced listener.

The little child seldom speaks in a monotonous pitch. Observe the conversations of little folk that you hear on the street or in the home, and note the continual changes of pitch. The unconscious speech of most adults is likewise full of pleasing variations.

Imagine someone speaking the following, and consider if the effect would not be just about as indicated. Remember, we are not now discussing the inflection of single words, but the general pitch in which phrases are spoken.

(High pitch) "I'd like to leave for my vacation tomorrow,—(lower) still, I have so much to do. (Higher) Yet I suppose if I wait until I have time I'll never go."

Repeat this, first in the pitches indicated, and then all in the one pitch, as many speakers would. Observe the difference in naturalness of effect.

The following exercise should be spoken in a purely conversational tone, with numerous changes of pitch. Practise it until your delivery would cause a stranger in the next room to think you were discussing an actual incident with a friend, instead of delivering a memorized monologue. If you are in doubt about the effect you have secured, repeat it to a friend and ask him if it sounds like memorized words. If it does, it is wrong.

# A Similar Case

Jack, I hear you've gone and done it.—Yes, I know; most fellows will; went and tried it once myself, sir, though you see I'm single still. And you met her—did you tell me—down at Newport, last July, and resolved to ask the question at a *soirée*? So did I.

I suppose you left the ball-room, with its music and its light; for they say love's flame is brightest in the darkness of the night. Well, you walked along together, overhead the starlit sky; and I'll bet—old man, confess it—you were frightened. So was I.

So you strolled along the terrace, saw the summer moonlight pour all its radiance on the waters, as they rippled on the shore, till at length you gathered courage, when you saw that none was nigh—did you draw her close and tell her that you loved her? So did I.

Well, I needn't ask you further, and I'm sure I wish you joy. Think I'll wander down and see you when you're married—eh, my boy? When the honeymoon is over and you're settled down, we'll try—What? the deuce you say! Rejected—you rejected? So was I.

—Anonymous

The necessity for changing pitch is so self-evident that it should be grasped and applied immediately. However, it requires patient drill to free yourself from monotony of pitch.

In natural conversation you think of an idea first, and then find words to express it. In memorized speeches you are liable to speak the words, and then think what they mean—and many speakers seem to trouble very little even about that. Is it any wonder that reversing the process should reverse the result? Get back to nature in your methods of expression.

Read the following selection in a nonchalant manner, never pausing to think what the words really mean. Try it again, carefully studying the thought you have assimilated. Believe the idea, desire to express it effectively, and imagine an audience before you. Look them earnestly in the face and repeat this truth. If you follow directions, you will note that you have made many changes of pitch after several readings.

It is not work that kills men; it is worry. Work is healthy; you can hardly put more upon a man than he can bear. Worry is rust upon the blade. It is not the revolution that destroys the machinery but the friction.

—Henry Ward Beecher

## Change of Pitch Produces Emphasis

This is a highly important statement. Variety in pitch maintains the hearer's interest, but one of the surest ways to compel attention—to secure unusual emphasis—is to change the pitch of your voice suddenly and in a marked degree. A great contrast always arouses attention. White shows whiter against black; a cannon roars louder in the Sahara silence than in the Chicago hurly burly—these are simple illustrations of the power of contrast.

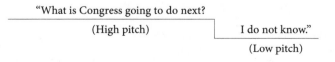

"What is Congress going to do next?
(High pitch)          I do not know."
                      (Low pitch)

By such sudden change of pitch during a sermon Dr. Newell Dwight Hillis recently achieved great emphasis and suggested the gravity of the question he had raised.

The foregoing order of pitch-change might be reversed with equally good effect, though with a slight change in seriousness—either method produces emphasis when used intelligently, that is, with a common-sense appreciation of the sort of emphasis to be attained.

In attempting these contrasts of pitch it is important to avoid unpleasant extremes. Most speakers pitch their voices too high. One of the secrets of Mr. Bryan's eloquence is his low, bell-like voice. Shakespeare said that a soft, gentle, low voice was "an excellent thing in woman;" it is no less so in man, for a voice need not be blatant to be powerful,— and *must* not be, to be pleasing.

In closing, let us emphasize anew the importance of using variety of pitch. You sing up and down the scale, first touching one note and then another above or below it. Do likewise in speaking.

Thought and individual taste must generally be your guide as to where to use a low, a moderate, or a high pitch.

## QUESTIONS AND EXERCISES

1. Name two methods of destroying monotony and gaining force in speaking.

2. Why is a continual change of pitch necessary in speaking?

3. Notice your habitual tones in speaking. Are they too high to be pleasant?

4. Do we express the following thoughts and emotions in a low or a high pitch? Which may be expressed in either high or low pitch? Excitement. Victory. Defeat. Sorrow. Love. Earnestness. Fear.

5. How would you naturally vary the pitch in introducing an explanatory or parenthetical expression like the following:

   He started—*that is, he made preparations to start*—on September third.

6. Speak the following lines with as marked variations in pitch as your interpretation of the sense may dictate. Try each line in two different ways. Which, in each instance, is the more effective—and why?

   What have I to gain from you? Nothing.

   To engage our nation in such a compact would be an infamy.

NOTE: In the foregoing sentence, experiment as to where the change in pitch would better be made.

   Once the flowers distilled their fragrance here, but now see the devastations of war.

   He had reckoned without one prime factor—his conscience.

7. Make a diagram of a conversation you have heard, showing where high and low pitches were used. Were these changes in pitch advisable? Why or why not?

**8.** Read the following selections, paying careful attention to the changes in pitch. Reread, substituting low pitch for high, and vice versa.

## SELECTIONS FOR PRACTISE

**NOTE:** In the following selections, those passages that may best be delivered in a moderate pitch are printed in ordinary (roman) type. Those which may be rendered in a high pitch—do not make the mistake of raising the voice too high—are printed *in italics*. Those which might well be spoken in a low pitch are printed in *CAPITALS*.

These arrangements, however, are merely suggestive—we cannot make it strong enough that you must use your own judgment in interpreting a selection. Before doing so, however, it is well to practise these passages as they are marked.

> *Yes, all men labor. RUFUS CHOATE AND DANIEL WEBSTER labor,* say the critics. But every man who reads of the labor question knows that it means the movement of the men that earn their living with their hands; *THAT ARE EMPLOYED, AND PAID WAGES: are gathered under roofs of factories, sent out on farms, sent out on ships, gathered on the walls.* In popular acceptation, the working class means the men that work with their hands, for wages, so many hours a day, employed by great capitalists; that work for everybody else. Why do we move for this class? "*Why,*" asks a critic, "*don't you move FOR ALL WORKINGMEN?" BECAUSE, WHILE DANIEL WEBSTER GETS FORTY THOUSAND DOLLARS FOR ARGUING THE MEXICAN CLAIMS, there is no need of anybody's moving for him. BECAUSE, WHILE RUFUS CHOATE GETS FIVE THOUSAND DOLLARS FOR MAKING ONE ARGUMENT TO A JURY, there is no need of moving for him, or for the men that work with their brains,*—that do highly disciplined and skilled labor, invent, and write books. The reason why the Labor movement confines itself to a single class is because that class of work *DOES NOT GET PAID, does not get protection. MENTAL LABOR is adequately paid,* and *MORE THAN ADEQUATELY protected. IT CAN SHIFT ITS CHANNELS; it can vary according to the supply and demand.*
>
> *IF A MAN FAILS AS A MINISTER, why, he becomes a railway conductor. IF THAT DOESN'T SUIT HIM, he goes West, and becomes governor of a territory. AND IF HE FINDS HIMSELF INCAPABLE OF EITHER OF THESE POSITIONS, he comes home, and gets to be a city editor.* He varies his occupation as he pleases, and doesn't need protection. *BUT THE GREAT MASS, CHAINED TO A TRADE, DOOMED TO BE GROUND UP IN THE MILL OF SUPPLY AND DEMAND, THAT WORK SO MANY HOURS A DAY, AND MUST RUN IN THE GREAT RUTS OF BUSINESS,—they are the men whose inadequate protection, whose unfair share of the general product, claims a movement in their behalf.*
>
> —WENDELL PHILLIPS

*KNOWING THE PRICE WE MUST PAY, THE SACRIFICE WE MUST MAKE, THE BURDENS WE MUST CARRY, THE ASSAULTS WE MUST ENDURE—KNOWING FULL WELL THE COST—yet we enlist, and we enlist for the war. FOR WE KNOW THE JUSTICE OF OUR CAUSE, and we know, too, its certain triumph.*

*NOT RELUCTANTLY THEN, but eagerly, not with faint hearts BUT STRONG, do we now advance upon the enemies of the people. FOR THE CALL THAT COMES TO US is the call that came to our fathers. As they responded so shall we.*

*"HE HATH SOUNDED FORTH A TRUMPET that shall never call retreat.*
*HE IS SIFTING OUT THE HEARTS OF MEN before His judgment seat.*
*OH, BE SWIFT OUR SOULS TO ANSWER HIM, BE JUBILANT OUR FEET,*
*Our God is marching on."*

—ALBERT J. BEVERIDGE

Remember that two sentences, or two parts of the same sentence, which contain changes of thought, cannot possibly be given effectively in the same key. Let us repeat, every big change of thought requires a big change of pitch. What the beginning student will think are big changes of pitch will be monotonously alike. Learn to speak some thoughts in a very high tone—others in a *very, very* low tone. *DEVELOP RANGE.* It is almost impossible to use too much of it.

*HAPPY AM I THAT THIS MISSION HAS BROUGHT MY FEET AT LAST TO PRESS NEW ENGLAND'S HISTORIC SOIL and my eyes to the knowledge of her beauty and her thrift.* Here within touch of Plymouth Rock and Bunker Hill—*WHERE WEBSTER THUNDERED and Longfellow sang, Emerson thought AND CHANNING PREACHED—HERE IN THE CRADLE OF AMERICAN LETTERS and almost of American liberty,* I hasten to make the obeisance that every American owes New England when first he stands uncovered in her mighty presence. *Strange apparition!* This stern and unique figure—carved from the ocean and the wilderness—its majesty kindling and growing amid the storms of winter and of wars—until at last the gloom was broken, *ITS BEAUTY DISCLOSED IN THE SUNSHINE, and the heroic workers rested at its base*—while startled kings and emperors gazed and marveled that from the rude touch of this handful cast on a bleak and unknown shore should have come the *embodied genius of human government AND THE PERFECTED MODEL OF HUMAN LIBERTY!* God bless the memory of those immortal workers, and prosper the fortunes of their living sons— and perpetuate the inspiration of their handiwork. . . .

Far to the South, Mr. President, separated from this section by a line—*once defined in irrepressible difference, once traced in fratricidal blood, AND NOW, THANK GOD, BUT A VANISHING SHADOW*—lies the fairest and richest domain *of this earth. It is the home of a brave and hospitable people. THERE IS CENTERED ALL THAT CAN PLEASE OR PROSPER HUMANKIND. A PERFECT CLIMATE ABOVE a fertile soil* yields to the husbandman every product of the temperate zone.

There, by night *the cotton whitens beneath the stars*, and by day *THE WHEAT LOCKS THE SUNSHINE IN ITS BEARDED SHEAF.* In the same field the clover steals the fragrance of the wind, and tobacco catches the quick aroma of the rains. *THERE ARE MOUNTAINS STORED WITH EXHAUSTLESS TREASURES: forests—vast and primeval;* and rivers that, *tumbling or loitering, run wanton to the sea.* Of the three essential items of all industries—cotton, iron and wood—that region has easy control. *IN COTTON, a fixed monopoly—IN IRON, proven supremacy—IN TIMBER, the reserve supply of the Republic.* From this assured and permanent advantage, against which artificial conditions cannot much longer prevail, has grown an amazing system of industries. Not maintained by human contrivance of tariff or capital, afar off from the fullest and cheapest source of supply, but resting in divine assurance, within touch of field and mine and forest—not set amid costly farms from which competition has driven the farmer in despair, but amid cheap and sunny lands, rich with agriculture, to which neither season nor soil has set a limit—this system of industries is mounting to a splendor that shall dazzle and illumine the world. *THAT, SIR, is the picture and the promise of my home—A LAND BETTER AND FAIRER THAN I HAVE TOLD YOU,* and *yet but fit setting in its material excellence for the loyal and gentle quality of its citizenship.*

This hour little needs the *LOYALTY THAT IS LOYAL TO ONE SECTION and yet holds the other in enduring suspicion and estrangement.* Give us the *broad* and *perfect loyalty that loves and trusts GEORGIA* alike with *Massachusetts*—that knows no *SOUTH,* no *North,* no *EAST,* no *West,* but *endears with equal and patriotic love* every foot of our soil, every State of our Union.

*A MIGHTY DUTY, SIR, AND A MIGHTY INSPIRATION impels every one of us to-night to lose in patriotic consecration WHATEVER ESTRANGES, WHATEVER DIVIDES.*

*WE, SIR, are Americans—AND WE STAND FOR HUMAN LIBERTY!* The uplifting force of the American idea is under every throne on earth. *France, Brazil— THESE ARE OUR VICTORIES. To redeem the earth from kingcraft and oppression— THIS IS OUR MISSION! AND WE SHALL NOT FAIL.* God has sown in our soil the seed of His millennial harvest, and He will not lay the sickle to the ripening crop until His full and perfect day has come. *OUR HISTORY, SIR, has been a constant and expanding miracle, FROM PLYMOUTH ROCK AND JAMESTOWN,* all the way—aye, even from the hour when from the voiceless and traceless ocean a new world rose to the sight of the inspired sailor. As we approach the fourth centennial of that stupendous day—when the old world will come to *marvel* and to *learn* amid our gathered treasures—let us resolve to crown the miracles of our past with the spectacle of a Republic, *compact, united INDISSOLUBLE IN THE BONDS OF LOVE*—loving from the Lakes to the Gulf—the wounds of war healed in every heart as on every hill, *serene and resplendent AT THE SUMMIT OF HUMAN ACHIEVEMENT AND EARTHLY GLORY, blazing out the path and making clear the way up which all the nations of the earth, must come in God's appointed time!*

—HENRY W. GRADY, *The Race Problem*

*. . . I WOULD CALL HIM NAPOLEON*, but Napoleon made his way to empire *over broken oaths and through a sea of blood.* This man never broke his word. "No Retaliation" was his great motto and the rule of his life; *AND THE LAST WORDS UTTERED TO HIS SON IN FRANCE WERE THESE: "My boy, you will one day go back to Santo Domingo; forget that France murdered your father." I WOULD CALL HIM CROMWELL*, but Cromwell *was only a soldier, and the state he founded went down with him into his grave. I WOULD CALL HIM WASHINGTON,* but the great Virginian *held slaves. THIS MAN RISKED HIS EMPIRE rather than permit the slave-trade in the humblest village of his dominions.*

*YOU THINK ME A FANATIC TO-NIGHT*, for you read history, *not with your eyes, BUT WITH YOUR PREJUDICES.* But fifty years hence, when Truth gets a hearing, the Muse of History will put *PHOCION for the Greek*, and *BRUTUS for the Roman, HAMPDEN for England, LAFAYETTE for France*, choose *WASHINGTON as the bright, consummate flower of our EARLIER civilization, AND JOHN BROWN the ripe fruit of our NOONDAY*, then, dipping her pen in the sunlight, will write in the clear blue, above them all, the name of *THE SOLDIER, THE STATESMAN, THE MARTYR, TOUSSAINT L'OUVERTURE.*

—WENDELL PHILLIPS, *Toussaint l'Ouverture*

Drill on the following selections for change of pitch: Beecher's "Abraham Lincoln," page 48; Seward's "Irrepressible Conflict," page 42; Everett's "History of Liberty," page 50; Grady's "The Race Problem," page 22; and Beveridge's "Pass Prosperity Around," page 305.

## CHAPTER V

# *Efficiency Through Change of Pace*

Hear how he clears the points o' Faith
Wi' rattlin' an' thumpin'!
Now meekly calm, now wild in wrath,
He's stampin' an' he's jumpin'.

—ROBERT BURNS, *Holy Fair*

THE LATINS HAVE BEQUEATHED TO US A WORD THAT HAS NO PRECISE EQUIVALENT IN our tongue, therefore we have accepted it, body unchanged—it is the word tempo, and means rate of movement, as measured by the time consumed in executing that movement.

Thus far its use has been largely limited to the vocal and musical arts, but it would not be surprising to hear tempo applied to more concrete matters, for it perfectly illustrates the real meaning of the word to say that an ox-cart moves in slow tempo, an express train in a fast tempo. Our guns that fire six hundred times a minute, shoot at a fast tempo; the old muzzle loader that required three minutes to load, shot at a slow tempo. Every musician understands this principle: it requires longer to sing a half note than it does an eighth note.

Now tempo is a tremendously important element in good platform work, for when a speaker delivers a whole address at very nearly the same rate of speed he is depriving himself of one of his chief means of emphasis and power. The baseball pitcher, the bowler in cricket, the tennis server, all know the value of change of pace—change of tempo—in delivering their ball, and so must the public speaker observe its power.

### Change of Tempo Lends Naturalness to the Delivery

Naturalness, or at least seeming naturalness, as was explained in the chapter on "Monotony," is greatly to be desired, and a continual change of tempo will go a long way towards establishing it. Mr. Howard Lindsay, Stage Manager for Miss Margaret Anglin, recently said to the present writer that change of pace was one of the most effective tools of the actor. While it must be admitted that the stilted mouthings of many actors indicate cloudy mirrors, still the public speaker would do well to study the actor's use of tempo.

There is, however, a more fundamental and effective source at which to study naturalness—a trait which, once lost, is shy of recapture: that source is the common conversation of any well-bred circle. *This* is the standard we strive to reach on both stage and platform—with certain differences, of course, which will appear as we go on. If speaker and actor were to reproduce with absolute fidelity every variation of utterance—every whisper, grunt, pause, silence, and explosion—of conversation as we find it typically in everyday life, much of the interest would leave the public utterance. Naturalness in public address is something more than faithful reproduction of nature—it is the reproduction of those *typical* parts of nature's work which are truly representative of the whole.

The realistic story-writer understands this in writing dialogue, and we must take it into account in seeking for naturalness through change of tempo.

Suppose you speak the first of the following sentences in a slow tempo, the second quickly, observing how natural is the effect. Then speak both with the same rapidity and note the difference.

I can't recall what I did with my knife. Oh, now I remember I gave it to Mary.

We see here that a change of tempo often occurs in the same sentence—for tempo applies not only to single words, groups of words, and groups of sentences, but to the major parts of a public speech as well.

## QUESTIONS AND EXERCISES

1. In the following, speak the words "long, long while" very slowly; the rest of the sentence is spoken in moderately rapid tempo.

> When you and I behind the Veil are past,
> Oh but the long, long while the world shall last,
> Which of our coming and departure heeds,
> As the seven seas should heed a pebble cast.

**NOTE:** In the following selections the passages that should be given a fast tempo are in italics; those that should be given in a slow tempo are in small capitals. Practise these selections, and then try others, changing from fast to slow tempo on different parts, carefully noting the effect.

2. No MIRABEAU, NAPOLEON, BURNS, CROMWELL, NO *man* ADEQUATE *to* DO ANYTHING *but is first of all in* RIGHT EARNEST *about it—what I call* A SINCERE *man. I should say* SINCERITY, *a* GREAT, DEEP, GENUINE SINCERITY, *is the first* CHARACTERISTIC *of a man in any way* HEROIC. *Not the sincerity that* CALLS *itself sincere. Ah no. That is a very poor matter indeed—*A SHALLOW, BRAGGART, CONSCIOUS *sincerity, oftenest* self-conceit *mainly. The* GREAT MAN'S SINCERITY *is of a kind he* CANNOT SPEAK OF. IS NOT CONSCIOUS *of.*

> —THOMAS CARLYLE

3. TRUE WORTH *is in* BEING—NOT SEEMING—*in doing each day that goes by* SOME LITTLE GOOD, *not in* DREAMING *of* GREAT THINGS *to do by and by. For whatever men say in their* BLINDNESS, *and in spite of the* FOLLIES *of* YOUTH, *there is nothing so* KINGLY *as* KINDNESS, *and nothing so* ROYAL *as* TRUTH.

> —ANONYMOUS

**4.** To get a natural effect, where would you use slow and where fast tempo in the following?

# Fool's Gold

See him there, cold and gray,
Watch him as he tries to play;
No, he doesn't know the way—
He began to learn too late.
She's a grim old hag, is Fate,
For she let him have his pile,
Smiling to herself the while,
Knowing what the cost would be,
When he'd found the Golden Key.
Multimillionaire is he,
Many times more rich than we;
But at that I wouldn't trade
With the bargain that he made.
Came here many years ago,
Not a person did he know;
Had the money-hunger bad—
Mad for money, piggish mad;
Didn't let a joy divert him,
Didn't let a sorrow hurt him,
Let his friends and kin desert him,
While he planned and plugged
    and hurried
On his quest for gold and power.
Every single wakeful hour
With a money thought he'd dower;
All the while as he grew older,
And grew bolder, he grew colder.
And he thought that some day
He would take the time to play;
But, say—he was wrong.
Life's a song;
In the spring
Youth can sing and can fling;
But joys wing
When we're older,
Like birds when it's colder.
The roses were red as he went
    rushing by,

And glorious tapestries hung in the sky,
And the clover was waving
'Neath honey-bees' slaving;
A bird over there
Roundelayed a soft air;
But the man couldn't spare
Time for gathering flowers,
Or resting in bowers,
Or gazing at skies
That gladdened the eyes.
So he kept on and swept on
Through mean, sordid years.
Now he's up to his ears
In the choicest of stocks.
He owns endless blocks
Of houses and shops,
And the stream never stops
Pouring into his banks.
I suppose that he ranks
Pretty near to the top.
What I have wouldn't sop
His ambition one tittle;
And yet with my little
I don't care to trade
With the bargain he made.
Just watch him to-day—
See him trying to play.
He's come back for blue skies.
But they're in a new guise—
Winter's here, all is gray,
The birds are away,
The meadows are brown,
The leaves lie aground,
And the gay brook that wound
With a swirling and whirling
Of waters, is furling
Its bosom in ice.
And he hasn't the price,

| | |
|---|---|
| With all of his gold, | And, say, |
| To buy what he sold. | He'd pay |
| He knows now the cost | Any price if the day |
| Of the spring-time he lost, | Could be made not so gray. |
| Of the flowers he tossed | *He can't play.* |
| From his way, | |

—HERBERT KAUFMAN
*Used by permission of* Everybody's Magazine

## Change of Tempo Prevents Monotony

The canary in the cage before the window is adding to the beauty and charm of his singing by a continual change of tempo. If King Solomon had been an orator he undoubtedly would have gathered wisdom from the song of the wild birds as well as from the bees. Imagine a song written with but quarter notes. Imagine an auto with only one speed.

### EXERCISES

1. Note the change of tempo indicated in the following, and how it gives a pleasing variety. Read it aloud. (Fast tempo is indicated by italics, slow by small capitals.)

   *And he thought that some day he would take the time to play; but, say—*HE WAS WRONG. LIFE'S A SONG; *in the* SPRING YOUTH *can* SING *and can* FLING; BUT JOYS WING WHEN WE'RE OLDER, LIKE THE BIRDS *when it's* COLDER. *The roses were red as he went rushing by, and glorious tapestries hung in the sky.*

2. Turn to "Fools Gold," on page 27, and deliver it in an unvaried tempo: note how monotonous is the result. This poem requires a great many changes of tempo, and is an excellent one for practise.

3. Use the changes of tempo indicated in the following, noting how they prevent monotony. Where no change of tempo is indicated, use a moderate speed. Too much of variety would really be a return to monotony.

## The Mob

"A MOB KILLS THE WRONG MAN" *was flashed in a newspaper headline lately. The mob is an* IRRESPONSIBLE, UNTHINKING MASS. *It always destroys* BUT NEVER CONSTRUCTS. *It criticises* BUT NEVER CREATES.

*Utter a great truth* AND THE MOB WILL HATE YOU. *See how it condemned* DANTE *to* EXILE. *Encounter the dangers of the unknown world for its benefit,* AND THE MOB WILL DECLARE YOU CRAZY. *It ridiculed* COLUMBUS, *and for discovering a new world* GAVE HIM PRISON AND CHAINS.

*Write a poem to thrill human hearts with pleasure,* AND THE MOB WILL ALLOW YOU TO GO HUNGRY: THE BLIND HOMER BEGGED BREAD THROUGH THE STREETS.

*Invent a machine to save labor* AND THE MOB WILL DECLARE YOU ITS ENEMY. *Less than a hundred years ago a furious rabble smashed Thimonier's invention, the sewing machine.*

BUILD A STEAMSHIP TO CARRY MERCHANDISE AND ACCELERATE TRAVEL *and the mob will call you a fool.* A MOB LINED THE SHORES OF THE HUDSON RIVER TO LAUGH AT THE MAIDEN ATTEMPT OF "FULTON'S FOLLY," *as they called his little steamboat.*

Emerson says: "A mob is a society of bodies voluntarily bereaving themselves of reason and traversing its work. The mob is man voluntarily descended to the nature of the beast. *Its fit hour of activity* IS NIGHT. ITS ACTIONS ARE INSANE, *like its whole constitution. It persecutes a principle*—IT WOULD WHIP A RIGHT. It would tar and feather justice by inflicting fire and outrage upon the house and persons of those who have these."

The mob spirit stalks abroad in our land today. Every week gives a fresh victim to its malignant cry for blood. There were 48 persons killed by mobs in the United States in 1913; 64 in 1912, and 71 in 1911. Among the 48 last year were a woman and a child. Two victims were proven innocent after their death.

In 399 B.C. A DEMAGOG APPEALED TO THE POPULAR MOB TO HAVE SOCRATES PUT TO DEATH *and he was sentenced to the hemlock cup.* FOURTEEN HUNDRED YEARS AFTERWARD AN ENTHUSIAST APPEALED TO THE POPULAR MOB *and all Europe plunged into the Holy Land to kill and mangle the heathen. In the seventeenth century a demagog appealed to the ignorance of men* AND TWENTY PEOPLE WERE EXECUTED AT SALEM, MASS., WITHIN SIX MONTHS FOR WITCHCRAFT. *Two thousand years ago the mob yelled, "RELEASE UNTO US BARABBAS"*—AND BARABBAS WAS A MURDERER!

—From an Editorial by D. C. in Leslie's Weekly, by permission

*Present-day business* is as unlike OLD-TIME BUSINESS as the OLD-TIME OX-CART is unlike the *present-day locomotive.* INVENTION has made the *whole world over again. The railroad, telegraph, telephone* have bound the people of MODERN NATIONS into FAMILIES. *To do the business of these closely knit millions in every modern country* GREAT BUSINESS CONCERNS CAME INTO BEING. *What we call big business is the* CHILD OF THE ECONOMIC PROGRESS OF MANKIND. *So warfare to destroy big business* IS FOOLISH BECAUSE IT CAN NOT SUCCEED *and wicked* BECAUSE IT OUGHT NOT TO SUCCEED. *Warfare to destroy big business does not hurt big business, which always comes out on top,* SO MUCH AS IT HURTS ALL OTHER BUSINESS WHICH, IN SUCH A WARFARE, NEVER COME OUT ON TOP.

—A. J. BEVERIDGE

## Change of Tempo Produces Emphasis

Any big change of tempo is emphatic and will catch the attention. You may scarcely be conscious that a passenger train is moving when it is flying over the rails at ninety miles an hour, but if it slows down very suddenly to a ten-mile gait your attention will be drawn to it very decidedly. You may forget that you are listening to music as you dine, but let the orchestra either increase or diminish its tempo in a very marked degree and your attention will be arrested at once.

This same principle will procure emphasis in a speech. If you have a point that you want to bring home to your audience forcefully, make a sudden and great change of tempo, and they will be powerless to keep from paying attention to that point. Recently the present writer saw a play in which these lines were spoken:

"I don't want you to forget what I said. I want you to remember it the longest day you—I don't care if you've got six guns." The part up to the dash was delivered in a very slow tempo, the remainder was named out at lightning speed, as the character who was spoken to drew a revolver. The effect was so emphatic that the lines are remembered six months afterwards, while most of the play has faded from memory. The student who has powers of observation will see this principle applied by all our best actors in their efforts to get emphasis where emphasis is due. But remember that the emotion in the matter must warrant the intensity in the manner, or the effect will be ridiculous. Too many public speakers are impressive over nothing.

Thought rather than rules must govern you while practising change of pace. It is often a matter of no consequence which part of a sentence is spoken slowly and which is given in fast tempo. The main thing to be desired is the change itself. For example, in the selection, "The Mob," on page 28, note the last paragraph. Reverse the instructions given, delivering everything that is marked for slow tempo, quickly; and everything that is marked for quick tempo, slowly. You will note that the force or meaning of the passage has not been destroyed.

However, many passages cannot be changed to a slow tempo without destroying their force. Instances: The Patrick Henry speech on page 67, and the following passage from Whittier's "Barefoot Boy."

O for boyhood's time of June, crowding years in one brief moon, when all things
I heard or saw, me, their master, waited for. I was rich in flowers and trees, humming-
birds and honey-bees; for my sport the squirrel played; plied the snouted mole his
spade; for my taste the blackberry cone purpled over hedge and stone; laughed the
brook for my delight through the day and through the night, whispering at the garden
wall, talked with me from fall to fall; mine the sand-rimmed pickerel pond; mine the
walnut slopes beyond; mine, an bending orchard trees, apples of Hesperides! Still, as
my horizon grew, larger grew my riches, too; all the world I saw or knew seemed a
complex Chinese toy, fashioned for a barefoot boy!

—J. G. WHITTIER

Be careful in regulating your tempo not to get your movement too fast. This is a common fault with amateur speakers. Mrs. Siddons rule was, "Take time." A hundred years ago there was used in medical circles a preparation known as "the shot gun remedy;" it was a mixture of about fifty different ingredients, and was given to the patient in the hope that at least one of them would prove efficacious! That seems a rather poor scheme for medical practice, but it is good to use "shot gun" tempo for most speeches, as it gives a variety. Tempo, like diet, is best when mixed.

## QUESTIONS AND EXERCISES

1. Define tempo.
2. What words come from the same root?
3. What is meant by a change of tempo?
4. What effects are gained by it?
5. Name three methods of destroying monotony and gaining force in speaking.
6. Note the changes of tempo in a conversation or speech that you hear. Were they well made? Why? Illustrate.
7. Read selections on pages 21–24, paying careful attention to change of tempo.
8. As a rule, excitement, joy, or intense anger take a fast tempo, while sorrow, and sentiments of great dignity or solemnity tend to a slow tempo. Try to deliver Lincoln's Gettysburg speech (below), in a fast tempo, or Patrick Henry's speech (page 67), in a slow tempo, and note how ridiculous the effect will be.

PRACTISE the following selections, noting carefully where the tempo may be changed to advantage. Experiment, making numerous changes. Which one do you like best?

## Dedication of Gettysburg Cemetery

Fourscore and seven years ago, our fathers brought forth upon this continent a new nation, conceived in liberty and dedicated to the proposition that all men are created equal. Now we are engaged in a great civil war, testing whether that nation—or any nation so conceived and so dedicated—can long endure.

We are met on a great battlefield of that war. We are met to dedicate a portion of it as the final resting-place of those who have given their lives that that nation might live. It is altogether fitting and proper that we should do this.

But, in a larger sense, we cannot dedicate, we cannot consecrate, we cannot hallow, this ground. The brave men, living and dead, who struggled here, have consecrated it, far above our power to add or to detract. The world will very little note nor long remember what we say here; but it can never forget what they did here.

It is for us, the living, rather, to be dedicated here to the unfinished work they have thus far so nobly carried on. It is rather for us to be here dedicated to the great task remaining before us: that from these honored dead we take increased devotion to that cause for which they here gave the last full measure of devotion; that we here highly resolve that these dead shall not have died in vain; that the nation shall, under God, have a new birth of freedom, and that government of the people, by the people, for the people, shall not perish from the earth.

—ABRAHAM LINCOLN

# A Plea for Cuba

*[This deliberative oration was delivered by Senator Thurston in the United States Senate
on March 24, 1898. It is recorded in full in the* Congressional Record *of that date. Mrs.
Thurston died in Cuba. As a dying request she urged her husband, who was investigating
affairs in the island, to do his utmost to induce the United States to intervene—hence
this oration.]*

Mr. President, I am here by command of silent lips to speak once and for all upon
the Cuban situation. I shall endeavor to be honest, conservative, and just. I have
no purpose to stir the public passion to any action not necessary and imperative to
meet the duties and necessities of American responsibility, Christian humanity, and
national honor. I would shirk this task if I could, but I dare not. I cannot satisfy my
conscience except by speaking, and speaking now.

I went to Cuba firmly believing that the condition of affairs there had been greatly
exaggerated by the press, and my own efforts were directed in the first instance to the
attempted exposure of these supposed exaggerations. There has undoubtedly been
much sensationalism in the journalism of the time, but as to the condition of affairs in
Cuba, there has been no exaggeration, because exaggeration has been impossible.

Under the inhuman policy of Weyler not less than four hundred thousand
self-supporting, simple, peaceable, defenseless country people were driven from
their homes in the agricultural portions of the Spanish provinces to the cities, and
imprisoned upon the barren waste outside the residence portions of these cities and
within the lines of intrenchment established a little way beyond. Their humble homes
were burned, their fields laid waste, their implements of husbandry destroyed, their
live stock and food supplies for the most part confiscated. Most of the people were
old men, women, and children. They were thus placed in hopeless imprisonment,
without shelter or food. There was no work for them in the cities to which they were
driven. They were left with nothing to depend upon except the scanty charity of the
inhabitants of the cities and with slow starvation their inevitable fate. . . .

The pictures in the American newspapers of the starving reconcentrados are
true. They can all be duplicated by the thousands. I never before saw, and please God
I may never again see, so deplorable a sight as the reconcentrados in the suburbs of
Matanzas. I can never forget to my dying day the hopeless anguish in their despairing
eyes. Huddled about their little bark huts, they raised no voice of appeal to us for alms
as we went among them. . . .

Men, women, and children stand silent, famishing with hunger. Their only appeal
comes from their sad eyes, through which one looks as through an open window into
their agonizing souls.

The government of Spain has not appropriated and will not appropriate one dollar
to save these people. They are now being attended and nursed and administered to by
the charity of the United States. Think of the spectacle! We are feeding these citizens of
Spain; we are nursing their sick; we are saving such as can be saved, and yet there are

those who still say it is right for us to send food, but we must keep hands off. I say that the time has come when muskets ought to go with the food.

We asked the governor if he knew of any relief for these people except through the charity of the United States. He did not. We asked him, "When do you think the time will come that these people can be placed in a position of self-support?" He replied to us, with deep feeling, "Only the good God or the great government of the United States will answer that question." I hope and believe that the good God by the great government of the United States will answer that question.

I shall refer to these horrible things no further. They are there. God pity me, I have seen them; they will remain in my mind forever—and this is almost the twentieth century. Christ died nineteen hundred years ago, and Spain is a Christian nation. She has set up more crosses in more lands, beneath more skies, and under them has butchered more people than all the other nations of the earth combined. Europe may tolerate her existence as long as the people of the Old World wish. God grant that before another Christmas morning the last vestige of Spanish tyranny and oppression will have vanished from the Western Hemisphere! . . .

The time for action has come. No greater reason for it can exist to-morrow than exists to-day. Every hour's delay only adds another chapter to the awful story of misery and death. Only one power can intervene—the United States of America. Ours is the one great nation in the world, the mother of American republics. She holds a position of trust and responsibility toward the peoples and affairs of the whole Western Hemisphere. It was her glorious example which inspired the patriots of Cuba to raise the flag of liberty in her eternal hills. We cannot refuse to accept this responsibility which the God of the universe has placed upon us as the one great power in the New World. We must act! What shall our action be?

Against the intervention of the United States in this holy cause there is but one voice of dissent; that voice is the voice of the money-changers. They fear war! Not because of any Christian or ennobling sentiment against war and in favor of peace, but because they fear that a declaration of war, or the intervention which might result in war, would have a depressing effect upon the stock market. Let them go. They do not represent American sentiment; they do not represent American patriotism. Let them take their chances as they can. Their weal or woe is of but little importance to the liberty-loving people of the United States. They will not do the fighting; their blood will not flow; they will keep on dealing in options on human life. Let the men whose loyalty is to the dollar stand aside while the men whose loyalty is to the flag come to the front.

Mr. President, there is only one action possible, if any is taken; that is, intervention for the independence of the island. But we cannot intervene and save Cuba without the exercise of force, and force means war; war means blood. The lowly Nazarene on the shores of Galilee preached the divine doctrine of love, "Peace on earth, good will toward men." Not peace on earth at the expense of liberty and humanity. Not good will toward men who despoil, enslave, degrade, and starve to death their fellow-men.

I believe in the doctrine of Christ. I believe in the doctrine of peace; but, Mr. President, men must have liberty before there can come abiding peace.

Intervention means force. Force means war. War means blood. But it will be God's force. When has a battle for humanity and liberty ever been won except by force? What barricade of wrong, injustice, and oppression has ever been carried except by force?

Force compelled the signature of unwilling royalty to the great Magna Charta; force put life into the Declaration of Independence and made effective the Emancipation Proclamation; force beat with naked hands upon the iron gateway of the Bastile and made reprisal in one awful hour for centuries of kingly crime; force waved the flag of revolution over Bunker Hill and marked the snows of Valley Forge with blood-stained feet; force held the broken line of Shiloh, climbed the flame-swept hill at Chattanooga, and stormed the clouds on Lookout Heights; force marched with Sherman to the sea, rode with Sheridan in the valley of the Shenandoah, and gave Grant victory at Appomattox; force saved the Union, kept the stars in the flag, made "niggers" men. The time for God's force has come again. Let the impassioned lips of American patriots once more take up the song:—

> "In the beauty of the lilies, Christ was born across the sea.
> With a glory in His bosom that transfigures you and me;
> As He died to make men holy, let us die to make men free.
> While God is marching on."

Others may hesitate, others may procrastinate, others may plead for further diplomatic negotiation, which means delay; but for me, I am ready to act now, and for my action I am ready to answer to my conscience, my country, and my God.

—James Mellen Thurston

# CHAPTER VI

# *Pause and Power*

The true business of the literary artist is to plait or weave his meaning, involving it around itself; so that each sentence, by successive phrases, shall first come into a kind of knot, and then, after a moment of suspended meaning, solve and clear itself.

—GEORGE SAINTSBURY, from "English Prose Style," in *Miscellaneous Essays*

... pause ... has a distinctive value, expressed in silence; in other words, while the voice is waiting, the music of the movement is going on ... To manage it, with its delicacies and compensations, requires that same fineness of ear on which we must depend for all faultless prose rhythm. When there is no compensation, when the pause is inadvertent ... there is a sense of jolting and lack, as if some pin or fastening had fallen out.

—JOHN FRANKLIN GENUNG, *The Working Principles of Rhetoric*

PAUSE, IN PUBLIC SPEECH, IS NOT MERE SILENCE—IT IS SILENCE MADE DESIGNEDLY eloquent.

When a man says: "I-uh-it is with profound-ah-pleasure that-er-I have been permitted to speak to you tonight and-uh-uh-I should say-er"—that is not pausing; that is stumbling. It is conceivable that a speaker may be effective in spite of stumbling—but never because of it.

On the other hand, one of the most important means of developing power in public speaking is to pause either before or after, or both before and after, an important word or phrase. No one who would be a forceful speaker can afford to neglect this principle—one of the most significant that has ever been inferred from listening to great orators. Study this potential device until you have absorbed and assimilated it.

It would seem that this principle of rhetorical pause ought to be easily grasped and applied, but a long experience in training both college men and maturer speakers has demonstrated that the device is no more readily understood by the average man when it is first explained to him than if it were spoken in Hindoostani. Perhaps this is because we do not eagerly devour the fruit of experience when it is impressively set before us on the platter of authority; we like to pluck fruit for ourselves—it not only tastes better, but we never forget that tree! Fortunately, this is no difficult task, in this instance, for the trees stand thick all about us.

One man is pleading the cause of another:

"This man, my friends, has made this wonderful sacrifice—for you and me."

Did not the pause surprisingly enhance the power of this statement? See how he gathered up reserve force and impressiveness to deliver the words "for you and me." Repeat this passage without making a pause. Did it lose in effectiveness?

Naturally enough, during a premeditated pause of this kind the mind of the speaker is concentrated on the thought to which he is about to give expression. He will not dare to allow his thoughts to wander for an instant—he will rather supremely center his thought and his emotion upon the sacrifice whose service, sweetness and divinity he is enforcing by his appeal.

*Concentration*, then, is the big word here—no pause without it can perfectly hit the mark.

Efficient pausing accomplishes one or all of four results:

## 1. *Pause Enables the Mind of the Speaker to Gather His Forces Before Delivering the Final Volley*

It is often dangerous to rush into battle without pausing for preparation or waiting for recruits. Consider Custer's massacre as an instance.

You can light a match by holding it beneath a lens and concentrating the sun's rays. You would not expect the match to flame if you jerked the lens back and forth quickly. Pause, and the lens gathers the heat. Your thoughts will not set fire to the minds of your hearers unless you pause to gather the force that comes by a second or two of concentration. Maple trees and gas wells are rarely tapped continually; when a stronger flow is wanted, a pause is made, nature has time to gather her reserve forces, and when the tree or the well is reopened, a stronger flow is the result.

Use the same common sense with your mind. If you would make a thought particularly effective, pause just before its utterance, concentrate your mind-energies, and then give it expression with renewed vigor. Carlyle was right: "Speak not, I passionately entreat thee, till thy thought has silently matured itself. Out of silence comes thy strength. Speech is silvern, Silence is golden; Speech is human, Silence is divine."

Silence has been called the father of speech. It should be. Too many of our public speeches have no fathers. They ramble along without pause or break. Like Tennyson's brook, they run on forever. Listen to little children, the policeman on the corner, the family conversation around the table, and see how many pauses they naturally use, for they are unconscious of effects. When we get before an audience, we throw most of our natural methods of expression to the wind, and strive after artificial effects. Get back to the methods of nature—and pause.

## 2. *Pause Prepares the Mind of the Auditor to Receive Your Message*

Herbert Spencer said that all the universe is in motion. So it is—and all perfect motion is rhythm. Part of rhythm is rest. Rest follows activity all through nature. Instances: day and night; spring—summer—autumn—winter; a period of rest between breaths; an instant of complete rest between heart beats. Pause, and give the attention-powers of your audience a rest. What you say after such a silence will then have a great deal more effect.

When your country cousins come to town, the noise of a passing car will awaken them, though it seldom affects a seasoned city dweller. By the continual passing of cars his attention-power has become deadened. In one who visits the city but seldom, attention-value is insistent. To him the noise comes after a long pause; hence its power. To you, dweller in the city, there is no pause; hence the low attention-value. After riding on a train several hours you will become so accustomed to its roar that it will lose its attention-value, unless the train should stop for a while and start again. If you attempt to listen to a clock-tick that is so far away that you can barely hear it, you will find that at times you are unable to distinguish it, but in a few moments the sound becomes distinct again. Your mind will pause for rest whether you desire it to do so or not.

The attention of your audience will act in quite the same way. Recognize this law and prepare for it—by pausing. Let it be repeated: the thought that follows a pause is much more dynamic than if no pause had occurred. What is said to you of a night will not have the same effect on your mind as if it had been uttered in the morning when your attention had been lately refreshed by the pause of sleep. We are told on the first page of the Bible that even the Creative Energy of God rested on the "seventh day." You may be sure, then, that the frail finite mind of your audience will likewise demand rest. Observe nature, study her laws, and obey them in your speaking.

## 3. *Pause Creates Effective Suspense*

Suspense is responsible for a great share of our interest in life; it will be the same with your speech. A play or a novel is often robbed of much of its interest if you know the plot beforehand. We like to keep guessing as to the outcome. The ability to create suspense is part of woman's power to hold the other sex. The circus acrobat employs this principle when he fails purposely in several attempts to perform a feat, and then achieves it. Even the deliberate manner in which he arranges the preliminaries increases our expectation—we like to be kept waiting. In the last act of the play, "Polly of the Circus," there is a circus scene in which a little dog turns a backward somersault on the back of a running pony. One night when he hesitated and had to be coaxed and worked with a long time before he would perform his feat he got a great deal more applause than when he did his trick at once. We not only like to wait but we appreciate what we wait for. If fish bite too readily the sport soon ceases to be a sport.

It is this same principle of suspense that holds you in a Sherlock Holmes story—you wait to see how the mystery is solved, and if it is solved too soon you throw down the tale unfinished. Wilkie Collins' receipt for fiction writing well applies to public speech: "Make 'em laugh; make 'em weep; make 'em wait." Above all else make them wait; if they will not do that you may be sure they will neither laugh nor weep.

Thus pause is a valuable instrument in the hands of a trained speaker to arouse and maintain suspense. We once heard Mr. Bryan say in a speech: "It was my privilege to hear"—and he paused, while the audience wondered for a second whom it was his privilege to hear—"the great evangelist"—and he paused again; we knew a little more about the man he had heard, but still wondered to which evangelist he referred; and then he concluded: "Dwight L. Moody." Mr. Bryan paused slightly again and continued: "I came to regard him"—here he paused again and held the audience in a brief moment of suspense as to how he had regarded Mr. Moody, then continued—"as the greatest preacher of his day." Let the dashes illustrate pauses and we have the following:

"It was my privilege to hear—the great evangelist—Dwight L. Moody.—I came to regard him—as the greatest preacher of his day."

The unskilled speaker would have rattled this off with neither pause nor suspense, and the sentences would have fallen flat upon the audience. It is precisely the application of these small things that makes much of the difference between the successful and the unsuccessful speaker.

### 4. *Pausing After An Important Idea Gives It Time to Penetrate*

Any Missouri farmer will tell you that a rain that falls too fast will run off into the creeks and do the crops but little good. A story is told of a country deacon praying for rain in this manner: "Lord, don't send us any chunk floater. Just give us a good old drizzle-drazzle." A speech, like a rain, will not do anybody much good if it comes too fast to soak in. The farmer's wife follows this same principle in doing her washing when she puts the clothes in water—and pauses for several hours that the water may soak in. The physician puts cocaine on your turbinates—and pauses to let it take hold before he removes them. Why do we use this principle everywhere except in the communication of ideas? If you have given the audience a big idea, pause for a second or two and let them turn it over. See what effect it has. After the smoke clears away you may have to fire another 14-inch shell on the same subject before you demolish the citadel of error that you are trying to destroy. Take time. Don't let your speech resemble those tourists who try "to do" New York in a day. They spend fifteen minutes looking at the masterpieces in the Metropolitan Museum of Arts, ten minutes in the Museum of Natural History, take a peep into the Aquarium, hurry across the Brooklyn Bridge, rush up to the Zoo, and back by Grant's Tomb—and call that "Seeing New York." If you hasten by your important points without pausing, your audience will have just about as adequate an idea of what you have tried to convey.

Take time, you have just as much of it as our richest multimillionaire. Your audience will wait for you. It is a sign of smallness to hurry. The great redwood trees of California had burst through the soil five hundred years before Socrates drank his cup of hemlock poison, and are only in their prime today. Nature shames us with our petty haste. Silence is one of the most eloquent things in the world. Master it, and use it through pause.

In the following selections dashes have been inserted where pauses may be used effectively. Naturally, you may omit some of these and insert others without going wrong—one speaker would interpret a passage in one way, one in another; it is largely a matter of personal preference. A dozen great actors have played Hamlet well, and yet each has played the part differently. Which comes the nearest to perfection is a question of opinion. You will succeed best by daring to follow your own course—if you are individual enough to blaze an original trail.

> A moment's halt—a momentary taste of being from the well amid the waste—and
> lo! the phantom caravan has reached—the nothing it set out from—Oh make haste!

> The worldly hope men set their hearts upon—turns ashes—or it prospers;—and
> anon like snow upon the desert's dusty face—lighting a little hour or two—is gone.

> The bird of time has but a little way to flutter,—and the bird is on the wing.

You will note that the punctuation marks have nothing to do with the pausing. You may run by a period very quickly and make a long pause where there is no kind of punctuation. Thought is greater than punctuation. It must guide you in your pauses.

> A book of verses underneath the bough,—a jug of wine, a loaf of bread—and thou
> beside me singing in the wilderness—Oh—wilderness were paradise enow.

You must not confuse the pause for emphasis with the natural pauses that come through taking breath and phrasing. For example, note the pauses indicated in this selection from Byron:

> But *hush!—hark!*—that deep sound breaks in once more,
> And *nearer!—clearer!—deadlier* than before.
> *Arm,* ARM!—it is—it is the cannon's opening roar!

It is not necessary to dwell at length upon these obvious distinctions. You will observe that in natural conversation our words are gathered into clusters or phrases, and we often pause to take breath between them. So in public speech, breathe naturally and do not talk until you must gasp for breath; nor until the audience is equally winded.

A serious word of caution must here be uttered: do not overwork the pause. To do so will make your speech heavy and stilted. And do not think that pause can transmute commonplace thoughts into great and dignified utterance. A grand manner combined with insignificant ideas is like harnessing a Hambletonian with an ass. You remember the farcical old school declamation, "A Midnight Murder," that proceeded in grandiose manner to a thrilling climax, and ended—"and relentlessly murdered—a mosquito!"

The pause, dramatically handled, always drew a laugh from the tolerant hearers. This is all very well in farce, but such anti-climax becomes painful when the speaker falls from the sublime to the ridiculous quite unintentionally. The pause, to be effective in some other manner than in that of the boomerang, must precede or follow a thought that is really worth while, or at least an idea whose bearing upon the rest of the speech is important.

William Pittenger relates in his volume, "Extempore Speech," an instance of the unconsciously farcical use of the pause by a really great American statesman and orator. "He had visited Niagara Falls and was to make an oration at Buffalo the same day, but, unfortunately, he sat too long over the wine after dinner. When he arose to speak, the oratorical instinct struggled with difficulties, as he declared, 'Gentlemen, I have been to look upon your mag—mag—magnificent cataract, one hundred—and forty—seven—feet high! Gentlemen, Greece and Rome in their palmiest days never had a cataract one hundred—and forty—seven—feet high!'"

## QUESTIONS AND EXERCISES

1. Name four methods for destroying monotony and gaining power in speaking.

2. What are the four special effects of pause?

3. Note the pauses in a conversation, play, or speech. Were they the best that could have been used? Illustrate.

4. Read aloud selections on pages 31–34, paying special attention to pause.

5. Read the following without making any pauses. Reread correctly and note the difference:

> Soon the night will pass; and when, of the Sentinel on the ramparts of Liberty the anxious ask: | "Watchman, what of the night?" his answer will be | "Lo, the morn appeareth."
>
> Knowing the price we must pay, | the sacrifice | we must make, | the burdens | we must carry, | the assaults | we must endure, | knowing full well the cost, | yet we enlist, and we enlist | for the war. | For we know the justice of our cause, | and we know, too, its certain triumph. |
>
> Not reluctantly, then, | but eagerly, | not with faint hearts, | but strong, do we now advance upon the enemies of the people. | For the call that comes to us is the call that came to our fathers. | As they responded, so shall we.
>
> "He hath sounded forth a trumpet | that shall never call retreat,
> He is sifting out the hearts of men | before His judgment seat.
> Oh, be swift | our souls to answer Him, | be jubilant our feet,
> Our God | is marching on."
>
> —ALBERT J. BEVERIDGE, *from his speech as temporary chairman*
> *of Progressive National Convention, Chicago, 1912*

**6.** Bring out the contrasting ideas in the following by using the pause:

Contrast now the circumstances of your life and mine, gently and with temper, Æschines; and then ask these people whose fortune they would each of them prefer. You taught reading, I went to school: you performed initiations, I received them: you danced in the chorus, I furnished it: you were assembly-clerk, I was a speaker: you acted third parts, I heard you: you broke down, and I hissed: you have worked as a statesman for the enemy, I for my country. I pass by the rest; but this very day I am on my probation for a crown, and am acknowledged to be innocent of all offence; while you are already judged to be a pettifogger, and the question is, whether you shall continue that trade, or at once be silenced by not getting a fifth part of the votes. A happy fortune, do you see, you have enjoyed, that you should denounce mine as miserable!

—DEMOSTHENES

**7.** After careful study and practice, mark the pauses in the following:

The past rises before me like a dream. Again we are in the great struggle for national life. We hear the sounds of preparation—the music of the boisterous drums, the silver voices of heroic bugles. We see thousands of assemblages, and hear the appeals of orators; we see the pale cheeks of women and the flushed faces of men; and in those assemblages we see all the dead whose dust we have covered with flowers. We lose sight of them no more. We are with them when they enlist in the great army of freedom. We see them part from those they love. Some are walking for the last time in quiet woody places with the maiden they adore. We hear the whisperings and the sweet vows of eternal love as they lingeringly part forever. Others are bending over cradles, kissing babies that are asleep. Some are receiving the blessings of old men. Some are parting from those who hold them and press them to their hearts again and again, and say nothing; and some are talking with wives, and endeavoring with brave words spoken in the old tones to drive from their hearts the awful fear. We see them part. We see the wife standing in the door, with the babe in her arms—standing in the sunlight sobbing; at the turn of the road a hand waves—she answers by holding high in her loving hands the child. He is gone—and forever.

—ROBERT J. INGERSOLL, *to the Soldiers of Indianapolis*

**8.** Where would you pause in the following selections? Try pausing in different places and note the effect it gives.

The moving finger writes; and having writ moves on: nor all your piety nor wit shall lure it back to cancel half a line, nor all your tears wash out a word of it.

The history of womankind is a story of abuse. For ages men beat, sold, and abused their wives and daughters like cattle. The Spartan mother that gave birth to one of her own sex disgraced herself; the girl babies were often deserted in the mountains to starve; China bound and deformed their feet; Turkey veiled their faces; America denied them equal educational advantages with men. Most of the world still refuses them the right to participate in the government and everywhere women bear the brunt of an unequal standard of morality.

But the women are on the march. They are walking upward to the sunlit plains where the thinking people rule. China has ceased binding their feet. In the shadow of the Harem Turkey has opened a school for girls. America has given the women equal educational advantages, and America, we believe, will enfranchise them.

We can do little to help and not much to hinder this great movement. The thinking people have put their O.K. upon it. It is moving forward to its goal just as surely as this old earth is swinging from the grip of winter toward the spring's blossoms and the summer's harvest.

—*From an editorial by D. C. in* Leslie's Weekly,
*June 4, 1914. Used by permission*

**9.** Read aloud the following address, paying careful attention to pause wherever the emphasis may thereby be heightened.

## The Irrepressible Conflict

. . . At last, the Republican party has appeared. It avows, now, as the Republican party of 1800 did, in one word, its faith and its works, "Equal and exact justice to all men." Even when it first entered the field, only half organized, it struck a blow which only just failed to secure complete and triumphant victory. In this, its second campaign, it has already won advantages which render that triumph now both easy and certain. The secret of its assured success lies in that very characteristic which, in the mouth of scoffers, constitutes its great and lasting imbecility and reproach. It lies in the fact that it is a party of one idea; but that is a noble one—an idea that fills and expands all generous souls; the idea of equality of all men before human tribunals and human laws, as they all are equal before the Divine tribunal and Divine laws.

I know, and you know, that a revolution has begun. I know, and all the world knows, that revolutions never go backward. Twenty senators and a hundred representatives proclaim boldly in Congress to-day sentiments and opinions and principles of freedom which hardly so many men, even in this free State, dared to utter in their own homes twenty years ago. While the government of the United States, under the conduct of the Democratic party, has been all that time surrendering one plain and castle after another to slavery, the people of the United States have been no less steadily and perseveringly gathering together the forces with which to recover back again all the fields and all the castles which have been lost, and to confound and overthrow, by one decisive blow, the betrayers of the Constitution and freedom forever.

—W. H. Seward

# CHAPTER VII

# Efficiency Through Inflection

How soft the music of those village bells,
Falling at intervals upon the ear
In cadence sweet; now dying all away,
Now pealing loud again, and louder still,
Clear and sonorous, as the gale comes on!
With easy force it opens all the cells
Where Memory slept.

—WILLIAM COWPER, *The Task*

HERBERT SPENCER REMARKED THAT "CADENCE"—BY WHICH HE MEANT THE MOD-ulation of the tones of the voice in speaking—"is the running commentary of the emotions upon the propositions of the intellect." How true this is will appear when we reflect that the little upward and downward shadings of the voice tell more truly what we mean than our words. The expressiveness of language is literally multiplied by this subtle power to shade the vocal tones, and this voice-shading we call inflection.

The change of pitch *within* a word is even more important, because more delicate, than the change of pitch from phrase to phrase. Indeed, one cannot be practised without the other. The bare words are only so many bricks—inflection will make of them a pavement, a garage, or a cathedral. It is the power of inflection to change the meaning of words that gave birth to the old saying: "It is not so much what you say, as how you say it."

Mrs. Jameson, the Shakespearean commentator, has given us a penetrating example of the effect of inflection; "In her impersonation of the part of Lady Macbeth, Mrs. Siddons adopted successively three different intonations in giving the words 'We fail.' At first a quick contemptuous interrogation—'We fail?' Afterwards, with the note of admiration—'We fail,' an accent of indignant astonishment laying the principal emphasis on the word 'we'—'*we* fail.' Lastly, she fixed on what I am convinced is the true reading—*We fail*—with the simple period, modulating the voice to a deep, low, resolute tone which settles the issue at once as though she had said: 'If we fail, why then we fail, and all is over.'"

This most expressive element of our speech is the last to be mastered in attaining to naturalness in speaking a foreign language, and its correct use is the main element in a natural, flexible utterance of our native tongue. Without varied inflections speech becomes wooden and monotonous.

There are but two kinds of inflection, the rising and the falling, yet these two may be so shaded or so combined that they are capable of producing as many varieties of modulation as maybe illustrated by either one or two lines, straight or curved, thus:

| | |
|---|---|
| Sharp rising | |
| Long rising | |
| Level | |
| Long falling | |
| Sharp falling | |
| Sharp rising and falling | |
| Sharp falling and rising | |
| Hesitating | |

These may be varied indefinitely, and serve merely to illustrate what wide varieties of combination may be effected by these two simple inflections of the voice.

It is impossible to tabulate the various inflections which serve to express various shades of thought and feeling. A few suggestions are offered here, together with abundant exercises for practise, but the only real way to master inflection is to observe, experiment, and practise.

For example, take the common sentence, "Oh, he's all right." Note how a rising inflection may be made to express faint praise, or polite doubt, or uncertainty of opinion. Then note how the same words, spoken with a generally falling inflection may denote certainty, or good-natured approval, or enthusiastic praise, and so on.

In general, then, we find that a bending upward of the voice will suggest doubt and uncertainty, while a decided falling inflection will suggest that you are certain of your ground.

Students dislike to be told that their speeches are "not so bad," spoken with a rising inflection. To enunciate these words with a long falling inflection would indorse the speech rather heartily.

Say good-bye to an imaginary person whom you expect to see again tomorrow; then to a dear friend you never expect to meet again. Note the difference in inflection.

"I have had a delightful time," when spoken at the termination of a formal tea by a frivolous woman takes altogether different inflection than the same words spoken between lovers who have enjoyed themselves. Mimic the two characters in repeating this and observe the difference.

Note how light and short the inflections are in the following brief quotation from "Anthony the Absolute," by Samuel Mervin.

## At Sea—March 28th.

This evening I told Sir Robert What's His Name he was a fool.

I was quite right in this. He is.

Every evening since the ship left Vancouver he has presided over the round table in the middle of the smoking-room. There he sips his coffee and liqueur, and holds forth on every subject known to the mind of man. Each subject is *his* subject. He is an elderly person, with a bad face and a drooping left eyelid.

They tell me that he is in the British Service—a judge somewhere down in Malaysia, where they drink more than is good for them.

Deliver the two following selections with great earnestness, and note how the inflections differ from the foregoing. Then reread these selections in a light, superficial manner, noting that the change of attitude is expressed through a change of inflection.

When I read a sublime fact in Plutarch, or an unselfish deed in a line of poetry, or thrill beneath some heroic legend, it is no longer fairyland—I have seen it matched.

—WENDELL PHILLIPS

Thought is deeper than all speech,
  Feeling deeper than all thought;
Souls to souls can never teach
  What unto themselves was taught.

—CRANCH

It must be made perfectly clear that inflection deals mostly in subtle, delicate shading *within single words*, and is not by any means accomplished by a general rise or fall in the voice in speaking a sentence. Yet certain sentences may be effectively delivered with just such inflection. Try this sentence in several ways, making no modulation until you come to the last two syllables, as indicated,

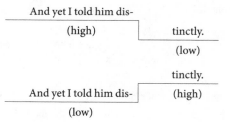

Now try this sentence by inflecting the important words so as to bring out various shades of meaning. The first forms, illustrated above, show change of pitch *within a single word*; the forms you will work out for yourself should show a number of such inflections throughout the sentence.

One of the chief means of securing emphasis is to employ a long falling inflection on the emphatic words—that is, to let the voice fall to a lower pitch on an *interior* vowel sound in a word. Try it on the words "every," "eleemosynary," and "destroy."

Use long falling inflections on the italicized words in the following selection, noting their emphatic power. Are there any other words here that long falling inflections would help to make expressive?

# Address in the Dartmouth College Case

This, sir, is my case. It is the case not merely of that humble institution; it is the case of *every* college in our land. It is *more*; it is the case of *every eleemosynary* institution throughout our country—of *all* those great charities founded by the piety of our ancestors to alleviate human misery and scatter blessings along the pathway of life. Sir, you may *destroy* this little institution—it is *weak*, it is in your hands. I know it is one of the lesser lights in the literary horizon of our country. You may put it out. But if you do you must carry through your work; you must extinguish, one after another, *all* those great lights of science which, for more than a century, have thrown their radiance over our land!

It is, sir, as I have said, a small college, and yet—there are those who *love* it!

Sir, I know not how others may feel, but as for myself when I see my alma mater surrounded, like Cæsar in the senate house, by those who are reiterating *stab* after *stab*, I would not for this right hand have her turn to me and say, And *thou, too*, my son!

—Daniel Webster

Be careful not to over-inflect. Too much modulation produces an unpleasant effect of artificiality, like a mature matron trying to be kittenish. It is a short step between true expression and unintentional burlesque. Scrutinize your own tones. Take a single expression like "Oh, no!" or "Oh, I see," or "Indeed," and by patient self-examination see how many shades of meaning may be expressed by inflection. This sort of common-sense practise will do you more good than a book of rules. *But don't forget to listen to your own voice.*

## QUESTIONS AND EXERCISES

1. In your own words define (*a*) cadence, (*b*) modulation, (*c*) inflection, (*d*) emphasis.

2. Name five ways of destroying monotony and gaining effectiveness in speech.

3. What states of mind does falling inflection signify? Make as full a list as you can.

4. Do the same for the rising inflection.

5. How does the voice bend in expressing (*a*) surprise? (*b*) shame? (*c*) hate? (*d*) formality? (*e*) excitement?

6. Reread some sentence several times and by using different inflections change the meaning with each reading.

7. Note the inflections employed in some speech or conversation. Were they the best that could be used to bring out the meaning? Criticise and illustrate.

8. Render the following passages:

   Has the gentleman done? Has he completely done?
   And God said, Let there be light: and there was light.

9. Invent an indirect question and show how it would naturally be inflected.

10. Does a direct question always require a rising inflection? Illustrate.

11. Illustrate how the complete ending of an expression or of a speech is indicated by inflection.

12. Do the same for incompleteness of idea.

13. Illustrate (*a*) trembling, (*b*) hesitation, and (*c*) doubt by means of inflection.

14. Show how contrast may be expressed.

15. Try the effects of both rising and falling inflections on the italicized words in the following sentences. State your preference.

> Gentlemen, I am *persuaded*, nay, I am *resolved* to speak.

> It is sown a *natural* body; it is raised a *spiritual* body.

## SELECTIONS FOR PRACTISE

In the following selections secure emphasis by means of long falling inflections rather than loudness.

Repeat these selections, attempting to put into practise all the technical principles that we have thus far had; emphasizing important words, subordinating unimportant words, variety of pitch, changing tempo, pause, and inflection. If these principles are applied you will have no trouble with monotony.

Constant practise will give great facility in the use of inflection and will render the voice itself flexible.

## Charles I

We charge him with having broken his coronation oath; and we are told that he kept his marriage vow! We accuse him of having given up his people to the merciless inflictions of the most hot-headed and hard-hearted of prelates; and the defence is, that he took his little son on his knee and kissed him! We censure him for having violated the articles of the Petition of Right, after having, for good and valuable consideration, promised to observe them; and we are informed that he was accustomed to hear prayers at six o'clock in the morning! It is to such considerations as these, together with his Vandyke dress, his handsome face, and his peaked beard, that he owes, we verily believe, most of his popularity with the present generation.

—T. B. Macaulay

## Abraham Lincoln

We needed not that he should put on paper that he believed in slavery, who, with treason, with murder, with cruelty infernal, hovered around that majestic man to destroy his life. He was himself but the long sting with which slavery struck at liberty; and he carried the poison that belonged to slavery. As long as this nation lasts, it will never be forgotten that we have one martyred President—never! Never, while time lasts, while heaven lasts, while hell rocks and groans, will it be forgotten that slavery, by its minions, slew him, and in slaying him made manifest its whole nature and tendency.

But another thing for us to remember is that this blow was aimed at the life of the government and of the nation. Lincoln was slain; America was meant. The man was cast down; the government was smitten at. It was the President who was killed. It was national life, breathing freedom and meaning beneficence, that was sought. He, the man of Illinois, the private man, divested of robes and the insignia of authority, representing nothing but his personal self, might have been hated; but that would not have called forth the murderer's blow. It was because he stood in the place of government, representing government and a government that represented right and liberty, that he was singled out.

This, then, is a crime against universal government. It is not a blow at the foundations of our government, more than at the foundations of the English government, of the French government, of every compact and well-organized government. It was a crime against mankind. The whole world will repudiate and stigmatize it as a deed without a shade of redeeming light . . .

The blow, however, has signally failed. The cause is not stricken; it is strengthened. This nation has dissolved,—but in tears only. It stands, four-square, more solid, to-day, than any pyramid in Egypt. This people are neither wasted, nor daunted, nor disordered. Men hate slavery and love liberty with stronger hate and love to-day than ever before. The Government is not weakened, it is made stronger. . . .

And now the martyr is moving in triumphal march, mightier than when alive. The nation rises up at every stage of his coming. Cities and states are his pall-bearers, and the cannon beats the hours with solemn progression. Dead—dead—dead—he yet speaketh! Is Washington dead? Is Hampden dead? Is David dead? Is any man dead that ever was fit to live? Disenthralled of flesh, and risen to the unobstructed sphere where passion never comes, he begins his illimitable work. His life now is grafted upon the Infinite, and will be fruitful as no earthly life can be. Pass on, thou that hast overcome! Your sorrows O people, are his peace! Your bells, and bands, and muffled drums sound triumph in his ear. Wail and weep here; God makes it echo joy and triumph there. Pass on, victor!

Four years ago, O Illinois, we took from your midst an untried man, and from among the people; we return him to you a mighty conqueror. Not thine any more, but the nation's; not ours, but the world's. Give him place, ye prairies! In the midst of this great Continent his dust shall rest, a sacred treasure to myriads who shall make pilgrimage to that shrine to kindle anew their zeal and patriotism. Ye winds, that move over the mighty places of the West, chant his requiem! Ye people, behold a martyr, whose blood, as so many inarticulate words, pleads for fidelity, for law, for liberty!

—Henry Ward Beecher

# The History of Liberty

The event which we commemorate is all-important, not merely in our own annals, but in those of the world. The sententious English poet has declared that "the proper study of mankind is man," and of all inquiries of a temporal nature, the history of our fellow-beings is unquestionably among the most interesting. But not all the chapters of human history are alike important. The annals of our race have been filled up with incidents which concern not, or at least ought not to concern, the great company of mankind. History, as it has often been written, is the genealogy of princes, the field-book of conquerors; and the fortunes of our fellow-men have been treated only so far as they have been affected by the influence of the great masters and destroyers of our race. Such history is, I will not say a worthless study, for it is necessary for us to know the dark side as well as the bright side of our condition. But it is a melancholy study which fills the bosom of the philanthropist and the friend of liberty with sorrow.

But the history of liberty—the history of men struggling to be free—the history of men who have acquired and are exercising their freedom—the history of those great movements in the world, by which liberty has been established and perpetuated, forms a subject which we cannot contemplate too closely. This is the real history of man, of the human family, of rational immortal beings. . . .

The trial of adversity was theirs; the trial of prosperity is ours. Let us meet it as men who know their duty and prize their blessings. Our position is the most enviable, the most responsible, which men can fill. If this generation does its duty, the cause of constitutional freedom is safe. If we fail—if we fail—not only do we defraud our children of the inheritance which we received from our fathers, but we blast the hopes of the friends of liberty throughout our continent, throughout Europe, throughout the world, to the end of time.

History is not without her examples of hard-fought fields, where the banner of liberty has floated triumphantly on the wildest storm of battle. She is without her examples of a people by whom the dear-bought treasure has been wisely employed and safely handed down. The eyes of the world are turned for that example to us. . . .

Let us, then, as we assemble on the birthday of the nation, as we gather upon the green turf, once wet with precious blood—let us devote ourselves to the sacred cause of constitutional liberty! Let us abjure the interests and passions which divide the great family of American freemen! Let the rage of party spirit sleep to-day! Let us resolve that our children shall have cause to bless the memory of their fathers, as we have cause to bless the memory of ours!

—Edward Everett

# CHAPTER VIII

# *Concentration in Delivery*

Attention is the microscope of the mental eye. Its power may be high
or low; its field of view narrow or broad. When high power is used
attention is confined within very circumscribed limits, but its action
is exceedingly intense and absorbing. It sees but few things, but these
few are observed "through and through" . . . Mental energy and activity,
whether of perception or of thought, thus concentrated, act like the sun's
rays concentrated by the burning glass. The object is illumined, heated,
set on fire. Impressions are so deep that they can never be effaced.
Attention of this sort is the prime condition of the most productive
mental labor.

—DANIEL PUTNAM, *Psychology*

TRY TO RUB THE TOP OF YOUR HEAD FORWARD AND BACKWARD AT THE SAME TIME
that you are patting your chest. Unless your powers of coördination are well developed you will find it confusing, if not impossible. The brain needs special training before
it can do two or more things efficiently at the same instant. It may seem like splitting a hair
between its north and northwest corner, but some psychologists argue that no brain can
think two distinct thoughts, absolutely simultaneously—that what seems to be simultane-
ous is really very rapid rotation from the first thought to the second and back again, just
as in the above-cited experiment the attention must shift from one hand to the other until
one or the other movement becomes partly or wholly automatic.

Whatever is the psychological truth of this contention it is undeniable that the mind
measurably loses grip on one idea the moment the attention is projected decidedly ahead
to a second or a third idea.

A fault in public speakers that is as pernicious as it is common is that they try to think
of the succeeding sentence while still uttering the former, and in this way their concentration trails off; in consequence, they start their sentences strongly and end them weakly.
In a well-prepared written speech the emphatic word usually comes at one end of the sentence. But an emphatic word needs emphatic expression, and this is precisely what it does
not get when concentration flags by leaping too soon to that which is next to be uttered.
Concentrate all your mental energies on the present sentence. Remember that the mind
of your audience follows yours very closely, and if you withdraw your attention from what

you are saying to what you are going to say, your audience will also withdraw theirs. They may not do so consciously and deliberately, but they will surely cease to give importance to the things that you yourself slight. It is fatal to either the actor or the speaker to cross his bridges too soon.

Of course, all this is not to say that in the natural pauses of your speech you are not to take swift forward surveys—they are as important as the forward look in driving a motor car; the caution is of quite another sort: *while speaking one sentence do not think of the sentence to follow.* Let it come from its proper source—within yourself. You cannot deliver a broadside without concentrated force—that is what produces the explosion. In preparation you store and concentrate thought and feeling; in the pauses during delivery you swiftly look ahead and gather yourself for effective attack; during the moments of actual speech, *SPEAK—DON'T ANTICIPATE.* Divide your attention and you divide your power.

This matter of the effect of the inner man upon the outer needs a further word here, particularly as touching concentration.

"What do you read, my lord?" Hamlet replied, "Words. Words. Words." That is a world-old trouble. The mechanical calling of words is not expression, by a long stretch. Did you ever notice how hollow a memorized speech usually sounds? You have listened to the ranting, mechanical cadence of inefficient actors, lawyers and preachers. Their trouble is a mental one—they are not concentratedly thinking thoughts that cause words to issue with sincerity and conviction, but are merely enunciating word-sounds mechanically. Painful experience alike to audience and to speaker! A parrot is equally eloquent. Again let Shakespeare instruct us, this time in the insincere prayer of the King, Hamlet's uncle. He laments thus pointedly:

> My words fly up, my thoughts remain below:
> Words without thoughts never to heaven go.

The truth is, that as a speaker your words must be born again every time they are spoken, then they will not suffer in their utterance, even though perforce committed to memory and repeated, like Dr. Russell Conwell's lecture, "Acres of Diamonds," five thousand times. Such speeches lose nothing by repetition for the perfectly patent reason that they arise from concentrated thought and feeling and not a mere necessity for saying something—which usually means anything, and that, in turn, is tantamount to nothing. If the thought beneath your words is warm, fresh, spontaneous, a part of your *self*, your utterance will have breath and life. Words are only a result. Do not try to get the result without stimulating the cause.

Do you ask *how* to concentrate? Think of the word itself, and of its philological brother, *concentric.* Think of how a lens gathers and concenters the rays of light within a given circle. It centers them by a process of withdrawal. It may seem like a harsh saying, but the man who cannot concentrate is either weak of will, a nervous wreck, or has never learned what will-power is good for.

You must concentrate by resolutely withdrawing your attention from everything else. If you concentrate your thought on a pain which may be afflicting you, that pain will grow more intense. "Count your blessings" and they will multiply. Center your thought on your strokes and your tennis play will gradually improve. To concentrate is simply to attend to one thing, and attend to nothing else. If you find that you cannot do that, there is something wrong—attend to that first. Remove the cause and the symptom will disappear. Read the chapter on "Will Power." Cultivate your will by willing and then doing, at all costs. Concentrate—and you will win.

## QUESTIONS AND EXERCISES

1. Select from any source several sentences suitable for speaking aloud; deliver them first in the manner condemned in this chapter, and second with due regard for emphasis toward the close of each sentence.

2. Put into about one hundred words your impression of the effect produced.

3. Tell of any peculiar methods you may have observed or heard of by which speakers have sought to aid their powers of concentration, such as looking fixedly at a blank spot in the ceiling, or twisting a watch charm.

4. What effect do such habits have on the audience?

5. What relation does pause bear to concentration?

6. Tell why concentration naturally helps a speaker to change pitch, tempo, and emphasis.

7. Read the following selection through to get its meaning and spirit clearly in your mind. Then read it aloud, concentrating solely on the thought that you are expressing—do not trouble about the sentence or thought that is coming. Half the troubles of mankind arise from anticipating trials that never occur. Avoid this in speaking. Make the end of your sentences just as strong as the beginning. *CONCENTRATE.*

## War!

The last of the savage instincts is war. The cave man's club made law and procured food. Might decreed right. Warriors were saviours.

In Nazareth a carpenter laid down the saw and preached the brotherhood of man. Twelve centuries afterwards his followers marched to the Holy Land to destroy all who differed with them in the worship of the God of Love. Triumphantly they wrote "In Solomon's Porch and in his temple our men rode in the blood of the Saracens up to the knees of their horses."

History is an appalling tale of war. In the seventeenth century Germany, France, Sweden, and Spain warred for thirty years. At Magdeburg 30,000 out of 36,000 were killed regardless of sex or age. In Germany schools were closed for a third of a century, homes burned, women outraged, towns demolished, and the untilled land became a wilderness.

Two-thirds of Germany's property was destroyed and 18,000,000 of her citizens were killed, because men quarrelled about the way to glorify "The Prince of Peace." Marching through rain and snow, sleeping on the ground, eating stale food or starving, contracting diseases and facing guns that fire six hundred times a minute, for fifty cents a day—this is the soldier's life.

At the window sits the widowed mother crying. Little children with tearful faces pressed against the pane watch and wait. Their means of livelihood, their home, their happiness is gone. Fatherless children, broken-hearted women, sick, disabled and dead men—this is the wage of war.

We spend more money preparing men to kill each other than we do in teaching them to live. We spend more money building one battleship than in the annual maintenance of all our state universities. The financial loss resulting from destroying one another's homes in the civil war would have built 15,000,000 houses, each costing $2,000. We pray for love but prepare for hate. We preach peace but equip for war.

> Were half the power that fills the world with terror,
> Were half the wealth bestowed on camp and court
> Given to redeem this world from error,
> There would be no need of arsenal and fort.

War only defers a question. No issue will ever really be settled until it is settled rightly. Like rival "gun gangs" in a back alley, the nations of the world, through the bloody ages, have fought over their differences. Denver cannot fight Chicago and Iowa cannot fight Ohio. Why should Germany be permitted to fight France, or Bulgaria fight Turkey?

When mankind rises above creeds, colors and countries, when we are citizens, not of a nation, but of the world, the armies and navies of the earth will constitute an international police force to preserve the peace and the dove will take the eagle's place.

Our differences will be settled by an international court with the power to enforce its mandates. In times of peace prepare for peace. The wages of war are the wages of sin, and the "wages of sin is death."

—*Editorial by D. C.,* Leslie's Weekly. *Used by permission*

# CHAPTER IX

# *Force*

However, 'tis expedient to be wary:
Indifference, certes, don't produce distress;
And rash enthusiasm in good society
Were nothing but a moral inebriety.

—BYRON, *Don Juan*

YOU HAVE ATTENDED PLAYS THAT SEEMED FAIR, YET THEY DID NOT MOVE YOU, GRIP you. In theatrical parlance, they failed to "get over," which means that their message did not get over the foot-lights to the audience. There was no punch, no jab to them—they had no force.

Of course, all this spells disaster, in big letters, not only in a stage production but in any platform effort. Every such presentation exists solely for the audience, and if it fails to hit them—and the expression is a good one—it has no excuse for living; nor will it live long.

## What Is Force?

Some of our most obvious words open up secret meanings under scrutiny, and this is one of them.

To begin with, we must recognize the distinction between inner and outer force. The one is cause, the other effect. The one is spiritual, the other physical. In this important particular, animate force differs from inanimate force—the power of man, coming from within and expressing itself outwardly, is of another sort from the force of Shimose powder, which awaits some influence from without to explode it. However susceptive to outside stimuli, the true source of power in man lies within himself. This may seem like "mere psychology," but it has an intensely practical bearing on public speaking, as will appear.

Not only must we discern the difference between human force and mere physical force, but we must not confuse its real essence with some of the things that may—and may not—accompany it. For example, loudness is not force, though force at times may be attended by noise. Mere roaring never made a good speech, yet there are moments—moments, mind you, not minutes—when big voice power may be used with tremendous effect.

Nor is violent motion force—yet force may result in violent motion. Hamlet counseled the players:

Nor do not saw the air too much with your hand, thus; but use all gently; for in the very torrent, tempest, and (as I may say) whirlwind of your passion, you must acquire and beget a temperance, that may give it smoothness. Oh, it offends me to the soul, to hear a robustious periwig-pated fellow tear a passion to tatters, to very rags, to split the ears of the groundlings[1]; who, for the most part, are capable of nothing but inexplicable dumb show, and noise. I would have such a fellow whipped for o'er-doing Termagant; it out-herods Herod. Pray you avoid it.

Be not too tame, neither, but let your discretion be your tutor: suit the action to the word, the word to the action; with this special observance, that you o'erstep not the modesty of nature; for anything so overdone is from the purpose of playing, whose end, both at the first, and now, was, and is, to hold, as 'twere, the mirror up to Nature, to show Virtue her own feature, Scorn her own image, and the very age and body of the time his form and pressure. Now, this overdone, or come tardy off, though it make the unskillful laugh, cannot but make the judicious grieve; the censure of the which one must, in your allowance, o'erweigh a whole theater of others. Oh, there be players that I have seen play—and heard others praise, and that highly—not to speak it profanely, that, neither having the accent of Christians, nor the gait of Christian, pagan, or man, have so strutted and bellowed that I have thought some of Nature's journeymen had made men, and not made them well, they imitated humanity so abominably.

—HAMLET, *Act III, Scene 2*

Force is both a cause and an effect. Inner force, which must precede outer force, is a combination of four elements, acting progressively. First of all, *force arises from conviction*. You must be convinced of the truth, or the importance, or the meaning, of what you are about to say before you can give it forceful delivery. It must lay strong hold upon your convictions before it can grip your audience. Conviction convinces.

*The Saturday Evening Post* in an article on "England's T. R."—Winston Spencer Churchill—attributed much of Churchill's and Roosevelt's public platform success to their forceful delivery. No matter what is in hand, these men make themselves believe for the time being that that one thing is the most important on earth. Hence they speak to their audiences in a Do-this-or-you-*PERISH* manner.

That kind of speaking wins, and it is that virile, strenuous, aggressive attitude which both distinguishes and maintains the platform careers of our greatest leaders.

But let us look a little closer at the origins of inner force. How does conviction affect the man who feels it? We have answered the inquiry in the very question itself—he *feels* it: *Conviction produces emotional tension*. Study the pictures of Theodore Roosevelt and of Billy Sunday in action—*action* is the word. Note the tension of their jaw muscles, the taut lines of sinews in their entire bodies when reaching a climax of force. Moral and phys-ical force are alike in being both preceded and accompanied by in-*tens*-ity—tension—tightness of the cords of power.

---

1 Those who sat in the pit or the parquet.

It is this tautness of the bow-string, this knotting of the muscles, this contraction before the spring, that makes an audience *feel*—almost see—the reserve power in a speaker. In some really wonderful way it is more what a speaker does *not* say and do that reveals the dynamo within. *Anything* may come from such stored-up force once it is let loose; and that keeps an audience alert, hanging on the lips of a speaker for his next word. After all, it is all a question of manhood, for a stuffed doll has neither convictions nor emotional tension. If you are upholstered with sawdust, keep off the platform, for your own speech will puncture you.

Growing out of this conviction-tension comes *resolve to make the audience share that conviction-tension*. Purpose is the backbone of force; without it speech is flabby—it may glitter, but it is the iridescence of the spineless jellyfish. You must hold fast to your resolve if you would hold fast to your audience.

Finally, all this conviction-tension-purpose is lifeless and useless unless it results in *propulsion*. You remember how Young in his wonderful "Night Thoughts" delineates the man who

> Pushes his prudent purpose to resolve,
> Resolves, and re-resolves, and dies the same.

Let not your force "die a-borning,"—bring it to full life in its conviction, emotional tension, resolve, and propulsive power.

## Can Force be Acquired?

Yes, if the acquirer has any such capacities as we have just outlined. How to acquire this vital factor is suggested in its very analysis: Live with your subject until you are convinced of its importance.

If your message does not of itself arouse you to tension, *PULL* yourself together. When a man faces the necessity of leaping across a crevasse he does not wait for inspiration, he *wills* his muscles into tensity for the spring—it is not without purpose that our English language uses the same word to depict a mighty though delicate steel contrivance and a quick leap through the air. Then resolve—and let it all end in actual *punch*.

This truth is worth reiteration: The man within is the final factor. He must supply the fuel. The audience, or even the man himself, may add the match—it matters little which, only so that there be fire. However skillfully your engine is constructed, however well it works, you will have no force if the fire has gone out under the boiler. It matters little how well you have mastered poise, pause, modulation, and tempo, if your speech lacks fire it is dead. Neither a dead engine nor a dead speech will move anybody.

Four factors of force are measurably within your control, and in that far may be acquired: *ideas, feeling about the subject, wording,* and *delivery*. Each of these is more or less fully discussed in this volume, except wording, which really requires a fuller rhetorical study than can here be ventured. It is, however, of the utmost importance that you should be aware of precisely how wording bears upon force in a sentence. Study "The Working Principles of Rhetoric," by John Franklin Genung, or the rhetorical treatises of Adams

Sherman Hill, of Charles Sears Baldwin, or any others whose names may easily be learned from any teacher.

Here are a few suggestions on the use of words to attain force:

## CHOICE OF WORDS

PLAIN words are more forceful than words less commonly used—*juggle* has more vigor than *prestidigitate.*

SHORT words are stronger than long words—*end* has more directness than *terminate.*

SAXON words are usually more forceful than Latinistic words—for force, use *wars against* rather than *militate against.*

SPECIFIC words are stronger than general words—*pressman* is more definite than *printer.*

CONNOTATIVE words, those that suggest more than they say, have more power than ordinary words—"She *let* herself be married" expresses more than "She *married.*"

EPITHETS, figuratively descriptive words, are more effective than direct names—"Go tell that *old fox,*" has more "punch" than "Go tell that *sly fellow.*"

ONOMATOPOETIC words, words that convey the sense by the sound, are more powerful than other words—*crash* is more effective than *cataclysm.*

## ARRANGEMENT OF WORDS

- Cut out modifiers.
- Cut out connectives.
- Begin with words that demand attention.
- "End with words that deserve distinction," says Prof. Barrett Wendell.
- Set strong ideas over against weaker ones, so as to gain strength by the contrast.
- Avoid elaborate sentence structure—short sentences are stronger than long ones.
- Cut out every useless word, so as to give prominence to the really important ones.
- Let each sentence be a condensed battering ram, swinging to its final blow on the attention.
- A familiar, homely idiom, if not worn by much use, is more effective than a highly formal, scholarly expression.
- Consider well the relative value of different positions in the sentence so that you may give the prominent place to ideas you wish to emphasize.

"But," says someone, "is it not more honest to depend on the inherent interest in a subject, its native truth, clearness and sincerity of presentation, and beauty of utterance, to win your audience? Why not charm men instead of capturing them by assault?"

## Why Use Force?

There is much truth in such an appeal, but not all the truth. Clearness, persuasion, beauty, simple statement of truth, are all essential—indeed, they are all definite parts of a forceful presentment of a subject, without being the only parts. Strong meat may not be as attractive as ices, but all depends on the appetite and the stage of the meal.

You can not deliver an aggressive message with caressing little strokes. No! Jab it in with hard, swift solar plexus punches. You cannot strike fire from flint or from an audience with love taps. Say to a crowded theatre in a lackadaisical manner: "It seems to me that the house is on fire," and your announcement may be greeted with a laugh. If you flash out the words: "The house's on fire!" they will crush one another in getting to the exits.

The spirit and the language of force are definite with conviction. No immortal speech in literature contains such expressions as "it seems to me," "I should judge," "in my opinion," "I suppose," "perhaps it is true." The speeches that will live have been delivered by men ablaze with the courage of their convictions, who uttered their words as eternal truth. Of Jesus it was said that "the common people heard Him gladly." Why? "He taught them as one having *AUTHORITY.*" An audience will never be moved by what "seems" to you to be truth or what in your "humble opinion" may be so. If you honestly can, assert convictions as your conclusions. Be sure you are right before you speak your speech, then utter your thoughts as though they were a Gibraltar of unimpeachable *truth.* Deliver them with the iron hand and confidence of a Cromwell. Assert them with the fire of *authority.* Pronounce them as an *ultimatum.* If you cannot speak with conviction, be silent.

What force did that young minister have who, fearing to be too dogmatic, thus exhorted his hearers: "My friends—as I assume that you are—it appears to be my duty to tell you that if you do not repent, so to speak, forsake your sins, as it were, and turn to righteousness, if I may so express it, you will be lost, in a measure"?

Effective speech must reflect the era. This is not a rose water age, and a tepid, half-hearted speech will not win. This is the century of trip hammers, of overland expresses that dash under cities and through mountain tunnels, and you must instill this spirit into your speech if you would move a popular audience. From a front seat listen to a first-class company present a modern Broadway drama—not a comedy, but a gripping, thrilling drama. Do not become absorbed in the story; reserve all your attention for the technique and the force of the acting. There is a kick and a crash as well as an infinitely subtle intensity in the big, climax-speeches that suggest this lesson: the same well-calculated, restrained, delicately shaded force would simply *rivet* your ideas in the minds of your audience. An air-gun will rattle bird-shot against a window pane—it takes a rifle to wing a bullet through plate glass and the oaken walls beyond.

## When to Use Force

An audience is unlike the kingdom of heaven—the violent do not always take it by force. There are times when beauty and serenity should be the only bells in your chime. Force is only one of the great extremes of contrast—use neither it nor quiet utterance to the exclusion of other tones: be various, and in variety find even greater force than you could attain by attempting its constant use. If you are reading an essay on the beauties of the dawn, talking about the dainty bloom of a honey-suckle, or explaining the mechanism of a gas engine, a vigorous style of delivery is entirely out of place. But when you are appealing to wills and consciences for immediate action, forceful delivery wins. In such cases, consider the minds of your audience as so many safes that have been locked and the keys lost. Do not try to figure out the combinations. Pour a little nitro glycerine into the cracks and light the fuse. As these lines are being written a contractor down the street is clearing away the rocks with dynamite to lay the foundations for a great building. When you want to get action, do not fear to use dynamite.

The final argument for the effectiveness of force in public speech is the fact that everything must be enlarged for the purposes of the platform—that is why so few speeches read well in the reports on the morning after: statements appear crude and exaggerated because they are unaccompanied by the forceful delivery of a glowing speaker before an audience heated to attentive enthusiasm. So in preparing your speech you must not err on the side of mild statement—your audience will inevitably tone down your words in the cold grey of afterthought. When Phidias was criticised for the rough, bold outlines of a figure he had submitted in competition, he smiled and asked that his statue and the one wrought by his rival should be set upon the column for which the sculpture was destined. When this was done all the exaggerations and crudities, toned by distances, melted into exquisite grace of line and form. Each speech must be a special study in suitability and proportion.

Omit the thunder of delivery, if you will, but like Wendell Phillips put "silent lightning" into your speech. Make your thoughts breathe and your words burn. Birrell said: "Emerson writes like an electrical cat emitting sparks and shocks in every sentence." Go thou and speak likewise. Get the "big stick" into your delivery—be forceful.

## QUESTIONS AND EXERCISES

1. Illustrate, by repeating a sentence from memory, what is meant by employing force in speaking.

2. Which in your opinion is the most important of the technical principles of speaking that you have studied so far? Why?

3. What is the effect of too much force in a speech? Too little?

4. Note some uninteresting conversation or ineffective speech, and tell why it failed.

5. Suggest how it might be improved.

6. Why do speeches have to be spoken with more force than do conversations?

7. Read aloud the selection on page 53, using the technical principles outlined in chapters III to VIII, but neglect to put any force behind the interpretation. What is the result?

8. Reread several times, doing your best to achieve force.

9. Which parts of the selection on page 53 require the most force?

10. Write a five-minute speech not only discussing the errors of those who exaggerate and those who minimize the use of force, but by imitation show their weaknesses. Do not burlesque, but closely imitate.

11. Give a list of ten themes for public addresses, saying which seem most likely to require the frequent use of force in delivery.

12. In your own opinion, do speakers usually err from the use of too much or too little force?

13. Define (*a*) bombast; (*b*) bathos; (*c*) sentimentality; (*d*) squeamish.

14. Say how the foregoing words describe weaknesses in public speech.

15. Recast in twentieth-century English "Hamlet's Directions to the Players," page 56.

16. Memorize the following extracts from Wendell Phillips' speeches, and deliver them with the of Wendell Phillips' "silent lightning" delivery.

> We are for a revolution! We say in behalf of these hunted lyings, whom God created, and who law-abiding Webster and Winthrop have sworn shall not find shelter in Massachusetts,—we say that they may make their little motions, and pass their little laws in Washington, but that Faneuil Hall repeals them in the name of humanity and the old Bay State!

> My advice to workingmen is this:
>
> If you want power in this country; if you want to make yourselves felt; if you do not want your children to wait long years before they have the bread on the table they ought to have, the leisure in their lives they ought to have, the opportunities in life they ought to have; if you don't want to wait yourselves,— write on your banner, so that every political trimmer can read it, so that every politician, no matter how short-sighted he may be, can read it, "WE NEVER FORGET! If you launch the arrow of sarcasm at labor, WE NEVER FORGET! If there is a division in Congress, and you throw your vote in the wrong scale, WE NEVER FORGET! You may go down on your knees, and say, 'I am sorry I did the act'—but we will say '*IT WILL AVAIL YOU IN HEAVEN TO BE SORRY, BUT ON THIS SIDE OF THE GRAVE, NEVER!*'" So that a man in taking up the labor question will know he is dealing with a hair-trigger pistol, and will say, "I am to be true to justice and to man; otherwise I am a dead duck."

> In Russia there is no press, no debate, no explanation of what government does, no remonstrance allowed, no agitation of public issues. Dead silence, like that which reigns at the summit of Mont Blanc, freezes the whole empire, long ago described as "a despotism tempered by assassination." Meanwhile, such despotism has unsettled the brains of the ruling family, as unbridled power doubtless made some of the twelve Cæsars insane; a madman, sporting with

the lives and comfort of a hundred millions of men. The young girl whispers in her mother's ear, under a ceiled roof, her pity for a brother knouted and dragged half dead into exile for his opinions. The next week she is stripped naked and flogged to death in the public square. No inquiry, no explanation, no trial, no protest, one dead uniform silence, the law of the tyrant. Where is there ground for any hope of peaceful change? No, no! in such a land dynamite and the dagger are the necessary and proper substitutes for Faneuil Hall. Anything that will make the madman quake in his bedchamber, and rouse his victims into reckless and desperate resistance. This is the only view an American, the child of 1620 and 1776, can take of Nihilism. Any other unsettles and perplexes the ethics of our civilization.

Born within sight of Bunker Hill—son of Harvard, whose first pledge was "Truth," citizen of a republic based on the claim that no government is rightful unless resting on the consent of the people, and which assumes to lead in asserting the rights of humanity—I at least can say nothing else and nothing less—no, not if every tile on Cambridge roofs were a devil hooting my words!

For practise on forceful selections, use "The Irrepressible Conflict," page 42; "Abraham Lincoln," page 48, "Pass Prosperity Around," page 305; "A Plea for Cuba," page 32.

# CHAPTER X

# Feeling and Enthusiasm

Enthusiasm is that secret and harmonious spirit that hovers over the production of genius.

—ISAAC DISRAELI, *Literary Character*

IF YOU ARE ADDRESSING A BODY OF SCIENTISTS ON SUCH A SUBJECT AS THE VEINS IN A butterfly's wings, or on road structure, naturally your theme will not arouse much feeling in either you or your audience. These are purely mental subjects. But if you want men to vote for a measure that will abolish child labor, or if you would inspire them to take up arms for freedom, you must strike straight at their feelings. We lie on soft beds, sit near the radiator on a cold day, eat cherry pie, and devote our attention to one of the opposite sex, not because we have reasoned out that it is the right thing to do, but because it feels right. No one but a dyspeptic chooses his diet from a chart. Our feelings dictate what we shall eat and generally how we shall act. Man is a feeling animal, hence the public speaker's ability to arouse men to action depends almost wholly on his ability to touch their emotions.

Negro mothers on the auction-block seeing their children sold away from them into slavery have flamed out some of America's most stirring speeches. True, the mother did not have any knowledge of the technique of speaking, but she had something greater than all technique, more effective than reason: feeling. The great speeches of the world have not been delivered on tariff reductions or post-office appropriations. The speeches that will live have been charged with emotional force. Prosperity and peace are poor developers of eloquence. When great wrongs are to be righted, when the public heart is flaming with passion, that is the occasion for memorable speaking. Patrick Henry made an immortal address, for in an epochal crisis he pleaded for liberty. He had roused himself to the point where he could honestly and passionately exclaim, "Give me liberty or give me death." His fame would have been different had he lived to-day and argued for the recall of judges.

## The Power of Enthusiasm

Political parties hire bands, and pay for applause—they argue that, for vote-getting, to stir up enthusiasm is more effective than reasoning. How far they are right depends on the hearers, but there can be no doubt about the contagious nature of enthusiasm. A watch manufacturer in New York tried out two series of watch advertisements; one argued the superior construction, workmanship, durability, and guarantee offered with the watch;

the other was headed, "A Watch to be Proud of," and dwelt upon the pleasure and pride of ownership. The latter series sold twice as many as the former. A salesman for a locomotive works informed the writer that in selling railroad engines emotional appeal was stronger than an argument based on mechanical excellence.

Illustrations without number might be cited to show that in all our actions we are emotional beings. The speaker who would speak efficiently must develop the power to arouse feeling.

Webster, great debater that he was, knew that the real secret of a speaker's power was an emotional one. He eloquently says of eloquence:

> Affected passion, intense expression, the pomp of declamation, all may aspire after it; they cannot reach it. It comes, if it come at all, like the outbreak of a fountain from the earth, or the bursting forth of volcanic fires, with spontaneous, original, native force.
>
> The graces taught in the schools, the costly ornaments and studied contrivances of speech, shock and disgust men, when their own lives, and the fate of their wives, their children, and their country hang on the decision of the hour. Then words have lost their power, rhetoric is in vain, and all elaborate oratory contemptible. Even genius itself then feels rebuked and subdued, as in the presence of higher qualities. Then patriotism is eloquent, then self-devotion is eloquent. The clear conception outrunning the deductions of logic, the high purpose, the firm resolve, the dauntless spirit, speaking on the tongue, beaming from the eye, informing every feature, and urging the whole man onward, right onward to his subject—this, this is eloquence; or rather, it is something greater and higher than all eloquence; it is action, noble, sublime, godlike action.

When traveling through the Northwest some time ago, one of the present writers strolled up a village street after dinner and noticed a crowd listening to a "faker" speaking on a corner from a goods-box. Remembering Emerson's advice about learning something from every man we meet, the observer stopped to listen to this speaker's appeal. He was selling a hair tonic, which he claimed to have discovered in Arizona. He removed his hat to show what this remedy had done for him, washed his face in it to demonstrate that it was as harmless as water, and enlarged on its merits in such an enthusiastic manner that the half-dollars poured in on him in a silver flood. When he had supplied the audience with hair tonic, he asked why a greater proportion of men than women were bald. No one knew. He explained that it was because women wore thinner-soled shoes, and so made a good electrical connection with mother earth, while men wore thick, dry-soled shoes that did not transmit the earth's electricity to the body. Men's hair, not having a proper amount of electrical food, died and fell out. Of course he had a remedy—a little copper plate that should be nailed on the bottom of the shoe. He pictured in enthusiastic and vivid terms the desirability of escaping baldness—and paid tributes to his copper plates. Strange as it may seem when the story is told in cold print, the speaker's enthusiasm had swept his audience with him, and they crushed around his stand with outstretched "quarters" in their anxiety to be the possessors of these magical plates!

Emerson's suggestion had been well taken—the observer had seen again the wonderful, persuasive power of enthusiasm!

Enthusiasm sent millions crusading into the Holy Land to redeem it from the Saracens. Enthusiasm plunged Europe into a thirty years' war over religion. Enthusiasm sent three small ships plying the unknown sea to the shores of a new world. When Napoleon's army were worn out and discouraged in their ascent of the Alps, the Little Corporal stopped them and ordered the bands to play the Marseillaise. Under its soul-stirring strains there were no Alps.

Listen! Emerson said: "Nothing great was ever achieved without enthusiasm." Carlyle declared that "Every great movement in the annals of history has been the triumph of enthusiasm." It is as contagious as measles. Eloquence is half inspiration. Sweep your audience with you in a pulsation of enthusiasm. Let yourself go. "A man," said Oliver Cromwell, "never rises so high as when he knows not whither he is going."

## How Are We to Acquire and Develop Enthusiasm?

It is not to be slipped on like a smoking jacket. A book cannot furnish you with it. It is a growth—an effect. But an effect of what? Let us see.

Emerson wrote: "A painter told me that nobody could draw a tree without in some sort becoming a tree; or draw a child by studying the outlines of his form merely,—but, by watching for a time his motion and plays, the painter enters his nature, and then can draw him at will in every attitude. So Roos 'entered into the inmost nature of his sheep.' I knew a draughtsman employed in a public survey, who found that he could not sketch the rocks until their geological structure was first explained to him."

When Sarah Bernhardt plays a difficult role she frequently will speak to no one from four o'clock in the afternoon until after the performance. From the hour of four she lives her character. Booth, it is reported, would not permit anyone to speak to him between the acts of his Shakesperean rôles, for he was Macbeth then—not Booth. Dante, exiled from his beloved Florence, condemned to death, lived in caves, half starved; then Dante wrote out his heart in "The Divine Comedy." Bunyan entered into the spirit of his "Pilgrim's Progress" so thoroughly that he fell down on the floor of Bedford jail and wept for joy. Turner, who lived in a garret, arose before daybreak and walked over the hills nine miles to see the sun rise on the ocean, that he might catch the spirit of its wonderful beauty. Wendell Phillips' sentences were full of "silent lightning" because he bore in his heart the sorrow of five million slaves.

There is only one way to get feeling into your speaking—and whatever else you forget, forget not this: *You must actually ENTER INTO* the character you impersonate, the cause you advocate, the case you argue—enter into it so deeply that it clothes you, enthralls you, possesses you wholly. Then you are, in the true meaning of the word, in *sympathy* with your subject, for its feeling is your feeling, you "feel with" it, and therefore your enthusiasm is both genuine and contagious. The Carpenter who spoke as "never man spake" uttered words born out of a passion of love for humanity—he had entered into humanity, and thus became Man.

But we must not look upon the foregoing words as a facile prescription for decocting a feeling which may then be ladled out to a complacent audience in quantities to suit the need of the moment. Genuine feeling in a speech is bone and blood of the speech itself and not something that may be added to it or substracted at will. In the ideal address theme, speaker and audience become one, fused by the emotion and thought of the hour.

## The Need of Sympathy for Humanity

It is impossible to lay too much stress on the necessity for the speaker's having a broad and deep tenderness for human nature. One of Victor Hugo's biographers attributes his power as an orator and writer to his wide sympathies and profound religious feelings. Recently we heard the editor of Collier's Weekly speak on short-story writing, and he so often emphasized the necessity for this broad love for humanity, this truly religious feeling, that he apologized twice for delivering a sermon. Few if any of the immortal speeches were ever delivered for a selfish or a narrow cause—they were born out of a passionate desire to help humanity; instances, Paul's address to the Athenians on Mars Hill, Lincoln's Gettysburg speech, The Sermon on the Mount, Henry's address before the Virginia Convention of Delegates.

The seal and sign of greatness is a desire to serve others. Self-preservation is the first law of life, but self-abnegation is the first law of greatness—and of art. Selfishness is the fundamental cause of all sin, it is the thing that all great religions, all worthy philosophies, have struck at. Out of a heart of real sympathy and love come the speeches that move humanity.

Former United States Senator Albert J. Beveridge in an introduction to one of the volumes of "Modern Eloquence," says: "The profoundest feeling among the masses, the most influential element in their character, is the religious element. It is as instinctive and elemental as the law of self-preservation. It informs the whole intellect and personality of the people. And he who would greatly influence the people by uttering their unformed thoughts must have this great and unanalyzable bond of sympathy with them."

When the men of Ulster armed themselves to oppose the passage of the Home Rule Act, one of the present writers assigned to a hundred men "Home Rule" as the topic for an address to be prepared by each. Among this group were some brilliant speakers, several of them experienced lawyers and political campaigners. Some of their addresses showed a remarkable knowledge and grasp of the subject; others were clothed in the most attractive phrases. But a clerk, without a great deal of education and experience, arose and told how he spent his boyhood days in Ulster, how his mother while holding him on her lap had pictured to him Ulster's deeds of valor. He spoke of a picture in his uncle's home that showed the men of Ulster conquering a tyrant and marching on to victory. His voice quivered, and with a hand pointing upward he declared that if the men of Ulster went to war they would not go alone—a great God would go with them.

The speech thrilled and electrified the audience. It thrills yet as we recall it. The high-sounding phrases, the historical knowledge, the philosophical treatment, of the other speakers largely failed to arouse any deep interest, while the genuine conviction and feeling of the modest clerk, speaking on a subject that lay deep in his heart, not only electri-fied his audience but won their personal sympathy for the cause he advocated.

As Webster said, it is of no use to try to pretend to sympathy or feelings. It cannot be done successfully. "Nature is forever putting a premium on reality." What is false is soon detected as such. The thoughts and feelings that create and mould the speech in the study must be born again when the speech is delivered from the platform. Do not let your words say one thing, and your voice and attitude another. There is no room here for half-hearted, nonchalant methods of delivery. Sincerity is the very soul of eloquence. Carlyle was right: "No Mirabeau, Napoleon, Burns, Cromwell, no man adequate to do anything, but is first of all in right earnest about it; what I call a sincere man. I should say sincerity, a great, deep, genuine sincerity, is the first characteristic of all men in any way heroic. Not the sin-cerity that calls itself sincere; ah no, that is a very poor matter indeed; a shallow braggart, conscious sincerity, oftenest self-conceit mainly. The great man's sincerity is of the kind he cannot speak of—is not conscious of."

## QUESTIONS AND EXERCISES

It is one thing to convince the would-be speaker that he ought to put feeling into his speeches; often it is quite another thing for him to do it. The average speaker is afraid to let himself go, and continually suppresses his emotions. When you put enough feeling into your speeches they will sound overdone to you, unless you are an experienced speaker. They will sound too strong, if you are not used to enlarging for platform or stage, for the delineation of the emotions must be enlarged for public delivery.

1. Study the following speech, going back in your imagination to the time and circumstances that brought it forth. Make it not a memorized historical document, but feel the emotions that gave it birth. The speech is only an effect; live over in your own heart the causes that produced it and try to deliver it at white heat. It is not possible for you to put too much real feeling into it, though of course it would be quite easy to rant and fill it with false emotion. This speech, according to Thomas Jefferson, started the ball of the Revolution rolling. Men were then willing to go out and die for liberty.

### Patrick Henry's Speech
#### Before the Virginia Convention of Delegates

Mr. President, it is natural to man to indulge in the illusions of hope. We are apt to shut our eyes against a painful truth, and listen to the song of that siren, till she transforms us to beasts. Is this the part of wise men, engaged in a great and arduous struggle for liberty? Are we disposed to be of the number of those who, having eyes, see not, and having ears, hear not, the things which so nearly concern our temporal salvation? For my part, whatever anguish of spirit it may cost, I am willing to know the whole truth; to know the worst, and to provide for it.

I have but one lamp by which my feet are guided; and that is the lamp of experience. I know of no way of judging of the future but by the past. And judging by the past, I wish to know what there has been in the conduct of the British Ministry for the last ten years to justify those hopes with which gentlemen have been pleased to solace themselves and the House? Is it that insidious smile with which our petition has been lately received? Trust it not, sir; it will prove a snare to your feet. Suffer not yourselves to be "betrayed with a kiss"! Ask yourselves, how this gracious reception of our petition comports with those warlike preparations which cover our waters and darken our land. Are fleets and armies necessary to a work of love and reconciliation? Have we shown ourselves so unwilling to be reconciled, that force must be called in to win back our love? Let us not deceive ourselves, sir. These are the implements of war and subjugation, the last "arguments" to which kings resort.

I ask gentlemen, sir, what means this martial array, if its purpose be not to force us to submission? Can gentlemen assign any other possible motive for it? Has Great Britain any enemy in this quarter of the world, to call for all this accumulation of navies and armies? No, sir, she has none. They are meant for us; they can be meant for no other. They are sent over to bind and to rivet upon us those chains which the British Ministry have been so long forging. And what have we to oppose to them? Shall we try argument? Sir, we have been trying that for the last ten years. Have we anything new to offer upon the subject? Nothing. We have held the subject up in every light of which it is capable; but it has been all in vain. Shall we resort to entreaty and humble supplication? What terms shall we find which have not been already exhausted? Let us not, I beseech you, sir, deceive ourselves longer. Sir, we have done everything that could be done, to avert the storm which is now coming on. We have petitioned, we have remonstrated, we have supplicated, we have prostrated ourselves before the throne, and have implored its interposition to arrest the tyrannical hands of the Ministry and Parliament. Our petitions have been slighted; our remonstrances have produced additional violence and insult; our supplications have been disregarded, and we have been spurned with contempt from the foot of the throne. In vain, after these things, may we indulge in the fond hope of peace and reconciliation. There is no longer any room for hope. If we wish to be free, if we mean to preserve inviolate those inestimable privileges for which we have been so long contending; if we mean not basely to abandon the noble struggle in which we have been so long engaged, and which we have pledged ourselves never to abandon until the glorious object of our contest shall be obtained, we must fight; I repeat it, sir, we must fight! An appeal to arms, and to the God of Hosts, is all that is left us!

They tell us, sir, that we are weak—"unable to cope with so formidable an adversary"! But when shall we be stronger? Will it be the next week, or the next year? Will it be when we are totally disarmed, and when a British guard shall be stationed in every house? Shall we gather strength by irresolution and inaction? Shall we acquire the means of effectual resistance, by lying supinely on our backs, and hugging the delusive phantom of hope, until our enemies have bound us hand and foot? Sir, we are not weak, if we make a proper use of those means which the God of Nature hath placed in our power. Three millions of people, armed in the holy cause of Liberty, and in such a country as that which we possess, are invincible by any force which our enemy can send against us. Besides, sir, we shall not fight our battles alone. There is a just Power who presides over the destinies of nations, and who will raise up friends to fight our battles for us. The battle, sir, is not to the strong alone; it is to the vigilant, the active, the brave. Besides, sir, we have no election. If we were base enough to desire it, it is now too late to retire from the contest. There is no retreat, but in submission and slavery. Our chains are forged. Their clanking may be heard on the plains of Boston. The war is inevitable; and let it come! I repeat it, sir, let it come! It is in vain, sir, to extenuate the matter. Gentlemen may cry "Peace, peace!" but there is no peace! The war is actually begun! The next gale that sweeps from the north will bring to our ears the clash of resounding arms! Our brethren are already in the field! Why stand we here idle? What is it that gentlemen wish? What would they have? Is life so dear, or peace so sweet, as to be purchased at the price of chains and slavery? Forbid it, Almighty Powers!—I know not what course others may take; but as for me, give me liberty or give me death!

2. Live over in your imagination all the solemnity and sorrow that Lincoln felt at the Gettysburg cemetery. The feeling in this speech is very deep, but it is quieter and more subdued than the preceding one. The purpose of Henry's address was to get action; Lincoln's speech was meant only to dedicate the last resting place of those who had acted. Read it over and over (see page 31) until it burns in your soul. Then commit it and repeat it for emotional expression.

3. Beecher's speech on Lincoln, page 48; Thurston's speech on "A Plea for Cuba," page 32; and the following selection, are recommended for practise in developing feeling in delivery.

A living force that brings to itself all the resources of imagination, all the inspirations of feeling, all that is influential in body, in voice, in eye, in gesture, in posture, in the whole animated man, is in strict analogy with the divine thought and the divine arrangement; and there is no misconstruction more utterly untrue and fatal than this: that oratory is an artificial thing, which deals with baubles and trifles, for the sake of making bubbles of pleasure for transient effect on mercurial audiences. So far from that, it is the consecration of the whole man to the noblest purposes to which one can address himself— the education and inspiration of his fellow men by all that there is in learning, by all that there is in thought, by all that there is in feeling, by all that there is in all of them, sent home through the channels of taste and of beauty.

—Henry Ward Beecher

4. What in your opinion are the relative values of thought and feeling in a speech?

5. Could we dispense with either?

6. What kinds of selections or occasions require much feeling and enthusiasm? Which require little?

7. Invent a list of ten subjects for speeches, saying which would give most room for pure thought and which for feeling.

8. Prepare and deliver a ten-minute speech denouncing the (imaginary) unfeeling plea of an attorney; he may be either the counsel for the defense or the prosecuting attorney, and the accused may be assumed to be either guilty or innocent, at your option.

9. Is feeling more important than the technical principles expounded in chapters III to VII? Why?

10. Analyze the secret of some effective speech or speaker. To what is the success due?

11. Give an example from your own observation of the effect of feeling and enthusiasm on listeners.

12. Memorize Carlyle's and Emerson's remarks on enthusiasm.

13. Deliver Patrick Henry's address, page 67, and Thurston's speech, page 32, without show of feeling or enthusiasm. What is the result?

14. Repeat, with all the feeling these selections demand. What is the result?

15. What steps do you intend to take to develop the power of enthusiasm and feeling in speaking?

16. Write and deliver a five-minute speech ridiculing a speaker who uses bombast, pomposity and over-enthusiasm. Imitate him.

## CHAPTER XI

# Fluency Through Preparation

*Animis opibusque parati*—Ready in mind and resources.

—Motto of South Carolina

*In omnibus negotiis prius quam aggrediare, adhibenda est præparatio diligens*—In all matters before beginning a diligent preparation should be made.

—Cicero, *De Officiis*

Take your dictionary and look up the words that contain the Latin stem flu—the results will be suggestive.

At first blush it would seem that fluency consists in a ready, easy use of words. Not so—the flowing quality of speech is much more, for it is a composite effect, with each of its prior conditions deserving of careful notice.

## The Sources of Fluency

Speaking broadly, fluency is almost entirely a matter of preparation. Certainly, native gifts figure largely here, as in every art, but even natural facility is dependent on the very same laws of preparation that hold good for the man of supposedly small native endowment. Let this encourage you if, like Moses, you are prone to complain that you are not a ready speaker.

Have you ever stopped to analyze that expression, "a ready speaker?" Readiness, in its prime sense, is preparedness, and they are most ready who are best prepared. Quick firing depends more on the alert finger than on the hair trigger. Your fluency will be in direct ratio to two important conditions: your knowledge of what you are going to say, and your being accustomed to telling what you know to an audience. This gives us the second great element of fluency—to preparation must be added the ease that arises from practise; of which more presently.

## Knowledge Is Essential

Mr. Bryan is a most fluent speaker when he speaks on political problems, tendencies of the time, and questions of morals. It is to be supposed, however, that he would not be so fluent in speaking on the bird life of the Florida Everglades. Mr. John Burroughs might be at his best on this last subject, yet entirely lost in talking about international law. Do not expect to speak fluently on a subject that you know little or nothing about. Ctesiphon boasted that he could speak all day (a sin in itself) on any subject that an audience would suggest. He was banished by the Spartans.

But preparation goes beyond the getting of the facts in the case you are to present: it includes also the ability to think and arrange your thoughts, a full and precise vocabulary, an easy manner of speech and breathing, absence of self-consciousness, and the several other characteristics of efficient delivery that have deserved special attention in other parts of this book rather than in this chapter.

Preparation may be either general or specific; usually it should be both. A life-time of reading, of companionship with stirring thoughts, of wrestling with the problems of life—this constitutes a general preparation of inestimable worth. Out of a well-stored mind, and—richer still—a broad experience, and—best of all—a warmly sympathetic heart, the speaker will have to draw much material that no *immediate* study could provide. General preparation consists of all that a man has put into himself, all that heredity and environment have instilled into him, and—that other rich source of preparedness for speech—the friendship of wise companions. When Schiller returned home after a visit with Goethe a friend remarked: "I am amazed by the progress Schiller can make within a single fort-night." It was the progressive influence of a new friendship. Proper friendships form one of the best means for the formation of ideas and ideals, for they enable one to practise in giving expression to thought. The speaker who would speak fluently before an audience should learn to speak fluently and entertainingly with a friend. Clarify your ideas by putting them in words; the talker gains as much from his conversation as the listener. You sometimes begin to converse on a subject thinking you have very little to say, but one idea gives birth to another, and you are surprised to learn that the more you give the more you have to give. This give-and-take of friendly conversation develops mentality, and fluency in expression. Longfellow said: "A single conversation across the table with a wise man is better than ten years' study of books," and Holmes whimsically yet none the less truthfully declared that half the time he talked to find out what he thought. But that method must not be applied on the platform!

After all this enrichment of life by storage, must come the special preparation for the particular speech. This is of so definite a sort that it warrants separate chapter-treatment later.

## Practise

But preparation must also be of another sort than the gathering, organizing, and shaping of materials—it must include *practise*, which, like mental preparation, must be both general and special.

Do not feel surprised or discouraged if practise on the principles of delivery herein laid down seems to retard your fluency. For a time, this will be inevitable. While you are working for proper inflection, for instance, inflection will be demanding your first thoughts, and the flow of your speech, for the time being, will be secondary. This warning, however, is strictly for the closet, for your practise at home. Do not carry any thoughts of inflection with you to the platform. There you must *think* only of your subject. There is an absolute telepathy between the audience and the speaker. If your thought goes to your gesture, their thought will too. If your interest goes to the quality of your voice, they will be regarding that instead of what your voice is uttering.

You have doubtless been adjured to "forget everything but your subject." This advice says either too much or too little. The truth is that while on the platform you must not *forget* a great many things that are not in your subject, but you must not *think* of them. Your attention must consciously go only to your message, but subconsciously you will be attending to the points of technique which have become more or less *habitual by practise.*

A nice balance between these two kinds of attention is important.

You can no more escape this law than you can live without air: Your platform gestures, your voice, your inflection, will all be just as good as your *habit* of gesture, voice, and inflection makes them—no better. Even the thought of whether you are speaking fluently or not will have the effect of marring your flow of speech.

Return to the opening chapter, on self-confidence, and again lay its precepts to heart. Learn by rules to speak without thinking of rules. It is not—or ought not to be—necessary for you to stop to think how to say the alphabet correctly, as a matter of fact it is slightly more difficult for you to repeat Z, Y, X than it is to say X, Y, Z—habit has established the order. Just so you must master the laws of efficiency in speaking until it is a second nature for you to speak correctly rather than otherwise. A beginner at the piano has a great deal of trouble with the mechanics of playing, but as time goes on his fingers become trained and almost instinctively wander over the keys correctly. As an inexperienced speaker you will find a great deal of difficulty at first in putting principles into practise, for you will be scared, like the young swimmer, and make some crude strokes, but if you persevere you will "win out."

Thus, to sum up, the vocabulary you have enlarged by study,[2] the ease in speaking you have developed by practise, the economy of your well-studied emphasis all will sub-consciously come to your aid on the platform. Then the habits you have formed will be earning you a splendid dividend. The fluency of your speech will be at the speed of flow your practise has made habitual.

But this means work. What good habit does not? No philosopher's stone that will act as a substitute for laborious practise has ever been found. If it were, it would be thrown away, because it would kill our greatest joy—the delight of acquisition. If public-speaking means to you a fuller life, you will know no greater happiness than a well-spoken speech. The time you have spent in gathering ideas and in private practise of speaking you will find amply rewarded.

---

2 See chapter on "Growing a Vocabulary."

## QUESTIONS AND EXERCISES

1. What advantages has the fluent speaker over the hesitating talker?

2. What influences, within and without the man himself, work against fluency?

3. Select from the daily paper some topic for an address and make a three-minute address on it. Do your words come freely and your sentences flow out rhythmically? Practise *on the same topic* until they do.

4. Select some subject with which you are familiar and test your fluency by speaking extemporaneously.

5. Take one of the sentiments given below and, following the advice given on pages 72–73, construct a short speech beginning with the last word in the sentence.

   Machinery has created a new economic world.

   The Socialist Party is a strenuous worker for peace.

   He was a crushed and broken man when he left prison.

   War must ultimately give way to world-wide arbitration.

   The labor unions demand a more equal distribution of the wealth that labor creates.

6. Put the sentiments of Mr. Bryan's "Prince of Peace," on page 287, into your own words. Honestly criticise your own effort.

7. Take any of the following quotations and make a five-minute speech on it without pausing to prepare. The first efforts may be very lame, but if you want speed on a typewriter, a record for a hundred-yard dash, or facility in speaking, you must practise, *practise, PRACTISE.*

   There lives more faith in honest doubt,
   Believe me, than in half the creeds.
   —TENNYSON, *In Memoriam*

   Howe'er it be, it seems to me,
       'Tis only noble to be good.
   Kind hearts are more than coronets,
       And simple faith than Norman blood.
   —TENNYSON, *Lady Clara Vere de Vere*

   'Tis distance lends enchantment to the view
   And robes the mountain in its azure hue.
   —CAMPBELL, *Pleasures of Hope*

His best companions, innocence and health,
And his best riches, ignorance of wealth.
                    —GOLDSMITH, *The Deserted Village*

Beware of desperate steps! The darkest day,
Live till tomorrow, will have passed away.
                    —COWPER, *Needless Alarm*

My country is the world, and my religion is to do good.
                    —PAINE, *Rights of Man*

Trade it may help, society extend,
But lures the pirate, and corrupts the friend:
It raises armies in a nation's aid,
But bribes a senate, and the land's betray'd.
                    —POPE, *Moral Essays*

O God, that men should put an enemy in their mouths to steal away
their brains!
                    —SHAKESPEARE, *Othello*

It matters not how strait the gate,
How charged with punishment the scroll,
I am the master of my fate,
I am the captain of my soul.
                    —HENLEY, *Invictus*

The world is so full of a number of things,
I am sure we should all be happy as kings.
                    —STEVENSON, *A Child's Garden of Verses*

If your morals are dreary, depend upon it they are wrong.
                    —STEVENSON, *Essays*

Every advantage has its tax. I learn to be content.
                    —EMERSON, *Essays*

8. Make a two-minute speech on any of the following general subjects, but you will
   find that your ideas will come more readily if you narrow your subject by taking
   some specific phase of it. For instance, instead of trying to speak on "Law" in
   general, take the proposition, "The Poor Man Cannot Afford to Prosecute;" or
   instead of dwelling on "Leisure," show how modern speed is creating more leisure.
   In this way you may expand this subject list indefinitely.

## GENERAL THEMES

Law

Politics

Woman's Suffrage

Initiative and
    Referendum

A Larger Navy

War

Peace

Foreign Immigration

The Liquor Traffic

Labor Unions

Strikes

Socialism

Single Tax

Tariff

Honesty

Courage

Hope

Love

Mercy

Kindness

Justice

Progress

Machinery

Invention

Wealth

Poverty

Agriculture

Science

Surgery

Haste

Leisure

Happiness

Health

Business

America

The Far East

Mobs

Colleges

Sports

Matrimony

Divorce

Child Labor

Education

Books

The Theater

Literature

Electricity

Achievement

Failure

Public Speaking

Ideals

Conversation

The Most Dramatic
    Moment of My Life

My Happiest Days

Things Worth While

What I Hope to Achieve

My Greatest Desire

What I Would Do with a
    Million Dollars

Is Mankind Progressing?

Our Greatest Need

# CHAPTER XII

# *The Voice*

Oh, there is something in that voice that reaches
The innermost recesses of my spirit!

—LONGFELLOW, *Christus*

THE DRAMATIC CRITIC OF THE LONDON TIMES ONCE DECLARED THAT ACTING IS nine-tenths voice work. Leaving the message aside, the same may justly be said of public speaking. A rich, correctly-used voice is the greatest physical factor of persuasiveness and power, often over-topping the effects of reason.

But a good voice, well handled, is not only an effective possession for the professional speaker, it is a mark of personal culture as well, and even a distinct commercial asset. Gladstone, himself the possessor of a deep, musical voice, has said: "Ninety men in every hundred in the crowded professions will probably never rise above mediocrity because the training of the voice is entirely neglected and considered of no importance." These are words worth pondering.

There are three fundamental requisites for a good voice:

## 1. *Ease*

Signor Bonci of the Metropolitan Opera Company says that the secret of good voice is relaxation; and this is true, for relaxation is the basis of ease. The air waves that produce voice result in a different kind of tone when striking against relaxed muscles than when striking constricted muscles. Try this for yourself. Contract the muscles of your face and throat as you do in hate, and flame out "I hate you!" Now relax as you do when thinking gentle, tender thoughts, and say, "I love you." How different the voice sounds.

In practising voice exercises, and in speaking, never force your tones. Ease must be your watchword. The voice is a delicate instrument, and you must not handle it with hammer and tongs. Don't *make* your voice go—*let* it go. Don't work. Let the yoke of speech be easy and its burden light.

Your throat should be free from strain during speech, therefore it is necessary to avoid muscular contraction. The throat must act as a sort of chimney or funnel for the voice, hence any unnatural constriction will not only harm its tones but injure its health.

Nervousness and mental strain are common sources of mouth and throat constriction, so make the battle for poise and self-confidence for which we pleaded in the opening chapter.

But *how* can I relax? you ask. By simply *willing* to relax. Hold your arm out straight from your shoulder. Now—withdraw all power and let it fall. Practise relaxation of the muscles of the throat by letting your neck and head fall forward. Roll the upper part of your body around, with the waist line acting as a pivot. Let your head fall and roll around as you shift the torso to different positions. Do not force your head around— simply relax your neck and let gravity pull it around as your body moves.

Again, let your head fall forward on your breast; raise your head, letting your jaw hang. Relax until your jaw feels heavy, as though it were a weight hung to your face. Remember, you must relax the jaw to obtain command of it. It must be free and flexible for the moulding of tone, and to let the tone pass out unobstructed.

The lips also must be made flexible, to aid in the moulding of clear and beautiful tones. For flexibility of lips repeat the syllables, *mo—me.* In saying *mo*, bring the lips up to resemble the shape of the letter O. In repeating *me,* draw them back as you do in a grin. Repeat this exercise rapidly, giving the lips as much exercise as possible.

Try the following exercise in the same manner:

Mo—E—O—E—OO—Ah.

After this exercise has been mastered, the following will also be found excellent for flexibility of lips:

Memorize these *sounds* indicated (not the *expressions*) so that you can repeat them rapidly.

| A as in *may* | E as in *eat* | OO as in *foot* | OO as in *ooze* |
| A as in *ah* | E as in *met* | OO as in *ooze* | A as in *ah* |
| A as in *at* | I as in *ice* | U as in *use* | E as in *eat* |
| O as in *no* | I as in *it* | Oi as in *oil* | |
| A as in *all* | O as in *no* | Ou as in *our* | |

All the activity of breathing must be centered, not in the throat, but in the middle of the body—you must breathe from the diaphragm. Note the way you breathe when lying flat on the back, undressed in bed. You will observe that all the activity then centers around the diaphragm. This is the natural and correct method of breathing. By constant watchfulness make this your habitual manner, for it will enable you to relax more perfectly the muscles of the throat.

The next fundamental requisite for good voice is

## 2. *Openness*

If the muscles of the throat are constricted, the tone passage partially closed, and the mouth kept half-shut, how can you expect the tone to come out bright and clear, or even to come out at all? Sound is a series of waves, and if you make a prison of your mouth, holding the jaws and lips rigidly, it will be very difficult for the tone to squeeze through, and even when it does escape it will lack force and carrying power. Open your mouth wide, relax all the organs of speech, and let the tone flow out easily.

Start to yawn, but instead of yawning, speak while your throat is open. Make this open-feeling habitual when speaking—we say *make* because it is a matter of resolution and of practise, if your vocal organs are healthy. Your tone passages may be partly closed by enlarged tonsils, adenoids, or enlarged turbinate bones of the nose. If so, a skilled physician should be consulted.

The nose is an important tone passage and should be kept open and free for perfect tones. What we call "talking through the nose" is not talking through the nose, as you can easily demonstrate by holding your nose as you talk. If you are bothered with nasal tones caused by growths or swellings in the nasal passages, a slight, painless operation will remove the obstruction. This is quite important, aside from voice, for the general health will be much lowered if the lungs are continually starved for air.

The final fundamental requisite for good voice is

### 3. *Forwardness*

A voice that is pitched back in the throat is dark, sombre, and unattractive. The tone must be pitched forward, but do not *force* it forward. You will recall that our first principle was ease. *Think* the tone forward and out. Believe it is going forward, and allow it to flow easily. You can tell whether you are placing your tone forward or not by inhaling a deep breath and singing *ah* with the mouth wide open, trying to feel the little delicate sound waves strike the bony arch of the mouth just above the front teeth. The sensation is so slight that you will probably not be able to detect it at once, but persevere in your practise, always thinking the tone forward, and you will be rewarded by feeling your voice strike the roof of your mouth. A correct forward-placing of the tone will do away with the dark, throaty tones that are so unpleasant, inefficient, and harmful to the throat.

Close the lips, humming *ng, im,* or *an.* Think the tone forward. Do you feel it strike the lips?

Hold the palm of your hand in front of your face and say vigorously *crash, dash, whirl, buzz.* Can you feel the forward tones strike against your hand? Practise until you can. Remember, the only way to get your voice forward is to *put* it forward.

## How to Develop the Carrying Power of the Voice

It is not necessary to speak loudly in order to be heard at a distance. It is necessary only to speak correctly. Edith Wynne Matthison's voice will carry in a whisper throughout a large theater. A paper rustling on the stage of a large auditorium can be heard distinctly in the furthermost seat in the gallery. If you will only use your voice correctly, you will not have much difficulty in being heard. Of course it is always well to address your speech to your furthest auditors; if they get it, those nearer will have no trouble, but aside from this obvious suggestion, you must observe these laws of voice production:

Remember to apply the principles of ease, openness and forwardness—they are the prime factors in enabling your voice to be heard at a distance.

Do not gaze at the floor as you talk. This habit not only gives the speaker an amateurish appearance but if the head is hung forward the voice will be directed towards the ground instead of floating out over the audience.

Voice is a series of air vibrations. To strengthen it two things are necessary: more air or breath, and more vibration.

Breath is the very basis of voice. As a bullet with little powder behind it will not have force and carrying power, so the voice that has little breath behind it will be weak. Not only will deep breathing—breathing from the diaphragm—give the voice a better support, but it will give it a stronger resonance by improving the general health.

Usually, ill health means a weak voice, while abundant physical vitality is shown through a strong, vibrant voice. Therefore anything that improves the general vitality is an excellent voice strengthener, provided you *use* the voice properly. Authorities differ on most of the rules of hygiene but on one point they all agree: vitality and longevity are increased by deep breathing. Practise this until it becomes second nature. Whenever you are speaking, take in deep breaths, but in such a manner that the inhalations will be silent.

Do not try to speak too long without renewing your breath. Nature cares for this pretty well unconsciously in conversation, and she will do the same for you in platform speaking if you do not interfere with her premonitions.

A certain very successful speaker developed voice carrying power by running across country, practising his speeches as he went. The vigorous exercise forced him to take deep breaths, and developed lung power. A hard-fought basketball or tennis game is an efficient way of practising deep breathing. When these methods are not convenient, we recommend the following:

Place your hands at your sides, on the waist line.

By trying to encompass your waist with your fingers and thumbs, force all the air out of the lungs.

Take a deep breath. Remember, all the activity is to be centered in the *middle* of the body; do not raise the shoulders. As the breath is taken your hands will be forced out.

Repeat the exercise, placing your hands on the small of the back and forcing them out as you inhale.

Many methods for deep breathing have been given by various authorities. Get the air into your lungs—that is the important thing.

The body acts as a sounding board for the voice just as the body of the violin acts as a sounding board for its tones. You can increase its vibrations by practise.

Place your finger on your lip and hum the musical scale, thinking and placing the voice forward on the lips. Do you feel the lips vibrate? After a little practise they will vibrate, giving a tickling sensation.

Repeat this exercise, throwing the humming sound into the nose. Hold the upper part of the nose between the thumb and forefinger. Can you feel the nose vibrate?

Placing the palm of your hand on top of your head, repeat this humming exercise. Think the voice there as you hum in head tones. Can you feel the vibration there?

Now place the palm of your hand on the back of your head, repeating the foregoing process. Then try it on the chest. Always remember to think your tone where you desire to feel the vibrations. The mere act of thinking about any portion of your body will tend to make it vibrate.

Repeat the following, after a deep inhalation, endeavoring to feel all portions of your body vibrate at the same time. When you have attained this you will find that it is a pleasant sensation.

> What ho, my jovial mates. Come on! We will frolic it like fairies, frisking in the merry moonshine.

## Purity of Voice

This quality is sometimes destroyed by wasting the breath. Carefully control the breath, using only as much as is necessary for the production of tone. Utilize all that you give out. Failure to do this results in a breathy tone. Take in breath like a prodigal; in speaking, give it out like a miser.

## Voice Suggestions

Never attempt to force your voice when hoarse.

Do not drink cold water when speaking. The sudden shock to the heated organs of speech will injure the voice.

Avoid pitching your voice too high—it will make it raspy. This is a common fault. When you find your voice in too high a range, lower it. Do not wait until you get to the platform to try this. Practise it in your daily conversation. Repeat the alphabet, beginning A on the lowest scale possible and going up a note on each succeeding letter, for the development of range. A wide range will give you facility in making numerous changes of pitch.

Do not form the habit of listening to your voice when speaking. You will need your brain to think of what you are saying—reserve your observation for private practise.

## QUESTIONS AND EXERCISES

1. What are the prime requisites for good voice?
2. Tell why each one is necessary for good voice production.
3. Give some exercises for development of these conditions.
4. Why is range of voice desirable?
5. Tell how range of voice may be cultivated.
6. How much daily practise do you consider necessary for the proper development of your voice?
7. How can resonance and carrying power be developed?
8. What are your voice faults?
9. How are you trying to correct them?

# CHAPTER XIII

# *Voice Charm*

A cheerful temper joined with innocence will make beauty attractive, knowledge delightful, and wit good-natured.

—Joseph Addison, *The Tattler*

POE SAID THAT "THE TONE OF BEAUTY IS SADNESS," BUT HE WAS EVIDENTLY THINKING from cause to effect, not contrariwise, for sadness is rarely a producer of beauty—that is peculiarly the province of joy.

The exquisite beauty of a sunset is not exhilarating but tends to a sort of melancholy that is not far from delight. The haunting beauty of deep, quiet music holds more than a tinge of sadness. The lovely minor cadences of bird song at twilight are almost depressing.

The reason we are affected to sadness by certain forms of placid beauty is twofold: movement is stimulating and joy-producing, while quietude leads to reflection, and reflection in turn often brings out the tone of regretful longing for that which is past; secondly, quiet beauty produces a vague aspiration for the relatively unattainable, yet does not stimulate to the tremendous effort necessary to make the dimly desired state or object ours.

We must distinguish, for these reasons, between the sadness of beauty and the joy of beauty. True, joy is a deep, inner thing and takes in much more than the idea of bounding, sanguine spirits, for it includes a certain active contentedness of heart. In this chapter, however, the word will have its optimistic, exuberant connotation—we are thinking now of vivid, bright-eyed, laughing joy.

Musical, joyous tones constitute voice charm, a subtle magnetism that is delightfully contagious. Now it might seem to the desultory reader that to take the lancet and cut into this alluring voice quality would be to dissect a butterfly wing and so destroy its charm. Yet how can we induce an effect if we are not certain as to the cause?

## Nasal Resonance Produces the Bell-tones of the Voice

The tone passages of the nose must be kept entirely free for the bright tones of voice—and after our warning in the preceding chapter you will not confuse what is popularly and erroneously called a "nasal" tone with the true nasal quality, which is so well illustrated by the voice work of trained French singers and speakers.

To develop nasal resonance sing the following, dwelling as long as possible on the *ng* sounds. Pitch the voice in the nasal cavity. Practise both in high and low registers, and develop range—*with brightness.*

Sing-song. Ding-dong. Hong-kong. Long-thong.

Practise in the falsetto voice develops a bright quality in the normal speaking-voice. Try the following, and any other selections you choose, in a falsetto voice. A man's falsetto voice is extremely high and womanish, so men should not practise in falsetto after the exercise becomes tiresome.

She perfectly scorned the best of his clan, and declared the ninth of any man, a perfectly vulgar fraction.

The actress Mary Anderson asked the poet Longfellow what she could do to improve her voice. He replied, "Read aloud daily, joyous, lyric poetry."

The joyous tones are the bright tones. Develop them by exercise. Practise your voice exercises in an attitude of joy. Under the influence of pleasure the body expands, the tone passages open, the action of heart and lungs is accelerated, and all the primary conditions for good tone are established.

More songs float out from the broken windows of the negro cabins in the South than from the palatial homes on Fifth Avenue. Henry Ward Beecher said the happiest days of his life were not when he had become an international character, but when he was an unknown minister out in Lawrenceville, Ohio, sweeping his own church, and working as a carpenter to help pay the grocer. Happiness is largely an attitude of mind, of viewing life from the right angle. The optimistic attitude can be cultivated, and it will express itself in voice charm. A telephone company recently placarded this motto in their booths: "The Voice with the Smile Wins." It does. Try it.

Reading joyous prose, or lyric poetry, will help put smile and joy of soul into your voice. The following selections are excellent for practise.

*REMEMBER* that when you first practise these classics you are to give sole attention to two things: a joyous attitude of heart and body, and bright tones of voice. After these ends have been attained to your satisfaction, carefully review the principles of public speaking laid down in the preceding chapters and put them into practise as you read these passages again and again. *It would be better to commit each selection to memory.*

## SELECTIONS FOR PRACTISE

### From Milton's "L'allegro"

Haste thee, Nymph, and bring with thee
Jest, and youthful Jollity,
Quips and Cranks and wanton Wiles,
Nods and Becks, and wreathèd Smiles,
Such as hang on Hebe's cheek,

And love to live in dimple sleek,—
Sport that wrinkled Care derides,
And Laughter holding both his sides.

Come, and trip it as ye go
On the light fantastic toe;
And in thy right hand lead with thee
The mountain nymph, sweet Liberty:
And, if I give thee honor due,
Mirth, admit me of thy crew,
To live with her, and live with thee,
In unreprovèd pleasures free;

To hear the lark begin his flight,
And singing, startle the dull Night
From his watch-tower in the skies,
Till the dappled Dawn doth rise;
Then to come in spite of sorrow,
And at my window bid good-morrow
Through the sweetbrier, or the vine,
Or the twisted eglantine;
While the cock with lively din
Scatters the rear of darkness thin,
And to the stack, or the barn-door,
Stoutly struts his dames before;

Oft listening how the hounds and horn
Cheerly rouse the slumbering Morn,
From the side of some hoar hill,
Through the high wood echoing shrill;
Sometime walking, not unseen,
By hedge-row elms, on hillocks green,
Right against the eastern gate,
Where the great Sun begins his state,
Robed in flames and amber light,
The clouds in thousand liveries dight,
While the plowman near at hand
Whistles o'er the furrowed land,
And the milkmaid singing blithe,
And the mower whets his scythe,
And every shepherd tells his tale,
Under the hawthorn in the dale.

# The Sea

The sea, the sea, the open sea,
The blue, the fresh, the fever free;
Without a mark, without a bound,
It runneth the earth's wide regions round;
It plays with the clouds, it mocks the skies,
Or like a cradled creature lies.

I'm on the sea, I'm on the sea,
I am where I would ever be,
With the blue above and the blue below,
And silence wheresoe'er I go.
If a storm should come and awake the deep,
What matter? I shall ride and sleep.

I love, oh! how I love to ride
On the fierce, foaming, bursting tide,
Where every mad wave drowns the moon,
And whistles aloft its tempest tune,
And tells how goeth the world below,
And why the southwest wind doth blow!

I never was on the dull, tame shore
But I loved the great sea more and more,
And backward flew to her billowy breast,
Like a bird that seeketh her mother's nest,—
And a mother she was and is to me,
For I was born on the open sea.

The waves were white, and red the morn,
In the noisy hour when I was born;
The whale it whistled, the porpoise rolled,
And the dolphins bared their backs of gold;
And never was heard such an outcry wild,
As welcomed to life the ocean child.

I have lived, since then, in calm and strife,
Full fifty summers a rover's life,
With wealth to spend, and a power to range,
But never have sought or sighed for change:
And death, whenever he comes to me,
Shall come on the wide, unbounded sea!

—Barry Cornwall

The sun does not shine for a few trees and flowers, but for the wide world's joy. The lonely pine upon the mountain-top waves its sombre boughs, and cries, "Thou art my sun." And the little meadow violet lifts its cup of blue, and whispers with its perfumed breath, "Thou art my sun." And the grain in a thousand fields rustles in the wind, and makes answer, "Thou art my sun." And so God sits effulgent in Heaven, not for a favored few, but for the universe of life; and there is no creature so poor or so low that he may not look up with child-like confidence and say, "My Father! Thou art mine."

—HENRY WARD BEECHER

## The Lark

Bird of the wilderness,
Blithesome and cumberless,
Sweet be thy matin o'er moorland and lea!
Emblem of happiness,
Blest is thy dwelling-place:
Oh, to abide in the desert with thee!

Wild is thy lay, and loud,
Far in the downy cloud,—
Love gives it energy; love gave it birth.
Where, on thy dewy wing
Where art thou journeying?
Thy lay is in heaven; thy love is on earth.

O'er fell and fountain sheen,
O'er moor and mountain green,
O'er the red streamer that heralds the day;
Over the cloudlet dim,
Over the rainbow's rim,
Musical cherub, soar, singing, away!

Then, when the gloaming comes,
Low in the heather blooms,
Sweet will thy welcome and bed of love be!
Emblem of happiness,
Blest is thy dwelling-place.
Oh, to abide in the desert with thee!

—JAMES HOGG

In joyous conversation there is an elastic touch, a delicate stroke, upon the central ideas, generally following a pause. This elastic touch adds vivacity to the voice. If you try repeatedly, it can be sensed by feeling the tongue strike the teeth. The entire absence of elastic touch in the voice can be observed in the thick tongue of the intoxicated man. Try to talk with the tongue lying still in the bottom of the mouth, and you will obtain largely the same effect. Vivacity of utterance is gained by using the tongue to strike off the emphatic idea with a decisive, elastic touch.

Deliver the following with decisive strokes on the emphatic ideas. Deliver it in a vivacious manner, noting the elastic touch-action of the tongue. A flexible, responsive tongue is absolutely essential to good voice work.

## From Napoleon's Address to the Directory on His Return from Egypt

What have you done with that brilliant France which I left you? I left you at peace, and I find you at war. I left you victorious and I find you defeated. I left you the millions of Italy, and I find only spoliation and poverty. What have you done with the hundred thousand Frenchmen, my companions in glory? They are dead! . . . This state of affairs cannot last long; in less than three years it would plunge us into despotism.

Practise the following selection, for the development of elastic touch; say it in a joyous spirit, using the exercise to develop voice charm in *all* the ways suggested in this chapter.

## The Brook

I come from haunts of coot and hern,
    I make a sudden sally,
And sparkle out among the fern,
    To bicker down a valley.

By thirty hills I hurry down,
    Or slip between the ridges;
By twenty thorps, a little town,
    And half a hundred bridges.

Till last by Philip's farm I flow
    To join the brimming river;
For men may come and men may go,
    But I go on forever.

I chatter over stony ways,
    In little sharps and trebles,
I bubble into eddying bays,
    I babble on the pebbles.

With many a curve my banks I fret,
   By many a field and fallow,
And many a fairy foreland set
   With willow-weed and mallow.

I chatter, chatter, as I flow
   To join the brimming river;
For men may come and men may go,
   But I go on forever.

I wind about, and in and out,
   With here a blossom sailing,
And here and there a lusty trout,
   And here and there a grayling,

And here and there a foamy flake
   Upon me, as I travel,
With many a silvery water-break
   Above the golden gravel,

And draw them all along, and flow
   To join the brimming river,
For men may come and men may go,
   But I go on forever.

I steal by lawns and grassy plots,
   I slide by hazel covers,
I move the sweet forget-me-nots
   That grow for happy lovers.

I slip, I slide, I gloom, I glance,
   Among my skimming swallows;
I make the netted sunbeam dance
   Against my sandy shallows,

I murmur under moon and stars
   In brambly wildernesses,
I linger by my shingly bars,
   I loiter round my cresses;

And out again I curve and flow
   To join the brimming river;
For men may come and men may go,
   But I go on forever.

—ALFRED TENNYSON

The children at play on the street, glad from sheer physical vitality, display a resonance and charm in their voices quite different from the voices that float through the silent halls of the hospitals. A skilled physician can tell much about his patient's condition from the mere sound of the voice. Failing health, or even physical weariness, tells through the voice. It is always well to rest and be entirely refreshed before attempting to deliver a public address. As to health, neither scope nor space permits us to discuss here the laws of hygiene. There are many excellent books on this subject. In the reign of the Roman emperor Tiberius, one senator wrote to another: "To the wise, a word is sufficient."

"The apparel oft proclaims the man;" the voice always does—it is one of the greatest revealers of character. The superficial woman, the brutish man, the reprobate, the person of culture, often discloses inner nature in the voice, for even the cleverest dissembler cannot entirely prevent its tones and qualities being affected by the slightest change of thought or emotion. In anger it becomes high, harsh, and unpleasant; in love low, soft, and melodious—the variations are as limitless as they are fascinating to observe. Visit a theatrical hotel in a large city, and listen to the buzz-saw voices of the chorus girls from some burlesque "attraction." The explanation is simple—buzz-saw lives. Emerson said: "When a man lives with God his voice shall be as sweet as the murmur of the brook or the rustle of the corn." It is impossible to think selfish thoughts and have either an attractive personality, a lovely character, or a charming voice. If you want to possess voice charm, cultivate a deep, sincere sympathy for mankind. Love will shine out through your eyes and proclaim itself in your tones. One secret of the sweetness of the canary's song may be his freedom from tainted thoughts. Your character beautifies or mars your voice. As a man thinketh in his heart so is his voice.

## QUESTIONS AND EXERCISES

1. Define (a) charm; (b) joy; (c) beauty.

2. Make a list of all the words related to *joy*.

3. Write a three-minute eulogy of "The Joyful Man."

4. Deliver it without the use of notes. Have you carefully considered all the qualities that go to make up voice charm in its delivery?

5. Tell briefly in your own words what means may be employed to develop a charming voice.

6. Discuss the effect of voice on character.

7. Discuss the effect of character on voice.

8. Analyze the voice charm of any speaker or singer you choose.

9. Analyze the defects of any given voice.

10. Make a short humorous speech imitating certain voice defects, pointing out reasons.

**11.** Commit the following stanza and interpret each phase of delight suggested or expressed by the poet.

> An infant when it gazes on a light,
>   A child the moment when it drains the breast,
> A devotee when soars the Host in sight,
>   An Arab with a stranger for a guest,
> A sailor when the prize has struck in fight,
>   A miser filling his most hoarded chest,
> Feel rapture; but not such true joy are reaping
> As they who watch o'er what they love while sleeping.
>
> —BYRON, *Don Juan*

# CHAPTER XIV

# *Distinctness and Precision of Utterance*

In man speaks God.

—HESIOD, *Words and Days*

And endless are the modes of speech, and far
Extends from side to side the field of words.

—HOMER, *Iliad*

IN POPULAR USAGE THE TERMS "PRONUNCIATION," "ENUNCIATION," AND "ARTICULA-tion" are synonymous, but real pronunciation includes three distinct processes, and may therefore be defined as, *the utterance of a syllable or a group of syllables with regard to articulation, accentuation, and enunciation.*

Distinct and precise utterance is one of the most important considerations of public speech. How preposterous it is to hear a speaker making sounds of "inarticulate earnest-ness" under the contented delusion that he is telling something to his audience! Telling? Telling means communicating, and how can he actually communicate without making every word distinct?

Slovenly pronunciation results from either physical deformity or habit. A surgeon or a surgeon dentist may correct a deformity, but your own will, working by self-observation and resolution in drill, will break a habit. All depends upon whether you think it worth while.

Defective speech is so widespread that freedom from it is the exception. It is painfully common to hear public speakers mutilate the king's English. If they do not actually mur-der it, as Curran once said, they often knock an *I* out.

A Canadian clergyman, writing in the *Homiletic Review*, relates that in his student days "a classmate who was an Englishman supplied a country church for a Sunday. On the following Monday he conducted a missionary meeting. In the course of his address he said some farmers thought they were doing their duty toward missions when they gave their 'hodds and hends' to the work, but the Lord required more. At the close of the meet-ing a young woman seriously said to a friend: 'I am sure the farmers do well if they give their hogs and hens to missions. It is more than most people can afford.'"

It is insufferable effrontery for any man to appear before an audience who persists in driving the *h* out of happiness, home and heaven, and, to paraphrase Waldo Messaros, will not let it rest in hell. He who does not show enough self-knowledge to see in himself such glaring faults, nor enough self-mastery to correct them, has no business to instruct others. If he *can* do no better, he should be silent. If he *will* do no better, he should also be silent.

Barring incurable physical defects—and few are incurable nowadays—the whole matter is one of will. The catalogue of those who have done the impossible by faithful work is as inspiring as a roll-call of warriors. "The less there is of you," says Nathan Sheppard, "the more need for you to make the most of what there is of you."

## *Articulation*

Articulation is the forming and joining of the elementary sounds of speech. It seems an appalling task to utter articulately the third-of-a million words that go to make up our English vocabulary, but the way to make a beginning is really simple: *learn to utter correctly, and with easy change from one to the other, each of the forty-four elementary sounds in our language.*

The reasons why articulation is so painfully slurred by a great many public speakers are four: ignorance of the elemental sounds; failure to discriminate between sounds nearly alike; a slovenly, lazy use of the vocal organs; and a torpid will. Anyone who is still master of himself will know how to handle each of these defects.

The vowel sounds are the most vexing source of errors, especially where diphthongs are found. Who has not heard such errors as are hit off in this inimitable verse by Oliver Wendell Holmes:

> Learning condemns beyond the reach of hope
> The careless lips that speak of sŏap for sōap;
> Her edict exiles from her fair abode
> The clownish voice that utters rŏad for rōad;
> Less stern to him who calls his cōat, a cŏat
> And steers his bōat believing it a bŏat.
> She pardoned one, our classic city's boast.
> Who said at Cambridge, mŏst instead of mōst,
> But knit her brows and stamped her angry foot
> To hear a Teacher call a rōōt a rŏŏt.

The foregoing examples are all monosyllables, but bad articulation is frequently the result of joining sounds that do not belong together. For example, no one finds it difficult to say *beauty*, but many persist in pronouncing *duty* as though it were spelled either *dooty* or *juty*. It is not only from untaught speakers that we hear such slovenly articulations as *colyum* for *column*, and *pritty* for *pretty*, but even great orators occasionally offend quite as unblushingly as less noted mortals.

Nearly all such are errors of carelessness, not of pure ignorance—of carelessness because the ear never tries to hear what the lips articulate. It must be exasperating to a foreigner to find that the elemental sound *ou* gives him no hint for the pronunciation of *bough, cough, rough, thorough,* and *through,* and we can well forgive even a man of culture who occasionally loses his way amidst the intricacies of English articulation, but there can be no excuse for the slovenly utterance of the simple vowel sounds which form at once the life and the beauty of our language. He who is too lazy to speak distinctly should hold his tongue.

The consonant sounds occasion serious trouble only for those who do not look with care at the spelling of words about to be pronounced. Nothing but carelessness can account for saying *Jacop, Babtist, sevem, alwus,* or *sadisfy.*

"He that hath yaws to yaw, let him yaw," is the rendering which an Anglophobiac clergyman gave of the familiar scripture, "He that hath ears to hear, let him hear." After hearing the name of Sir Humphry Davy pronounced, a Frenchman who wished to write to the eminent Englishman thus addressed the letter: "Serum Fridavi."

## Accentuation

Accentuation is the stressing of the proper syllables in words. This it is that is popularly called *pronunciation.* For instance, we properly say that a word is mispronounced when it is accented *in'-vite* instead of *in-vite',* though it is really an offense against only one form of pronunciation—accentuation.

It is the work of a lifetime to learn the accents of a large vocabulary and to keep pace with changing usage; but an alert ear, the study of word-origins, and the dictionary habit, will prove to be mighty helpers in a task that can never be finally completed.

## Enunciation

Correct enunciation is the complete utterance of all the sounds of a syllable or a word. Wrong articulation gives the wrong sound to the vowel or vowels of a word or a syllable, as *doo* for *dew;* or unites two sounds improperly, as *hully* for *wholly.* Wrong enunciation is the *incomplete* utterance of a syllable or a word, the sound omitted or added being usually consonantal. To say *needcessity* instead of *necessity* is a wrong articulation; to say *doin* for *doing* is improper enunciation. The one articulates—that is, joints—two sounds that should not be joined, and thus gives the word a positively wrong sound; the other fails to touch all the sounds in the word, and *in that particular way* also sounds the word incorrectly.

"My tex' may be foun' in the fif' and six' verses of the secon' chapter of Titus; and the subjec' of my discourse is 'The Gover'ment of ar Homes.'"[3]

What did this preacher do with his final consonants? This slovenly dropping of essential sounds is as offensive as the common habit of running words together so that they lose their individuality and distinctness. *Lighten dark, uppen down, doncher know, partic'lar, zamination,* are all too common to need comment.

Imperfect enunciation is due to lack of attention and to lazy lips. It can be corrected by resolutely attending to the formation of syllables as they are uttered. Flexible lips will

---

3 *School and College Speaker,* Mitchell.

enunciate difficult combinations of sounds without slighting any of them, but such flexibility cannot be attained except by habitually uttering words with distinctness and accuracy. A daily exercise in enunciating a series of sounds will in a short time give flexibility to the lips and alertness to the mind, so that no word will be uttered without receiving its due complement of sound.

Returning to our definition, we see that when the sounds of a word are properly articulated, the right syllables accented, and full value given to each sound in its enunciation, we have correct pronunciation. Perhaps one word of caution is needed here, lest any one, anxious to bring out clearly every sound, should overdo the matter and neglect the unity and smoothness of pronunciation. Be careful not to bring syllables into so much prominence as to make words seem long and angular. The joints must be kept decently dressed.

Before delivery, do not fail to go over your manuscript and note every sound that may possibly be mispronounced. Consult the dictionary and make assurance doubly sure. If the arrangement of words is unfavorable to clear enunciation, change either words or order, and do not rest until you can follow Hamlet's directions to the players.

## QUESTIONS AND EXERCISES

1. Practise repeating the following rapidly, paying particular attention to the consonants.

   "Foolish Flavius, flushing feverishly, fiercely found fault with Flora's frivolity.[4]"
   Mary's matchless mimicry makes much mischief.
   Seated on shining shale she sells sea shells.
   You youngsters yielded your youthful yule-tide yearnings yesterday.

2. Sound the *l* in each of the following words, repeated in sequence:

   Blue black blinkers blocked Black Blondin's eyes.

3. Do you say a *bloo* sky or a *blue* sky?

4. Compare the *u* sound in *few* and in *new*. Say each aloud, and decide which is correct, *Noo York*, *New Yawk*, or *New York*?

5. Pay careful heed to the directions of this chapter in reading the following, from *Hamlet*. After the interview with the ghost of his father, Hamlet tells his friends Horatio and Marcellus that he intends to act a part:

   > *Horatio.* O day and night, but this is wondrous strange!
   > *Hamlet.* And therefore as a stranger give it welcome.
   > There are more things in heaven and earth, Horatio,
   > Than are dreamt of in your philosophy.
   > But come;
   > Here, as before, never, so help you mercy,
   > How strange or odd so'er I bear myself,—

---

4 *School and College Speaker*, Mitchell.

As I perchance hereafter shall think meet
To put an antic disposition on,—
That you, at such times seeing me, never shall,
With arms encumber'd thus, or this head-shake,
Or by pronouncing of some doubtful phrase,
As "Well, well, we know," or "We could, an if we would,"
Or "If we list to speak," or "There be, an if there might,"
Or such ambiguous giving-out, to note
That you know aught of me: this not to do,
So grace and mercy at your most need help you,
Swear.

—ACT I. SCENE V

6. Make a list of common errors of pronunciation, saying which are due to faulty articulation, wrong accentuation, and incomplete enunciation. In each case make the correction.

7. Criticise any speech you may have heard which displayed these faults.

8. Explain how the false shame of seeming to be too precise may hinder us from cultivating perfect verbal utterance.

9. Over-precision is likewise a fault. To bring out any syllable unduly is to caricature the word. Be *moderate* in reading the following:

## The Last Speech of Maximilian de Robespierre

The enemies of the Republic call me tyrant! Were I such they would grovel at my feet. I should gorge them with gold, I should grant them immunity for their crimes, and they would be grateful. Were I such, the kings we have vanquished, far from denouncing Robespierre, would lend me their guilty support; there would be a covenant between them and me. Tyranny must have tools. But the enemies of tyranny,—whither does their path tend? To the tomb, and to immortality! What tyrant is my protector? To what faction do I belong? Yourselves! What faction, since the beginning of the Revolution, has crushed and annihilated so many detected traitors? You, the people,—our principles— are that faction—a faction to which I am devoted, and against which all the scoundrelism of the day is banded!

The confirmation of the Republic has been my object; and I know that the Republic can be established only on the eternal basis of morality. Against me, and against those who hold kindred principles, the league is formed. My life? Oh! my life I abandon without a regret! I have seen the past; and I foresee the future. What friend of this country would wish to survive the moment when he could no longer serve it,—when he could no longer defend innocence against oppression? Wherefore should I continue in an order of things, where intrigue eternally triumphs over truth; where justice is mocked; where passions the most abject, or fears the most absurd, over-ride the sacred interests of humanity? In witnessing the multitude of vices which the torrent of the Revolution has rolled in turbid communion with its civic virtues, I confess that I have sometimes feared that I should be sullied, in the eyes of posterity, by the impure neighborhood of unprincipled men, who had thrust themselves into association with the sincere friends of humanity; and I rejoice that these conspirators against my country have now, by their reckless rage, traced deep the line of demarcation between themselves and all true men.

Question history, and learn how all the defenders of liberty, in all times, have been overwhelmed by calumny. But their traducers died also. The good and the bad disappear alike from the earth; but in very different conditions. O Frenchmen! O my countrymen! Let not your enemies, with their desolating doctrines, degrade your souls, and enervate your virtues! No, Chaumette, no! Death is not "an eternal sleep!" Citizens! efface from the tomb that motto, graven by sacrilegious hands, which spreads over all nature a funereal crape, takes from oppressed innocence its support, and affronts the beneficent dispensation of death! Inscribe rather thereon these words: "Death is the commencement of immortality!" I leave to the oppressors of the People a terrible testament, which I proclaim with the independence befitting one whose career is so nearly ended; it is the awful truth—"Thou shalt die!"

# CHAPTER XV

# *The Truth About Gesture*

When Whitefield acted an old blind man advancing by slow steps
toward the edge of the precipice, Lord Chesterfield started up and cried:
"Good God, he is gone!"

—NATHAN SHEPPARD, *Before an Audience*

GESTURE IS REALLY A SIMPLE MATTER THAT REQUIRES OBSERVATION AND COMMON sense rather than a book of rules. Gesture is an outward expression of an inward condition. It is merely an effect—the effect of a mental or an emotional impulse struggling for expression through physical avenues.

You must not, however, begin at the wrong end: if you are troubled by your gestures, or a lack of gestures, attend to the cause, not the effect. It will not in the least help matters to tack on to your delivery a few mechanical movements. If the tree in your front yard is not growing to suit you, fertilize and water the soil and let the tree have sunshine. Obviously it will not help your tree to nail on a few branches. If your cistern is dry, wait until it rains; or bore a well. Why plunge a pump into a dry hole?

The speaker whose thoughts and emotions are welling within him like a mountain spring will not have much trouble to make gestures; it will be merely a question of properly directing them. If his enthusiasm for his subject is not such as to give him a natural impulse for dramatic action, it will avail nothing to furnish him with a long list of rules. He may tack on some movements, but they will look like the wilted branches nailed to a tree to simulate life. Gestures must be born, not built. A wooden horse may amuse the children, but it takes a live one to go somewhere.

It is not only impossible to lay down definite rules on this subject, but it would be silly to try, for everything depends on the speech, the occasion, the personality and feelings of the speaker, and the attitude of the audience. It is easy enough to forecast the result of multiplying seven by six, but it is impossible to tell any man what kind of gestures he will be impelled to use when he wishes to show his earnestness. We may tell him that many speakers close the hand, with the exception of the forefinger, and pointing that finger straight at the audience pour out their thoughts like a volley; or that others stamp one foot for emphasis; or that Mr. Bryan often slaps his hands together for great force, holding one palm upward in an easy manner; or that Gladstone would sometimes make a rush at the clerk's table in Parliament and smite it with his hand so forcefully that D'israeli once brought down the house by grimly congratulating himself that such a barrier stood between himself and "the honorable gentleman."

All these things, and a bookful more, may we tell the speaker, but we cannot know whether he can use these gestures or not, any more than we can decide whether he could wear Mr. Bryan's clothes. The best that can be done on this subject is to offer a few practical suggestions, and let personal good taste decide as to where effective dramatic action ends and extravagant motion begins.

### Any Gesture That Merely Calls Attention to Itself Is Bad

The purpose of a gesture is to carry your thought and feeling into the minds and hearts of your hearers; this it does by emphasizing your message, by interpreting it, by expressing it in action, by striking its tone in either a physically descriptive, a suggestive, or a typical gesture—and let it be remembered all the time that gesture includes *all* physical movement, from facial expression and the tossing of the head to the expressive movements of hand and foot. A shifting of the pose may be a most effective gesture.

What is true of gesture is true of all life. If the people on the street turn around and watch your walk, your walk is more important than you are—change it. If the attention of your audience is called to your gestures, they are not convincing, because they *appear* to be—what they have a doubtful right to be in reality—studied. Have you ever seen a speaker use such grotesque gesticulations that you were fascinated by their frenzy of oddity, but could not follow his thought? Do not smother ideas with gymnastics. Savonarola would rush down from the high pulpit among the congregation in the *duomo* at Florence and carry the fire of conviction to his hearers; Billy Sunday slides to base on the platform carpet in dramatizing one of his baseball illustrations. Yet in both instances the message has somehow stood out bigger than the gesture—it is chiefly in calm afterthought that men have remembered the *form* of dramatic expression. When Sir Henry Irving made his famous exit as "Shylock" the last thing the audience saw was his pallid, avaricious hand extended skinny and claw-like against the background. At the time, every one was overwhelmed by the tremendous typical quality of this gesture; now, we have time to think of its art, and discuss its realistic power.

Only when gesture is subordinated to the absorbing importance of the idea—a spontaneous, living expression of living truth—is it justifiable at all; and when it is remembered for itself—as a piece of unusual physical energy or as a poem of grace—it is a dead failure as dramatic expression. There is a place for a unique style of walking—it is the circus or the cake-walk; there is a place for surprisingly rhythmical evolutions of arms and legs—it is on the dance floor or the stage. Don't let your agility and grace put your thoughts out of business.

One of the present writers took his first lessons in gesture from a certain college president who knew far more about what had happened at the Diet of Worms than he did about how to express himself in action. His instructions were to start the movement on a certain word, continue it on a precise curve, and unfold the fingers at the conclusion, ending with the forefinger—just so. Plenty, and more than plenty, has been published on this subject, giving just such silly directions. Gesture is a thing of mentality and feeling—not a matter of geometry. Remember, whenever a pair of shoes, a method of pronunciation, or a gesture calls attention to itself, it is bad. When you have made really good gestures in a good speech your hearers will not go away saying, "What beautiful gestures he made!" but they will say, "I'll vote for that measure." "He is right—I believe in that."

## Gestures Should Be Born of the Moment

The best actors and public speakers rarely know in advance what gestures they are going to make. They make one gesture on certain words tonight, and none at all tomorrow night at the same point—their various moods and interpretations govern their gestures. It is all a matter of impulse and intelligent feeling with them—don't overlook that word *intelligent*. Nature does not always provide the same kind of sunsets or snow flakes, and the movements of a good speaker vary almost as much as the creations of nature.

Now all this is not to say that you must not take some thought for your gestures. If that were meant, why this chapter? When the sergeant despairingly besought the recruit in the awkward squad to step out and look at himself, he gave splendid advice—and worthy of personal application. Particularly while you are in the learning days of public speaking you must learn to criticise your own gestures. Recall them—see where they were useless, crude, awkward, what not, and do better next time. There is a vast deal of difference between being conscious of self and being self-conscious.

It will require your nice discrimination in order to cultivate spontaneous gestures and yet give due attention to practise. While you depend upon the moment it is vital to remember that only a dramatic genius can effectively accomplish such feats as we have related of Whitefield, Savonarola, and others: and doubtless the first time they were used they came in a burst of spontaneous feeling, yet Whitefield declared that not until he had delivered a sermon forty times was its delivery perfected. What spontaneity initiates let practise complete. Every effective speaker and every vivid actor has observed, considered and practised gesture until his dramatic actions are a sub-conscious possession, just like his ability to pronounce correctly without especially concentrating his thought. Every able platform man has possessed himself of a dozen ways in which he might depict in gesture any given emotion; in fact, the means for such expression are endless—and this is precisely why it is both useless and harmful to make a chart of gestures and enforce them as the ideals of what may be used to express this or that feeling. Practise descriptive, suggestive, and typical movements until they come as naturally as a good articulation; and rarely forecast the gestures you will use at a given moment: leave something to that moment.

## Avoid Monotony in Gesture

Roast beef is an excellent dish, but it would be terrible as an exclusive diet. No matter how effective one gesture is, do not overwork it. Put variety in your actions. Monotony will destroy all beauty and power. The pump handle makes one effective gesture, and on hot days that one is very eloquent, but it has its limitations.

### Any Movement That Is Not Significant, Weakens

Do not forget that. Restlessness is not expression. A great many useless movements will only take the attention of the audience from what you are saying. A widely-noted man introduced the speaker of the evening one Sunday lately to a New York audience. The only thing remembered about that introductory speech is that the speaker played nervously with the covering of the table as he talked. We naturally watch moving objects. A janitor putting down a window can take the attention of the hearers from Mr. Roosevelt. By making a few movements at one side of the stage a chorus girl may draw the interest of the spectators from a big scene between the "leads." When our forefathers lived in caves they had to watch moving objects, for movements meant danger. We have not yet overcome the habit. Advertisers have taken advantage of it—witness the moving electric light signs in any city. A shrewd speaker will respect this law and conserve the attention of his audience by eliminating all unnecessary movements.

### Gesture Should Either Be Simultaneous with or Precede the Words—Not Follow Them

Lady Macbeth says: "Bear welcome in your eye, your hand, your tongue." Reverse this order and you get comedy. Say, "There he goes," pointing at him after you have finished your words, and see if the result is not comical.

### Do Not Make Short, Jerky Movements

Some speakers seem to be imitating a waiter who has failed to get a tip. Let your movements be easy, and from the shoulder, as a rule, rather than from the elbow. But do not go to the other extreme and make too many flowing motions—that savors of the lackadaisical.

Put a little "punch" and life into your gestures. You can not, however, do this mechanically. The audience will detect it if you do. They may not know just what is wrong, but the gesture will have a false appearance to them.

### Facial Expression Is Important

Have you ever stopped in front of a Broadway theater and looked at the photographs of the cast? Notice the row of chorus girls who are supposed to be expressing fear. Their attitudes are so mechanical that the attempt is ridiculous. Notice the picture of the "star" expressing the same emotion: his muscles are drawn, his eyebrows lifted, he shrinks, and fear shines through his eyes. That actor *felt* fear when the photograph was taken. The chorus girls felt that it was time for a rarebit, and more nearly expressed that emotion than they did fear. Incidentally, that is one reason why they *stay* in the chorus.

The movements of the facial muscles may mean a great deal more than the movements of the hand. The man who sits in a dejected heap with a look of despair on his face is expressing his thoughts and feelings just as effectively as the man who is waving his arms and shouting from the back of a dray wagon. The eye has been called the window of the soul. Through it shines the light of our thoughts and feelings.

## Do Not Use Too Much Gesture

As a matter of fact, in the big crises of life we do not go through many actions. When your closest friend dies you do not throw up your hands and talk about your grief. You are more likely to sit and brood in dry-eyed silence. The Hudson River does not make much noise on its way to the sea—it is not half so loud as the little creek up in Bronx Park that a bullfrog could leap across. The barking dog never tears your trousers—at least they say he doesn't. Do not fear the man who waves his arms and shouts his anger, but the man who comes up quietly with eyes flaming and face burning may knock you down. Fuss is not force. Observe these principles in nature and practise them in your delivery.

The writer of this chapter once observed an instructor drilling a class in gesture. They had come to the passage from *Henry VIII* in which the humbled Cardinal says: "Farewell, a long farewell to all my greatness." It is one of the pathetic passages of literature. A man uttering such a sentiment would be crushed, and the last thing on earth he would do would be to make flamboyant movements. Yet this class had an elocutionary manual before them that gave an appropriate gesture for every occasion, from paying the gas bill to death-bed farewells. So they were instructed to throw their arms out at full length on each side and say: "Farewell, a long farewell to all my greatness." Such a gesture might possibly be used in an after-dinner speech at the convention of a telephone company whose lines extended from the Atlantic to the Pacific, but to think of Wolsey's using that movement would suggest that his fate was just.

## Posture

The physical attitude to be taken before the audience really is included in gesture. Just what that attitude should be depends, not on rules, but on the spirit of the speech and the occasion. Senator La Follette stood for three hours with his weight thrown on his forward foot as he leaned out over the footlights, ran his fingers through his hair, and flamed out a denunciation of the trusts. It was very effective. But imagine a speaker taking that kind of position to discourse on the development of road-making machinery. If you have a fiery, aggressive message, and will let yourself go, nature will naturally pull your weight to your forward foot. A man in a hot political argument or a street brawl never has to stop to think upon which foot he should throw his weight. You may sometimes place your weight on your back foot if you have a restful and calm message—but don't worry about it: just stand like a man who genuinely feels what he is saying. Do not stand with your heels close together, like a soldier or a butler. No more should you stand with them wide apart like a traffic policeman. Use simple good manners and common sense.

Here a word of caution is needed. We have advised you to allow your gestures and postures to be spontaneous and not woodenly prepared beforehand, but do not go to the extreme of ignoring the importance of acquiring mastery of your physical movements. A muscular hand made flexible by free movement, is far more likely to be an effective instrument in gesture than a stiff, pudgy bunch of fingers. If your shoulders are lithe and carried well, while your chest does not retreat from association with your chin, the chances of using good extemporaneous gestures are so much the better. Learn to keep the *back* of your neck touching your collar, hold your chest high, and keep down your waist measure.

So attention to strength, poise, flexibility, and grace of body are the foundations of good gesture, for they are expressions of vitality, and without vitality no speaker can enter the kingdom of power. When an awkward giant like Abraham Lincoln rose to the sublimest heights of oratory he did so because of the greatness of his soul—his very ruggedness of spirit and artless honesty were properly expressed in his gnarly body. The fire of character, of earnestness, and of message swept his hearers before him when the tepid words of an insincere Apollo would have left no effect. But be sure you are a second Lincoln before you despise the handicap of physical awkwardness.

"Ty" Cobb has confided to the public that when he is in a batting slump he even stands before a mirror, bat in hand, to observe the "swing" and "follow through" of his batting form. If you would learn to stand well before an audience, look at yourself in a mirror—but not too often. Practise walking and standing before the mirror so as to conquer awkwardness—not to cultivate a pose. Stand on the platform in the same easy manner that you would use before guests in a drawing-room. If your position is not graceful, make it so by dancing, gymnasium work, and *by getting grace and poise in your mind.*

Do not continually hold the same position. Any big change of thought necessitates a change of position. Be at home. There are no rules—it is all a matter of taste. While on the platform forget that you have any hands until you desire to use them—then remember them effectively. Gravity will take care of them. Of course, if you want to put them behind you, or fold them once in awhile, it is not going to ruin your speech. Thought and feeling are the big things in speaking—not the position of a foot or a hand. Simply *put* your limbs where you want them to be—you have a will, so do not neglect to use it.

Let us reiterate, do not despise practise. Your gestures and movements may be spontaneous and still be wrong. No matter how natural they are, it is possible to improve them.

It is impossible for anyone—even yourself—to criticise your gestures until after they are made. You can't prune a peach tree until it comes up; therefore speak much, and observe your own speech. While you are examining yourself, do not forget to study statuary and paintings to see how the great portrayers of nature have made their subjects express ideas through action. Notice the gestures of the best speakers and actors. Observe the physical expression of life everywhere. The leaves on the tree respond to the slightest breeze. The muscles of your face, the light of your eyes, should respond to the slightest change of feeling. Emerson says: "Every man that I meet is my superior in some way. In that I learn of him." Illiterate Italians make gestures so wonderful and beautiful that Booth or Barrett might have sat at their feet and been instructed. Open your eyes. Emerson says again: "We are immersed in beauty, but our eyes have no clear vision." Toss this book to one side; go out and watch one child plead with another for a bite of apple; see a street brawl; observe life in action. Do you want to know how to express victory? Watch the victors' hands go high on election night. Do you want to plead a cause? Make a composite photograph of all the pleaders in daily life you constantly see. Beg, borrow, and steal the best you can get, *BUT DON'T GIVE IT OUT AS THEFT.* Assimilate it until it becomes a part of you—then *let* the expression come out.

## QUESTIONS AND EXERCISES

1. From what source do you intend to study gesture?

2. What is the first requisite of good gestures? Why?

3. Why is it impossible to lay down steel-clad rules for gesturing?

4. Describe (*a*) a graceful gesture that you have observed; (*b*) a forceful one; (*c*) an extravagant one; (*d*) an inappropriate one.

5. What gestures do you use for emphasis? Why?

6. How can grace of movement be acquired?

7. When in doubt about a gesture what would you do?

8. What, according to your observations before a mirror, are your faults in gesturing?

9. How do you intend to correct them?

10. What are some of the gestures, if any, that you might use in delivering Thurston's speech, page 32; Grady's speech, page 22? Be specific.

11. Describe some particularly appropriate gesture that you have observed. Why was it appropriate?

12. Cite at least three movements in nature that might well be imitated in gesture.

13. What would you gather from the expressions: *descriptive* gesture, *suggestive* gesture, and *typical* gesture?

14. Select any elemental emotion, such as fear, and try, by picturing in your mind at least five different situations that might call forth this emotion, to express its several phases by gesture—including posture, movement, and facial expression.

15. Do the same thing for such other emotions as you may select.

16. Select three passages from any source, only being sure that they are suitable for public delivery, memorize each, and then devise gestures suitable for each. Say why.

17. Criticise the gestures in any speech you have heard recently.

18. Practise flexible movement of the hand. What exercises did you find useful?

19. Carefully observe some animal; then devise several typical gestures.

20. Write a brief dialogue between any two animals; read it aloud and invent expressive gestures.

21. Deliver, with appropriate gestures, the quotation that heads this chapter.

22. Read aloud the following incident, using dramatic gestures:

> When Voltaire was preparing a young actress to appear in one of his tragedies, he tied her hands to her sides with pack thread in order to check her tendency toward exuberant gesticulation. Under this condition of compulsory immobility she commenced to rehearse, and for some time she bore herself calmly enough; but at last, completely carried away by her feelings, she burst

her bonds and flung up her arms. Alarmed at her supposed neglect of his instructions, she began to apologize to the poet; he smilingly reassured her, however; the gesture was *then* admirable, because it was irrepressible.

—REDWAY, *The Actor's Art*

**23.** Render the following with suitable gestures:

One day, while preaching, Whitefield "suddenly assumed a nautical air and manner that were irresistible with him," and broke forth in these words: "Well, my boys, we have a clear sky, and are making fine headway over a smooth sea before a light breeze, and we shall soon lose sight of land. But what means this sudden lowering of the heavens, and that dark cloud arising from beneath the western horizon? Hark! Don't you hear distant thunder? Don't you see those flashes of lightning? There is a storm gathering! Every man to his duty! The air is dark!—the tempest rages!—our masts are gone!—the ship is on her beam ends! What next?" At this a number of sailors in the congregation, utterly swept away by the dramatic description, leaped to their feet and cried: "The longboat!—take to the longboat!"

—NATHAN SHEPPARD, *Before an Audience*

CHAPTER XVI

# Methods of Delivery

The crown, the consummation, of the discourse is its delivery. Toward it all preparation looks, for it the audience waits, by it the speaker is judged. . . . All the forces of the orator's life converge in his oratory. The logical acuteness with which he marshals the facts around his theme, the rhetorical facility with which he orders his language, the control to which he has attained in the use of his body as a single organ of expression, whatever richness of acquisition and experience are his—these all are now incidents; *the fact* is the sending of his message home to his hearers. . . . The hour of delivery is the "supreme, inevitable hour" for the orator. It is this fact that makes lack of adequate preparation such an impertinence. And it is this that sends such thrills of indescribable joy through the orator's whole being when he has achieved a success—it is like the mother forgetting her pangs for the joy of bringing a son into the world.

—J. B. E., *How to Attract and Hold an Audience*

THERE ARE FOUR FUNDAMENTAL METHODS OF DELIVERING AN ADDRESS; ALL OTHers are modifications of one or more of these: reading from manuscript, committing the written speech and speaking from memory, speaking from notes, and extemporaneous speech. It is impossible to say which form of delivery is best for all speakers in all circumstances—in deciding for yourself you should consider the occasion, the nature of the audience, the character of your subject, and your own limitations of time and ability. However, it is worth while warning you not to be lenient in self-exaction. Say to yourself courageously: What others can do, I can attempt. A bold spirit conquers where others flinch, and a trying task challenges pluck.

## Reading from Manuscript

This method really deserves short shrift in a book on public speaking, for, delude yourself as you may, public reading is not public speaking. Yet there are so many who grasp this broken reed for support that we must here discuss the "read speech"—apologetic misnomer as it is.

Certainly there are occasions—among them, the opening of Congress, the presentation of a sore question before a deliberative body, or a historical commemoration—when it may seem not alone to the "orator" but to all those interested that the chief thing is to express certain thoughts in precise language—in language that *must* not be either misunderstood or misquoted. At such times oratory is unhappily elbowed to a back bench, the manuscript is solemnly withdrawn from the capacious inner pocket of the new frock coat, and everyone settles himself resignedly, with only a feeble flicker of hope that the so-called speech may not be as long as it is thick. The words may be golden, but the hearers' (?) eyes are prone to be leaden, and in about one instance out of a hundred does the perpetrator really deliver an impressive address. His excuse is his apology—he is not to be blamed, as a rule, for some one decreed that it would be dangerous to cut loose from manuscript moorings and take his audience with him on a really delightful sail.

One great trouble on such "great occasions" is that the essayist—for such he is—has been chosen not because of his speaking ability but because his grandfather fought in a certain battle, or his constituents sent him to Congress, or his gifts in some line of endeavor other than speaking have distinguished him.

As well choose a surgeon from his ability to play golf. To be sure, it always interests an audience to see a great man; because of his eminence they are likely to listen to his words with respect, perhaps with interest, even when droned from a manuscript. But how much more effective such a deliverance would be if the papers were cast aside!

Nowhere is the read-address so common as in the pulpit—the pulpit, that in these days least of all can afford to invite a handicap. Doubtless many clergymen prefer finish to fervor—let them choose: they are rarely men who sway the masses to acceptance of their message. What they gain in precision and elegance of language they lose in force.

There are just four motives that can move a man to read his address or sermon:

1.  Laziness is the commonest. Enough said. Even Heaven cannot make a lazy man efficient.
2.  A memory so defective that he really cannot speak without reading. Alas, he is not speaking when he is reading, so his dilemma is painful—and not to himself alone. But no man has a right to assume that his memory is utterly bad until he has buckled down to memory culture—and failed. A weak memory is oftener an excuse than a reason.
3.  A genuine lack of time to do more than write the speech. There are such instances— but they do not occur every week! The disposition of your time allows more flexibility than you realize. Motive 3 too often harnesses up with Motive 1.
4.  A conviction that the speech is too important to risk forsaking the manuscript. But, if it is vital that every word should be so precise, the style so polished, and the thoughts so logical, that the preacher must write the sermon entire, is not the message important enough to warrant extra effort in perfecting its delivery? It is an insult to a congregation and disrespectful to Almighty God to put the phrasing of a message above the message itself. To reach the hearts of the hearers the sermon must be delivered—it is only half delivered when the speaker cannot utter it with original fire and force, when he merely repeats words that were conceived hours or weeks before and hence are like champagne that has lost its fizz. The reading preacher's eyes are tied down to his manuscript; he cannot give the audience the benefit of his expression. How long would a play fill a theater if the actors held their cue-books in hand and read their parts? Imagine Patrick Henry

reading his famous speech; Peter-the-Hermit, manuscript in hand, exhorting the crusaders; Napoleon, constantly looking at his papers, addressing the army at the Pyramids; or Jesus reading the Sermon on the Mount! These speakers were so full of their subjects, their general preparation had been so richly adequate, that there was no necessity for a manuscript, either to refer to or to serve as "an outward and visible sign" of their preparedness. No event was ever so dignified that it required an *artificial* attempt at speech making. Call an essay by its right name, but never call it a speech. Perhaps the most dignified of events is a supplication to the Creator. If you ever listened to the reading of an original prayer you must have felt its superficiality.

Regardless of what the theories may be about manuscript delivery, the fact remains that it does not work out with efficiency. *Avoid it whenever at all possible.*

## Committing the Written Speech and Speaking from Memory

This method has certain points in its favor. If you have time and leisure, it is possible to polish and rewrite your ideas until they are expressed in clear, concise terms. Pope sometimes spent a whole day in perfecting one couplet. Gibbon consumed twenty years gathering material for and rewriting the "Decline and Fall of the Roman Empire." Although you cannot devote such painstaking preparation to a speech, you should take time to eliminate useless words, crowd whole paragraphs into a sentence and choose proper illustrations. Good speeches, like plays, are not written; they are rewritten. The National Cash Register Company follows this plan with their most efficient selling organization: they require their salesmen to memorize verbatim a selling talk. They maintain that there is one best way of putting their selling arguments, and they insist that each salesman use this ideal way rather than employ any haphazard phrases that may come into his mind at the moment.

The method of writing and committing has been adopted by many noted speakers; Julius Cæsar, Robert Ingersoll, and, on some occasions, Wendell Phillips, were distinguished examples. The wonderful effects achieved by famous actors were, of course, accomplished through the delivery of memorized lines.

The inexperienced speaker must be warned before attempting this method of delivery that it is difficult and trying. It requires much skill to make it efficient. The memorized lines of the young speaker will usually *sound* like memorized words, and repel.

If you want to hear an example, listen to a department store demonstrator repeat her memorized lingo about the newest furniture polish or breakfast food. It requires training to make a memorized speech sound fresh and spontaneous, and, unless you have a fine native memory, in each instance the finished product necessitates much labor. Should you forget a part of your speech or miss a few words, you are liable to be so confused that, like Mark Twain's guide in Rome, you will be compelled to repeat your lines from the beginning.

On the other hand, you may be so taken up with trying to recall your written words that you will not abandon yourself to the spirit of your address, and so fail to deliver it with that spontaneity which is so vital to forceful delivery.

But do not let these difficulties frighten you. If committing seems best to you, give it a faithful trial. Do not be deterred by its pitfalls, but by resolute practise avoid them.

One of the best ways to rise superior to these difficulties is to do as Dr. Wallace Radcliffe often does: commit without writing the speech, making practically all the preparation mentally, without putting pen to paper—a laborious but effective way of cultivating both mind and memory.

You will find it excellent practise, both for memory and delivery, to commit the specimen speeches found in this volume and declaim them, with all attention to the principles we have put before you. William Ellery Channing, himself a distinguished speaker, years ago had this to say of practise in declamation:

"Is there not an amusement, having an affinity with the drama, which might be usefully introduced among us? I mean, Recitation. A work of genius, recited by a man of fine taste, enthusiasm, and powers of elocution, is a very pure and high gratification. Were this art cultivated and encouraged, great numbers, now insensible to the most beautiful compositions, might be waked up to their excellence and power."

## Speaking from Notes

The third, and the most popular method of delivery, is probably also the best one for the beginner. Speaking from notes is not ideal delivery, but we learn to swim in shallow water before going out beyond the ropes.

Make a definite plan for your discourse (for a fuller discussion see Chapter XVIII) and set down the points somewhat in the fashion of a lawyer's brief, or a preacher's outline. Here is a sample of very simple notes:

### Attention

I. INTRODUCTION.
   Attention indispensable to the performance of any great work.
   *Anecdote.*

II. DEFINED AND ILLUSTRATED.
   1. From common observation.
   2. From the lives of great men (Carlyle, Robert E. Lee).

III. ITS RELATION TO OTHER MENTAL POWERS.
   1. Reason.
   2. Imagination.
   3. Memory.
   4. Will. *Anecdote.*

IV. ATTENTION MAY BE CULTIVATED.
   1. Involuntary attention.
   2. Voluntary attention. *Examples.*

V. CONCLUSION.
   The consequences of inattention and of attention.

Few briefs would be so precise as this one, for with experience a speaker learns to use little tricks to attract his eye—he may underscore a catch-word heavily, draw a red circle around a pivotal idea, enclose the key-word of an anecdote in a wavy-lined box, and so on indefinitely. These points are worth remembering, for nothing so eludes the swift-glancing eye of the speaker as the sameness of typewriting, or even a regular pen-script. So unintentional a thing as a blot on the page may help you to remember a big "point" in your brief—perhaps by association of ideas.

An inexperienced speaker would probably require fuller notes than the specimen given. Yet that way lies danger, for the complete manuscript is but a short remove from the copious outline. Use as few notes as possible.

They may be necessary for the time being, but do not fail to look upon them as a necessary evil; and even when you lay them before you, refer to them only when compelled to do so. Make your notes as full as you please in preparation, but by all means condense them for platform use.

## Extemporaneous Speech

Surely this is the ideal method of delivery. It is far and away the most popular with the audience, and the favorite method of the most efficient speakers.

"Extemporaneous speech" has sometimes been made to mean unprepared speech, and indeed it is too often precisely that; but in no such sense do we recommend it strongly to speakers old and young. On the contrary, to speak well without notes requires all the preparation which we discussed so fully in the chapter on "Fluency," while yet relying upon the "inspiration of the hour" for some of your thoughts and much of your language. You had better remember, however, that the most effective inspiration of the hour is the inspiration you yourself bring to it, bottled up in your spirit and ready to infuse itself into the audience.

If you extemporize you can get much closer to your audience. In a sense, they appreciate the task you have before you and send out their sympathy. Extemporize, and you will not have to stop and fumble around amidst your notes—you can keep your eye afire with your message and hold your audience with your very glance. You yourself will feel their response as you read the effects of your warm, spontaneous words, written on their countenances.

Sentences written out in the study are liable to be dead and cold when resurrected before the audience. When you create as you speak you conserve all the native fire of your thought. You can enlarge on one point or omit another, just as the occasion or the mood of the audience may demand. It is not possible for every speaker to use this, the most difficult of all methods of delivery, and least of all can it be used successfully without much practise, but it is the ideal towards which all should strive.

One danger in this method is that you may be led aside from your subject into by-paths. To avoid this peril, firmly stick to your mental outline. Practise speaking from a memorized brief until you gain control. Join a debating society—talk, *talk*, TALK, and always extemporize. You may "make a fool of yourself" once or twice, but is that too great a price to pay for success?

Notes, like crutches, are only a sign of weakness. Remember that the power of your speech depends to some extent upon the view your audience holds of you. General Grant's words as president were more powerful than his words as a Missouri farmer. If you would appear in the light of an authority, be one. Make notes on your brain instead of on paper.

## Joint Methods of Delivery

A modification of the second method has been adopted by many great speakers, particularly lecturers who are compelled to speak on a wide variety of subjects day after day; such speakers often commit their addresses to memory but keep their manuscripts in flexible book form before them, turning several pages at a time. They feel safer for having a sheet-anchor to windward—but it is an anchor, nevertheless, and hinders rapid, free sailing, though it drag never so lightly.

Other speakers throw out a still lighter anchor by keeping before them a rather full outline of their written and committed speech.

Others again write and commit a few important parts of the address—the introduction, the conclusion, some vital argument, some pat illustration—and depend on the hour for the language of the rest. This method is well adapted to speaking either with or without notes.

Some speakers read from manuscript the most important parts of their speeches and utter the rest extemporaneously.

Thus, what we have called "joint methods of delivery" are open to much personal variation. You must decide for yourself which is best for you, for the occasion, for your subject, for your audience—for these four factors all have their individual claims.

Whatever form you choose, do not be so weakly indifferent as to prefer the easy way— choose the *best* way, whatever it cost you in time and effort. And of this be assured: only the practised speaker can hope to gain *both* conciseness of argument and conviction in manner, polish of language and power in delivery, finish of style and fire in utterance.

### QUESTIONS AND EXERCISES

1. Which in your judgment is the most suitable form of delivery for you? Why?

2. What objections can you offer to, (*a*) memorizing the entire speech; (*b*) reading from manuscript; (*c*) using notes; (*d*) speaking from memorized outline or notes; (*e*) any of the "joint methods"?

3. What is there to commend in delivering a speech in any of the foregoing methods?

4. Can you suggest any combination of methods that you have found efficacious?

5. What methods, according to your observation, do most successful speakers use?

6. Select some topic from the list on page 76, narrow the theme so as to make it specific (see page 75), and deliver a short address, utilizing the four methods mentioned, in four different deliveries of the speech.

7. Select one of the joint methods and apply it to the delivery of the same address.

8. Which method do you prefer, and why?

9. From the list of subjects in the Appendix select a theme and deliver a five-minute address without notes, but make careful preparation without putting your thoughts on paper.

**NOTE:** It is earnestly hoped that instructors will not pass this stage of the work without requiring of their students much practise in the delivery of original speeches, in the manner that seems, after some experiment, to be best suited to the student's gifts. Students who are studying alone should be equally exacting in demand upon themselves. One point is most important: It is easy to learn to read a speech, therefore it is much more urgent that the pupil should have much practise in speaking from Notes and speaking without Notes. At this stage, pay more attention to manner than to matter—the succeeding chapters take up the composition of the address. Be particularly insistent upon *frequent* and *thorough* review of the principles of delivery discussed in the preceding chapters.

# CHAPTER XVII

# *Thought and Reserve Power*

Providence is always on the side of the last reserve.

—NAPOLEON BONAPARTE

So mightiest powers by deepest calms are fed,
And sleep, how oft, in things that gentlest be!

—BARRY CORNWALL, *The Sea in Calm*

WHAT WOULD HAPPEN IF YOU SHOULD OVERDRAW YOUR BANK ACCOUNT? AS A rule the check would be protested; but if you were on friendly terms with the bank, your check might be honored, and you would be called upon to make good the overdraft.

Nature has no such favorites, therefore extends no credits. She is as relentless as a gasoline tank—when the "gas" is all used the machine stops. It is as reckless for a speaker to risk going before an audience without having something in reserve as it is for the motorist to essay a long journey in the wilds without enough gasoline in sight.

But in what does a speaker's reserve power consist? In a well-founded reliance on his general and particular grasp of his subject; in the quality of being alert and resourceful in thought—particularly in the ability to think while on his feet; and in that self-possession which makes one the captain of all his own forces, bodily and mental.

The first of these elements, adequate preparation, and the last, self-reliance, were discussed fully in the chapters on "Self-Confidence" and "Fluency," so they will be touched only incidentally here; besides, the next chapter will take up specific methods of preparation for public speaking. Therefore the central theme of this chapter is the second of the elements of reserve power—Thought.

## The Mental Storehouse

An empty mind, like an empty larder, may be a serious matter or not—all will depend on the available resources. If there is no food in the cupboard the housewife does not nervously rattle the empty dishes; she telephones the grocer. If you have no ideas, do not rattle your empty *ers* and *ahs*, but *get* some ideas, and don't speak until you do get them.

This, however, is not being what the old New England housekeeper used to call "forehanded." The real solution of the problem of what to do with an empty head is never to let it become empty. In the artesian wells of Dakota the water rushes to the surface and leaps a score of feet above the ground. The secret of this exuberant flow is of course the great supply below, crowding to get out.

What is the use of stopping to prime a mental pump when you can fill your life with the resources for an artesian well? It is not enough to have merely enough; you must have more than enough. Then the pressure of your mass of thought and feeling will maintain your flow of speech and give you the confidence and poise that denote reserve power. To be away from home with only the exact return fare leaves a great deal to circumstances!

Reserve power is magnetic. It does not consist in giving the idea that you are holding something in reserve, but rather in the suggestion that the audience is getting the cream of your observation, reading, experience, feeling, thought. To have reserve power, therefore, you must have enough milk of material on hand to supply sufficient cream.

But how shall we get the milk? There are two ways: the one is first-hand—from the cow; the other is second-hand—from the milkman.

## The Seeing Eye

Some sage has said: "For a thousand men who can speak, there is only one who can think; for a thousand men who can think, there is only one who can see." To see and to think is to get your milk from your own cow.

When the one man in a million who can see comes along, we call him Master. Old Mr. Holbrook, of "Cranford," asked his guest what color ash-buds were in March; she confessed she did not know, to which the old gentleman answered: "I knew you didn't. No more did I—an old fool that I am!—till this young man comes and tells me. 'Black as ash-buds in March.' And I've lived all my life in the country. More shame for me not to know. Black; they are jet-black, madam."

"This young man" referred to by Mr. Holbrook was Tennyson.

Henry Ward Beecher said: "I do not believe that I have ever met a man on the street that I did not get from him some element for a sermon. I never see anything in nature which does not work towards that for which I give the strength of my life. The material for my sermons is all the time following me and swarming up around me."

Instead of saying only one man in a million can see, it would strike nearer the truth to say that none of us sees with perfect understanding more than a fraction of what passes before our eyes, yet this faculty of acute and accurate observation is so important that no man ambitious to lead can neglect it. The next time you are in a car, look at those who sit opposite you and see what you can discover of their habits, occupations, ideals, nationalities, environments, education, and so on. You may not see a great deal the first time, but practise will reveal astonishing results. Transmute every incident of your day into a subject for a speech or an illustration. Translate all that you see into terms of speech. When you can describe all that you have seen in definite words, you are seeing clearly. You are becoming the millionth man.

De Maupassant's description of an author should also fit the public-speaker: "His eye is like a suction pump, absorbing everything; like a pickpocket's hand, always at work.

Nothing escapes him. He is constantly collecting material, gathering-up glances, gestures, intentions, everything that goes on in his presence—the slightest look, the least act, the merest trifle." De Maupassant was himself a millionth man, a Master.

"Ruskin took a common rock-crystal and saw hidden within its stolid heart lessons which have not yet ceased to move men's lives. Beecher stood for hours before the window of a jewelry store thinking out analogies between jewels and the souls of men. Gough saw in a single drop of water enough truth wherewith to quench the thirst of five thousand souls. Thoreau sat so still in the shadowy woods that birds and insects came and opened up their secret lives to his eye. Emerson observed the soul of a man so long that at length he could say, 'I cannot hear what you say, for seeing what you are.' Preyer for three years studied the life of his babe and so became an authority upon the child mind. Observation! Most men are blind. There are a thousand times as many hidden truths and undiscovered facts about us to-day as have made discoverers famous—facts waiting for some one to 'pluck out the heart of their mystery.' But so long as men go about the search with eyes that see not, so long will these hidden pearls lie in their shells. Not an orator but who could more effectively point and feather his shafts were he to search nature rather than libraries. Too few can see 'sermons in stones' and 'books in the running brooks,' because they are so used to seeing merely sermons in books and only stones in running brooks. Sir Philip Sidney had a saying, 'Look in thy heart and write;' Massillon explained his astute knowledge of the human heart by saying, 'I learned it by studying myself;' Byron says of John Locke that 'all his knowledge of the human understanding was derived from studying his own mind.' Since multiform nature is all about us, originality ought not to be so rare."[5]

## *The Thinking Mind*

Thinking is doing mental arithmetic with facts. Add this fact to that and you reach a certain conclusion. Subtract this truth from another and you have a definite result. Multiply this fact by another and have a precise product. See how many times this occurrence happens in that space of time and you have reached a calculable dividend. In thought-processes you perform every known problem of arithmetic and algebra. That is why mathematics are such excellent mental gymnastics. But by the same token, thinking is work. Thinking takes energy. Thinking requires time, and patience, and broad information, and clearheadedness. Beyond a miserable little surface-scratching, few people really think at all—only one in a thousand, according to the pundit already quoted. So long as the present system of education prevails and children are taught through the ear rather than through the eye, so long as they are expected to remember thoughts of others rather than think for themselves, this proportion will continue—one man in a million will be able to see, and one in a thousand to think.

But, however thought-less a mind has been, there is promise of better things so soon as the mind detects its own lack of thought-power. The first step is to stop regarding thought as "the magic of the mind," to use Byron's expression, and see it as thought truly

5 *How to Attract and Hold an Audience*, J. Berg Esenwein.

is—*a weighing of ideas and a placing of them in relationships to each other*. Ponder this definition and see if you have learned to think efficiently.

Habitual thinking is just that—a habit. Habit comes of doing a thing repeatedly. The lower habits are acquired easily, the higher ones require deeper grooves if they are to persist. So we find that the thought-habit comes only with resolute practise; yet no effort will yield richer dividends. Persist in practise, and whereas you have been able to think only an inch-deep into a subject, you will soon find that you can penetrate it a foot.

Perhaps this homely metaphor will suggest how to begin the practise of consecutive thinking, by which we mean *welding a number of separate thought-links into a chain that will hold*. Take one link at a time, see that each naturally belongs with the ones you link to it, and remember that a single missing link means *no chain*.

Thinking is the most fascinating and exhilarating of all mental exercises. Once realize that your opinion on a subject does not represent the choice you have made between what Dr. Cerebrum has written and Professor Cerebellum has said, but is the result of your own earnestly-applied brain-energy, and you will gain a confidence in your ability to speak on that subject that nothing will be able to shake. Your thought will have given you both power and reserve power.

Someone has condensed the relation of thought to knowledge in these pungent, homely lines:

> Don't give me the man who thinks he thinks,
> Don't give me the man who thinks he knows,
> But give me the man who knows he thinks,
> And I have the man who knows he knows!

## Reading as a Stimulus to Thought

No matter how dry the cow, however, nor how poor our ability to milk, there is still the milkman—we can read what others have seen and felt and thought. Often, indeed, such records will kindle within us that pre-essential and vital spark, the *desire* to be a thinker.

The following selection is taken from one of Dr. Newell Dwight Hillis's lectures, as given in "A Man's Value to Society." Dr. Hillis is a most fluent speaker—he never refers to notes. He has reserve power. His mind is a veritable treasure-house of facts and ideas. See how he draws from a knowledge of fifteen different general or special subjects: geology, plant life, Palestine, chemistry, Eskimos, mythology, literature, The Nile, history, law, wit, evolution, religion, biography, and electricity. Surely, it needs no sage to discover that the secret of this man's reserve power is the old secret of our artesian well whose abundance surges from unseen depths.

## The Uses of Books and Reading[6]

Each Kingsley approaches a stone as a jeweler approaches a casket to unlock the hidden gems. Geikie causes the bit of hard coal to unroll the juicy bud, the thick odorous leaves, the pungent boughs, until the bit of carbon enlarges into the beauty of a tropic forest. That little book of Grant Allen's called "How Plants Grow" exhibits trees and shrubs as eating, drinking and marrying. We see certain date groves in Palestine, and other date groves in the desert a hundred miles away, and the pollen of the one carried upon the trade winds to the branches of the other. We see the tree with its strange system of water-works, pumping the sap up through pipes and mains; we see the chemical laboratory in the branches mixing flavor for the orange in one bough, mixing the juices of the pineapple in another; we behold the tree as a mother making each infant acorn ready against the long winter, rolling it in swaths soft and warm as wool blankets, wrapping it around with garments impervious to the rain, and finally slipping the infant acorn into a sleeping bag, like those the Eskimos gave Dr. Kane.

At length we come to feel that the Greeks were not far wrong in thinking each tree had a dryad in it, animating it, protecting it against destruction, dying when the tree withered. Some Faraday shows us that each drop of water is a sheath for electric forces sufficient to charge 800,000 Leyden jars, or drive an engine from Liverpool to London. Some Sir William Thomson tells us how hydrogen gas will chew up a large iron spike as a child's molars will chew off the end of a stick of candy. Thus each new book opens up some new and hitherto unexplored realm of nature. Thus books fulfill for us the legend of the wondrous glass that showed its owner all things distant and all things hidden. Through books our world becomes as "a bud from the bower of God's beauty; the sun as a spark from the light of His wisdom; the sky as a bubble on the sea of His Power." Therefore Mrs. Browning's words, "No child can be called fatherless who has God and his mother; no youth can be called friendless who has God and the companionship of good books."

Books also advantage us in that they exhibit the unity of progress, the solidarity of the race, and the continuity of history. Authors lead us back along the pathway of law, of liberty or religion, and set us down in front of the great man in whose brain the principle had its rise. As the discoverer leads us from the mouth of the Nile back to the headwaters of Nyanza, so books exhibit great ideas and institutions, as they move forward, ever widening and deepening, like some Nile feeding many civilizations. For all the reforms of to-day go back to some reform of yesterday. Man's art goes back to Athens and Thebes. Man's laws go back to Blackstone and Justinian. Man's reapers and plows go back to the savage scratching the ground with his forked stick, drawn by the wild bullock. The heroes of liberty march forward in a solid column. Lincoln grasps the hand of Washington. Washington

---

6 Used by permission.

received his weapons at the hands of Hampden and Cromwell. The great Puritans lock hands with Luther and Savonarola.

The unbroken procession brings us at length to Him whose Sermon on the Mount was the very charter of liberty. It puts us under a divine spell to perceive that we are all coworkers with the great men, and yet single threads in the warp and woof of civilization. And when books have related us to our own age, and related all the epochs to God, whose providence is the gulf stream of history, these teachers go on to stimulate us to new and greater achievements. Alone, man is an unlighted candle. The mind needs some book to kindle its faculties. Before Byron began to write he used to give half an hour to reading some favorite passage. The thought of some great writer never failed to kindle Byron into a creative glow, even as a match lights the kindlings upon the grate. In these burning, luminous moods Byron's mind did its best work. The true book stimulates the mind as no wine can ever quicken the blood. It is reading that brings us to our best, and rouses each faculty to its most vigorous life.

We recognize this as pure cream, and if it seems at first to have its secondary source in the friendly milkman, let us not forget that the theme is "The Uses of Books and Reading." Dr. Hillis both sees and thinks.

It is fashionable just now to decry the value of reading. We read, we are told, to avoid the necessity of thinking for ourselves. Books are for the mentally lazy.

Though this is only a half-truth, the element of truth it contains is large enough to make us pause. Put yourself through a good old Presbyterian soul-searching self-examination, and if reading-from-thought-laziness is one of your sins, confess it. No one can shrive you of it—but yourself. Do penance for it by using your own brains, for it is a transgression that dwarfs the growth of thought and destroys mental freedom. At first the penance will be trying—but at the last you will be glad in it.

Reading should entertain, give information, or stimulate thought. Here, however, we are chiefly concerned with information, and stimulation of thought.

What shall I read for information?

The ample page of knowledge, as Grey tells us, is "rich with the spoils of time," and these are ours for the price of a theatre ticket. You may command Socrates and Marcus Aurelius to sit beside you and discourse of their choicest, hear Lincoln at Gettysburg and Pericles at Athens, storm the Bastile with Hugo, and wander through Paradise with Dante. You may explore darkest Africa with Stanley, penetrate the human heart with Shakespeare, chat with Carlyle about heroes, and delve with the Apostle Paul into the mysteries of faith. The general knowledge and the inspiring ideas that men have collected through ages of toil and experiment are yours for the asking. The Sage of Chelsea was right: "The true university of these days is a collection of books."

To master a worth-while book is to master much else besides; few of us, however, make perfect conquest of a volume without first owning it physically. To read a borrowed book may be a joy, but to assign your own book a place of its own on your own shelves— be they few or many—to love the book and feel of its worn cover, to thumb it over slowly, page by page, to pencil its margins in agreement or in protest, to smile or thrill with its remembered pungencies—no mere book borrower could ever sense all that delight.

The reader who possesses books in this double sense finds also that his books possess him, and the volumes which most firmly grip his life are likely to be those it has cost him some sacrifice to own. These lightly-come-by titles, which Mr. Fatpurse selects, perhaps by proxy, can scarcely play the guide, philosopher and friend in crucial moments as do the books—long coveted, joyously attained—that are welcomed into the lives, and not merely the libraries, of us others who are at once poorer and richer.

So it is scarcely too much to say that of all the many ways in which an owned—a mastered—book is like to a human friend, the truest ways are these: A friend is worth making sacrifices for, both to gain and to keep; and our loves go out most dearly to those into whose inmost lives we have sincerely entered.

When you have not the advantage of the test of time by which to judge books, investigate as thoroughly as possible the authority of the books you read. Much that is printed and passes current is counterfeit. "I read it in a book" is to many a sufficient warranty of truth, but not to the thinker. "What book?" asks the careful mind. "Who wrote it? What does he know about the subject and what right has he to speak on it? Who recognizes him as authority? With what other recognized authorities does he agree or disagree?" Being caught trying to pass counterfeit money, even unintentionally, is an unpleasant situation. Beware lest you circulate spurious coin.

Above all, seek reading that makes you use your own brains. Such reading must be alive with fresh points of view, packed with special knowledge, and deal with subjects of vital interest. Do not confine your reading to what you already know you will agree with. Opposition wakes one up. The other road may be the better, but you will never know it unless you "give it the once over." Do not do all your thinking and investigating in front of given "Q.E.D.'s;" merely assembling reasons to fill in between your theorem and what you want to prove will get you nowhere. Approach each subject with an open mind and—once sure that you have thought it out thoroughly and honestly—have the courage to abide by the decision of your own thought. But don't brag about it afterward.

No book on public speaking will enable you to discourse on the tariff if you know nothing about the tariff. Knowing more about it than the other man will be your only hope for making the other man listen to you.

Take a group of men discussing a governmental policy of which some one says: "It is socialistic." That will commend the policy to Mr. A., who believes in socialism, but condemn it to Mr. B., who does not. It may be that neither had considered the policy beyond noticing that its surface-color was socialistic. The chances are, furthermore, that neither Mr. A. nor Mr. B. has a definite idea of what socialism really is, for as Robert Louis Stevenson says, "Man lives not by bread alone but chiefly by catch words." If you are of this group of men, and have observed this proposed government policy, and investigated it, and thought about it, what you have to say cannot fail to command their respect and approval, for you will have shown them that you possess a grasp of your subject and—to adopt an exceedingly expressive bit of slang—*then* some.

## QUESTIONS AND EXERCISES

1. Robert Houdin trained his son to give one swift glance at a shop window in passing and be able to report accurately a surprising number of its contents. Try this several times on different windows and report the result.

2. What effect does reserve power have on an audience?

3. What are the best methods for acquiring reserve power?

4. What is the danger of too much reading?

5. Analyze some speech that you have read or heard and notice how much real information there is in it. Compare it with Dr. Hillis's speech on "Brave Little Belgium," page 242.

6. Write out a three-minute speech on any subject you choose. How much information, and what new ideas, does it contain? Compare your speech with the extract on page 116 from Dr. Hillis's "The Uses of Books and Reading."

7. Have you ever read a book on the practise of thinking? If so, give your impressions of its value.

NOTE: There are a number of excellent books on the subject of thought and the management of thought. The following are recommended as being especially helpful: "Thinking and Learning to Think," Nathan C. Schaeffer; "Talks to Students on the Art of Study," Cramer; "As a Man Thinketh," Allen.

8. Define (a) logic; (b) mental philosophy (or mental science); (c) psychology; (d) abstract.

# CHAPTER XVIII

# *Subject and Preparation*

Suit your topics to your strength,
And ponder well your subject, and its length;
Nor lift your load, before you're quite aware
What weight your shoulders will, or will not, bear.

—BYRON, *Hints from Horace*

Look to this day, for it is life—the very life of life. In its brief course
lie all the verities and realities of your existence: the bliss of growth,
the glory of action, the splendor of beauty. For yesterday is already a
dream and tomorrow is only a vision; but today, well lived, makes every
yesterday a dream of happiness and every tomorrow a vision of hope.
Look well, therefore, to this day. Such is the salutation of the dawn.

—FROM THE SANSKRIT

IN THE CHAPTER PRECEDING WE HAVE SEEN THE INFLUENCE OF "THOUGHT AND Reserve Power" on general preparedness for public speech. But preparation consists in something more definite than the cultivation of thought-power, whether from original or from borrowed sources—it involves a specifically acquisitive attitude of the whole life. If you would become a full soul you must constantly take in and assimilate, for in that way only may you hope to give out that which is worth the hearing; but do not confuse the acquisition of general information with the mastery of specific knowledge. Information consists of a fact or a group of facts; knowledge is organized information—knowledge knows a fact in relation to other facts.

Now the important thing here is that you should set all your faculties to take in the things about you with the particular object of correlating them and storing them for use in public speech. You must hear with the speaker's ear, see with the speaker's eye, and choose books and companions and sights and sounds with the speaker's purpose in view. At the same time, be ready to receive unplanned-for knowledge. One of the fascinating elements in your life as a public speaker will be the conscious growth in power that casual daily experiences bring. If your eyes are alert you will be constantly discovering facts, illustrations, and ideas without having set out in search of them. These all may be turned to account on the platform; even the leaden events of hum-drum daily life may be melted into bullets for future battles.

## Conservation of Time in Preparation

But, you say, I have so little time for preparation—my mind must be absorbed by other matters. Daniel Webster never let an opportunity pass to gather material for his speeches. When he was a boy working in a sawmill he read out of a book in one hand and busied himself at some mechanical task with the other. In youth Patrick Henry roamed the fields and woods in solitude for days at a time unconsciously gathering material and impressions for his later service as a speaker. Dr. Russell H. Conwell, the man who, the late Charles A. Dana said, had addressed more hearers than any living man, used to memorize long passages from Milton while tending the boiling syrup-pans in the silent New England woods at night. The modern employer would discharge a Webster of today for inattention to duty, and doubtless he would be justified, and Patrick Henry seemed only an idle chap even in those easy-going days; but the truth remains: those who take in power and have the purpose to use it efficiently will some day win to the place in which that stored-up power will revolve great wheels of influence.

Napoleon said that quarter hours decide the destinies of nations. How many quarter hours do we let drift by aimlessly! Robert Louis Stevenson conserved *all* his time; *every* experience became capital for his work—for capital may be defined as "the results of labor stored up to assist future production." He continually tried to put into suitable language the scenes and actions that were in evidence about him. Emerson says: "Tomorrow will be like today. Life wastes itself whilst we are preparing to live."

Why wait for a more convenient season for this broad, general preparation? The fifteen minutes that we spend on the car could be profitably turned into speech-capital.

Procure a cheap edition of modern speeches, and by cutting out a few pages each day, and reading them during the idle minute here and there, note how soon you can make yourself familiar with the world's best speeches. If you do not wish to mutilate your book, take it with you—most of the epoch-making books are now printed in small volumes. The daily waste of natural gas in the Oklahoma fields is equal to ten thousand tons of coal. Only about three per cent of the power of the coal that enters the furnace ever diffuses itself from your electric bulb as light—the other ninety-seven per cent is wasted. Yet these wastes are no larger, nor more to be lamented than the tremendous waste of time which, if conserved would increase the speaker's powers to their $n$th degree. Scientists are making three ears of corn grow where one grew before; efficiency engineers are eliminating useless motions and products from our factories: catch the spirit of the age and apply efficiency to the use of the most valuable asset you possess— time. What do you do mentally with the time you spend in dressing or in shaving? Take some subject and concentrate your energies on it for a week by utilizing just the spare moments that would otherwise be wasted. You will be amazed at the result. One passage a day from the Book of Books, one golden ingot from some master mind, one fully-possessed thought of your own might thus be added to the treasury of your life. Do not waste your time in ways that profit you nothing. Fill "the unforgiving minute" with "sixty seconds' worth of distance run" and on the platform you will be immeasurably the gainer.

Let no word of this, however, seem to decry the value of recreation. Nothing is more vital to a worker than rest—yet nothing is so vitiating to the shirker. Be sure that your recreation re-creates. A pause in the midst of labors gathers strength for new effort. The mistake is to pause too long, or to fill your pauses with ideas that make life flabby.

## Choosing a Subject

Subject and materials tremendously influence each other.

"This arises from the fact that there are two distinct ways in which a subject may be chosen: by arbitrary choice, or by development from thought and reading.

"Arbitrary choice . . . of one subject from among a number involves so many important considerations that no speaker ever fails to appreciate the tone of satisfaction in him who triumphantly announces: 'I have a subject!'

"'Do give me a subject!' How often the weary school teacher hears that cry. Then a list of themes is suggested, gone over, considered, and, in most instances, rejected, because the teacher can know but imperfectly what is in the pupil's mind. To suggest a subject in this way is like trying to discover the street on which a lost child lives, by naming over a number of streets until one strikes the little one's ear as sounding familiar.

"Choice by development is a very different process. It does not ask, What shall I say? It turns the mind in upon itself and asks, What do I think? Thus, the subject may be said to choose itself, for in the process of thought or of reading one theme rises into prominence and becomes a living germ, soon to grow into the discourse. He who has not learned to reflect is not really acquainted with his own thoughts; hence, his thoughts are not productive. Habits of reading and reflection will supply the speaker's mind with an abundance of subjects of which he already knows something from the very reading and reflection which gave birth to his theme. This is not a paradox, but sober truth.

"It must be already apparent that the choice of a subject by development savors more of collection than of conscious selection. The subject 'pops into the mind.' . . . In the intellect of the trained thinker it concentrates—by a process which we have seen to be induction—the facts and truths of which he has been reading and thinking. This is most often a gradual process. The scattered ideas may be but vaguely connected at first, but more and more they concentrate and take on a single form until at length one strong idea seems to grasp the soul with irresistible force, and to cry aloud, 'Arise, I am your *theme*! Henceforth, until you transmute me by the alchemy of your inward fire into vital speech, you shall know no rest!' Happy, then, is that speaker, for he has found a subject that grips him.

"Of course, experienced speakers use both methods of selection. Even a reading and reflective man is sometimes compelled to hunt for a theme from Dan to Beersheba, and then the task of gathering materials becomes a serious one. But even in such a case there is a sense in which the selection comes by development, because no careful speaker settles upon a theme which does not represent at least some matured thought."[7]

---

7 *How to Attract and Hold an Audience*, J. Berg Esenwein.

## Deciding on the Subject Matter

Even when your theme has been chosen for you by someone else, there remains to you a considerable field for choice of subject matter. The same considerations, in fact, that would govern you in choosing a theme must guide in the selection of the material. Ask yourself—or someone else—such questions as these:

What is the precise nature of the occasion? How large an audience may be expected? From what walks of life do they come? What is their probable attitude toward the theme? Who else will speak? Do I speak first, last, or where, on the program? What are the other speakers going to talk about? What is the nature of the auditorium? Is there a desk? Could the subject be more effectively handled if somewhat modified? Precisely how much time am I to fill?

It is evident that many speech-misfits of subject, speaker, occasion and place are due to failure to ask just such pertinent questions. *What* should be said, by *whom*, and *in what circumstances*, constitute ninety per cent of efficiency in public address. No matter who asks you, refuse to be a square peg in a round hole.

## Questions of Proportion

Proportion in a speech is attained by a nice adjustment of time. How fully you may treat your subject it is not always for you to say. Let ten minutes mean neither nine nor eleven— though better nine than eleven, at all events. You wouldn't steal a man's watch; no more should you steal the time of the succeeding speaker, or that of the audience. There is no need to overstep time-limits if you make your preparation adequate and divide your subject so as to give each thought its due proportion of attention—and no more. Blessed is the man that maketh short speeches, for he shall be invited to speak again.

Another matter of prime importance is, what part of your address demands the most emphasis. This once decided, you will know where to place that pivotal section so as to give it the greatest strategic value, and what degree of preparation must be given to that central thought so that the vital part may not be submerged by non-essentials. Many a speaker has awakened to find that he has burnt up eight minutes of a ten-minute speech in merely getting up steam. That is like spending eighty percent of your building-money on the vestibule of the house.

The same sense of proportion must tell you to stop precisely when you are through— and it is to be hoped that you will discover the arrival of that period before your audience does.

## Tapping Original Sources

The surest way to give life to speech-material is to gather your facts at first hand. Your words come with the weight of authority when you can say, "I have examined the employment rolls of every mill in this district and find that thirty-two per cent of the children employed are under the legal age." No citation of authorities can equal that. You must adopt the methods of the reporter and find out the facts underlying your argument or appeal. To do so may prove laborious, but it should not be irksome, for the great world of fact teems with interest, and over and above all is the sense of power that will come to you from original investigation. To see and feel the facts you are discussing will react upon you much more powerfully than if you were to secure the facts at second hand.

Live an active life among people who are doing worth-while things, keep eyes and ears and mind and heart open to absorb truth, and then tell of the things you know, as if you know them. The world will listen, for the world loves nothing so much as real life.

## How to Use a Library

Unsuspected treasures lie in the smallest library. Even when the owner has read every last page of his books it is only in rare instances that he has full indexes to all of them, either in his mind or on paper, so as to make available the vast number of varied subjects touched upon or treated in volumes whose titles would never suggest such topics.

For this reason it is a good thing to take an odd hour now and then to browse. Take down one volume after another and look over its table of contents and its index. (It is a reproach to any author of a serious book not to have provided a full index, with cross references.) Then glance over the pages, making notes, mental or physical, of material that looks interesting and usable. Most libraries contain volumes that the owner is "going to read some day." A familiarity with even the contents of such books on your own shelves will enable you to refer to them when you want help. Writings read long ago should be treated in the same way—in every chapter some surprise lurks to delight you.

In looking up a subject do not be discouraged if you do not find it indexed or outlined in the table of contents—you are pretty sure to discover some material under a related title.

Suppose you set to work somewhat in this way to gather references on "Thinking:" First you look over your book titles, and there is Schaeffer's "Thinking and Learning to Think." Near it is Kramer's "Talks to Students on the Art of Study"—that seems likely to provide some material, and it does. Naturally you think next of your book on psychology, and there is help there. If you have a volume on the human intellect you will have already turned to it. Suddenly you remember your encyclopedia and your dictionary of quotations—and now material fairly rains upon you; the problem is what *not* to use. In the encyclopedia you turn to every reference that includes or touches or even suggests "thinking;" and in the dictionary of quotations you do the same. The latter volume you find peculiarly helpful because it suggests several volumes to you that are on your own shelves—you never would have thought to look in them for references on this subject. Even fiction will supply help, but especially books of essays and biography. Be aware of your own resources.

To make a general index to your library does away with the necessity for indexing individual volumes that are not already indexed.

To begin with, keep a note-book by you; or small cards and paper cuttings in your pocket and on your desk will serve as well. The same note-book that records the impressions of your own experiences and thoughts will be enriched by the ideas of others.

To be sure, this note-book habit means labor, but remember that more speeches have been spoiled by half-hearted preparation than by lack of talent. Laziness is an own-brother to Over-confidence, and both are your inveterate enemies, though they pretend to be soothing friends.

Conserve your material by indexing every good idea on cards, thus:

| Socialism |
| --- |
| Progress of S., Env. 16 |
| S. a fallacy, 96/210 |
| General article on S., Howells', Dec. 1913 |
| "Socialism and the Franchise," Forbes |
| "Socialism in Ancient Life," Original Ms., Env. 102 |
| |

On the card illustrated above, clippings are indexed by giving the number of the envelope in which they are filed. The envelopes may be of any size desired and kept in any convenient receptacle. On the foregoing example, "Progress of S., Envelope 16," will represent a clipping, filed in Envelope 16, which is, of course, numbered arbitrarily.

The fractions refer to books in your library—the numerator being the book-number, the denominator referring to the page. Thus, "S. a fallacy, 96/210," refers to page 210 of volume 96 in your library. By some arbitrary sign—say red ink—you may even index a reference in a public library book.

If you preserve your magazines, important articles may be indexed by month and year. An entire volume on a subject may be indicated like the imaginary book by "Forbes." If you clip the articles, it is better to index them according to the envelope system.

Your own writings and notes may be filed in envelopes with the clippings or in a separate series.

Another good indexing system combines the library index with the "scrap," or clipping, system by making the outside of the envelope serve the same purpose as the card for the indexing of books, magazines, clippings and manuscripts, the latter two classes of material being enclosed in the envelopes that index them, and all filed alphabetically.

When your cards accumulate so as to make ready reference difficult under a single alphabet, you may subdivide each letter by subordinate guide cards marked by the vowels, A, E, I, O, U. Thus, "Antiquities" would be filed under *i* in A, because A begins the word, and the second letter, *n*, comes after the vowel *i* in the alphabet, but before *o*. In the same manner, "Beecher" would be filed under *e* in B; and "Hydrogen" would come under *u* in H.

## Outlining the Address

No one can advise you how to prepare the notes for an address. Some speakers get the best results while walking out and ruminating, jotting down notes as they pause in their walk. Others never put pen to paper until the whole speech has been thought out. The great majority, however, will take notes, classify their notes, write a hasty first draft, and then revise the speech. Try each of these methods and choose the one that is best—*for you*. Do not allow any man to force you to work in *his* way; but do not neglect to consider his way, for it may be better than your own.

For those who make notes and with their aid write out the speech, these suggestions may prove helpful:

After having read and thought enough, classify your notes by setting down the big, central thoughts of your material on separate cards or slips of paper. These will stand in the same relation to your subject as chapters do to a book.

Then arrange these main ideas or heads in such an order that they will lead effectively to the result you have in mind, so that the speech may rise in argument, in interest, in power, by piling one fact or appeal upon another until the climax—the highest point of influence on your audience—has been reached.

Next group all your ideas, facts, anecdotes, and illustrations under the foregoing main heads, each where it naturally belongs.

You now have a skeleton or outline of your address that in its polished form might serve either as the brief, or manuscript notes, for the speech or as the guide-outline which you will expand into the written address, if written it is to be.

Imagine each of the main ideas in the brief on page 127 as being separate; then picture your mind as sorting them out and placing them in order; finally, conceive of how you would fill in the facts and examples under each head, giving special prominence to those you wish to emphasize and subduing those of less moment. In the end, you have the outline complete. The simplest form of outline—not very suitable for use on the platform, however—is the following:

## Why Prosperity Is Coming

What prosperity means.—The real tests of prosperity.—Its basis in the soil.— American agricultural progress.—New interest in farming.—Enormous value of our agricultural products.—Reciprocal effect on trade.—Foreign countries affected.—Effects of our new internal economy—the regulation of banking and "big business"—on prosperity.—Effects of our revised attitude toward foreign markets, including our merchant marine.—Summary.

Obviously, this very simple outline is capable of considerable expansion under each head by the addition of facts, arguments, inferences and examples.

Here is an outline arranged with more regard for argument:

## Foreign Immigration Should Be Restricted[8]

I. FACT AS CAUSE: Many immigrants are practically paupers. (Proofs involving statistics or statements of authorities.)

II. FACT AS EFFECT: They sooner or later fill our alms-houses and become public charges. (Proofs involving statistics or statements of authorities.)

III. FACT AS CAUSE: Some of them are criminals. (Examples of recent cases.)

IV. FACT AS EFFECT: They reënforce the criminal classes. (Effects on our civic life.)

---

8 Adapted from *Competition-Rhetoric*, Scott and Denny, p. 241.

V. FACT AS CAUSE: Many of them know nothing of the duties of free citizenship. (Examples.)

VI. FACT AS EFFECT: Such immigrants recruit the worst element in our politics. (Proofs.)

A more highly ordered grouping of topics and subtopics is shown in the following:

## Ours a Christian Nation

I. INTRODUCTION: Why the subject is timely. Influences operative against this contention today.

II. CHRISTIANITY PRESIDED OVER THE EARLY HISTORY OF AMERICA.
1. First practical discovery by a Christian explorer. Columbus worshiped god on the new soil.
2. The Cavaliers.
3. The French Catholic settlers.
4. The Huguenots.
5. The Puritans.

III. THE BIRTH OF OUR NATION WAS UNDER CHRISTIAN AUSPICES.
1. Christian character of Washington.
2. Other Christian patriots.
3. The Church in our Revolutionary struggle. Muhlenberg.

IV. OUR LATER HISTORY HAS ONLY EMPHASIZED OUR NATIONAL ATTITUDE. Examples of dealings with foreign nations show Christian magnanimity. Returning the Chinese Indemnity; fostering the Red Cross; attitude toward Belgium.

V. OUR GOVERNMENTAL FORMS AND MANY OF OUR LAWS ARE OF A CHRISTIAN TEMPER.
1. The use of the Bible in public ways, oaths, etc.
2. The Bible in our schools.
3. Christian chaplains minister to our law-making bodies, to our army, and to our navy.
4. The Christian Sabbath is officially and generally recognized.
5. The Christian family and the Christian system of morality are at the basis of our laws.

VI. THE LIFE OF THE PEOPLE TESTIFIES OF THE POWER OF CHRISTIANITY. Charities, education, etc., have Christian tone.

VII. OTHER NATIONS REGARD US AS A CHRISTIAN PEOPLE.

VIII. CONCLUSION: The attitude which may reasonably be expected of all good citizens toward questions touching the preservation of our standing as a Christian nation.

## Writing and Revision

After the outline has been perfected comes the time to write the speech, if write it you must. Then, whatever you do, write it at white heat, with not *too* much thought of anything but the strong, appealing expression of your ideas.

The final stage is the paring down, the re-vision—the seeing again, as the word implies—when all the parts of the speech must be impartially scrutinized for clearness, precision, force, effectiveness, suitability, proportion, logical climax; and in all this you must *imagine yourself to be before your audience*, for a speech is not an essay and what will convince and arouse in the one will not prevail in the other.

## The Title

Often last of all will come that which in a sense is first of all—the title, the name by which the speech is known. Sometimes it will be the simple theme of the address, as "The New Americanism," by Henry Watterson; or it may be a bit of symbolism typifying the spirit of the address, as "Acres of Diamonds," by Russell H. Conwell; or it may be a fine phrase taken from the body of the address, as "Pass Prosperity Around," by Albert J. Beveridge. All in all, from whatever motive it be chosen, let the title be fresh, short, suited to the subject, and likely to excite interest.

## QUESTIONS AND EXERCISES

1. Define (*a*) introduction; (*b*) climax; (*c*) peroration.

2. If a thirty-minute speech would require three hours for specific preparation, would you expect to be able to do equal justice to a speech one-third as long in one-third the time for preparation? Give reasons.

3. Relate briefly any personal experience you may have had in conserving time for reading and thought.

4. In the manner of a reporter or investigator, go out and get first-hand information on some subject of interest to the public. Arrange the results of your research in the form of an outline, or brief.

5. From a private or a public library gather enough authoritative material on one of the following questions to build an outline for a twenty-minute address. Take one definite side of the question. (*a*) "The Housing of the Poor;" (*b*) "The Commission Form of Government for Cities as a Remedy for Political Graft;" (*c*) "The Test of Woman's Suffrage in the West;" (*d*) "Present Trends of Public Taste in Reading;" (*e*) "Municipal Art;" (*f*) "Is the Theatre Becoming more Elevated in Tone?" (*g*) "The Effects of the Magazine on Literature;" (*h*) "Does Modern Life Destroy Ideals?" (*i*) "Is Competition 'the Life of Trade?'" (*j*) "Baseball is too Absorbing to be a Wholesome National Game;" (*k*) "Summer Baseball and Amateur Standing;" (*l*) "Does College Training Unfit a Woman for Domestic Life?" (*m*) "Does Woman's Competition with Man in Business Dull the Spirit of Chivalry?" (*n*) "Are Elective

Studies Suited to High School Courses?" (*o*) "Does the Modern College Prepare Men for Preeminent Leadership?" (*p*) "The Y.M.C.A. in Its Relation to the Labor Problem;" (*q*) "Public Speaking as Training in Citizenship."

6. Construct the outline, examining it carefully for interest, convincing character, proportion, and climax of arrangement.

NOTE: This exercise should be repeated until the student shows facility in synthetic arrangement.

7. Deliver the address, if possible before an audience.

8. Make a three-hundred word report on the results, as best you are able to estimate them.

9. Tell something of the benefits of using a periodical (or cumulative) index.

10. Give a number of quotations, suitable for a speaker's use, that you have memorized in off moments.

11. In the manner of the outline on page 127, analyze the address on page 50, "The History of Liberty."

12. Give an outline analysis, from notes or memory, of an address or sermon to which you have listened for this purpose.

13. Criticise the address from a structural point of view.

14. Invent titles for any five of the themes in Exercise 5.

15. Criticise the titles of any five chapters of this book, suggesting better ones.

16. Criticise the title of any lecture or address of which you know.

# CHAPTER XIX

## *Influencing by Exposition*

Speak not at all, in any wise, till you have somewhat to speak; care not
for the reward of your speaking, but simply and with undivided mind
for the truth of your speaking.

—THOMAS CARLYLE, *Essay on* Biography

A COMPLETE DISCUSSION OF THE RHETORICAL STRUCTURE OF PUBLIC SPEECHES
requires a fuller treatise than can be undertaken in a work of this nature, yet in
this chapter, and in the succeeding ones on "Description," "Narration," "Argument," and
"Pleading," the underlying principles are given and explained as fully as need be for a
working knowledge, and adequate book references are given for those who would perfect
themselves in rhetorical art.

### *The Nature of Exposition*

In the word "expose"—*to lay bare, to uncover, to show the true inwardness of*—we see the
foundation-idea of "Exposition." It is the clear and precise setting forth of what the subject
really is—it is explanation.

Exposition does not draw a picture, for that would be description. To tell in exact
terms what the automobile is, to name its characteristic parts and explain their workings,
would be exposition; so would an explanation of the nature of "fear." But to create a mental
image of a particular automobile, with its glistening body, graceful lines, and great speed,
would be description; and so would a picturing of fear acting on the emotions of a child at
night. Exposition and description often intermingle and overlap, but fundamentally they
are distinct. Their differences will be touched upon again in the chapter on "Description."

Exposition furthermore does not include an account of how events happened—that
is narration. When Peary lectured on his polar discoveries he explained the instruments
used for determining latitude and longitude—that was exposition. In picturing his equip-
ment he used description. In telling of his adventures day by day he employed narration.
In supporting some of his contentions he used argument. Yet he mingled all these forms
throughout the lecture.

Neither does exposition deal with reasons and inferences—that is the field of argument. A series of connected statements intended to convince a prospective buyer that one
automobile is better than another, or proofs that the appeal to fear is a wrong method of

discipline, would not be exposition. The plain facts as set forth in expository speaking or writing are nearly always the basis of argument, yet the processes are not one. True, the statement of a single significant fact without the addition of one other word may be convincing, but a moment's thought will show that the inference, which completes a chain of reasoning, is made in the mind of the hearer and presupposes other facts held in consideration.[9]

In like manner, it is obvious that the field of persuasion is not open to exposition, for exposition is entirely an intellectual process, with no emotional element.

## The Importance of Exposition

The importance of exposition in public speech is precisely the importance of setting forth a matter so plainly that it cannot be misunderstood.

> To master the process of exposition is to become a clear thinker. "I know, when you do not ask me,"[10] replied a gentleman upon being requested to define a highly complex idea. Now some large concepts defy explicit definition; but no mind should take refuge behind such exceptions, for where definition fails, other forms succeed. Sometimes we feel confident that we have perfect mastery of an idea, but when the time comes to express it, the clearness becomes a haze. Exposition, then, is the test of clear understanding. To speak effectively you must be able to see your subject clearly and comprehensively, and to make your audience see it as you do.[11]

There are pitfalls on both sides of this path. To explain too little will leave your audience in doubt as to what you mean. It is useless to argue a question if it is not perfectly clear just what is meant by the question. Have you never come to a blind lane in conversation by finding that you were talking of one aspect of a matter while your friend was thinking of another? If two do not agree in their definitions of a Musician, it is useless to dispute over a certain man's right to claim the title.

On the other side of the path lies the abyss of tediously explaining too much. That offends because it impresses the hearers that you either do not respect their intelligence or are trying to blow a breeze into a tornado. Carefully estimate the probable knowledge of your audience, both in general and of the particular point you are explaining. In trying to simplify, it is fatal to "sillify." To explain more than is needed for the purposes of your argument or appeal is to waste energy all around. In your efforts to be explicit do not press exposition to the extent of dulness—the confines are not far distant and you may arrive before you know it.

## Some Purposes of Exposition

From what has been said it ought to be clear that, primarily, exposition weaves a cord of understanding between you and your audience. It lays, furthermore, a foundation of fact

---

9 Argumentation will be outlined fully in subsequent chapter.
10 *The Working Principles of Rhetoric*, J. F. Genung.
11 *How to Attract and Hold an Audience*, J. Berg Esenwein.

on which to build later statements, arguments, and appeals. In scientific and purely "information" speeches exposition may exist by itself and for itself, as in a lecture on biology, or on psychology; but in the vast majority of cases it is used to accompany and prepare the way for the other forms of discourse.

Clearness, precision, accuracy, unity, truth, and necessity—these must be the *constant* standards by which you test the efficiency of your expositions, and, indeed, that of every explanatory statement. This dictum should be written on your brain in letters most plain. And let this apply not alone to the *purposes* of exposition but in equal measure to your use of the

## Methods of Exposition

The various ways along which a speaker may proceed in exposition are likely to touch each other now and then, and even when they do not meet and actually overlap they run so nearly parallel that the roads are sometimes distinct rather in theory than in any more practical respect.

**Definition**, the primary expository method, is a statement of precise limits.[12] Obviously, here the greatest care must be exercised that the terms of definition should not themselves demand too much definition; that the language should be concise and clear; and that the definition should neither exclude nor include too much. The following is a simple example:

> To expound is to set forth the nature, the significance, the characteristics, and the bearing of an idea or a group of ideas.
>
> —ARLO BATES, *Talks on Writing English*

**Contrast and Antithesis** are often used effectively to amplify definition, as in this sentence, which immediately follows the above-cited definition:

> Exposition therefore differs from Description in that it deals directly with the meaning or intent of its subject instead of with its appearance.

This antithesis forms an expansion of the definition, and as such it might have been still further extended. In fact, this is a frequent practise in public speech, where the minds of the hearers often ask for reiteration and expanded statement to help them grasp a subject in its several aspects. This is the very heart of exposition—to amplify and clarify all the terms by which a matter is defined.

**Example** is another method of amplifying a definition or of expounding an idea more fully. The following sentences immediately succeed Mr. Bates's definition and contrast just quoted:

> A good deal which we are accustomed inexactly to call description is really exposition. Suppose that your small boy wishes to know how an engine works, and should say: "Please describe the steam-engine to me." If you insist on taking

---

12 On the various types of definition see any college manual of Rhetoric.

his words literally—and are willing to run the risk of his indignation at being wilfully misunderstood—you will to the best of your ability picture to him this familiarly wonderful machine. If you explain it to him, you are not describing but expounding it.

The chief value of example is that it makes clear the unknown by referring the mind to the known. Readiness of mind to make illuminating, apt comparisons for the sake of clearness is one of the speaker's chief resources on the platform—it is the greatest of all teaching gifts. It is a gift, moreover, that responds to cultivation. Read the three extracts from Arlo Bates as their author delivered them, as one passage, and see how they melt into one, each part supplementing the other most helpfully.

**Analogy**, which calls attention to similar relationships in objects not otherwise similar, is one of the most useful methods of exposition. The following striking specimen is from Beecher's Liverpool speech:

> A savage is a man of one story, and that one story a cellar. When a man begins to be civilized he raises another story. When you Christianize and civilize the man, you put story upon story, for you develop faculty after faculty; and you have to supply every story with your productions.

**Discarding** is a less common form of platform explanation. It consists in clearing away associated ideas so that the attention may be centered on the main thought to be discussed. Really, it is a negative factor in exposition though a most important one, for it is fundamental to the consideration of an intricately related matter that subordinate and side questions should be set aside in order to bring out the main issue. Here is an example of the method:

> I cannot allow myself to be led aside from the only issue before this jury. It is not pertinent to consider that this prisoner is the husband of a heartbroken woman and that his babes will go through the world under the shadow of the law's extremest penalty worked upon their father. We must forget the venerable father and the mother whom Heaven in pity took before she learned of her son's disgrace. What have these matters of heart, what have the blenched faces of his friends, what have the prisoner's long and honorable career to say before this bar when you are sworn to weigh only the direct evidence before you? The one and only question for you to decide on the evidence is whether this man did with revengeful intent commit the murder that every impartial witness has solemnly laid at his door.

**Classification** assigns a subject to its class. By an allowable extension of the definition it may be said to assign it also to its order, genus, and species. Classification is useful in public speech in narrowing the issue to a desired phase. It is equally valuable for showing a thing in its relation to other things, or in correlation. Classification is closely akin to Definition and Division.

This question of the liquor traffic, sirs, takes its place beside the grave moral issues of all times. Whatever be its economic significance—and who is there to question it—whatever vital bearing it has upon our political system—and is there one who will deny it?—the question of the licensed saloon must quickly be settled as the world in its advancement has settled the questions of constitutional government for the masses, of the opium traffic, of the serf, and of the slave—not as matters of economic and political expediency but as questions of right and wrong.

**Analysis** separates a subject into its essential parts. This it may do by various principles; for example, analysis may follow the order of time (geologic eras), order of place (geographic facts), logical order (a sermon outline), order of increasing interest, or procession to a climax (a lecture on 20th century poets); and so on. A classic example of analytical exposition is the following:

> In philosophy the contemplations of man do either penetrate unto God, or are circumferred to nature, or are reflected or reverted upon himself. Out of which several inquiries there do arise three knowledges: divine philosophy, natural philosophy, and human philosophy or humanity. For all things are marked and stamped with this triple character, of the power of God, the difference of nature, and the use of man.
>
> —Lord Bacon, *The Advancement of Learning*[13]

**Division** differs only from analysis in that analysis follows the inherent divisions of a subject, as illustrated in the foregoing passage, while division arbitrarily separates the subject for convenience of treatment, as in the following none-too-logical example:

> For civil history, it is of three kinds; not unfitly to be compared with the three kinds of pictures or images. For of pictures or images, we see some are unfinished, some are perfect, and some are defaced. So of histories we may find three kinds, memorials, perfect histories, and antiquities; for memorials are history unfinished, or the first or rough drafts of history; and antiquities are history defaced, or some remnants of history which have casually escaped the shipwreck of time.
>
> —Lord Bacon, *The Advancement of Learning*[13]

**Generalization** states a broad principle, or a general truth, derived from examination of a considerable number of individual facts. This synthetic exposition is not the same as argumentative generalization, which supports a general contention by citing instances in proof. Observe how Holmes begins with one fact, and by adding another and another reaches a complete whole. This is one of the most effective devices in the public speaker's repertory.

---

13 Quoted in *The Working Principles of Rhetoric,* J. F. Genung.

Take a hollow cylinder, the bottom closed while the top remains open, and pour in water to the height of a few inches. Next cover the water with a flat plate or piston, which fits the interior of the cylinder perfectly; then apply heat to the water, and we shall witness the following phenomena. After the lapse of some minutes the water will begin to boil, and the steam accumulating at the upper surface will make room for itself by raising the piston slightly. As the boiling continues, more and more steam will be formed, and raise the piston higher and higher, till all the water is boiled away, and nothing but steam is left in the cylinder. Now this machine, consisting of cylinder, piston, water, and fire, is the steam-engine in its most elementary form. For a steam-engine may be defined as an apparatus for doing work by means of heat applied to water; and since raising such a weight as the piston is a form of doing work, this apparatus, clumsy and inconvenient though it may be, answers the definition precisely.[14]

**Reference to Experience** is one of the most vital principles in exposition—as in every other form of discourse.

"Reference to experience," as here used, means reference to the known. The known is that which the listener has seen, heard, read, felt, believed or done, and which still exists in his consciousness—his stock of knowledge. It embraces all those thoughts, feelings and happenings which are to him real. Reference to Experience, then, means *coming into the listener's life.*[15]

The vast results obtained by science are won by no mystical faculties, by no mental processes, other than those which are practised by every one of us in the humblest and meanest affairs of life. A detective policeman discovers a burglar from the marks made by his shoe, by a mental process identical with that by which Cuvier restored the extinct animals of Montmartre from fragments of their bones. Nor does that process of induction and deduction by which a lady, finding a stain of a particular kind upon her dress, concludes that somebody has upset the inkstand thereon, differ in any way from that by which Adams and Leverrier discovered a new planet. The man of science, in fact, simply uses with scrupulous exactness the methods which we all habitually, and at every moment, use carelessly.

—THOMAS HENRY HUXLEY, *Lay Sermons*

Do you set down your name in the scroll of youth, that are written down old with all the characters of age? Have you not a moist eye? a dry hand? a yellow cheek? a white beard? a decreasing leg? an increasing belly? is not your voice broken? your wind short? your chin double? your wit single? and every part about you blasted with antiquity? and will you yet call yourself young? Fie, fie, fie, Sir John!

—SHAKESPEARE, *The Merry Wives of Windsor*

---

14 G. C. V. Holmes, quoted in *Specimens of Exposition*, H. Lamont.
15 *Effective Speaking*, Arthur Edward Phillips. This work covers the preparation of public speech in a very helpful way.

Finally, in preparing expository material ask yourself these questions regarding your subject:

What is it, and what is it not?

What is it like, and unlike?

What are its causes, and effects?

How shall it be divided?

With what subjects is it correlated?

What experiences does it recall?

What examples illustrate it?

## QUESTIONS AND EXERCISES

1. What would be the effect of adhering to any one of the forms of discourse in a public address?

2. Have you ever heard such an address?

3. Invent a series of examples illustrative of the distinctions made on pages 138 and 139.

4. Make a list of ten subjects that might be treated largely, if not entirely, by exposition.

5. Name the six standards by which expository writing should be tried.

6. Define any one of the following: (a) storage battery; (b) "a free hand;" (c) sail boat; (d) "The Big Stick;" (e) nonsense; (f) "a good sport;" (g) short-story; (h) novel; (i) newspaper; (j) politician; (k) jealousy; (l) truth; (m) matinée girl; (n) college honor system; (o) modish; (p) slum; (q) settlement work; (r) forensic.

7. Amplify the definition by antithesis.

8. Invent two examples to illustrate the definition (question 6).

9. Invent two analogies for the same subject (question 6).

10. Make a short speech based on one of the following: (a) wages and salary; (b) master and man; (c) war and peace; (d) home and the boarding house; (e) struggle and victory; (f) ignorance and ambition.

11. Make a ten-minute speech on any of the topics named in question 6, using all the methods of exposition already named.

12. Explain what is meant by discarding topics collateral and subordinate to a subject.

13. Rewrite the jury-speech on page 133.

14. Define correlation.

15. Write an example of "classification," on any political, social, economic, or moral issue of the day.

16. Make a brief analytical statement of Henry W. Grady's "The Race Problem," page 22.

**17.** By what analytical principle did you proceed? (See page 134.)

**18.** Write a short, carefully generalized speech from a large amount of data on one of the following subjects: (*a*) The servant girl problem; (*b*) cats; (*c*) the baseball craze; (*d*) reform administrations; (*e*) sewing societies; (*f*) coeducation; (*g*) the traveling salesman.

**19.** Observe this passage from Newton's "Effective Speaking:"

> That man is a cynic. He sees goodness nowhere. He sneers at virtue, sneers at love; to him the maiden plighting her troth is an artful schemer, and he sees even in the mother's kiss nothing but an empty conventionality.

Write, commit and deliver two similar passages based on your choice from this list: (*a*) "the egotist;" (*b*) "the sensualist;" (*c*) "the hypocrite;" (*d*) "the timid man;" (*e*) "the joker;" (*f*) "the flirt;" (*g*) "the ungrateful woman;" (*h*) "the mournful man." In both cases use the principle of "Reference to Experience."

**20.** Write a passage on any of the foregoing characters in imitation of the style of Shakespeare's characterization of Sir John Falstaff, page 135.

# CHAPTER XX

# *Influencing by Description*

The groves of Eden vanish'd now so long,
Live in description, and look green in song.

—ALEXANDER POPE, *Windsor Forest*

The moment our discourse rises above the ground-line of familiar facts, and is inflamed with passion or exalted thought, it clothes itself in images. A man conversing in earnest, if he watch his intellectual processes, will find that always a material image, more or less luminous, arises in his mind, contemporaneous with every thought, which furnishes the vestment of the thought. . . . This imagery is spontaneous. It is the blending of experience with the present action of the mind. It is proper creation.

—RALPH WALDO EMERSON, *Nature*

LIKE OTHER VALUABLE RESOURCES IN PUBLIC SPEAKING, DESCRIPTION LOSES ITS power when carried to an extreme. Over-ornamentation makes the subject ridiculous. A dust-cloth is a very useful thing, but why embroider it? Whether description shall be restrained within its proper and important limits, or be encouraged to run riot, is the personal choice that comes before every speaker, for man's earliest literary tendency is to depict.

## *The Nature of Description*

To describe is to call up a picture in the mind of the hearer. "In talking of description we naturally speak of portraying, delineating, coloring, and all the devices of the picture painter. To describe is to visualize, hence we must look at description as a pictorial process, whether the writer deals with material or with spiritual objects."[16]

If you were asked to describe the rapid-fire gun you might go about it in either of two ways: give a cold technical account of its mechanism, in whole and in detail, or else describe it as a terrible engine of slaughter, dwelling upon its effects rather than upon its structure.

---

16 *Writing the Short-Story,* J. Berg Esenwein.

The former of these processes is exposition, the latter is true description. Exposition deals more with the *general*, while description must deal with the *particular*. Exposition elucidates *ideas*, description treats of *things*. Exposition deals with the *abstract*, description with the *concrete*. Exposition is concerned with the *internal*, description with the *external*. Exposition is *enumerative*, description *literary*. Exposition is *intellectual*, description *sensory*. Exposition is *impersonal*, description *personal*.

If description is a visualizing process for the hearer, it is first of all such for the speaker—he cannot describe what he has never seen, either physically or in fancy. It is this personal quality—this question of the personal eye which sees the things later to be described—that makes description so interesting in public speech. Given a speaker of personality, and we are interested in his personal view—his view adds to the natural interest of the scene, and may even be the sole source of that interest to his auditors.

The seeing eye has been praised in an earlier chapter (on "Subject and Preparation") and the imagination will be treated in a subsequent one (on "Riding the Winged Horse"), but here we must consider the *picturing mind*: the mind that forms the double habit of seeing things clearly—for we see more with the mind than we do with the physical eye— and then of re-imaging these things for the purpose of getting them before the minds' eyes of the hearers. No habit is more useful than that of visualizing clearly the object, the scene, the situation, the action, the person, about to be described. Unless that primary process is carried out clearly, the picture will be blurred for the hearer-beholder.

In a work of this nature we are concerned with the rhetorical analysis of description, and with its methods, only so far as may be needed for the practical purposes of the speaker.[17] The following grouping, therefore, will not be regarded as complete, nor will it here be necessary to add more than a word of explanation:

## Description for Public Speakers

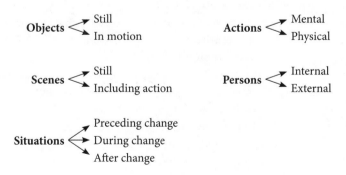

Some of the foregoing processes will overlap, in certain instances, and all are more likely to be found in combination than singly.

---

[17] For fuller treatment of Description see Genung's *Working Principles of Rhetoric*, Albright's *Descriptive Writing*, Bates' *Talks on Writing English*, first and second series, and any advanced rhetoric.

When description is intended solely to give accurate information—as to delineate the appearance, not the technical construction, of the latest Zeppelin airship—it is called "scientific description," and is akin to exposition. When it is intended to present a free picture for the purpose of making a vivid impression, it is called "artistic description." With both of these the public speaker has to deal, but more frequently with the latter form. Rhetoricians make still further distinctions.

## Methods of Description

In public speaking, *description should be mainly by suggestion*, not only because suggestive description is so much more compact and time-saving but because it is so vivid. Suggestive expressions connote more than they literally say—they suggest ideas and pictures to the mind of the hearer which supplement the direct words of the speaker. When Dickens, in his "Christmas Carol," says: "In came Mrs. Fezziwig, one vast substantial smile," our minds complete the picture so deftly begun—a much more effective process than that of a minutely detailed description because it leaves a unified, vivid impression, and that is what we need. Here is a present-day bit of suggestion: "General Trinkle was a gnarly oak of a man—rough, solid, and safe; you always knew where to find him." Dickens presents Miss Peecher as: "A little pin-cushion, a little housewife, a little book, a little work-box, a little set of tables and weights and measures, and a little woman all in one." In his "Knickerbocker's History of New York," Irving portrays Wouter van Twiller as "a robustious beer-barrel, standing on skids."

Whatever forms of description you neglect, be sure to master the art of suggestion.

*Description may be by simple hint.* Lowell notes a happy instance of this sort of picturing by intimation when he says of Chaucer: "Sometimes he describes amply by the merest hint, as where the Friar, before setting himself down, drives away the cat. We know without need of more words that he has chosen the snuggest corner."

*Description may depict a thing by its effects.* "When the spectator's eye is dazzled, and he shades it," says Mozley in his "Essays," "we form the idea of a splendid object; when his face turns pale, of a horrible one; from his quick wonder and admiration we form the idea of great beauty; from his silent awe, of great majesty."

*Brief description may be by epithet.* "Blue-eyed," "white-armed," "laughter-loving," are now conventional compounds, but they were fresh enough when Homer first conjoined them. The centuries have not yet improved upon "Wheels round, brazen, eight-spoked," or "Shields smooth, beautiful, brazen, well-hammered." Observe the effective use of epithet in Will Levington Comfort's "The Fighting Death," when he speaks of soldiers in a Philippine skirmish as being "leeched against a rock."

*Description uses figures of speech.* Any advanced rhetoric will discuss their forms and give examples for guidance.[18] This matter is most important, be assured. A brilliant yet carefully restrained figurative style, a style marked by brief, pungent, witty, and humorous comparisons and characterizations, is a wonderful resource for all kinds of platform work.

---

18 See also *The Art of Versification*, J. Berg Esenwein and Mary Eleanor Roberts, pp. 28–35; and *Writing the Short-Story*, J. Berg Esenwein, pp. 152–162; 231–240.

*Description may be direct.* This statement is plain enough without exposition. Use your own judgment as to whether in picturing you had better proceed from a general view to the details, or first give the details and thus build up the general picture, but by all means BE BRIEF.

Note the vivid compactness of these delineations from Washington Irving's "Knickerbocker:"

> He was a short, square, brawny old gentleman, with a double chin, a mastiff mouth, and a broad copper nose, which was supposed in those days to have acquired its fiery hue from the constant neighborhood of his tobacco pipe.
>
> He was exactly five feet six inches in height, and six feet five inches in circumference. His head was a perfect sphere, and of such stupendous dimensions, that Dame Nature, with all her sex's ingenuity, would have been puzzled to construct a neck capable of supporting it; wherefore she wisely declined the attempt, and settled it firmly on the top of his backbone, just between the shoulders. His body was of an oblong form, particularly capacious at bottom; which was wisely ordered by Providence, seeing that he was a man of sedentary habits, and very averse to the idle labor of walking.

The foregoing is too long for the platform, but it is so good-humored, so full of delightful exaggeration, that it may well serve as a model of humorous character picturing, for here one inevitably sees the inner man in the outer.

Direct description for platform use may be made vivid by the *sparing* use of the "historical present." The following dramatic passage, accompanied by the most lively action, has lingered in the mind for thirty years after hearing Dr. T. De Witt Talmage lecture on "Big Blunders." The crack of the bat sounds clear even today:

> Get ready the bats and take your positions. Now, give us the ball. Too low. Don't strike. Too high. Don't strike. There it comes like lightning. Strike! Away it soars! Higher! Higher! Run! Another base! Faster! Faster! Good! All around at one stroke!

Observe the remarkable way in which the lecturer fused speaker, audience, spectators, and players into one excited, ecstatic whole—just as you have found yourself starting forward in your seat at the delivery of the ball with "three on and two down" in the ninth inning. Notice, too, how—perhaps unconsciously—Talmage painted the scene in Homer's characteristic style: not as having already happened, but as happening before your eyes.

If you have attended many travel talks you must have been impressed by the painful extremes to which the lecturers go—with a few notable exceptions, their language is either over-ornate or crude. If you would learn the power of words to make scenery, yes, even houses, palpitate with poetry and human appeal, read Lafcadio Hearn, Robert Louis Stevenson, Pierre Loti, and Edmondo De Amicis.

Blue-distant, a mountain of carven stone appeared before them,—the Temple, lifting to heaven its wilderness of chiseled pinnacles, flinging to the sky the golden spray of its decoration.

—LAFCADIO HEARN, *Chinese Ghosts*

The stars were clear, colored, and jewel-like, but not frosty. A faint silvery vapour stood for the Milky Way. All around me the black fir-points stood upright and stock-still. By the whiteness of the pack-saddle I could see Modestine walking round and round at the length of her tether; I could hear her steadily munching at the sward; but there was not another sound save the indescribable quiet talk of the runnel over the stones.

—ROBERT LOUIS STEVENSON, *Travels with a Donkey*

It was full autumn now, late autumn—with the nightfalls gloomy, and all things growing dark early in the old cottage, and all the Breton land looking sombre, too. The very days seemed but twilight; immeasurable clouds, slowly passing, would suddenly bring darkness at broad noon. The wind moaned constantly—it was like the sound of a great cathedral organ at a distance, but playing profane airs, or despairing dirges; at other times it would come close to the door, and lift up a howl like wild beasts.

—PIERRE LOTI, *An Iceland Fisherman*

I see the great refectory,[19] where a battalion might have drilled; I see the long tables, the five hundred heads bent above the plates, the rapid motion of five hundred forks, of a thousand hands, and sixteen thousand teeth; the swarm of servants running here and there, called to, scolded, hurried, on every side at once; I hear the clatter of dishes, the deafening noise, the voices choked with food crying out: "Bread—bread!" and I feel once more the formidable appetite, the herculean strength of jaw, the exuberant life and spirits of those far-off days.[20]

—EDMONDO DE AMICIS, *College Friends*

## Suggestions for the Use of Description

Decide, on beginning a description, what point of view you wish your hearers to take. One cannot see either a mountain or a man on all sides at once. Establish a view-point, and do not shift without giving notice.

Choose an attitude toward your subject—shall it be idealized? caricatured? ridiculed? exaggerated? defended? or described impartially?

Be sure of your mood, too, for it will color the subject to be described. Melancholy will make a rose-garden look gray.

---

19 In the Military College of Modena.
20 This figure of speech is known as "Vision."

Adopt an order in which you will proceed—do not shift backward and forward from near to far, remote to close in time, general to particular, large to small, important to unimportant, concrete to abstract, physical to mental; but follow your chosen order. Scattered and shifting observations produce hazy impressions just as a moving camera spoils the time-exposure.

Do not go into needless minutiæ. Some details identify a thing with its class, while other details differentiate it from its class. Choose only the significant, suggestive characteristics and bring those out with terse vividness. Learn a lesson from the few strokes used by the poster artist.

In determining what to describe and what merely to name, seek to read the knowledge of your audience. The difference to them between the unknown and the known is a vital one also to you.

Relentlessly cut out all ideas and words not necessary to produce the effect you desire. Each element in a mental picture either helps or hinders. Be sure they do not hinder, for they cannot be passively present in any discourse.

Interruptions of the description to make side-remarks are as powerful to destroy unity as are scattered descriptive phrases. The only visual impression that can be effective is one that is unified.

In describing, try to call up the emotions you felt when first you saw the scene, and then try to reproduce those emotions in your hearers. Description is primarily emotional in its appeal; nothing can be more deadly dull than a cold, unemotional outline, while nothing leaves a warmer impression than a glowing, spirited description.

Give a swift and vivid general view at the close of the portrayal. First and final impressions remain the longest. The mind may be trained to take in the characteristic points of a subject, so as to view in a single scene, action, experience, or character, a unified impression of the whole. To describe a thing as a whole you must first see it as a whole. Master that art and you have mastered description to the last degree.

## SELECTIONS FOR PRACTISE

# The Homes of the People

I went to Washington the other day, and I stood on the Capitol Hill; my heart beat quick as I looked at the towering marble of my country's Capitol and the mist gathered in my eyes as I thought of its tremendous significance, and the armies and the treasury, and the judges and the President, and the Congress and the courts, and all that was gathered there. And I felt that the sun in all its course could not look down on a better sight than that majestic home of a republic that had taught the world its best lessons of liberty. And I felt that if honor and wisdom and justice abided therein, the world would at last owe to that great house in which the ark of the covenant of my country is lodged, its final uplifting and its regeneration.

Two days afterward, I went to visit a friend in the country, a modest man, with a quiet country home. It was just a simple, unpretentious house, set about with big trees, encircled in meadow and field rich with the promise of harvest. The fragrance of the pink and hollyhock in the front yard was mingled with the aroma of the orchard and of the gardens, and resonant with the cluck of poultry and the hum of bees.

Inside was quiet, cleanliness, thrift, and comfort. There was the old clock that had welcomed, in steady measure, every newcomer to the family, that had ticked the solemn requiem of the dead, and had kept company with the watcher at the bedside. There were the big, restful beds and the old, open fireplace, and the old family Bible, thumbed with the fingers of hands long since still, and wet with the tears of eyes long since closed, holding the simple annals of the family and the heart and the conscience of the home.

Outside, there stood my friend, the master, a simple, upright man, with no mortgage on his roof, no lien on his growing crops, master of his land and master of himself. There was his old father, an aged, trembling man, but happy in the heart and home of his son. And as they started to their home, the hands of the old man went down on the young man's shoulder, laying there the unspeakable blessing of the honored and grateful father and ennobling it with the knighthood of the fifth commandment.

And as they reached the door the old mother came with the sunset falling fair on her face, and lighting up her deep, patient eyes, while her lips, trembling with the rich music of her heart, bade her husband and son welcome to their home. Beyond was the housewife, busy with her household cares, clean of heart and conscience, the buckler and helpmeet of her husband. Down the lane came the children, trooping home after the cows, seeking as truant birds do the quiet of their home nest.

And I saw the night come down on that house, falling gently as the wings of the unseen dove. And the old man—while a startled bird called from the forest, and the trees were shrill with the cricket's cry, and the stars were swarming in the sky— got the family around him, and, taking the old Bible from the table, called them to their knees, the little baby hiding in the folds of its mother's dress, while he closed the record of that simple day by calling down God's benediction on that family and that home. And while I gazed, the vision of that marble Capitol faded. Forgotten were its treasures and its majesty and I said, "Oh, surely here in the homes of the people are lodged at last the strength and the responsibility of this government, the hope and the promise of this republic."

—Henry W. Grady

## Suggestive Scenes

One thing in life calls for another; there is a fitness in events and places. The sight of a pleasant arbor puts it in our mind to sit there. One place suggests work, another idleness, a third early rising and long rambles in the dew. The effect of night, of any flowing water, of lighted cities, of the peep of day, of ships, of the open ocean, calls up in the mind an army of anonymous desires and pleasures. Something, we feel, should happen; we know not what, yet we proceed in quest of it. And many of the happiest hours in life fleet by us in this vain attendance on the genius of the place and moment. It is thus that tracts of young fir, and low rocks that reach into deep soundings, particularly delight and torture me. Something must have happened in such places, and perhaps ages back, to members of my race; and when I was a child I tried to invent appropriate games for them, as I still try, just as vainly, to fit them with the proper story. Some places speak distinctly. Certain dank gardens cry aloud for a murder; certain old houses demand to be haunted; certain coasts are set aside for shipwreck. Other spots again seem to abide their destiny, suggestive and impenetrable, "miching mallecho." The inn at Burford Bridge, with its arbours and green garden and silent, eddying river—though it is known already as the place where Keats wrote some of his *Endymion* and Nelson parted from his Emma—still seems to wait the coming of the appropriate legend. Within these ivied walls, behind these old green shutters, some further business smoulders, waiting for its hour. The old Hawes Inn at the Queen's ferry makes a similar call upon my fancy. There it stands, apart from the town, beside the pier, in a climate of its own, half inland, half marine—in front, the ferry bubbling with the tide and the guard-ship swinging to her anchor; behind, the old garden with the trees. Americans seek it already for the sake of Lovel and Oldbuck, who dined there at the beginning of the *Antiquary*. But you need not tell me—that is not all; there is some story, unrecorded or not yet complete, which must express the meaning of that inn more fully. . . . I have lived both at the Hawes and Burford in a perpetual flutter, on the heel, as it seemed, of some adventure that should justify the place; but though the feeling had me to bed at night and called me again at morning in one unbroken round of pleasure and suspense, nothing befell me in either worth remark. The man or the hour had not yet come; but some day, I think, a boat shall put off from the Queen's ferry, fraught with a dear cargo, and some frosty night a horseman, on a tragic errand, rattle with his whip upon the green shutters at the inn at Burford.

—R. L. Stevenson, *A Gossip on Romance*

# From "Midnight In London"

Clang! Clang! Clang! the fire-bells! Bing! Bing! Bing! the alarm! In an instant quiet turns to uproar—an outburst of noise, excitement, clamor—bedlam broke loose; Bing! Bing! Bing! Rattle, clash and clatter. Open fly the doors; brave men mount their boxes. Bing! Bing! Bing! They're off! The horses tear down the street like mad. Bing! Bing! Bing! goes the gong!

"Get out of the track! The engines are coming! For God's sake, snatch that child from the road!"

On, on, wildly, resolutely, madly fly the steeds. Bing! Bing! the gong. Away dash the horses on the wings of fevered fury. On whirls the machine, down streets, around corners, up this avenue and across that one, out into the very bowels of darkness, whiffing, wheezing, shooting a million sparks from the stack, paving the path of startled night with a galaxy of stars. Over the house-tops to the north, a volcanic burst of flame shoots out, belching with blinding effect. The sky is ablaze. A tenement house is burning. Five hundred souls are in peril. Merciful Heaven! Spare the victims! Are the engines coming? Yes, here they are, dashing down the street. Look! the horses ride upon the wind; eyes bulging like balls of fire; nostrils wide open. A palpitating billow of fire, rolling, plunging, bounding, rising, falling, swelling, heaving, and with mad passion bursting its red-hot sides asunder, reaching out its arms, encircling, squeezing, grabbing up, swallowing everything before it with the hot, greedy mouth of an appalling monster.

How the horses dash around the corner! Animal instinct say you? Aye, more. Brute reason.

"Up the ladders, men!"

The towering building is buried in bloated banks of savage, biting elements. Forked tongues dart out and in, dodge here and there, up and down, and wind their cutting edges around every object. A crash, a dull, explosive sound, and a puff of smoke leaps out. At the highest point upon the roof stands a dark figure in a desperate strait, the hands making frantic gestures, the arms swinging wildly—and then the body shoots off into frightful space, plunging upon the pavement with a revolting thud. The man's arm strikes a bystander as he darts down. The crowd shudders, sways, and utters a low murmur of pity and horror. The faint-hearted lookers-on hide their faces. One woman swoons away.

"Poor fellow! Dead!" exclaims a laborer, as he looks upon the man's body.

"Aye, Joe, and I knew him well, too! He lived next door to me, five flights back. He leaves a widowed mother and two wee bits of orphans. I helped him bury his wife a fortnight ago. Ah, Joe! but it's hard lines for the orphans."

A ghastly hour moves on, dragging its regiment of panic in its trail and leaving crimson blotches of cruelty along the path of night.

"Are they all out, firemen?"

"Aye, aye, sir!"

"No, they're not! There's a woman in the top window holding a child in her arms—over yonder in the right-hand corner! The ladders, there! A hundred pounds to the man who makes the rescue!"

A dozen start. One man more supple than the others, and reckless in his bravery, clambers to the top rung of the ladder.

"Too short!" he cries. "Hoist another!"

Up it goes. He mounts to the window, fastens the rope, lashes mother and babe, swings them off into ugly emptiness, and lets them down to be rescued by his comrades.

"Bravo, fireman!" shouts the crowd.

A crash breaks through the uproar of crackling timbers.

"Look alive, up there! Great God! The roof has fallen!"

The walls sway, rock, and tumble in with a deafening roar. The spectators cease to breathe. The cold truth reveals itself. The fireman has been carried into the seething furnace. An old woman, bent with the weight of age, rushes through the fire line, shrieking, raving, and wringing her hands and opening her heart of grief.

"Poor John! He was all I had! And a brave lad he was, too! But he's gone now. He lost his own life in savin' two more, and now—now he's there, away in there!" she repeats, pointing to the cruel oven.

The engines do their work. The flames die out. An eerie gloom hangs over the ruins like a formidable, blackened pall.

And the noon of night is passed.

—Ardennes Jones-Foster

## QUESTIONS AND ANSWERS

1. Write two paragraphs on one of these: the race horse, the motor boat, golfing, tennis; let the first be pure exposition and the second pure description.

2. Select your own theme and do the same in two short extemporaneous speeches.

3. Deliver a short original address in the over-ornamented style.

4. (a) Point out its defects; (b) recast it in a more effective style; (c) show how the one surpasses the other.

5. Make a list of ten subjects which lend themselves to description in the style you prefer.

6. Deliver a two-minute speech on any one of them, using chiefly, but not solely, description.

7. For one minute, look at any object, scene, action, picture, or person you choose, take two minutes to arrange your thoughts, and then deliver a short description— all without making written notes.

8. In what sense is description more *personal* than exposition?

**9.** Explain the difference between a scientific and an artistic description.

**10.** In the style of Dickens and Irving (pages 140–141), write five separate sentences describing five characters by means of suggestion—one sentence to each.

**11.** Describe a character by means of a hint, after the manner of Chaucer (page 140).

**12.** Read aloud the following with special attention to gesture:

His very throat was moral. You saw a good deal of it. You looked over a very low fence of white cravat (whereof no man had ever beheld the tie, for he fastened it behind), and there it lay, a valley between two jutting heights of collar, serene and whiskerless before you. It seemed to say, on the part of Mr. Pecksniff, "There is no deception, ladies and gentlemen, all is peace, a holy calm pervades me." So did his hair, just grizzled with an iron gray, which was all brushed off his forehead, and stood bolt upright, or slightly drooped in kindred action with his heavy eyelids. So did his person, which was sleek though free from corpulency. So did his manner, which was soft and oily. In a word, even his plain black suit, and state of widower, and dangling double eye-glass, all tended to the same purpose, and cried aloud, "Behold the moral Pecksniff!"

—CHARLES DICKENS, *Martin Chuzzlewit*

**13.** Which of the following do you prefer, and why?

She was a blooming lass of fresh eighteen, plump as a partridge, ripe and melting and rosy-cheeked as one of her father's peaches.

—IRVING

She was a splendidly feminine girl, as wholesome as a November pippin, and no more mysterious than a window-pane.

—O. HENRY

Small, shining, neat, methodical, and buxom was Miss Peecher; cherry-cheeked and tuneful of voice.

—DICKENS

**14.** Invent five epithets, and apply them as you choose (page 140).

**15.** (*a*) Make a list of five figures of speech; (*b*) define them; (*c*) give an example—preferably original—under each.

**16.** Pick out the figures of speech in the address by Grady, on page 143.

**17.** Invent an original figure to take the place of any one in Grady's speech.

**18.** What sort of figures do you find in the selection from Stevenson, on page 145?

**19.** What methods of description does he seem to prefer?

**20.** Write and deliver, without notes and with descriptive gestures, a description in imitation of any of the authors quoted in this chapter.

**21.** Reëxamine one of your past speeches and improve the descriptive work. Report on what faults you found to exist.

**22.** Deliver an extemporaneous speech describing any dramatic scene in the style of "Midnight in London."

**23.** Describe an event in your favorite sport in the style of Dr. Talmage. Be careful to make the delivery effective.

**24.** Criticise, favorably or unfavorably, the descriptions of any travel talk you may have heard recently.

**25.** Deliver a brief original travel talk, as though you were showing pictures.

**26.** Recast the talk and deliver it "without pictures."

# CHAPTER XXI

# *Influencing by Narration*

The art of narration is the art of writing in hooks and eyes. The principle consists in making the appropriate thought follow the appropriate thought, the proper fact the proper fact; in first preparing the mind for what is to come, and then letting it come.

—WALTER BAGEHOT, *Literary Studies*

Our very speech is curiously historical. Most men, you may observe, speak only to narrate; not in imparting what they have thought, which indeed were often a very small matter, but in exhibiting what they have undergone or seen, which is a quite unlimited one, do talkers dilate. Cut us off from Narrative, how would the stream of conversation, even among the wisest, languish into detached handfuls, and among the foolish utterly evaporate! Thus, as we do nothing but enact History, we say little but recite it

—THOMAS CARLYLE, *On History*

ONLY A SMALL SEGMENT OF THE GREAT FIELD OF NARRATION OFFERS ITS RESOURCES to the public speaker, and that includes the anecdote, biographical facts, and the narration of events in general.

Narration—more easily defined than mastered—is the recital of an incident, or a group of facts and occurrences, in such a manner as to produce a desired effect.

The laws of narration are few, but its successful practise involves more of art than would at first appear—so much, indeed, that we cannot even touch upon its technique here, but must content ourselves with an examination of a few examples of narration as used in public speech.

In a preliminary way, notice how radically the public speaker's use of narrative differs from that of the story-writer in the more limited scope, absence of extended dialogue and character drawing, and freedom from elaboration of detail, which characterize platform narrative. On the other hand, there are several similarities of method: the frequent combination of narration with exposition, description, argumentation, and pleading; the care exercised in the arrangement of material so as to produce a strong effect at the close (cli-

INFLUENCING BY NARRATION  *&* 151

max); the very general practise of concealing the "point" (dénouement) of a story until the effective moment; and the careful suppression of needless, and therefore hurtful, details.

So we see that, whether for magazine or platform, the art of narration involves far more than the recital of annals; the succession of events recorded requires a *plan* in order to bring them out with real effect.

It will be noticed, too, that the literary style in platform narration is likely to be either less polished and more vigorously dramatic than in that intended for publication, or else more fervid and elevated in tone. In this latter respect, however, the best platform speaking of today differs from the models of the preceding generation, wherein a highly dignified, and sometimes pompous, style was thought the only fitting dress for a public deliverance. Great, noble and stirring as these older masters were in their lofty and impassioned eloquence, we are sometimes oppressed when we read their sounding periods for any great length of time—even allowing for all that we lose by missing the speaker's presence, voice, and fire. So let us model our platform narration, as our other forms of speech, upon the effective addresses of the moderns, without lessening our admiration for the older school.

## *The Anecdote*

An anecdote is a short narrative of a single event, told as being striking enough to bring out a point. The keener the point, the more condensed the form, and the more suddenly the application strikes the hearer, the better the story.

To regard an anecdote as an illustration—an interpretive picture—will help to hold us to its true purpose, for a purposeless story is of all offenses on the platform the most asinine. A perfectly capital joke will fall flat when it is dragged in by the nape without evident bearing on the subject under discussion. On the other hand, an apposite anecdote has saved many a speech from failure.

"There is no finer opportunity for the display of tact than in the introduction of witty or humorous stories into a discourse. Wit is keen and like a rapier, piercing deeply, sometimes even to the heart. Humor is good-natured, and does not wound. Wit is founded upon the sudden discovery of an unsuspected relation existing between two ideas. Humor deals with things out of relation—with the incongruous. It was wit in Douglass Jerrold to retort upon the scowl of a stranger whose shoulder he had familiarly slapped, mistaking him for a friend: 'I beg your pardon, I thought I knew you—but I'm glad I don't.' It was humor in the Southern orator, John Wise, to liken the pleasure of spending an evening with a Puritan girl to that of sitting on a block of ice in winter, cracking hailstones between his teeth."[21]

The foregoing quotation has been introduced chiefly to illustrate the first and simplest form of anecdote—the single sentence embodying a pungent saying.

Another simple form is that which conveys its meaning without need of "application," as the old preachers used to say. George Ade has quoted this one as the best joke he ever heard:

---

21 *How to Attract and Hold an Audience*, J. Berg Esenwein.

> Two solemn-looking gentlemen were riding together in a railway carriage. One gentleman said to the other: "Is your wife entertaining this summer?" Whereupon the other gentleman replied: "Not very."

Other anecdotes need harnessing to the particular truth the speaker wishes to carry along in his talk. Sometimes the application is made before the story is told and the audience is prepared to make the comparison, point by point, as the illustration is told. Henry W. Grady used this method in one of the anecdotes he told while delivering his great extemporaneous address, "The New South."

> Age does not endow all things with strength and virtue, nor are all new things to be despised. The shoemaker who put over his door, "John Smith's shop, founded 1760," was more than matched by his young rival across the street who hung out this sign: "Bill Jones. Established 1886. No old stock kept in this shop."

In two anecdotes, told also in "The New South," Mr. Grady illustrated another way of enforcing the application: in both instances he split the idea he wished to drive home, bringing in part before and part after the recital of the story. The fact that the speaker misquoted the words of Genesis in which the Ark is described did not seem to detract from the burlesque humor of the story.

> I bespeak the utmost stretch of your courtesy tonight. I am not troubled about those from whom I come. You remember the man whose wife sent him to a neighbor with a pitcher of milk, who, tripping on the top step, fell, with such casual interruptions as the landings afforded, into the basement, and, while picking himself up, had the pleasure of hearing his wife call out:
>    "John, did you break the pitcher?"
>    "No, I didn't," said John, "but I be dinged if I don't."
>    So, while those who call to me from behind may inspire me with energy, if not with courage, I ask an indulgent hearing from you. I beg that you will bring your full faith in American fairness and frankness to judgment upon what I shall say. There was an old preacher once who told some boys of the Bible lesson he was going to read in the morning. The boys, finding the place, glued together the connecting pages. The next morning he read on the bottom of one page: "When Noah was one hundred and twenty years old he took unto himself a wife, who was"—then turning the page—"one hundred and forty cubits long, forty cubits wide, built of gopher wood, and covered with pitch inside and out." He was naturally puzzled at this. He read it again, verified it, and then said, "My friends, this is the first time I ever met this in the Bible, but I accept it as an evidence of the assertion that we are fearfully and wonderfully made." If I could get you to hold such faith to-night, I could proceed cheerfully to the task I otherwise approach with a sense of consecration.

Now and then a speaker will plunge without introduction into an anecdote, leaving the application to follow. The following illustrates this method:

A large, slew-footed darky was leaning against the corner of the railroad station in a Texas town when the noon whistle in the canning factory blew and the hands hurried out, bearing their grub buckets. The darky listened, with his head on one side until the rocketing echo had quite died away. Then he heaved a deep sigh and remarked to himself:

"Dar she go. Dinner time for some folks—but jes' 12 o'clock fur me!"

That is the situation in thousands of American factories, large and small, today. And why? etc., etc.

Doubtless the most frequent platform use of the anecdote is in the pulpit. The sermon "illustration," however, is not always strictly narrative in form, but tends to extended comparison, as the following from Dr. Alexander Maclaren:

Men will stand as Indian fakirs do, with their arms above their heads until they stiffen there. They will perch themselves upon pillars like Simeon Stylites, for years, till the birds build their nests in their hair. They will measure all the distance from Cape Comorin to Juggernaut's temple with their bodies along the dusty road. They will wear hair shirts and scourge themselves. They will fast and deny themselves. They will build cathedrals and endow churches. They will do as many of you do, labor by fits and starts all thru your lives at the endless task of making yourselves ready for heaven, and winning it by obedience and by righteousness. They will do all these things and do them gladly, rather than listen to the humbling message that says, "You do not need to do anything—wash." Is it your washing, or the water, that will clean you? Wash and be clean! Naaman's cleaning was only a test of his obedience, and a token that it was God who cleansed him. There was no power in Jordan's waters to take away the taint of leprosy. Our cleansing is in that blood of Jesus Christ that has the power to take away all sin, and to make the foulest amongst us pure and clean.

One final word must be said about the introduction to the anecdote. A clumsy, inappropriate introduction is fatal, whereas a single apt or witty sentence will kindle interest and prepare a favorable hearing. The following extreme illustration, by the English humorist, Captain Harry Graham, well satirizes the stumbling manner:

The best story that I ever heard was one that I was told once in the fall of 1905 (or it may have been 1906), when I was visiting Boston—at least, I think it was Boston; it may have been Washington (my memory is so bad).

I happened to run across a most amusing man whose name I forget—Williams or Wilson or Wilkins; some name like that—and he told me this story while we were waiting for a trolley car.

I can still remember how heartily I laughed at the time; and again, that evening, after I had gone to bed, how I laughed myself to sleep recalling the humor of this incredibly humorous story. It was really quite extraordinarily funny. In fact, I can truthfully affirm that it is quite the most amusing story I have ever had the privilege of hearing. Unfortunately, I've forgotten it.

## Biographical Facts

Public speaking has much to do with personalities; naturally, therefore, the narration of a series of biographical details, including anecdotes among the recital of interesting facts, plays a large part in the eulogy, the memorial address, the political speech, the sermon, the lecture, and other platform deliverances. Whole addresses may be made up of such biographical details, such as a sermon on "Moses," or a lecture on "Lee."

The following example is in itself an expanded anecdote, forming a link in a chain:

## Marius in Prison

The peculiar sublimity of the Roman mind does not express itself, nor is it at all to be sought, in their poetry. Poetry, according to the Roman ideal of it, was not an adequate organ for the grander movements of the national mind. Roman sublimity must be looked for in Roman acts, and in Roman sayings. Where, again, will you find a more adequate expression of the Roman majesty, than in the saying of Trajan—*Imperatorem oportere stantem mori*—that Cæsar ought to die standing; a speech of imperatorial grandeur! Implying that he, who was "the foremost man of all this world,"—and, in regard to all other nations, the representative of his own,— should express its characteristic virtue in his farewell act—should die *in procinctu*— and should meet the last enemy as the first, with a Roman countenance and in a soldier's attitude. If this had an imperatorial—what follows had a consular majesty, and is almost the grandest story upon record.

Marius, the man who rose to be seven times consul, was in a dungeon, and a slave was sent in with commission to put him to death. These were the persons,— the two extremities of exalted and forlorn humanity, its vanward and its rearward man, a Roman consul and an abject slave. But their natural relations to each other were, by the caprice of fortune, monstrously inverted: the consul was in chains; the slave was for a moment the arbiter of his fate. By what spells, what magic, did Marius reinstate himself in his natural prerogatives? By what marvels drawn from heaven or from earth, did he, in the twinkling of an eye, again invest himself with the purple, and place between himself and his assassin a host of shadowy lictors? By the mere blank supremacy of great minds over weak ones. He *fascinated* the slave, as a rattlesnake does a bird. Standing "like Teneriffe," he smote him with his eye, and said, "*Tune, homo, audes occidere C. Marium?*"—"Dost thou, fellow, presume to kill Caius Marius?" Whereat, the reptile, quaking under the voice, nor daring to affront the consular eye, sank gently to the ground—turned round upon his hands and feet—and, crawling out of the prison like any other vermin, left Marius standing in solitude as steadfast and immovable as the capitol.

—Thomas De Quincy

Here is a similar example, prefaced by a general historical statement and concluding with autobiographical details:

# A Reminiscence of Lexington

One raw morning in spring—it will be eighty years the 19th day of this month— Hancock and Adams, the Moses and Aaron of that Great Deliverance, were both at Lexington; they also had "obstructed an officer" with brave words. British soldiers, a thousand strong, came to seize them and carry them over sea for trial, and so nip the bud of Freedom auspiciously opening in that early spring. The town militia came together before daylight, "for training." A great, tall man, with a large head and a high, wide brow, their captain,—one who had "seen service,"—marshalled them into line, numbering but seventy, and bade "every man load his piece with powder and ball. I will order the first man shot that runs away," said he, when some faltered. "Don't fire unless fired upon, but if they want to have a war, let it begin here."

Gentlemen, you know what followed; those farmers and mechanics "fired the shot heard round the world." A little monument covers the bones of such as before had pledged their fortune and their sacred honor to the Freedom of America, and that day gave it also their lives. I was born in that little town, and bred up amid the memories of that day. When a boy, my mother lifted me up, one Sunday, in her religious, patriotic arms, and held me while I read the first monumental line I ever saw—"Sacred to Liberty and the Rights of Mankind."

Since then I have studied the memorial marbles of Greece and Rome, in many an ancient town; nay, on Egyptian obelisks have read what was written before the Eternal raised up Moses to lead Israel out of Egypt; but no chiseled stone has ever stirred me to such emotion as these rustic names of men who fell "In the Sacred Cause of God and their Country."

Gentlemen, the Spirit of Liberty, the Love of Justice, were early fanned into a flame in my boyish heart. That monument covers the bones of my own kinsfolk; it was their blood which reddened the long, green grass at Lexington. It was my own name which stands chiseled on that stone; the tall captain who marshalled his fellow farmers and mechanics into stern array, and spoke such brave and dangerous words as opened the war of American Independence,—the last to leave the field,—was my father's father. I learned to read out of his Bible, and with a musket he that day captured from the foe, I learned another religious lesson, that "Rebellion to Tyrants is Obedience to God." I keep them both "Sacred to Liberty and the Rights of Mankind," to use them both "In the Sacred Cause of God and my Country."

—Theodore Parker

## Narration of Events in General

In this wider, emancipated narration we find much mingling of other forms of discourse, greatly to the advantage of the speech, for this truth cannot be too strongly emphasized: The efficient speaker cuts loose from form for the sake of a big, free effect. The present analyses are for no other purpose than to *acquaint* you with form—do not allow any such models to hang as a weight about your neck.

The following pure narration of events, from George William Curtis's "Paul Revere's Ride," varies the biographical recital in other parts of his famous oration:

> That evening, at ten o'clock, eight hundred British troops, under Lieutenant-Colonel Smith, took boat at the foot of the Common and crossed to the Cambridge shore. Gage thought his secret had been kept, but Lord Percy, who had heard the people say on the Common that the troops would miss their aim, undeceived him. Gage instantly ordered that no one should leave the town. But as the troops crossed the river, Ebenezer Dorr, with a message to Hancock and Adams, was riding over the Neck to Roxbury, and Paul Revere was rowing over the river to Charlestown, having agreed with his friend, Robert Newman, to show lanterns from the belfry of the Old North Church—"One if by land, and two if by sea"—as a signal of the march of the British.

The following, from the same oration, beautifully mingles description with narration:

> It was a brilliant night. The winter had been unusually mild, and the spring very forward. The hills were already green. The early grain waved in the fields, and the air was sweet with the blossoming orchards. Already the robins whistled, the bluebirds sang, and the benediction of peace rested upon the landscape. Under the cloudless moon the soldiers silently marched, and Paul Revere swiftly rode, galloping through Medford and West Cambridge, rousing every house as he went spurring for Lexington and Hancock and Adams, and evading the British patrols who had been sent out to stop the news.

In the succeeding extract from another of Mr. Curtis's addresses, we have a free use of allegory as illustration:

## The Leadership of Educated Men

> There is a modern English picture which the genius of Hawthorne might have inspired. The painter calls it, "How they met themselves." A man and a woman, haggard and weary, wandering lost in a somber wood, suddenly meet the shadowy figures of a youth and a maid. Some mysterious fascination fixes the gaze and stills the hearts of the wanderers, and their amazement deepens into awe as they gradually recognize themselves as once they were; the soft bloom of youth upon their rounded cheeks, the dewy light of hope in their trusting eyes, exulting

confidence in their springing step, themselves blithe and radiant with the glory of the dawn. Today, and here, we meet ourselves. Not to these familiar scenes alone— yonder college-green with its reverend traditions; the halcyon cove of the Seekonk, upon which the memory of Roger Williams broods like a bird of calm; the historic bay, beating forever with the muffled oars of Barton and of Abraham Whipple; here, the humming city of the living; there, the peaceful city of the dead;—not to these only or chiefly do we return, but to ourselves as we once were. It is not the smiling freshmen of the year, it is your own beardless and unwrinkled faces, that are looking from the windows of University Hall and of Hope College. Under the trees upon the hill it is yourselves whom you see walking, full of hopes and dreams, glowing with conscious power, and "nourishing a youth sublime;" and in this familiar temple, which surely has never echoed with eloquence so fervid and inspiring as that of your commencement orations, it is not yonder youths in the galleries who, as they fondly believe, are whispering to yonder maids; it is your younger selves who, in the days that are no more, are murmuring to the fairest mothers and grandmothers of those maids.

Happy the worn and weary man and woman in the picture could they have felt their older eyes still glistening with that earlier light, and their hearts yet beating with undiminished sympathy and aspiration. Happy we, brethren, whatever may have been achieved, whatever left undone, if, returning to the home of our earlier years, we bring with us the illimitable hope, the unchilled resolution, the inextinguishable faith of youth.

—GEORGE WILLIAM CURTIS

## QUESTIONS AND EXERCISES

1. Clip from any source ten anecdotes and state what truths they may be used to illustrate.

2. Deliver five of these in your own language, without making any application.

3. From the ten, deliver one so as to make the application before telling the anecdote.

4. Deliver another so as to split the application.

5. Deliver another so as to make the application after the narration.

6. Deliver another in such a way as to make a specific application needless.

7. Give three ways of introducing an anecdote, by saying where you heard it, etc.

8. Deliver an illustration that is not strictly an anecdote, in the style of Curtis's speech on pages 156–157.

9. Deliver an address on any public character, using the forms illustrated in this chapter.

10. Deliver an address on some historical event in the same manner.

11. Explain how the sympathies and viewpoint of the speaker will color an anecdote, a biography, or a historical account.

12. Illustrate how the same anecdote, or a section of a historical address, may be given two different effects by personal prejudice.

13. What would be the effect of shifting the viewpoint in the midst of a narration?

14. What is the danger of using too much humor in an address? Too much pathos?

# CHAPTER XXII

# *Influencing by Suggestion*

> Sometimes the feeling that a given way of looking at things is
> undoubtedly correct prevents the mind from thinking at all. . . .
> In view of the hindrances which certain kinds or degrees of feeling
> throw into the way of thinking, it might be inferred that the thinker
> must suppress the element of feeling in the inner life. No greater mistake
> could be made. If the Creator endowed man with the power to think,
> to feel, and to will, these several activities of the mind are not designed
> to be in conflict, and so long as any one of them is not perverted or
> allowed to run to excess, it necessarily aids and strengthens the others in
> their normal functions.
>
> —NATHAN C. SCHAEFFER, *Thinking and Learning to Think*

WHEN WE WEIGH, COMPARE, AND DECIDE UPON THE VALUE OF ANY GIVEN IDEAS, we reason; when an idea produces in us an opinion or an action, without first being subjected to deliberation, we are moved by suggestion.

Man was formerly thought to be a reasoning animal, basing his actions on the conclusions of natural logic. It was supposed that before forming an opinion or deciding on a course of conduct he weighed at least some of the reasons for and against the matter, and performed a more or less simple process of reasoning. But modern research has shown that quite the opposite is true. Most of our opinions and actions are not based upon conscious reasoning, but are the result of suggestion. In fact, some authorities declare that an act of pure reasoning is very rare in the average mind. Momentous decisions are made, far-reaching actions are determined upon, primarily by the force of suggestion.

Notice that word "primarily," for simple thought, and even mature reasoning, often follows a suggestion accepted in the mind, and the thinker fondly supposes that his conclusion is from first to last based on cold logic.

## The Basis of Suggestion

We must think of suggestion both as an effect and as a cause. Considered as an effect, or objectively, there must be something in the hearer that predisposes him to receive suggestion; considered as a cause, or subjectively, there must be some methods by which the speaker can move upon that particularly susceptible attitude of the hearer. How to do this honestly and fairly is our problem—to do it dishonestly and trickily, to use suggestion to bring about conviction and action without a basis of right and truth and in a bad cause, is to assume the terrible responsibility that must fall on the champion of error. Jesus scorned not to use suggestion so that he might move men to their benefit, but every vicious trickster has adopted the same means to reach base ends. Therefore honest men will examine well into their motives and into the truth of their cause, before seeking to influence men by suggestion.

Three fundamental conditions make us all susceptive to suggestion:

*We naturally respect authority.* In every mind this is only a question of degree, ranging from the subject who is easily hypnotized to the stubborn mind that fortifies itself the more strongly with every assault upon its opinion. The latter type is almost immune to suggestion.

One of the singular things about suggestion is that it is rarely a fixed quantity. The mind that is receptive to the authority of a certain person may prove inflexible to another; moods and environments that produce hypnosis readily in one instance may be entirely inoperative in another; and some minds can scarcely ever be thus moved. We do know, however, that the feeling of the subject that authority—influence, power, domination, control, whatever you wish to call it—lies in the person of the suggester, is the basis of all suggestion.

The extreme force of this influence is demonstrated in hypnotism. The hypnotic subject is told that he is in the water; he accepts the statement as true and makes swimming motions. He is told that a band is marching down the street, playing "The Star Spangled Banner;" he declares he hears the music, arises and stands with head bared.

In the same way some speakers are able to achieve a modified hypnotic effect upon their audiences. The hearers will applaud measures and ideas which, after individual reflection, they will repudiate unless such reflection brings the conviction that the first impression is correct.

A second important principle is that *our feelings, thoughts and wills tend to follow the line of least resistance.* Once open the mind to the sway of one feeling and it requires a greater power of feeling, thought, or will—or even all three—to unseat it. Our feelings influence our judgments and volitions much more than we care to admit. So true is this that it is a superhuman task to get an audience to reason fairly on a subject on which it feels deeply, and when this result is accomplished the success becomes noteworthy, as in the case of Henry Ward Beecher's Liverpool speech. Emotional ideas once accepted are soon cherished, and finally become our very inmost selves. Attitudes based on feelings alone are prejudices.

What is true of our feelings, in this respect, applies to our ideas: All thoughts that enter the mind tend to be accepted as truth unless a stronger and contradictory thought arises.

The speaker skilled in moving men to action manages to dominate the minds of his audience with his thoughts by subtly prohibiting the entertaining of ideas hostile to his own. Most of us are captured by the latest strong attack, and if we can be induced to act while under the stress of that last insistent thought, we lose sight of counter influences.

The fact is that almost all our decisions—if they involve thought at all—are of this sort: At the moment of decision the course of action then under contemplation usurps the attention, and conflicting ideas are dropped out of consideration.

The head of a large publishing house remarked only recently that ninety per cent of the people who bought books by subscription never read them. They buy because the salesman presents his wares so skillfully that every consideration but the attractiveness of the book drops out of the mind, and that thought prompts action. *Every* idea that enters the mind will result in action unless a contradictory thought arises to prohibit it. Think of singing the musical scale and it will result in your singing it unless the counter-thought of its futility or absurdity inhibits your action. If you bandage and "doctor" a horse's foot, he will go lame. You cannot think of swallowing, without the muscles used in that process being affected. You cannot think of saying "hello," without a slight movement of the muscles of speech. To warn children that they should not put beans up their noses is the surest method of getting them to do it. Every thought called up in the mind of your audience will work either for or against you. Thoughts are not dead matter; they radiate dynamic energy—the thoughts all tend to pass into action. "Thought is another name for fate." Dominate your hearers' thoughts, allay all contradictory ideas, and you will sway them as you wish.

Volitions as well as feelings and thoughts tend to follow the line of least resistance. That is what makes habit. Suggest to a man that it is impossible to change his mind and in most cases it becomes more difficult to do so—the exception is the man who naturally jumps to the contrary. Counter suggestion is the only way to reach him. Suggest subtly and persistently that the opinions of those in the audience who are opposed to your views are changing, and it requires an effort of the will—in fact, a summoning of the forces of feeling, thought and will—to stem the tide of change that has subconsciously set in.

But, not only are we moved by authority, and tend toward channels of least resistance: *We are all influenced by our environments.* It is difficult to rise above the sway of a crowd—its enthusiasms and its fears are contagious because they are suggestive. What so many feel, we say to ourselves, must have some basis in truth. Ten times ten makes more than one hundred. Set ten men to speaking to ten audiences of ten men each, and compare the aggregate power of those ten speakers with that of one man addressing one hundred men. The ten speakers may be more logically convincing than the single orator, but the chances are strongly in favor of the one man's reaching a greater total effect, for the hundred men will radiate conviction and resolution as ten small groups could not. We all know the truism about the enthusiasm of numbers. (See the chapter on "Influencing the Crowd.")

Environment controls us unless the contrary is strongly suggested. A gloomy day, in a drab room, sparsely tenanted by listeners, invites platform disaster. Everyone feels it in the air. But let the speaker walk squarely up to the issue and suggest by all his feeling, manner and words that this is going to be a great gathering in every vital sense, and see how the suggestive power of environment recedes before the advance of a more potent suggestion—if such the speaker is able to make it.

Now these three factors—respect for authority, tendency to follow lines of least resistance, and susceptibility to environment—all help to bring the auditor into a state of mind favorable to suggestive influences, but they also react on the speaker, and now we must consider those personally causative, or subjective, forces which enable him to use suggestion effectively.

## How the Speaker Can Make Suggestion Effective

We have seen that under the influence of authoritative suggestion the audience is inclined to accept the speaker's assertion without argument and criticism. But the audience is not in this state of mind unless it has implicit confidence in the speaker. If they lack faith in him, question his motives or knowledge, or even object to his manner they will not be moved by his most logical conclusion and will fail to give him a just hearing. *It is all a matter of their confidence in him.* Whether the speaker finds it already in the warm, expectant look of his hearers, or must win to it against opposition or coldness, he must gain that one great vantage point before his suggestions take on power in the hearts of his listeners. Confidence is the mother of Conviction.

Note in the opening of Henry W. Grady's after-dinner speech how he attempted to secure the confidence of his audience. He created a receptive atmosphere by a humorous story; expressed his desire to speak with earnestness and sincerity; acknowledged "the vast interests involved;" deprecated his "untried arm," and professed his humility. Would not such an introduction give you confidence in the speaker, unless you were strongly opposed to him? And even then, would it not partly disarm your antagonism?

> Mr. President:—Bidden by your invitation to a discussion of the race problem—forbidden by occasion to make a political speech—I appreciate, in trying to reconcile orders with propriety, the perplexity of the little maid, who, bidden to learn to swim, was yet adjured, "Now, go, my darling; hang your clothes on a hickory limb, and don't go near the water."
>
> The stoutest apostle of the Church, they say, is the missionary, and the missionary, wherever he unfurls his flag, will never find himself in deeper need of unction and address than I, bidden tonight to plant the standard of a Southern Democrat in Boston's banquet hall, and to discuss the problem of the races in the home of Phillips and of Sumner. But, Mr. President, if a purpose to speak in perfect frankness and sincerity; if earnest understanding of the vast interests involved; if a consecrating sense of what disaster may follow further misunderstanding and estrangement; if these may be counted to steady undisciplined speech and to strengthen an untried arm—then, sir, I shall find the courage to proceed.

Note also Mr. Bryan's attempt to secure the confidence of his audience in the following introduction to his "Cross of Gold" speech delivered before the National Democratic Convention in Chicago, 1896. He asserts his own inability to oppose the "distinguished gentleman;" he maintains the holiness of his cause; and he declares that he will speak in the interest of humanity—well knowing that humanity is likely to have confidence in the champion of their rights. This introduction completely dominated the audience, and the speech made Mr. Bryan famous.

> Mr. Chairman and Gentlemen of the Convention: I would be presumptuous indeed to present myself against the distinguished gentlemen to whom you have listened if this were a mere measuring of abilities; but this is not a contest between persons. The humblest citizen in all the land, when clad in the armor of a righteous cause, is stronger than all the hosts of error. I come to speak to you in defense of a cause as holy as the cause of liberty—the cause of humanity.

Some speakers are able to beget confidence by their very manner, while others can not.

*To secure confidence, be confident.* How can you expect others to accept a message in which you lack, or seem to lack, faith yourself? Confidence is as contagious as disease. Napoleon rebuked an officer for using the word "impossible" in his presence. The speaker who will entertain no idea of defeat begets in his hearers the idea of his victory. Lady Macbeth was so confident of success that Macbeth changed his mind about undertaking the assassination. Columbus was so certain in his mission that Queen Isabella pawned her jewels to finance his expedition. Assert your message with implicit assurance, and your own belief will act as so much gunpowder to drive it home.

Advertisers have long utilized this principle. "The machine you will eventually buy," "Ask the man who owns one," "Has the strength of Gibraltar," are publicity slogans so full of confidence that they give birth to confidence in the mind of the reader.

It should—but may not!—go without saying that confidence must have a solid ground of merit or there will be a ridiculous crash. It is all very well for the "spellbinder" to claim all the precincts—the official count is just ahead. The reaction against over-confidence and over-suggestion ought to warn those whose chief asset is mere bluff.

A short time ago a speaker arose in a public-speaking club and asserted that grass would spring from wood-ashes sprinkled over the soil, without the aid of seed. This idea was greeted with a laugh, but the speaker was so sure of his position that he reiterated the statement forcefully several times and cited his own personal experience as proof. One of the most intelligent men in the audience, who at first had derided the idea, at length came to believe in it. When asked the reason for his sudden change of attitude, he replied: "Because the speaker is so confident." In fact, he was so confident that it took a letter from the U.S. Department of Agriculture to dislodge his error.

If by a speaker's confidence, intelligent men can be made to believe such preposterous theories as this where will the power of self-reliance cease when plausible propositions are under consideration, advanced with all the power of convincing speech?

Note the utter assurance in these selections:

> I know not what course others may take, but as for me give me liberty or give me death.
>
> —PATRICK HENRY

I ne'er will ask ye quarter, and I ne'er will be your slave;
But I'll swim the sea of slaughter, till I sink beneath its wave.

—PATTEN

Come one, come all. This rock shall fly
From its firm base as soon as I.

—SIR WALTER SCOTT

# INVICTUS

Out of the night that covers me,
   Black as the pit from pole to pole,
I thank whatever Gods may be
   For my unconquerable soul.

In the fell clutch of circumstance
   I have not winced nor cried aloud;
Under the bludgeonings of chance
   My head is bloody, but unbowed.

Beyond this place of wrath and tears
   Looms but the Horror of the shade,
And yet the menace of the years
   Finds and shall find me unafraid.

It matters not how strait the gate,
   How charged with punishments the scroll,
I am the master of my fate;
   I am the captain of my soul.

—WILLIAM ERNEST HENLEY

*Authority is a factor in suggestion.* We generally accept as truth, and without criticism, the words of an authority. When he speaks, contradictory ideas rarely arise in the mind to inhibit the action he suggests. A judge of the Supreme Court has the power of his words multiplied by the virtue of his position. The ideas of the U.S. Commissioner of Immigration on his subject are much more effective and powerful than those of a soap manufacturer, though the latter may be an able economist.

This principle also has been used in advertising. We are told that the physicians to two Kings have recommended Sanatogen. We are informed that the largest bank in America, Tiffany and Co., and The State, War, and Navy Departments, all use the Encyclopedia Britannica. The shrewd promoter gives stock in his company to influential bankers or business men in the community in order that he may use their examples as a selling argument.

If you wish to influence your audience through suggestion, if you would have your statements accepted without criticism or argument, you should appear in the light of an authority—and *be* one. Ignorance and credulity will remain unchanged unless the suggestion of authority be followed promptly by facts. Don't claim authority unless you carry your license in your pocket. Let reason support the position that suggestion has assumed.

Advertising will help to establish your reputation—it is "up to you" to maintain it. One speaker found that his reputation as a magazine writer was a splendid asset as a speaker. Mr. Bryan's publicity, gained by three nominations for the presidency and his position as Secretary of State, helps him to command large sums as a speaker. But—back of it all, he *is* a great speaker. Newspaper announcements, all kinds of advertising, formality, impressive introductions, all have a capital effect on the attitude of the audience. But how ridiculous are all these if a toy pistol is advertised as a sixteen-inch gun!

Note how authority is used in the following to support the strength of the speaker's appeal:

Professor Alfred Russell Wallace has just celebrated his 90th birthday. Sharing with Charles Darwin the honor of discovering evolution, Professor Wallace has lately received many and signal honors from scientific societies. At the dinner given him in London his address was largely made up of reminiscences. He reviewed the progress of civilization during the last century and made a series of brilliant and startling contrasts between the England of 1813 and the world of 1913. He affirmed that our progress is only seeming and not real. Professor Wallace insists that the painters, the sculptors, the architects of Athens and Rome were so superior to the modern men that the very fragments of their marbles and temples are the despair of the present day artists. He tells us that man has improved his telescope and spectacles, but that he is losing his eyesight; that man is improving his looms, but stiffening his fingers; improving his automobile and his locomotive, but losing his legs; improving his foods, but losing his digestion. He adds that the modern white slave traffic, orphan asylums, and tenement house life in factory towns, make a black page in the history of the twentieth century.

Professor Wallace's views are reinforced by the report of the commission of Parliament on the causes of the deterioration of the factory-class people. In our own country Professor Jordan warns us against war, intemperance, overworking, underfeeding of poor children, and disturbs our contentment with his "Harvest of Blood." Professor Jenks is more pessimistic. He thinks that the pace, the climate, and the stress of city life, have broken down the Puritan stock, that in another century our old families will be extinct, and that the flood of immigration means a Niagara of muddy waters fouling the pure springs of American life. In his address in New Haven Professor Kellogg calls the roll of the signs of race degeneracy and tells us that this deterioration even indicates a trend toward race extinction.

—NEWELL DWIGHT HILLIS

From every side come warnings to the American people. Our medical journals are filled with danger signals; new books and magazines, fresh from the press, tell us plainly that our people are fronting a social crisis. Mr. Jefferson, who was once regarded as good Democratic authority, seems to have differed in opinion from the gentleman who has addressed us on the part of the minority. Those who are opposed to this proposition tell us that the issue of paper money is a function of the bank, and that the government ought to go out of the banking business. I stand with Jefferson rather than with them, and tell them, as he did, that the issue of money is a function of government, and that the banks ought to go out of the governing business.

—William Jennings Bryan

Authority is the great weapon against doubt, but even its force can rarely prevail against prejudice and persistent wrong-headedness. If any speaker has been able to forge a sword that is warranted to piece such armor, let him bless humanity by sharing his secret with his platform brethren everywhere, for thus far he is alone in his glory.

There is a middle-ground between the suggestion of authority and the confession of weakness that offers a wide range for tact in the speaker. No one can advise you when to throw your "hat in the ring" and say defiantly at the outstart, "Gentlemen, I am here to fight!" Theodore Roosevelt can do that—Beecher would have been mobbed if he had begun in that style at Liverpool. It is for your own tact to decide whether you will use the disarming grace of Henry W. Grady's introduction just quoted (even the time-worn joke was ingenuous and seemed to say, "Gentlemen, I come to you with no carefully-palmed coins"), or whether the solemn gravity of Mr. Bryan before the Convention will prove to be more effective. Only be sure that your opening attitude is well thought out, and if it change as you warm up to your subject, let not the change lay you open to a revulsion of feeling in your audience.

*Example is a powerful means of suggestion.* As we saw while thinking of environment in its effects on an audience, we do, without the usual amount of hesitation and criticism, what others are doing. Paris wears certain hats and gowns; the rest of the world imitates. The child mimics the actions, accents and intonations of the parent. Were a child never to hear anyone speak, he would never acquire the power of speech, unless under most arduous training, and even then only imperfectly. One of the biggest department stores in the United States spends fortunes on one advertising slogan: "Everybody is going to the big store." That makes everybody want to go.

You can reinforce the power of your message by showing that it has been widely accepted. Political organizations subsidize applause to create the impression that their speakers' ideas are warmly received and approved by the audience. The advocates of the commission-form of government of cities, the champions of votes for women, reserve as their strongest arguments the fact that a number of cities and states have already success-fully accepted their plans. Advertisements use the testimonial for its power of suggestion.

Observe how this principle has been applied in the following selections, and utilize it on every occasion possible in your attempts to influence through suggestion:

The war is actually begun. The next gale that sweeps from the North will bring to our ears the clash of resounding arms. Our brethren are already in the field. Why stand ye here idle?

—Patrick Henry

With a zeal approaching the zeal which inspired the Crusaders who followed Peter the Hermit, our silver Democrats went forth from victory unto victory until they are now assembled, not to discuss, not to debate, but to enter up the judgment already rendered by the plain people of this country. In this contest brother has been arrayed against brother, father against son. The warmest ties of love, acquaintance, and association have been disregarded; old leaders have been cast aside when they refused to give expression to the sentiments of those whom they would lead, and new leaders have sprung up to give direction to this cause of truth. Thus has the contest been waged, and we have assembled here under as binding and solemn instructions as were ever imposed upon representatives of the people.

—William Jennings Bryan

*Figurative and indirect language has suggestive force*, because it does not make statements that can be directly disputed. It arouses no contradictory ideas in the minds of the audience, thereby fulfilling one of the basic requisites of suggestion. By *implying* a conclusion in indirect or figurative language it is often asserted most forcefully.

Note that in the following Mr. Bryan did not say that Mr. McKinley would be defeated. He implied it in a much more effective manner:

Mr. McKinley was nominated at St. Louis upon a platform which declared for the maintenance of the gold standard until it can be changed into bimetallism by international agreement. Mr. McKinley was the most popular man among the Republicans, and three months ago everybody in the Republican party prophesied his election. How is it today? Why, the man who was once pleased to think that he looked like Napoleon—that man shudders today when he remembers that he was nominated on the anniversary of the battle of Waterloo. Not only that, but as he listens he can hear with ever-increasing distinctness the sound of the waves as they beat upon the lonely shores of St. Helena.

Had Thomas Carlyle said: "A false man cannot found a religion," his words would have been neither so suggestive nor so powerful, nor so long remembered as his implication in these striking words:

A false man found a religion? Why, a false man cannot build a brick house! If he does not know and follow truly the properties of mortar, burnt clay, and what else he works in, it is no house that he makes, but a rubbish heap. It will not stand for twelve centuries, to lodge a hundred and eighty millions; it will fall straightway. A man must conform himself to Nature's laws, be verily in communion with Nature and the truth of things, or Nature will answer him, No, not at all!

Observe how the picture that Webster draws here is much more emphatic and forceful than any mere assertion could be:

> Sir, I know not how others may feel, but as for myself when I see my *alma mater* surrounded, like Caesar in the senate house, by those who are reiterating stab after stab, I would not for this right hand have her turn to me and say, "And thou, too, my son!"
>
> —WEBSTER

A speech should be built on sound logical foundations, and no man should dare to speak in behalf of a fallacy. Arguing a subject, however, will necessarily arouse contradictory ideas in the mind of your audience. When immediate action or persuasion is desired, suggestion is more efficacious than argument—when both are judiciously mixed, the effect is irresistible.

## QUESTIONS AND EXERCISES

1. Make an outline, or brief, of the contents of this chapter.

2. Revise the introduction to any of your written addresses, with the teachings of this chapter in mind.

3. Give two original examples of the power of suggestion as you have observed it in each of these fields: (*a*) advertising; (*b*) politics; (*c*) public sentiment.

4. Give original examples of suggestive speech, illustrating two of the principles set forth in this chapter.

5. What reasons can you give that disprove the general contention of this chapter?

6. What reasons not already given seem to you to support it?

7. What effect do his own suggestions have on the speaker himself?

8. Can suggestion arise from the audience? If so, show how.

9. Select two instances of suggestion in the speeches found in the Appendix.

10. Change any two passages in the same, or other, speeches so as to use suggestion more effectively.

11. Deliver those passages in the revised form.

12. Choosing your own subject, prepare and deliver a short speech largely in the suggestive style.

# CHAPTER XXIII

# *Influencing by Argument*

Common sense is the common sense of mankind. It is the product
of common observation and experience. It is modest, plain, and
unsophisticated. It sees with everybody's eyes, and hears with
everybody's ears. It has no capricious distinctions, no perplexities, and
no mysteries. It never equivocates, and never trifles. Its language is
always intelligible. It is known by clearness of speech and singleness
of purpose.

—GEORGE JACOB HOLYOAKE, *Public Speaking and Debate*

THE VERY NAME OF LOGIC IS AWESOME TO MOST YOUNG SPEAKERS, BUT SO SOON AS
they come to realize that its processes, even when most intricate, are merely technical statements of the truths enforced by common sense, it will lose its terrors. In fact, logic[22] is a fascinating subject, well worth the public speaker's study, for it explains the principles that govern the use of argument and proof.

Argumentation is the process of producing conviction by means of reasoning. Other ways of producing conviction there are, notably suggestion, as we have just shown, but no means is so high, so worthy of respect, as the adducing of sound reasons in support of a contention.

Since more than one side of a subject must be considered before we can claim to have deliberated upon it fairly, we ought to think of argumentation under two aspects: building up an argument, and tearing down an argument; that is, you must not only examine into the stability of your structure of argument so that it may both support the proposition you intend to probe and yet be so sound that it cannot be overthrown by opponents, but you must also be so keen to detect defects in argument that you will be able to demolish the weaker arguments of those who argue against you.

We can consider argumentation only generally, leaving minute and technical discussions to such excellent works as George P. Baker's "The Principles of Argumentation," and George Jacob Holyoake's "Public Speaking and Debate." Any good college rhetoric also will give help on the subject, especially the works of John Franklin Genung and Adams Sherman Hill. The student is urged to familiarize himself with at least one of these texts.

---

22 McCosh's *Logic* is a helpful volume, and not too technical for the beginner. A brief digest of logical principles as applied to public speaking is contained in *How to Attract and Hold an Audience*, by J. Berg Esenwein.

The following series of questions will, it is hoped, serve a triple purpose: that of suggesting the forms of proof together with the ways in which they may be used; that of helping the speaker to test the strength of his arguments; and that of enabling the speaker to attack his opponent's arguments with both keenness and justice.

# Testing an Argument

I. THE QUESTION UNDER DISCUSSION

    1. *IS IT CLEARLY STATED?*

        (*a*) Do the terms of statement mean the same to each disputant? (For example, the meaning of the term "gentleman" may not be mutually agreed upon.)

        (*b*) Is confusion likely to arise as to its purpose?

    2. *Is it fairly stated?*

        (*a*) Does it include enough?

        (*b*) Does it include too much?

        (*c*) Is it stated so as to contain a trap?

    3. *Is it a debatable question?*

    4. *What is the pivotal point in the whole question?*

    5. *What are the subordinate points?*

II. THE EVIDENCE

    1. *The witnesses as to facts*

        (*a*) Is each witness impartial? What is his relation to the subject at issue?

        (*b*) Is he mentally competent?

        (*c*) Is he morally credible?

        (*d*) Is he in a position to know the facts? Is he an eye-witness?

        (*e*) Is he a willing witness?

        (*f*) Is his testimony contradicted?

        (*g*) Is his testimony corroborated?

        (*h*) Is his testimony contrary to well-known facts or general principles?

        (*i*) Is it probable?

    2. *The authorities cited as evidence*

        (*a*) Is the authority well-recognized as such?

        (*b*) What constitutes him an authority?

        (*c*) Is his interest in the case an impartial one?

        (*d*) Does he state his opinion positively and clearly?

        (*e*) Are the non-personal authorities cited (books, etc.) reliable and unprejudiced?

    3. *The facts adduced as evidence*

        (*a*) Are they sufficient in number to constitute proof?

        (*b*) Are they weighty enough in character?

        (*c*) Are they in harmony with reason?

        (*d*) Are they mutually harmonious or contradictory?

        (*e*) Are they admitted, doubted, or disputed?

    4. *The principles adduced as evidence*

(a) Are they axiomatic?

(b) Are they truths of general experience?

(c) Are they truths of special experience?

(d) Are they truths arrived at by experiment?

Were such experiments special or general?

Were the experiments authoritative and conclusive?

## III. THE REASONING

1. *Inductions*

(a) Are the facts numerous enough to warrant accepting the generalization as being conclusive?

(b) Do the facts agree *only* when considered in the light of this explanation as a conclusion?

(c) Have you overlooked any contradictory facts?

(d) Are the contradictory facts sufficiently explained when this inference is accepted as true?

(e) Are all contrary positions shown to be relatively untenable?

(f) Have you accepted mere opinions as facts?

2. *Deductions*

(a) Is the law or general principle a well-established one?

(b) Does the law or principle clearly include the fact you wish to deduce from it, or have you strained the inference?

(c) Does the importance of the law or principle warrant so important an inference?

(d) Can the deduction be shown to prove too much?

3. *Parallel cases*

(a) Are the cases parallel at enough points to warrant an inference of similar cause or effect?

(b) Are the cases parallel at the vital point at issue?

(c) Has the parallelism been strained?

(d) Are there no other parallels that would point to a stronger contrary conclusion?

4. *Inferences*

(a) Are the antecedent conditions such as would make the allegation probable? (Character and opportunities of the accused, for example.)

(b) Are the signs that point to the inference either clear or numerous enough to warrant its acceptance as fact?

(c) Are the signs cumulative, and agreeable one with the other?

(d) Could the signs be made to point to a contrary conclusion?

5. *Syllogisms*

(a) Have any steps been omitted in the syllogisms? (Such as in a syllogism *in enthymeme.*) If so, test any such by filling out the syllogisms.

(b) Have you been guilty of stating a conclusion that really does not follow? (A *non sequitur.*)

(c) Can your syllogism be reduced to an absurdity? (*Reductio ad absurdum.*)

## QUESTIONS AND EXERCISES

1. Show why an unsupported assertion is not an argument.

2. Illustrate how an irrelevant fact may be made to seem to support an argument.

3. What inferences may justly be made from the following?

> During the Boer War it was found that the average Englishman did not
> measure up to the standards of recruiting and the average soldier in the field
> manifested a low plane of vitality and endurance. Parliament, alarmed by
> the disastrous consequences, instituted an investigation. The commission
> appointed brought in a finding that alcoholic poisoning was the great cause
> of the national degeneracy. The investigations of the commission have been
> supplemented by investigations of scientific bodies and individual scientists,
> all arriving at the same conclusion. As a consequence, the British Government
> has placarded the streets of a hundred cities with billboards setting forth the
> destructive and degenerating nature of alcohol and appealing to the people
> in the name of the nation to desist from drinking alcoholic beverages. Under
> efforts directed by the Government the British Army is fast becoming an army
> of total abstainers.
>
> The Governments of continental Europe followed the lead of the British
> Government. The French Government has placarded France with appeals
> to the people, attributing the decline of the birth rate and increase in the
> death rate to the widespread use of alcoholic beverages. The experience of the
> German Government has been the same. The German Emperor has clearly
> stated that leadership in war and in peace will be held by the nation that roots
> out alcohol. He has undertaken to eliminate even the drinking of beer, so far
> as possible, from the German Army and Navy.
>
> —RICHMOND PEARSON HOBSON, *Before the U.S. Congress*

4. Since the burden of proof lies on him who attacks a position, or argues for a change in affairs, how would his opponent be likely to conduct his own part of a debate?

5. Define (*a*) syllogism; (*b*) rebuttal; (*c*) "begging the question;" (*d*) premise; (*e*) rejoinder; (*f*) surrejoinder; (*g*) dilemma; (*h*) induction; (*i*) deduction; (*j*) *a priori*; (*k*) *a posteriori*; (*l*) inference.

6. Criticise this reasoning:

> Men ought not to smoke tobacco, because to do so is contrary to best medical
> opinion. My physician has expressly condemned the practise, and is a medical
> authority in this country.

7. Criticise this reasoning:

> Men ought not to swear profanely, because it is wrong. It is wrong for the
> reason that it is contrary to the Moral Law, and it is contrary to the Moral Law

because it is contrary to the Scriptures. It is contrary to the Scriptures because it is contrary to the will of God, and we know it is contrary to God's will because it is wrong.

**8.** Criticise this syllogism:

MAJOR PREMISE: All men who have no cares are happy.
MINOR PREMISE: Slovenly men are careless.
CONCLUSION: Therefore, slovenly men are happy.

**9.** Criticise the following major, or foundation, premises:

All is not gold that glitters.

All cold may be expelled by fire.

**10.** Criticise the following fallacy (*non sequitur*):

MAJOR PREMISE: All strong men admire strength.
MINOR PREMISE: This man is not strong.
CONCLUSION: Therefore this man does not admire strength.

**11.** Criticise these statements:

Sleep is beneficial on account of its soporific qualities.

Fiske's histories are authentic because they contain accurate accounts of American history, and we know that they are true accounts for otherwise they would not be contained in these authentic works.

**12.** What do you understand from the terms "reasoning from effect to cause" and "from cause to effect?" Give examples.

**13.** What principle did Richmond Pearson Hobson employ in the following?

What is the police power of the States? The police power of the Federal Government or the State—any sovereign State—has been defined. Take the definition given by Blackstone, which is:

"The due regulation and domestic order of the Kingdom, whereby the inhabitants of a State, like members of a well-governed family, are bound to conform their general behavior to the rules of propriety, of neighborhood and good manners, and to be decent, industrious, and inoffensive in their respective stations."

Would this amendment interfere with any State carrying on the promotion of its domestic order?

Or you can take the definition in another form, in which it is given by Mr. Tiedeman, when he says:

"The object of government is to impose that degree of restraint upon human actions which is necessary to a uniform, reasonable enjoyment of private rights. The power of the government to impose this restraint is called the police power."

Judge Cooley says of the liquor traffic:

"The business of manufacturing and selling liquor is one that affects the public interests in many ways and leads to many disorders. It has a tendency to increase pauperism and crime. It renders a large force of peace officers essential, and it adds to the expense of the courts and of nearly all branches of civil administration."

Justice Bradley, of the United States Supreme Court, says:

"Licenses may be properly required in the pursuit of many professions and avocations, which require peculiar skill and training or supervision for the public welfare. The profession or avocation is open to all alike who will prepare themselves with the requisite qualifications or give the requisite security for preserving public order. This is in harmony with the general proposition that the ordinary pursuits of life, forming the greater per cent of the industrial pursuits, are and ought to be free and open to all, subject only to such general regulations, applying equally to all, as the general good may demand.

"All such regulations are entirely competent for the legislature to make and are in no sense an abridgment of the equal rights of citizens. But a license to do that which is odious and against common right is necessarily an outrage upon the equal rights of citizens."

**14.** What method did Jesus employ in the following:

Ye are the salt of the earth; but if the salt have lost his savour, wherewith shall it be salted? It is thenceforth good for nothing but to be cast out, and to be trodden under foot of men.

Behold the fowls of the air; for they sow not, neither do they reap nor gather into barns; yet your heavenly Father feedeth them. Are ye not much better than they?

And why take ye thought for raiment? Consider the lilies of the field; how they grow; they toil not, neither do they spin; And yet I say unto you, that even Solomon in all his glory was not arrayed like one of these. Wherefore, if God so clothe the grass of the field, which today is, and tomorrow is cast into the oven, shall he not much more clothe you, O ye of little faith?

Or what man is there of you, whom if his son ask bread, will he give him a stone? Or if he ask a fish, will he give him a serpent? If ye then, being evil, know how to give good gifts unto your children, how much more shall your Father which is in heaven give good things to them that ask him?

**15.** Make five original syllogisms[23] on the following models:

> MAJOR PREMISE: He who administers arsenic gives poison.
> MINOR PREMISE: The prisoner administered arsenic to the victim.
> CONCLUSION: Therefore the prisoner is a poisoner.

> MAJOR PREMISE: All dogs are quadrupeds.
> MINOR PREMISE: This animal is a biped.
> CONCLUSION: Therefore this animal is not a dog.

**16.** Prepare either the positive or the negative side of the following question for debate: *The recall of judges should be adopted as a national principle.*

**17.** Is this question debatable? *Benedict Arnold was a gentleman.* Give reasons for your answer.

**18.** Criticise any street or dinner-table argument you have heard recently.

**19.** Test the reasoning of any of the speeches given in this volume.

**20.** Make a short speech arguing in favor of instruction in public speaking in the public evening schools.

**21.** (*a*) Clip a newspaper editorial in which the reasoning is weak. (*b*) Criticise it. (*c*) Correct it.

**22.** Make a list of three subjects for debate, selected from the monthly magazines.

**23.** Do the same from the newspapers.

**24.** Choosing your own question and side, prepare a brief suitable for a ten-minute debating argument. The following models of briefs may help you:

---

23 For those who would make a further study of the syllogism the following rules are given: 1. In a syllogism there should be only three terms. 2. Of these three only one can be the middle term. 3. One premise must be affirmative. 4. The conclusion must be negative if either premise is negative. 5. To prove a negative, one of the premises must be negative.

 *Summary of Regulating Principles*: 1. Terms which agree with the same thing agree with each other; and when only one of two terms agrees with a third term, the two terms disagree with each other. 2. "Whatever is affirmed of a class may be affirmed of all the members of that class," and "Whatever is denied of a class may be denied of all the members of that class."

# Debate

**RESOLVED:** *That armed intervention is not justifiable on the part of any nation to collect, on behalf of private individuals, financial claims against any American nation.*[24]

## BRIEF OF AFFIRMATIVE ARGUMENT

### First speaker—Chafee

Armed intervention for collection of private claims from any American nation is not justifiable, for

1. *It is wrong in principle*, because
   (*a*) It violates the fundamental principles of international law for a very slight cause
   (*b*) It is contrary to the proper function of the State, and
   (*c*) It is contrary to justice, since claims are exaggerated.

### Second speaker—Hurley

2. *It is disastrous in its results*, because
   (*a*) It incurs danger of grave international complications
   (*b*) It tends to increase the burden of debt in the South American republics
   (*c*) It encourages a waste of the world's capital, and
   (*d*) It disturbs peace and stability in South America.

### Third speaker—Bruce

3. *It is unnecessary to collect in this way*, because
   (*a*) Peaceful methods have succeeded
   (*b*) If these should fail, claims should be settled by The Hague Tribunal
   (*c*) The fault has always been with European States when force has been used, and
   (*d*) In any case, force should not be used, for it counteracts the movement towards peace.

## BRIEF OF NEGATIVE ARGUMENT

### First speaker—Branch

Armed intervention for the collection of private financial claims against some American States is justifiable, for

1. *When other means of collection have failed, armed intervention against any nation is essentially proper*, because
   (*a*) Justice should always be secured
   (*b*) Non-enforcement of payment puts a premium on dishonesty

---

24 All the speakers were from Brown University. The affirmative briefs were used in debate with the Dartmouth College team, and the negative briefs were used in debate with the Williams College team. From *The Speaker*, by permission.

(c) Intervention for this purpose is sanctioned by the best international authority

(d) Danger of undue collection is slight and can be avoided entirely by submission of claims to The Hague Tribunal before intervening.

**Second speaker—Stone**

2. *Armed intervention is necessary to secure justice in tropical America*, for

(a) The governments of this section constantly repudiate just debts

(b) They insist that the final decision about claims shall rest with their own corrupt courts

(c) They refuse to arbitrate sometimes.

**Third speaker—Dennett**

3. *Armed intervention is beneficial in its results*, because

(a) It inspires responsibility

(b) In administering custom houses it removes temptation to revolutions

(c) It gives confidence to desirable capital.

Among others, the following books were used in the preparation of the arguments:

N. "The Monroe Doctrine," by T. B. Edgington. Chapters 22–28.

"Digest of International Law," by J. B. Moore.

Report of Penfield of proceedings before Hague Tribunal in 1903.

"Statesman's Year Book" (for statistics).

A. Minister Drago's appeal to the United States, in *Foreign Relations of United States,* 1903.

President Roosevelt's Message, 1905, pp. 33–37.

And articles in the following magazines (among many others):

"Journal of Political Economy," December, 1906.

"Atlantic Monthly," October, 1906.

"North American Review," Vol. 183, p. 602.

All of these contain material valuable for both sides, except those marked "N" and "A," which are useful only for the negative and affirmative, respectively.

**NOTE:** Practise in debating is most helpful to the public speaker, but if possible each debate should be under the supervision of some person whose word will be respected, so that the debaters might show regard for courtesy, accuracy, effective reasoning, and the necessity for careful preparation. The Appendix contains a list of questions for debate.

**25.** Are the following points well considered?

## The Inheritance Tax Is Not a Good Social Reform Measure

A. Does not strike at the root of the evil

1. *Fortunes not a menace in themselves.* A fortune of $500,000 may be a greater social evil than one of $500,000,000.

2. *Danger of wealth depends on its wrong accumulation and use.*

3. *Inheritance tax will not prevent rebates, monopoly, discrimination, bribery, etc.*

4. *Laws aimed at unjust accumulation and use of wealth furnish the true remedy.*

B. It would be evaded.

1. *Low rates are evaded.*

2. *Rate must be high to result in distribution of great fortunes.*

**26.** Class exercises: Mock Trial for (*a*) some serious political offense; (*b*) a burlesque offense.

# CHAPTER XXIV

## *Influencing by Persuasion*

She hath prosperous art
When she will play with reason and discourse,
And well she can persuade.

—SHAKESPEARE, *Measure for Measure*

Him we call an artist who shall play on an assembly of men as a master
on the keys of a piano,—who seeing the people furious, shall soften
and compose them, shall draw them, when he will, to laughter and to
tears. Bring him to his audience, and, be they who they may,—coarse or
refined, pleased or displeased, sulky or savage, with their opinions in the
keeping of a confessor or with their opinions in their bank safes,—he
will have them pleased and humored as he chooses; and they shall carry
and execute what he bids them

—RALPH WALDO EMERSON, *Essay on Eloquence*

MORE GOOD AND MORE ILL HAVE BEEN EFFECTED BY PERSUASION THAN BY ANY other form of speech. *It is an attempt to influence by means of appeal to some particular interest held important by the hearer.* Its motive may be high or low, fair or unfair, honest or dishonest, calm or passionate, and hence its scope is unparalleled in public speaking

This "instilment of conviction," to use Matthew Arnold's expression, is naturally a complex process in that it usually includes argumentation and often employs suggestion, as the next chapter will illustrate. In fact, there is little public speaking worthy of the name that is not in some part persuasive, for men rarely speak solely to alter men's opinions—the ulterior purpose is almost always action.

The nature of persuasion is not solely intellectual, but is largely emotional. It uses every principle of public speaking, and every "form of discourse," to use a rhetorician's expression, but argument supplemented by special appeal is its peculiar quality. This we may best see by examining

## *The Methods of Persuasion*

High-minded speakers often seek to move their hearers to action by an appeal to their highest motives, such as love of liberty. Senator Hoar, in pleading for action on the Philippine question, used this method:

> What has been the practical statesmanship which comes from your ideals and your sentimentalities? You have wasted nearly six hundred millions of treasure. You have sacrificed nearly ten thousand American lives—the flower of our youth. You have devastated provinces. You have slain uncounted thousands of the people you desire to benefit. You have established reconcentration camps. Your generals are coming home from their harvest bringing sheaves with them, in the shape of other thousands of sick and wounded and insane to drag out miserable lives, wrecked in body and mind. You make the American flag in the eyes of a numerous people the emblem of sacrilege in Christian churches, and of the burning of human dwellings, and of the horror of the water torture. Your practical statesmanship which disdains to take George Washington and Abraham Lincoln or the soldiers of the Revolution or of the Civil War as models, has looked in some cases to Spain for your example. I believe—nay, I know—that in general our officers and soldiers are humane. But in some cases they have carried on your warfare with a mixture of American ingenuity and Castilian cruelty.
>
> Your practical statesmanship has succeeded in converting a people who three years ago were ready to kiss the hem of the garment of the American and to welcome him as a liberator, who thronged after your men, when they landed on those islands, with benediction and gratitude, into sullen and irreconcilable enemies, possessed of a hatred which centuries cannot eradicate.
>
> Mr. President, this is the eternal law of human nature. You may struggle against it, you may try to escape it, you may persuade yourself that your intentions are benevolent, that your yoke will be easy and your burden will be light, but it will assert itself again. Government without the consent of the governed—authority which heaven never gave—can only be supported by means which heaven never can sanction.
>
> The American people have got this one question to answer. They may answer it now; they can take ten years, or twenty years, or a generation, or a century to think of it. But will not down. They must answer it in the end: Can you lawfully buy with money, or get by brute force of arms, the right to hold in subjugation an unwilling people, and to impose on them such constitution as you, and not they, think best for them?

Senator Hoar then went on to make another sort of appeal—the appeal to fact and experience:

> We have answered this question a good many times in the past. The fathers answered it in 1776, and founded the Republic upon their answer, which has been

the corner-stone. John Quincy Adams and James Monroe answered it again in the Monroe Doctrine, which John Quincy Adams declared was only the doctrine of the consent of the governed. The Republican party answered it when it took possession of the force of government at the beginning of the most brilliant period in all legislative history. Abraham Lincoln answered it when, on that fatal journey to Washington in 1861, he announced that as the doctrine of his political creed, and declared, with prophetic vision, that he was ready to be assassinated for it if need be. You answered it again yourselves when you said that Cuba, who had no more title than the people of the Philippine Islands had to their independence, of right ought to be free and independent.

—George F. Hoar

Appeal to the things that man holds dear is another potent form of persuasion. Joseph Story, in his great Salem speech (1828) used this method most dramatically:

I call upon you, fathers, by the shades of your ancestors—by the dear ashes which repose in this precious soil—by all you are, and all you hope to be—resist every object of disunion, resist every encroachment upon your liberties, resist every attempt to fetter your consciences, or smother your public schools, or extinguish your system of public instruction.

I call upon you, mothers, by that which never fails in woman, the love of your offspring; teach them, as they climb your knees, or lean on your bosoms, the blessings of liberty. Swear them at the altar, as with their baptismal vows, to be true to their country, and never to forget or forsake her.

I call upon you, young men, to remember whose sons you are; whose inheritance you possess. Life can never be too short, which brings nothing but disgrace and oppression. Death never comes too soon, if necessary in defence of the liberties of your country.

I call upon you, old men, for your counsels, and your prayers, and your benedictions. May not your gray hairs go down in sorrow to the grave, with the recollection that you have lived in vain. May not your last sun sink in the west upon a nation of slaves.

No; I read in the destiny of my country far better hopes, far brighter visions. We, who are now assembled here, must soon be gathered to the congregation of other days. The time of our departure is at hand, to make way for our children upon the theatre of life. May God speed them and theirs. May he who, at the distance of another century, shall stand here to celebrate this day, still look round upon a free, happy, and virtuous people. May he have reason to exult as we do. May he, with all the enthusiasm of truth as well as of poetry, exclaim, that here is still his country.

—Joseph Story

The appeal to prejudice is effective—though not often, if ever, justifiable; yet so long as special pleading endures this sort of persuasion will be resorted to. Rudyard Kipling uses this method—as have many others on both sides—in discussing the great European war. Mingled with the appeal to prejudice, Mr. Kipling uses the appeal to self-interest; though not the highest, it is a powerful motive in all our lives. Notice how at the last the pleader sweeps on to the highest ground he can take. This is a notable example of progressive appeal, beginning with a low motive and ending with a high one in such a way as to carry all the force of prejudice yet gain all the value of patriotic fervor.

Through no fault nor wish of ours we are at war with Germany, the power which owes its existence to three well-thought-out wars; the power which, for the last twenty years, has devoted itself to organizing and preparing for this war; the power which is now fighting to conquer the civilized world.

For the last two generations the Germans in their books, lectures, speeches and schools have been carefully taught that nothing less than this world-conquest was the object of their preparations and their sacrifices. They have prepared carefully and sacrificed greatly.

We must have men and men and men, if we, with our allies, are to check the onrush of organized barbarism.

Have no illusions. We are dealing with a strong and magnificently equipped enemy, whose avowed aim is our complete destruction. The violation of Belgium, the attack on France and the defense against Russia, are only steps by the way. The German's real objective, as she always has told us, is England, and England's wealth, trade and worldwide possessions.

If you assume, for an instant, that the attack will be successful, England will not be reduced, as some people say, to the rank of a second rate power, but we shall cease to exist as a nation. We shall become an outlying province of Germany, to be administered with that severity German safety and interest require.

We are against such a fate. We enter into a new life in which all the facts of war that we had put behind or forgotten for the last hundred years, have returned to the front and test us as they tested our fathers. It will be a long and a hard road, beset with difficulties and discouragements, but we tread it together and we will tread it together to the end.

Our petty social divisions and barriers have been swept away at the outset of our mighty struggle. All the interests of our life of six weeks ago are dead. We have but one interest now, and that touches the naked heart of every man in this island and in the empire.

If we are to win the right for ourselves and for freedom to exist on earth, every man must offer himself for that service and that sacrifice.

From these examples it will be seen that the particular way in which the speakers appealed to their hearers was *by coming close home to their interests, and by themselves showing emotion*—two very important principles which you must keep constantly in mind.

To accomplish the former requires a deep knowledge of human motive in general and an understanding of the particular audience addressed. What are the motives that arouse men to action? Think of them earnestly, set them down on the tablets of your mind, study how to appeal to them worthily. Then, what motives would be likely to appeal to *your* hearers? What are their ideals and interests in life? A mistake in your estimate may cost you your case. To appeal to pride in appearance would make one set of men merely laugh—to try to arouse sympathy for the Jews in Palestine would be wasted effort among others. Study your audience, feel your way, and when you have once raised a spark, fan it into a flame by every honest resource you possess.

The larger your audience the more sure you are to find a universal basis of appeal. A small audience of bachelors will not grow excited over the importance of furniture insurance; most men can be roused to the defense of the freedom of the press.

Patent medicine advertisement usually begins by talking about your pains—they begin on your interests. If they first discussed the size and rating of their establishment, or the efficacy of their remedy, you would never read the "ad." If they can make you think you have nervous troubles you will even plead for a remedy—they will not have to try to sell it.

The patent medicine men are pleading—asking you to invest your money in their commodity—yet they do not appear to be doing so. They get over on your side of the fence, and arouse a desire for their nostrums by appealing to your own interests.

Recently a book-salesman entered an attorney's office in New York and inquired: "Do you want to buy a book?" Had the lawyer wanted a book he would probably have bought one without waiting for a book-salesman to call. The solicitor made the same mistake as the representative who made his approach with: "I want to sell you a sewing machine." They both talked only in terms of their own interests.

The successful pleader must convert his arguments into terms of his hearers' advantage. Mankind are still selfish, are interested in what will serve them. Expunge from your address your own personal concern and present your appeal in terms of the general good, and to do this you need not be insincere, for you had better not plead any cause that is *not* for the hearers' good. Notice how Senator Thurston in his plea for intervention in Cuba and Mr. Bryan in his "Cross of Gold" speech constituted themselves the apostles of humanity.

*Exhortation* is a highly impassioned form of appeal frequently used by the pulpit in efforts to arouse men to a sense of duty and induce them to decide their personal courses, and by counsel in seeking to influence a jury. The great preachers, like the great jury-lawyers, have always been masters of persuasion.

Notice the difference among these four exhortations, and analyze the motives appealed to:

> Revenge! About! Seek! Burn! Fire! Kill! Slay! Let not a traitor live!
>
> SHAKESPEARE, *Julius Cæsar*

> Strike—till the last armed foe expires,
> Strike—for your altars and your fires,
> Strike—for the green graves of your sires,
> God—and your native land!
>
> —FITZ-GREENE HALLECK, *Marco Bozzaris*

Believe, gentlemen, if it were not for those children, he would not come here to-day to seek such remuneration; if it were not that, by your verdict, you may prevent those little innocent defrauded wretches from becoming wandering beggars, as well as orphans on the face of this earth. Oh, I know I need not ask this verdict from your mercy; I need not extort it from your compassion; I will receive it from your justice. I do conjure you, not as fathers, but as husbands:—not as husbands, but as citizens:—not as citizens, but as men:—not as men, but as Christians:—by all your obligations, public, private, moral, and religious; by the hearth profaned; by the home desolated; by the canons of the living God foully spurned;—save, oh: save your firesides from the contagion, your country from the crime, and perhaps thousands, yet unborn, from the shame, and sin, and sorrow of this example!

—CHARLES PHILLIPS, *Appeal to the jury in behalf of Guthrie*

So I appeal from the men in silken hose who danced to music made by slaves and called it freedom, from the men in bell-crown hats who led Hester Prynne to her shame and called it religion, to that Americanism which reaches forth its arms to smite wrong with reason and truth, secure in the power of both. I appeal from the patriarchs of New England to the poets of New England; from Endicott to Lowell; from Winthrop to Longfellow; from Norton to Holmes; and I appeal in the name and by the rights of that common citizenship—of that common origin, back of both the Puritan and the Cavalier, to which all of us owe our being. Let the dead past, consecrated by the blood of its martyrs, not by its savage hatreds, darkened alike by kingcraft and priestcraft—let the dead past bury its dead. Let the present and the future ring with the song of the singers. Blessed be the lessons they teach, the laws they make. Blessed be the eye to see, the light to reveal. Blessed be tolerance, sitting ever on the right hand of God to guide the way with loving word, as blessed be all that brings us nearer the goal of true religion, true republicanism, and true patriotism, distrust of watchwords and labels, shams and heroes, belief in our country and ourselves. It was not Cotton Mather, but John Greenleaf Whittier, who cried:

> Dear God and Father of us all,
> Forgive our faith in cruel lies,
> Forgive the blindness that denies.

> Cast down our idols—overturn
> Our Bloody altars—make us see
> Thyself in Thy humanity!
>> —HENRY WATTERSON, *Puritan and Cavalier*

Goethe, on being reproached for not having written war songs against the French, replied, "In my poetry I have never shammed. How could I have written songs of hate without hatred?" Neither is it possible to plead with full efficiency for a cause for which you do not feel deeply. Feeling is contagious as belief is contagious. The speaker who pleads with real feeling for his own convictions will instill his feelings into his listeners. Sincerity, force, enthusiasm, and above all, feeling—these are the qualities that move multitudes and make appeals irresistible. They are of far greater importance than technical principles of delivery, grace of gesture, or polished enunciation—important as all these elements must doubtless be considered. Base your appeal on reason, but do not end in the basement—let the building rise, full of deep emotion and noble persuasion.

## QUESTIONS AND EXERCISES

1. (*a*) What elements of appeal do you find in the following? (*b*) Is it too florid? (*c*) Is this style equally powerful today? (*d*) Are the sentences too long and involved for clearness and force?

Oh, gentlemen, am I this day only the counsel of my client? No, no; I am the advocate of humanity—of yourselves—your homes—your wives—your families—your little children. I am glad that this case exhibits such atrocity; unmarked as it is by any mitigatory feature, it may stop the frightful advance of this calamity; it will be met now, and marked with vengeance. If it be not, farewell to the virtues of your country; farewell to all confidence between man and man; farewell to that unsuspicious and reciprocal tenderness, without which marriage is but a consecrated curse. If oaths are to be violated, laws disregarded, friendship betrayed, humanity trampled, national and individual honor stained, and if a jury of fathers and of husbands will give such miscreancy a passport to their homes, and wives, and daughters,—farewell to all that yet remains of Ireland! But I will not cast such a doubt upon the character of my country. Against the sneer of the foe, and the skepticism of the foreigner, I will still point to the domestic virtues, that no perfidy could barter, and no bribery can purchase, that with a Roman usage, at once embellish and consecrate households, giving to the society of the hearth all the purity of the altar; that lingering alike in the palace and the cottage, are still to be found scattered over this land—the relic of what she was—the source perhaps of what she may be—the lone, the stately, and magnificent memorials, that rearing their majesty amid surrounding ruins, serve at once as the landmarks of the departed glory, and the models by which the future may be erected.

Preserve those virtues with a vestal fidelity; mark this day, by your verdict, your horror of their profanation; and believe me, when the hand which records that verdict shall be dust, and the tongue that asks it, traceless in the grave, many a happy home will bless its consequences, and many a mother teach her little child to hate the impious treason of adultery.

—CHARLES PHILLIPS

2. Analyze and criticise the forms of appeal used in the selections from Hoar, Story, and Kipling.

3. What is the type of persuasion used by Senator Thurston (page 32)?

4. Cite two examples each, from selections in this volume, in which speakers sought to be persuasive by securing the hearers' (a) sympathy for themselves; (b) sympathy with their subjects; (c) self-pity.

5. Make a short address using persuasion.

6. What other methods of persuasion than those here mentioned can you name?

7. Is it easier to persuade men to change their course of conduct than to persuade them to continue in a given course? Give examples to support your belief.

8. In how far are we justified in making an appeal to self-interest in order to lead men to adopt a given course?

9. Does the merit of the course have any bearing on the merit of the methods used?

10. Illustrate an unworthy method of using persuasion.

11. Deliver a short speech on the value of skill in persuasion.

12. Does effective persuasion always produce conviction?

13. Does conviction always result in action?

14. Is it fair for counsel to appeal to the emotions of a jury in a murder trial?

15. Ought the judge use persuasion in making his charge?

16. Say how self-consciousness may hinder the power of persuasion in a speaker.

17. Is emotion without words ever persuasive? If so, illustrate.

18. Might gestures without words be persuasive? If so, illustrate.

19. Has posture in a speaker anything to do with persuasion? Discuss.

20. Has voice? Discuss.

21. Has manner? Discuss.

22. What effect does personal magnetism have in producing conviction?

23. Discuss the relation of persuasion to (a) description; (b) narration; (c) exposition; (d) pure reason.

24. What is the effect of over-persuasion?

25. Make a short speech on the effect of the constant use of persuasion on the sincerity of the speaker himself.

26. Show by example how a general statement is not as persuasive as a concrete example illustrating the point being discussed.

27. Show by example how brevity is of value in persuasion.

28. Discuss the importance of avoiding an antagonistic attitude in persuasion.

29. What is the most persuasive passage you have found in the selections of this volume? On what do you base your decision?

30. Cite a persuasive passage from some other source. Read or recite it aloud.

31. Make a list of the emotional bases of appeal, grading them from low to high, according to your estimate.

32. Would circumstances make any difference in such grading? If so, give examples.

33. Deliver a short, passionate appeal to a jury, pleading for justice to a poor widow.

34. Deliver a short appeal to men to give up some evil way.

35. Criticise the structure of the sentence beginning the second paragraph of Senator Hoar's speech on page 180.

# CHAPTER XXV

# Influencing the Crowd

Success in business, in the last analysis, turns upon touching the imagination of crowds. The reason that preachers in this present generation are less successful in getting people to want goodness than business men are in getting them to want motorcars, hats, and pianolas, is that business men as a class are more close and desperate students of human nature, and have boned down harder to the art of touching the imaginations of the crowds.

GERALD STANLEY LEE, *Crowds*

IN THE EARLY PART OF JULY, 1914, A COLLECTION OF FRENCHMEN IN PARIS, OR Germans in Berlin, was not a crowd in a psychological sense. Each individual had his own special interests and needs, and there was no powerful common idea to unify them. A group then represented only a collection of individuals. A month later, any collection of Frenchmen or Germans formed a crowd: Patriotism, hate, a common fear, a pervasive grief, had unified the individuals.

The psychology of the crowd is far different from the psychology of the personal members that compose it. The crowd is a distinct entity. Individuals restrain and subdue many of their impulses at the dictates of reason. The crowd never reasons. It only feels. As persons there is a sense of responsibility attached to our actions which checks many of our incitements, but the sense of responsibility is lost in the crowd because of its numbers. The crowd is exceedingly suggestible and will act upon the wildest and most extreme ideas. The crowd-mind is primitive and will cheer plans and perform actions which its members would utterly repudiate.

A mob is only a highly-wrought crowd. Ruskin's description is fitting: "You can talk a mob into anything; its feelings may be—usually are—on the whole, generous and right, but it has no foundation for them, no hold of them. You may tease or tickle it into anything at your pleasure. It thinks by infection, for the most part, catching an opinion like a cold, and there is nothing so little that it will not roar itself wild about, when the fit is on, nothing so great but it will forget in an hour when the fit is past."[25]

---

25 *Sesame and Lilies.*

History will show us how the crowd-mind works. The medieval mind was not given to reasoning; the medieval man attached great weight to the utterance of authority; his religion touched chiefly the emotions. These conditions provided a rich soil for the propagation of the crowd-mind when, in the eleventh century, flagellation, a voluntary self-scourging, was preached by the monks. Substituting flagellation for reciting penitential psalms was advocated by the reformers. A scale was drawn up, making one thousand strokes equivalent to ten psalms, or fifteen thousand to the entire psalter. This craze spread by leaps—and crowds. Flagellant fraternities sprang up. Priests carrying banners led through the streets great processions reciting prayers and whipping their bloody bodies with leathern thongs fitted with four iron points. Pope Clement denounced this practise and several of the leaders of these processions had to be burned at the stake before the frenzy could be uprooted.

All western and central Europe was turned into a crowd by the preaching of the crusaders, and millions of the followers of the Prince of Peace rushed to the Holy Land to kill the heathen. Even the children started on a crusade against the Saracens. The mob-spirit was so strong that home affections and persuasion could not prevail against it and thousands of mere babes died in their attempts to reach and redeem the Sacred Sepulchre.

In the early part of the eighteenth century the South Sea Company was formed in England. Britain became a speculative crowd. Stock in the South Sea Company rose from 128½ points in January to 550 in May, and scored 1,000 in July. Five million shares were sold at this premium. Speculation ran riot. Hundreds of companies were organized. One was formed "for a wheel of perpetual motion." Another never troubled to give any reason at all for taking the cash of its subscribers—it merely announced that it was organized "for a design which will hereafter be promulgated." Owners began to sell, the mob caught the suggestion, a panic ensued, the South Sea Company stock fell 800 points in a few days, and more than a billion dollars evaporated in this era of frenzied speculation.

The burning of the witches at Salem, the Klondike gold craze, and the forty-eight people who were killed by mobs in the United States in 1913, are examples familiar to us in America.

## The Crowd Must Have a Leader

The leader of the crowd or mob is its determining factor. He becomes self-hynoptized with the idea that unifies its members, his enthusiasm is contagious—and so is theirs. The crowd acts as he suggests. The great mass of people do not have any very sharply-drawn conclusions on any subject outside of their own little spheres, but when they become a crowd they are perfectly willing to accept ready-made, hand-me-down opinions. They will follow a leader at all costs—in labor troubles they often follow a leader in preference to obeying their government, in war they will throw self-preservation to the bushes and follow a leader in the face of guns that fire fourteen times a second. The mob becomes shorn of will-power and blindly obedient to its dictator. The Russian Government, recognizing the menace of the crowd-mind to its autocracy, formerly prohibited public gatherings. History is full of similar instances.

## How the Crowd is Created

Today the crowd is as real a factor in our socialized life as are magnates and monopolies. It is too complex a problem merely to damn or praise it—it must be reckoned with, and mastered. The present problem is how to get the most and the best out of the crowd-spirit, and the public speaker finds this to be peculiarly his own question. His influence is multiplied if he can only transmute his audience into a crowd. His affirmations must be their conclusions.

This can be accomplished by unifying the minds and needs of the audience and arousing their emotions. Their feelings, not their reason, must be played upon—*it is "up to" him to do this nobly.* Argument has its place on the platform, but even its potencies must subserve the speaker's plan of attack to *win possession* of his audience.

Reread the chapter on "Feeling and Enthusiasm." It is impossible to make an audience a crowd without appealing to their emotions. Can you imagine the average group becoming a crowd while hearing a lecture on Dry Fly Fishing, or on Egyptian Art? On the other hand, it would not have required world-famous eloquence to have turned any audience in Ulster, in 1914, into a crowd by discussing the Home Rule Act. The crowd-spirit depends largely on the subject used to fuse their individualities into one glowing whole.

Note how Antony played upon the feelings of his hearers in the famous funeral oration given by Shakespeare in *Julius Cæsar.* From murmuring units the men became a unit—a mob.

## Antony's Oration Over Cæsar's Body

Friends, Romans, countrymen! Lend me your ears;
I come to bury Cæsar, not to praise him.
The evil that men do lives after them;
The good is oft interred with their bones:
So let it be with Cæsar! The Noble Brutus
Hath told you Cæsar was ambitious.
If it were so, it was a grievous fault,
And grievously hath Cæsar answered it.
Here, under leave of Brutus, and the rest—
For Brutus is an honorable man,
So are they all, all honorable men—
Come I to speak in Cæsar's funeral.
He was my friend, faithful and just to me:
But Brutus says he was ambitious;
And Brutus is an honorable man.
He hath brought many captives home to Rome,
Whose ransoms did the general coffers fill:
Did this in Cæsar seem ambitious?
When that the poor have cried, Cæsar hath wept;

Ambition should be made of sterner stuff:
Yet Brutus says, he was ambitious;
And Brutus is an honorable man.
You all did see, that, on the Lupercal,
I thrice presented him a kingly crown,
Which he did thrice refuse. Was this ambition?
Yet Brutus says he was ambitious;
And sure, he is an honorable man.
I speak not to disprove what Brutus spoke,
But here I am to speak what I do know.
You all did love him once, not without cause;
What cause withholds you then to mourn for him?
Oh, judgment, thou art fled to brutish beasts,
And men have lost their reason!—Bear with me;
My heart is in the coffin there with Cæsar,
And I must pause till it come back to me. [*Weeps.*

*1 Plebeian.* Methinks there is much reason in his sayings.

*2 Ple.* If thou consider rightly of the matter,
Cæsar has had great wrong.

*3 Ple.* Has he, masters?
I fear there will a worse come in his place.

*4 Ple.* Mark'd ye his words? He would not take the crown;
Therefore, 'tis certain, he was not ambitious.

*1 Ple.* If it be found so, some will dear abide it.

*2 Ple.* Poor soul, his eyes are red as fire with weeping.

*3 Ple.* There's not a nobler man in Rome than Antony.

*4 Ple.* Now mark him, he begins again to speak.

*Ant.* But yesterday, the word of Cæsar might
Have stood against the world: now lies he there,
And none so poor to do him reverence.

Oh, masters! if I were dispos'd to stir
Your hearts and minds to mutiny and rage,
I should do Brutus wrong, and Cassius wrong,
Who, you all know, are honorable men.
I will not do them wrong; I rather choose
To wrong the dead, to wrong myself, and you,
Than I will wrong such honorable men.

But here's a parchment, with the seal of Cæsar;
I found it in his closet; 'tis his will:
Let but the commons hear this testament—
 Which, pardon me, I do not mean to read—
And they would go and kiss dead Cæsar's wounds,
And dip their napkins in his sacred blood;
Yea, beg a hair of him for memory,
And, dying, mention it within their wills,
Bequeathing it as a rich legacy
Unto their issue.

*4 Ple.* We'll hear the will: Read it, Mark Antony.

*All.* The will! the will! we will hear Cæsar's will.

*Ant.* Have patience, gentle friends: I must not read it;
It is not meet you know how Cæsar lov'd you.
You are not wood, you are not stones, but men;
And, being men, hearing the will of Cæsar,
It will inflame you, it will make you mad:
'Tis good you know not that you are his heirs;
For if you should, oh, what would come of it!

*4 Ple.* Read the will; we'll hear it, Antony!
You shall read us the will! Cæsar's will!

*Ant.* Will you be patient? Will you stay awhile?
I have o'ershot myself, to tell you of it.
I fear I wrong the honorable men
Whose daggers have stab'd Cæsar; I do fear it.

*4 Ple.* They were traitors: Honorable men!

*All.* The will! the testament!

*2 Ple.* They were villains, murtherers! The will! Read the will!

*Ant.* You will compel me then to read the will?
Then, make a ring about the corpse of Cæsar,
And let me shew you him that made the will.
Shall I descend? And will you give me leave?

*All.* Come down.

*2 Ple.* Descend. [*He comes down from the Rostrum.*

*3 Ple.* You shall have leave.

*4 Ple.* A ring; stand round.

*1 Ple.* Stand from the hearse, stand from the body.

*2 Ple.* Room for Antony!—most noble Antony!

*Ant.* Nay, press not so upon me; stand far off.

*All.* Stand back! room! bear back!

*Ant.* If you have tears, prepare to shed them now;
You all do know this mantle: I remember
The first time ever Cæsar put it on;
'Twas on a summer's evening, in his tent,
That day he overcame the Nervii.
Look, in this place, ran Cassius' dagger through:
See, what a rent the envious Casca made:
Through this, the well-beloved Brutus stab'd;
And as he pluck'd his cursed steel away,
Mark how the blood of Cæsar follow'd it!—
As rushing out of doors, to be resolv'd
If Brutus so unkindly knock'd, or no;
For Brutus, as you know, was Cæsar's angel:
Judge, O you Gods, how Cæsar lov'd him!
This was the most unkindest cut of all!
For when the noble Cæsar saw him stab,
Ingratitude, more strong than traitors' arms,
Quite vanquish'd him: then burst his mighty heart;
And in his mantle muffling up his face,
Even at the base of Pompey's statue,
Which all the while ran blood, great Cæsar fell.
Oh what a fall was there, my countrymen!
Then I and you, and all of us, fell down,
Whilst bloody treason flourish'd over us.
Oh! now you weep; and I perceive you feel
The dint of pity; these are gracious drops.
Kind souls! what, weep you, when you but behold
Our Cæsar's vesture wounded? Look you here!
Here is himself, mar'd, as you see, by traitors.

*1 Ple.* Oh, piteous spectacle!

*2 Ple.* Oh, noble Cæsar!

*3 Ple.* Oh, woful day!

*4 Ple.* Oh, traitors, villains!

*1 Ple.* Oh, most bloody sight!

*2 Ple.* We will be reveng'd!

*All.* Revenge; about—seek—burn—fire—kill—slay!—Let not a traitor live!

*Ant.* Stay, countrymen.

*1 Ple.* Peace there! Hear the noble Antony.

*2 Ple.* We'll hear him, we'll follow him, we'll die with him.

*Ant.* Good friends, sweet friends, let me not stir you up
To such a sudden flood of mutiny:
They that have done this deed are honorable:
What private griefs they have, alas! I know not,
That made them do it; they are wise, and honorable,
And will, no doubt, with reasons answer you.
I come not, friends, to steal away your hearts;
I am no orator, as Brutus is;
But as you know me all, a plain blunt man,
That love my friend, and that they know full well
That gave me public leave to speak of him:
For I have neither wit, nor words, nor worth,
Action, nor utterance, nor the power of speech,
To stir men's blood. I only speak right on:
I tell you that which you yourselves do know;
Show your sweet Cæsar's wounds, poor, poor, dumb mouths,
And bid them speak for me. But were I Brutus,
And Brutus Antony, there were an Antony
Would ruffle up your spirits, and put a tongue
In every wound of Cæsar, that should move
The stones of Rome to rise and mutiny.

*All.* We'll mutiny!

*1 Ple.* We'll burn the house of Brutus.

*3 Ple.* Away, then! Come, seek the conspirators.

*Ant.* Yet hear me, countrymen; yet hear me speak.

*All.* Peace, ho! Hear Antony, most noble Antony.

*Ant.* Why, friends, you go to do you know not what.
Wherein hath Cæsar thus deserv'd your loves?

Alas! you know not!—I must tell you then.
You have forgot the will I told you of.

*Ple.* Most true;—the will!—let's stay, and hear the will.

*Ant.* Here is the will, and under Cæsar's seal.
To every Roman citizen he gives,
To every several man, seventy-five drachmas.

*2 Ple.* Most noble Cæsar!—we'll revenge his death.

*3 Ple.* O royal Cæsar!

*Ant.* Hear me with patience.

*All.* Peace, ho!

*Ant.* Moreover, he hath left you all his walks,
His private arbours, and new-planted orchards,
On this side Tiber; he hath left them you,
And to your heirs forever, common pleasures,
To walk abroad, and recreate yourselves.
Here was a Cæsar! When comes such another?

*1 Ple.* Never, never!—Come, away, away!
We'll burn his body in the holy place,
And with the brands fire the traitors' houses.
Take up the body.

*2 Ple.* Go, fetch fire.

*3 Ple.* Pluck down benches.

*4 Ple.* Pluck down forms, windows, anything.
  [*Exeunt Citizens, with the body.*

*Ant.* Now let it work. Mischief, thou art afoot,
Take thou what course thou wilt!

To unify single auditors into a crowd, express their common needs, aspirations, dangers, and emotions, deliver your message so that the interests of one shall appear to be the interests of all. The conviction of one man is intensified in proportion as he finds others sharing his belief—*and feeling.* Antony does not stop with telling the Roman populace that Cæsar fell—he makes the tragedy universal:

Then I, and you, and all of us fell down,
Whilst bloody treason flourished over us.

Applause, generally a sign of feeling, helps to unify an audience. The nature of the crowd is illustrated by the contagion of applause. Recently a throng in a New York moving-picture and vaudeville house had been applauding several songs, and when an advertisement for tailored skirts was thrown on the screen some one started the applause, and the crowd, like sheep, blindly imitated—until someone saw the joke and laughed; then the crowd again followed a leader and laughed at and applauded its own stupidity.

Actors sometimes start applause for their lines by snapping their fingers. Some one in the first few rows will mistake it for faint applause, and the whole theatre will chime in.

An observant auditor will be interested in noticing the various devices a monologist will use to get the first round of laughter and applause. He works so hard because he knows an audience of units is an audience of indifferent critics, but once get them to laughing together and each single laugher sweeps a number of others with him, until the whole theatre is aroar and the entertainer has scored. These are meretricious schemes, to be sure, and do not savor in the least of inspiration, but crowds have not changed in their nature in a thousand years and the one law holds for the greatest preacher and the pettiest stump-speaker—you must fuse your audience or they will not warm to your message. The devices of the great orator may not be so obvious as those of the vaudeville monologist, but the principle is the same: he tries to strike some universal note that will have all his hearers feeling alike at the same time.

The evangelist knows this when he has the soloist sing some touching song just before the address. Or he will have the entire congregation sing, and that is the psychology of "Now *every*body sing!" for he knows that they who will not join in the song are as yet outside the crowd. Many a time has the popular evangelist stopped in the middle of his talk, when he felt that his hearers were units instead of a molten mass (and a sensitive speaker can feel that condition most depressingly) and suddenly demanded that everyone arise and sing, or repeat aloud a familiar passage, or read in unison; or perhaps he has subtly left the thread of his discourse to tell a story that, from long experience, he knew would not fail to bring his hearers to a common feeling.

These things are important resources for the speaker, and happy is he who uses them worthily and not as a despicable charlatan. The difference between a demagogue and a leader is not so much a matter of method as of principle. Even the most dignified speaker must recognize the eternal laws of human nature. You are by no means urged to become a trickster on the platform—far from it!—but don't kill your speech with dignity. To be icily correct is as silly as to rant. Do neither, but appeal to those world-old elements in your audience that have been recognized by all great speakers from Demosthenes to Sam Small, and see to it that you never debase your powers by arousing your hearers unworthily.

It is as hard to kindle enthusiasm in a scattered audience as to build a fire with scattered sticks. An audience to be converted into a crowd must be made to appear as a crowd. This cannot be done when they are widely scattered over a large seating space or when many empty benches separate the speaker from his hearers. Have your audience seated compactly. How many a preacher has bemoaned the enormous edifice over which what would normally be a large congregation has scattered in chilled and chilling solitude Sunday after Sunday! Bishop Brooks himself could not have inspired a congregation of one thousand souls seated in the vastness of St. Peter's at Rome. In that colossal sanctuary it is only on great occasions which bring out the multitudes that the service is before the high altar—at other times the smaller side-chapels are used.

Universal ideas surcharged with feeling help to create the crowd-atmosphere. Examples: liberty, character, righteousness, courage, fraternity, altruism, country, and national heroes. George Cohan was making psychology practical and profitable when he introduced the flag and flag-songs into his musical comedies. Cromwell's regiments prayed before the battle and went into the fight singing hymns. The French corps, singing the Marseillaise in 1914, charged the Germans as one man. Such unifying devices arouse the feelings, make soldiers fanatical mobs—and, alas, more efficient murderers.

# CHAPTER XXVI

# *Riding the Winged Horse*

To think, and to feel, constitute the two grand divisions of men of
genius—the men of reasoning and the men of imagination.

—ISAAC DISRAELI, *Literary Character of Men of Genius*

And as imagination bodies forth
The forms of things unknown, the poet's pen
Turns them to shapes and gives to airy nothing
A local habitation and a name.

—SHAKESPEARE, *Midsummer-Night's Dream*

IT IS COMMON, AMONG THOSE WHO DEAL CHIEFLY WITH LIFE'S PRACTICALITIES, TO
think of imagination as having little value in comparison with direct thinking. They
smile with tolerance when Emerson says that "Science does not know its debt to the
imagination," for these are the words of a speculative essayist, a philosopher, a poet. But
when Napoleon—the indomitable welder of empires—declares that "The human race is
governed by its imagination," the authoritative word commands their respect.

Be it remembered, the faculty of forming *mental images* is as efficient a cog as may
be found in the whole mind-machine. True, it must fit into that other vital cog, pure
thought, but when it does so it may be questioned which is the more productive of
important results for the happiness and well-being of man. This should become more
apparent as we go on.

## I.  *What Is Imagination?*

Let us not seek for a definition, for a score of varying ones may be found, but let us grasp this
fact: By imagination we mean either the faculty or the process of forming mental images.

The subject-matter of imagination may be really existent in nature, or not at all real,
or a combination of both; it may be physical or spiritual, or both—the mental image is at
once the most lawless and the most law-abiding child that has ever been born of the mind.

First of all, as its name suggests, the process of imagination—for we are thinking of it
now as a process rather than as a faculty—is memory at work. Therefore we must consider
it primarily as

## 1. Reproductive Imagination

We see or hear or feel or taste or smell something and the sensation passes away. Yet we are conscious of a greater or lesser ability to reproduce such feelings at will. Two considerations, in general, will govern the vividness of the image thus evoked—the strength of the original impression, and the reproductive power of one mind as compared with another. Yet every normal person will be able to evoke images with some degree of clearness.

The fact that not all minds possess this imaging faculty in anything like equal measure will have an important bearing on the public speaker's study of this question. No man who does not feel at least some poetic impulses is likely to aspire seriously to be a poet, yet many whose imaging faculties are so dormant as to seem actually dead do aspire to be public speakers. To all such we say most earnestly: Awaken your image-making gift, for even in the most coldly logical discourse it is sure to prove of great service. It is important that you find out at once just how full and how trustworthy is your imagination, for it is capable of cultivation—as well as of abuse.

Francis Galton[26] says: "The French appear to possess the visualizing faculty in a high degree. The peculiar ability they show in pre-arranging ceremonials and fêtes of all kinds and their undoubted genius for tactics and strategy show that they are able to foresee effects with unusual clearness. Their ingenuity in all technical contrivances is an additional testimony in the same direction, and so is their singular clearness of expression. Their phrase *figurez-vous,* or *picture to yourself,* seems to express their dominant mode of perception. Our equivalent, of 'image,' is ambiguous."

But individuals differ in this respect just as markedly as, for instance, the Dutch do from the French. And this is true not only of those who are classified by their friends as being respectively imaginative or unimaginative, but of those whose gifts or habits are not well known.

Let us take for experiment six of the best-known types of imaging and see in practise how they arise in our own minds.

By all odds the most common type is, (*a*) *the visual image.* Children who more readily recall things seen than things heard are called by psychologists "eye-minded," and most of us are bent in this direction. Close your eyes now and re-call—the word thus hyphenated is more suggestive—the scene around this morning's breakfast table. Possibly there was nothing striking in the situation and the image is therefore not striking. Then image any notable table scene in your experience—how vividly it stands forth, because at the time you felt the impression strongly. Just then you may not have been conscious of how strongly the scene was laying hold upon you, for often we are so intent upon what we see that we give no particular thought to the fact that it is impressing us. It may surprise you to learn how accurately you are able to image a scene when a long time has elapsed between the conscious focussing of your attention on the image and the time when you saw the original.

(*b*) *The auditory image* is probably the next most vivid of our recalled experiences. Here association is potent to suggest similarities. Close out all the world beside and

---

**26** *Inquiries into Human Faculty.*

listen to the peculiar wood-against-wood sound of the sharp thunder among rocky mountains—the crash of ball against ten-pins may suggest it. Or image (the word is imperfect, for it seems to suggest only the eye) the sound of tearing ropes when some precious weight hangs in danger. Or recall the bay of a hound almost upon you in pursuit—choose your own sound, and see how pleasantly or terribly real it becomes when imaged in your brain.

(c) *The motor image* is a close competitor with the auditory for second place. Have you ever awakened in the night, every muscle taut and striving, to feel your self straining against the opposing football line that held like a stone-wall—or as firmly as the headboard of your bed? Or voluntarily recall the movement of the boat when you cried inwardly, "It's all up with me!" The perilous lurch of a train, the sudden sinking of an elevator, or the unexpected toppling of a rocking-chair may serve as further experiments.

(d) *The gustatory image* is common enough, as the idea of eating lemons will testify. Sometimes the pleasurable recollection of a delightful dinner will cause the mouth to water years afterward, or the "image" of particularly atrocious medicine will wrinkle the nose long after it made one day in boyhood wretched.

(e) *The olfactory image* is even more delicate. Some there are who are affected to illness by the memory of certain odors, while others experience the most delectable sensations by the rise of pleasing olfactory images.

(f) *The tactile image,* to name no others, is well nigh as potent. Do you shudder at the thought of velvet rubbed by short-nailed finger tips? Or were you ever "burned" by touching an ice-cold stove? Or, happier memory, can you still feel the touch of a well-loved absent hand?

Be it remembered that few of these images are present in our minds except in combination—the sight and sound of the crashing avalanche are one; so are the flash and report of the huntsman's gun that came so near "doing for us."

Thus, imaging—especially conscious reproductive imagination—will become a valuable part of our mental processes in proportion as we direct and control it.

## 2. Productive Imagination

All of the foregoing examples, and doubtless also many of the experiments you yourself may originate, are merely reproductive. Pleasurable or horrific as these may be, they are far less important than the images evoked by the productive imagination—though that does not infer a separate faculty.

Recall, again for experiment, some scene whose beginning you once saw enacted on a street corner but passed by before the dénouement was ready to be disclosed. Recall it all—that far the image is reproductive. But what followed? Let your fantasy roam at pleasure—the succeeding scenes are productive, for you have more or less consciously invented the unreal on the basis of the real.

And just here the fictionist, the poet, and the public speaker will see the value of productive imagery. True, the feet of the idol you build are on the ground, but its head pierces the clouds, it is a son of both earth and heaven.

One fact it is important to note here: Imagery is a valuable mental asset in proportion as it is controlled by the higher intellectual power of pure reason. The untutored child of nature thinks largely in images and therefore attaches to them undue importance. He readily confuses the real with the unreal—to him they are of like value. But the man of training readily distinguishes the one from the other and evaluates each with some, if not with perfect, justice.

So we see that unrestrained imaging may produce a rudderless steamer, while the trained faculty is the graceful sloop, skimming the seas at her skipper's will, her course steadied by the helm of reason and her lightsome wings catching every air of heaven.

The game of chess, the war-lord's tactical plan, the evolution of a geometrical theorem, the devising of a great business campaign, the elimination of waste in a factory, the dénouement of a powerful drama, the overcoming of an economic obstacle, the scheme for a sublime poem, and the convincing siege of an audience may—nay, indeed must—each be conceived in an image and wrought to reality according to the plans and specifications laid upon the trestle board by some modern imaginative Hiram. The farmer who would be content with the seed he possesses would have no harvest. Do not rest satisfied with the ability to recall images, but cultivate your creative imagination by building "what might be" upon the foundation of "what is."

## II. The Uses of Imaging in Public Speaking

By this time you will have already made some general application of these ideas to the art of the platform, but to several specific uses we must now refer.

### 1. Imaging in Speech-Preparation

(*a*) *Set the image of your audience before you while you prepare.* Disappointment may lurk here, and you cannot be forearmed for every emergency, but in the main you must meet your audience before you actually do—image its probable mood and attitude toward the occasion, the theme, and the speaker.

(*b*) *Conceive your speech as a whole while you are preparing its parts,* else can you not see—image—how its parts shall be fitly framed together.

(*c*) *Image the language you will use,* so far as written or extemporaneous speech may dictate. The habit of imaging will give you choice of varied figures of speech, for remember that an address without *fresh* comparisons is like a garden without blooms. Do not be content with the first hackneyed figure that comes flowing to your pen-point, but dream on until the striking, the unusual, yet the vividly real comparison points your thought like steel does the arrow-tip.

Note the freshness and effectiveness of the following description from the opening of O. Henry's story, "The Harbinger."

> Long before the springtide is felt in the dull bosom of the yokel does the city man
> know that the grass-green goddess is upon her throne. He sits at his breakfast eggs

and toast, begirt by stone walls, opens his morning paper and sees journalism leave vernalism at the post.

For whereas Spring's couriers were once the evidence of our finer senses, now the Associated Press does the trick.

The warble of the first robin in Hackensack, the stirring of the maple sap in Bennington, the budding of the pussy willows along the main street in Syracuse, the first chirp of the blue bird, the swan song of the blue point, the annual tornado in St. Louis, the plaint of the peach pessimist from Pompton, N.J., the regular visit of the tame wild goose with a broken leg to the pond near Bilgewater Junction, the base attempt of the Drug Trust to boost the price of quinine foiled in the House by Congressman Jinks, the first tall poplar struck by lightning and the usual stunned picknickers who had taken refuge, the first crack of the ice jamb in the Allegheny River, the finding of a violet in its mossy bed by the correspondent at Round Corners—these are the advanced signs of the burgeoning season that are wired into the wise city, while the farmer sees nothing but winter upon his dreary fields.

But these be mere externals. The true harbinger is the heart. When Strephon seeks his Chloe and Mike his Maggie, then only is Spring arrived and the newspaper report of the five foot rattler killed in Squire Pettregrew's pasture confirmed.

A hackneyed writer would probably have said that the newspaper told the city man about spring before the farmer could see any evidence of it, but that the real harbinger of spring was love and that "In the Spring a young man's fancy lightly turns to thoughts of love."

## 2. Imaging in Speech-Delivery

When once the passion of speech is on you and you are "warmed up"—perhaps by striking *till* the iron is hot so that you may not fail to strike *when* it is hot—your mood will be one of vision.

Then (*a*) *Re-image past emotion*—of which more elsewhere. The actor re-calls the old feelings every time he renders his telling lines.

(*b*) *Reconstruct in image the scenes you are to describe.*

(*c*) *Image the objects in nature whose tone you are delineating,* so that bearing and voice and movement (gesture) will picture forth the whole convincingly. Instead of merely stating the fact that whiskey ruins homes, the temperance speaker paints a drunkard coming home to abuse his wife and strike his children. It is much more effective than telling the truth in abstract terms. To depict the cruelness of war, do not assert the fact abstractly— "War is cruel." Show the soldier, an arm swept away by a bursting shell, lying on the battlefield pleading for water; show the children with tear-stained faces pressed against the window pane praying for their dead father to return. Avoid general and prosaic terms. Paint pictures. Evolve images for the imagination of your audience to construct into pictures of their own.

## III. *How to Acquire the Imaging Habit*

You remember the American statesman who asserted that "the way to resume is to resume"? The application is obvious. Beginning with the first simple analyses of this chapter, test your own qualities of image-making. One by one practise the several kinds of images; then add—even invent—others in combination, for many images come to us in complex form, like the combined noise and shoving and hot odor of a cheering crowd.

After practising on reproductive imaging, turn to the productive, beginning with the reproductive and adding productive features for the sake of cultivating invention.

Frequently, allow your originating gifts full swing by weaving complete imaginary fabrics—sights, sounds, scenes; all the fine world of fantasy lies open to the journeyings of your winged steed.

In like manner train yourself in the use of figurative language. Learn first to distinguish and then to use its varied forms. *When used with restraint,* nothing can be more effective than the trope; but once let extravagance creep in by the window, and power will flee by the door.

All in all, master your images—let not them master you.

### QUESTIONS AND EXERCISES

1. Give original examples of each kind of reproductive imagination.

2. Build two of these into imaginary incidents for platform use, using your productive, or creative, imagination.

3. Define (*a*) phantasy; (*b*) vision; (*c*) fantastic; (*d*) phantasmagoria; (*e*) transmogrify; (*f*) recollection.

4. What is a "figure of speech"?

5. Define and give two examples of each of the following figures of speech.[27] At least one of the examples under each type would better be original. (*a*) simile; (*b*) metaphor; (*c*) metonymy; (*d*) synecdoche; (*e*) apostrophe; (*f*) vision; (*g*) personification; (*h*) hyperbole; (*i*) irony.

6. (*a*) What is an allegory? (*b*) Name one example. (*c*) How could a short allegory be used as part of a public address?

7. Write a short fable[28] for use in a speech. Follow either the ancient form (Æsop) or the modern (George Ade, Josephine Dodge Daskam).

8. What do you understand by "the historical present?" Illustrate how it may be used (*ONLY* occasionally) in a public address.

9. Recall some disturbance on the street, (*a*) Describe it as you would on the platform; (*b*) imagine what preceded the disturbance; (*c*) imagine what followed it; (*d*)

---

27 Consult any good rhetoric. An unabridged dictionary will also be of help.
28 For a full discussion of the form see, *The Art of Story-Writing,* by J. Berg Esenwein and Mary D. Chambers.

connect the whole in a terse, dramatic narration for the platform and deliver it with careful attention to all that you have learned of the public speaker's art.

**10.** Do the same with other incidents you have seen or heard of, or read of in the newspapers.

NOTE: It is hoped that this exercise will be varied and expanded until the pupil has gained considerable mastery of imaginative narration. (See chapter on "Narration.")

**11.** Experiments have proved that the majority of people think most vividly in terms of visual images. However, some think more readily in terms of auditory and motor images. It is a good plan to mix all kinds of images in the course of your address for you will doubtless have all kinds of hearers. This plan will serve to give variety and strengthen your effects by appealing to the several senses of each hearer, as well as interesting many different auditors. For exercise, (*a*) give several original examples of compound images, and (*b*) construct brief descriptions of the scenes imagined. For example, the falling of a bridge in process of building.

**12.** Read the following observantly:

> The strikers suffered bitter poverty last winter in New York.
>
> Last winter a woman visiting the East Side of New York City saw another woman coming out of a tenement house wringing her hands. Upon inquiry the visitor found that a child had fainted in one of the apartments. She entered, and saw the child ill and in rags, while the father, a striker, was too poor to provide medical help. A physician was called and said the child had fainted from lack of food. The only food in the home was dried fish. The visitor provided groceries for the family and ordered the milkman to leave milk for them daily. A month later she returned. The father of the family knelt down before her, and calling her an angel said that she had saved their lives, for the milk she had provided was all the food they had had.

In the two preceding paragraphs we have substantially the same story, told twice. In the first paragraph we have a fact stated in general terms. In the second, we have an outline picture of a specific happening. Now expand this outline into a dramatic recital, drawing freely upon your imagination.

# CHAPTER XXVII

## *Growing a Vocabulary*

Boys flying kites haul in their white winged birds;
You can't do that way when you're flying words.
"Careful with fire," is good advice we know,
"Careful with words," is ten times doubly so.
Thoughts unexpressed many sometimes fall back dead;
But God Himself can't kill them when they're said.

—WILL CARLETON, *The First Settler's Story*

T HE TERM "VOCABULARY" HAS A SPECIAL AS WELL AS A GENERAL MEANING. TRUE, *all* vocabularies are grounded in the everyday words of the language, out of which grow the special vocabularies, but each such specialized group possesses a number of words of peculiar value for its own objects. These words may be used in other vocabularies also, but the fact that they are suited to a unique order of expression marks them as of special value to a particular craft or calling.

In this respect the public speaker differs not at all from the poet, the novelist, the scientist, the traveler. He must add to his everyday stock, words of value for the public presentation of thought. "A study of the discourses of effective orators discloses the fact that they have a fondness for words signifying power, largeness, speed, action, color, light, and all their opposites. They frequently employ words expressive of the various emotions. Descriptive words, adjectives used in *fresh* relations with nouns, and apt epithets, are freely employed. Indeed, the nature of public speech permits the use of mildly exaggerated words which, by the time they have reached the hearer's judgment, will leave only a just impression."[29]

### Form the Book-Note Habit

To possess a word involves three things: To know its special and broader meanings, to know its relation to other words, and to be able to use it. When you see or hear a familiar word used in an unfamiliar sense, jot it down, look it up, and master it. We have in mind a speaker of superior attainments who acquired his vocabulary by noting all new words he heard or read. These he mastered and *put into use*. Soon his vocabulary became large, varied, and exact. Use a new word accurately five times and it is yours. Professor Albert E.

---

29 *How to Attract and Hold an Audience,* J. Berg Esenwein.

Hancock says: "An author's vocabulary is of two kinds, latent and dynamic: latent—those words he understands; dynamic—those he can readily use. Every intelligent man *knows* all the words he needs, but he may not have them all ready for active service. The problem of literary diction consists in turning the latent into the dynamic." Your dynamic vocabulary is the one you must especially cultivate.

In his essay on "A College Magazine" in the volume, *Memories and Portraits,* Stevenson shows how he rose from imitation to originality in the use of words. He had particular reference to the formation of his literary style, but words are the raw materials of style, and his excellent example may well be followed judiciously by the public speaker. Words *in their relations* are vastly more important than words considered singly.

> Whenever I read a book or a passage that particularly pleased me, in which a thing was said or an effect rendered with propriety, in which there was either some conspicuous force or some happy distinction in the style, I must sit down at once and set myself to ape that quality. I was unsuccessful, and I knew it; and tried again, and was again unsuccessful, and always unsuccessful; but at least in these vain bouts I got some practice in rhythm, in harmony, in construction and coördination of parts.
>
> I have thus played the sedulous ape to Hazlitt, to Lamb, to Wordsworth, to Sir Thomas Browne, to Defoe, to Hawthorne, to Montaigne.
>
> That, like it or not, is the way to learn to write; whether I have profited or not, that is the way. It was the way Keats learned, and there never was a finer temperament for literature than Keats'.
>
> It is the great point of these imitations that there still shines beyond the student's reach, his inimitable model. Let him try as he please, he is still sure of failure; and it is an old and very true saying that failure is the only highroad to success.

## *Form the Reference-Book Habit*

Do not be content with your general knowledge of a word—press your study until you have mastered its individual shades of meaning and usage. Mere fluency is sure to become despicable, but accuracy never. The dictionary contains the crystallized usage of intellectual giants. No one who would write effectively dare despise its definitions and discriminations. Think, for example, of the different meanings of *mantle,* or *model,* or *quantity.* Any late edition of an unabridged dictionary is good, and is worth making sacrifices to own.

Books of synonyms and antonyms—used cautiously, for there are few *perfect* synonyms in any language—will be found of great help. Consider the shades of meanings among such word-groups as *thief, peculator, defaulter, embezzler, burglar, yeggman, robber, bandit, marauder, pirate,* and many more; or the distinctions among *Hebrew, Jew, Israelite,* and *Semite.* Remember that no book of synonyms is trustworthy unless used with a dictionary. "A Thesaurus of the English Language," by Dr. Francis A. March, is expensive, but full and authoritative. Of smaller books of synonyms and antonyms there are plenty.[30]

---

30 A book of synonyms and antonyms is in preparation for this series, "The Writer's Library."

Study the connectives of English speech. Fernald's book on this title is a mine of gems. Unsuspected pitfalls lie in the loose use of *and, or, for, while,* and a score of tricky little connectives.

Word derivations are rich in suggestiveness. Our English owes so much to foreign tongues and has changed so much with the centuries that whole addresses may grow out of a single root-idea hidden away in an ancient word-origin. Translation, also, is excellent exercise in word-mastery and consorts well with the study of derivations.

Phrase books that show the origins of familiar expressions will surprise most of us by showing how carelessly everyday speech is used. Brewer's "A Dictionary of Phrase, and Fable," Edwards' "Words, Facts, and Phrases," and Thornton's "An American Glossary," are all good—the last, an expensive work in three volumes.

A prefix or a suffix may essentially change the force of the stem, as in *master-ful* and *master-ly, contempt-ible* and *contempt-uous, envi-ous* and *envi-able.* Thus to study words in groups, according to their stems, prefixes, and suffixes is to gain a mastery over their shades of meaning, and introduce us to other related words.

## Do Not Favor One Set or Kind of Words More than Another

"Sixty years and more ago, Lord Brougham, addressing the students of the University of Glasgow, laid down the rule that the native (Anglo-Saxon) part of our vocabulary was to be favored at the expense of that other part which has come from the Latin and Greek. The rule was an impossible one, and Lord Brougham himself never tried seriously to observe it; nor, in truth, has any great writer made the attempt. Not only is our language highly composite, but the component words have, in De Quincey's phrase, 'happily coalesced.' It is easy to jest at words in *-osity* and *-ation*, as 'dictionary' words, and the like. But even Lord Brougham would have found it difficult to dispense with *pomposity* and *imagination*."[31]

The short, vigorous Anglo-Saxon will always be preferred for passages of special thrust and force, just as the Latin will continue to furnish us with flowing and smooth expressions; to mingle all sorts, however, will give variety—and that is most to be desired.

## Discuss Words with Those Who Know Them

Since the language of the platform follows closely the diction of everyday speech, many useful words may be acquired in conversation with cultivated men, and when such discussion takes the form of disputation as to the meanings and usages of words, it will prove doubly valuable. The development of word-power marches with the growth of individuality.

## Search Faithfully for the Right Word

Books of reference are tripled in value when their owner has a passion for getting the kernels out of their shells. Ten minutes a day will do wonders for the nut-cracker. "I am growing so peevish about my writing," says Flaubert. "I am like a man whose ear is true, but who plays falsely on the violin: his fingers refuse to reproduce precisely those sounds

---

31 *Composition and Rhetoric*, J. M. Hart.

of which he has the inward sense. Then the tears come rolling down from the poor scraper's eyes and the bow falls from his hand."

The same brilliant Frenchman sent this sound advice to his pupil, Guy de Maupassant: "Whatever may be the thing which one wishes to say, there is but one word for expressing it, only one verb to animate it, only one adjective to qualify it. It is essential to search for this word, for this verb, for this adjective, until they are discovered, and to be satisfied with nothing else."

Walter Savage Landor once wrote: "I hate false words, and seek with care, difficulty, and moroseness those that fit the thing." So did Sentimental Tommy, as related by James M. Barrie in his novel bearing his hero's name as a title. No wonder T. Sandys became an author and a lion!

Tommy, with another lad, is writing an essay on "A Day in Church," in competition for a university scholarship. He gets on finely until he pauses for lack of a word. For nearly an hour he searches for this elusive thing, until suddenly he is told that the allotted time is up, and he has lost! Barrie may tell the rest:

> Essay! It was no more an essay than a twig is a tree, for the gowk had stuck in the middle of his second page. Yes, stuck is the right expression, as his chagrined teacher had to admit when the boy was cross-examined. He had not been "up to some of his tricks;" he had stuck, and his explanations, as you will admit, merely emphasized his incapacity.
>
> He had brought himself to public scorn for lack of a word. What word? they asked testily; but even now he could not tell. He had wanted a Scotch word that would signify how many people were in church, and it was on the tip of his tongue, but would come no farther. Puckle was nearly the word, but it did not mean so many people as he meant. The hour had gone by just like winking; he had forgotten all about time while searching his mind for the word.
>
> The other five [examiners] were furious. . . . "You little tattie doolie," Cathro roared, "were there not a dozen words to wile from if you had an ill-will to puckle? What ailed you at manzy, or—"
>
> "I thought of manzy," replied Tommy, woefully, for he was ashamed of himself, "but—but a manzy's a swarm. It would mean that the folk in the kirk were buzzing thegither like bees, instead of sitting still."
>
> "Even if it does mean that," said Mr. Duthie, with impatience, "what was the need of being so particular? Surely the art of essay-writing consists in using the first word that comes and hurrying on."
>
> "That's how I did," said the proud McLauchlan [Tommy's successful competitor]. . . .
>
> "I see," interposed Mr. Gloag, "that McLauchlan speaks of there being a mask of people in the church. Mask is a fine Scotch word."
>
> "I thought of mask," whimpered Tommy, "but that would mean the kirk was crammed, and I just meant it to be middling full."
>
> "Flow would have done," suggested Mr. Lonimer.

"Flow's but a handful," said Tommy.

"Curran, then, you jackanapes!"

"Curran's no enough."

Mr. Lorrimer flung up his hands in despair.

"I wanted something between curran and mask," said Tommy, doggedly, yet almost at the crying.

Mr. Ogilvy, who had been hiding his admiration with difficulty, spread a net for him. "You said you wanted a word that meant middling full. Well, why did you not say middling full—or fell mask?"

"Yes, why not?" demanded the ministers, unconsciously caught in the net.

"I wanted one word," replied Tommy, unconsciously avoiding it.

"You jewel!" muttered Mr. Ogilvy under his breath, but Mr. Cathro would have banged the boy's head had not the ministers interfered.

"It is so easy, too, to find the right word," said Mr. Gloag.

"It's no; it's difficult as to hit a squirrel," cried Tommy, and again Mr. Ogilvy nodded approval.

And then an odd thing happened. As they were preparing to leave the school [Cathro having previously run Tommy out by the neck], the door opened a little and there appeared in the aperture the face of Tommy, tear-stained but excited. "I ken the word now," he cried, "it came to me a' at once; it is hantle!"

Mr. Ogilvy . . . . said in an ecstasy to himself, "He *had* to think of it till he got it—and he got it. The laddie is a genius!"

## QUESTIONS AND EXERCISES

1. What is the derivation of the word *vocabulary*?

2. Briefly discuss any complete speech given in this volume, with reference to (*a*) exactness, (*b*) variety, and (*c*) charm, in the use of words.

3. Give original examples of the kinds of word-studies referred to on pages 206–207.

4. Deliver a short talk on any subject, using at least five words which have not been previously in your "dynamic" vocabulary.

5. Make a list of the unfamiliar words found in any address you may select.

6. Deliver a short extemporaneous speech giving your opinions on the merits and demerits of the use of unusual words in public speaking.

7. Try to find an example of the over-use of unusual words in a speech.

8. Have you used reference books in word studies? If so, state with what result.

9. Find as many synonyms and antonyms as possible for each of the following words: Excess, Rare, Severe, Beautiful, Clear, Happy, Difference, Care, Skillful, Involve, Enmity, Profit, Absurd, Evident, Faint, Friendly, Harmony, Hatred, Honest, Inherent.

CHAPTER XXVIII

# Memory Training

Lulled in the countless chambers of the brain,
Our thoughts are linked by many a hidden chain;
Awake but one, and lo! what myriads rise!
Each stamps its image as the other flies!

Hail, memory, hail! in thy exhaustless mine
From age to age unnumber'd treasures shine!
Thought and her shadowy brood thy call obey,
And Place and Time are subject to thy sway!

—SAMUEL ROGERS, *Pleasures of Memory*

MANY AN ORATOR, LIKE THACKERAY, HAS MADE THE BEST PART OF HIS SPEECH TO himself—on the way home from the lecture hall. Presence of mind—it remained for Mark Twain to observe—is greatly promoted by absence of body. A hole in the memory is no less a common complaint than a distressing one.

Henry Ward Beecher was able to deliver one of the world's greatest addresses at Liverpool because of his excellent memory. In speaking of the occasion Mr. Beecher said that all the events, arguments and appeals that he had ever heard or read or written seemed to pass before his mind as oratorical weapons, and standing there he had but to reach forth his hand and "seize the weapons as they went smoking by." Ben Jonson could repeat all he had written. Scaliger memorized the *Iliad* in three weeks. Locke says: "Without memory, man is a perpetual infant." Quintilian and Aristotle regarded it as a measure of genius.

Now all this is very good. We all agree that a reliable memory is an invaluable possession for the speaker. We never dissent for a moment when we are solemnly told that his memory should be a storehouse from which at pleasure he can draw facts, fancies, and illustrations. But can the memory be trained to act as the warder for all the truths that we have gained from thinking, reading, and experience? And if so, how? Let us see.

Twenty years ago a poor immigrant boy, employed as a dish washer in New York, wandered into the Cooper Union and began to read a copy of Henry George's "Progress and Poverty." His passion for knowledge was awakened, and he became a habitual reader. But he found that he was not able to remember what he read, so he began to train his naturally poor memory until he became the world's greatest memory expert. This man was the late Mr. Felix Berol. Mr. Berol could tell the population of any town in the world, of more than five thousand inhabitants. He could recall the names of forty strangers who had just been introduced to him and was able to tell which had been presented third, eighth, seventeenth, or in any order. He knew the date of every important event in history, and could not only recall an endless array of facts but could correlate them perfectly.

To what extent Mr. Berol's remarkable memory was natural and required only attention, for its development, seems impossible to determine with exactness, but the evidence clearly indicates that, however useless were many of his memory feats, a highly retentive memory was developed where before only "a good forgettery" existed.

The freak memory is not worth striving for, but a good working memory decidedly is. Your power as a speaker will depend to a large extent upon your ability to retain impressions and call them forth when occasion demands, and that sort of memory is like muscle—it responds to training.

## What Not to Do

It is sheer misdirected effort to begin to memorize by learning words by rote, for that is beginning to build a pyramid at the apex. For years our schools were cursed by this vicious system—vicious not only because it is inefficient but for the more important reason that it hurts the mind. True, some minds are natively endowed with a wonderful facility in remembering strings of words, facts, and figures, but such are rarely good reasoning minds; the normal person must belabor and force the memory to acquire in this artificial way.

Again, it is hurtful to force the memory in hours of physical weakness or mental weariness. Health is the basis of the best mental action and the operation of memory is no exception.

Finally, do not become a slave to a system. Knowledge of a few simple facts of mind and memory will set you to work at the right end of the operation. Use these *principles*, whether included in a system or not, but do not bind yourself to a method that tends to lay more stress on the *way* to remember than on the development of memory itself. It is nothing short of ridiculous to memorize ten words in order to remember one fact.

## The Natural Laws of Memory

*Concentrated attention* at the time when you wish to store the mind is the first step in memorizing—and the most important one by far. You forgot the fourth of the list of articles your wife asked you to bring home chiefly because you allowed your attention to waver for an instant when she was telling you. Attention may not be concentrated attention. When a siphon is charged with gas it is sufficiently filled with the carbonic acid vapor to make its influence felt; a mind charged with an idea is charged to a degree sufficient to hold it. Too much charging will make the siphon burst; too much attention to trifles leads to insanity. Adequate attention, then, is the fundamental secret of remembering.

Generally we do not give a fact adequate attention when it does not seem important. Almost everyone has seen how the seeds in an apple point, and has memorized the date of Washington's death. Most of us have—perhaps wisely—forgotten both. The little nick in the bark of a tree is healed over and obliterated in a season, but the gashes in the trees around Gettysburg are still apparent after fifty years. Impressions that are gathered lightly are soon obliterated. Only deep impressions can be recalled at will. Henry Ward Beecher said: "One intense hour will do more than dreamy years." To memorize ideas and words, concentrate on them until they are fixed firmly and deeply in your mind and accord to them their true importance. LISTEN with the mind and you will remember.

How shall you concentrate? How would you increase the fighting-effectiveness of a man-of-war? One vital way would be to increase the size and number of its guns. To strengthen your memory, increase both the number and the force of your mental impressions by attending to them intensely. Loose, skimming reading, and drifting habits of reading destroy memory power. However, as most books and newspapers do not warrant any other kind of attention, it will not do altogether to condemn this method of reading; but avoid it when you are trying to memorize.

Environment has a strong influence upon concentration, until you have learned to be alone in a crowd and undisturbed by clamor. When you set out to memorize a fact or a speech, you may find the task easier away from all sounds and moving objects. All impressions foreign to the one you desire to fix in your mind must be eliminated.

The next great step in memorizing is to *pick out the essentials of the subject*, arrange them in order, and dwell upon them intently. Think clearly of each essential, one after the other. *Thinking* a thing—not allowing the mind to wander to non-essentials—is really memorizing.

*Association of ideas* is universally recognized as an essential in memory work; indeed, whole systems of memory training have been founded on this principle.

Many speakers memorize only the outlines of their addresses, filling in the words at the moment of speaking. Some have found it helpful to remember an outline by associating the different points with objects in the room. Speaking on "Peace," you may wish to dwell on the cost the cruelty, and the failure of war, and so lead to the justice of arbitration. Before going on the platform if you will associate four divisions of your outline with four objects in the room, this association may help you to recall them. You may be prone to forget your third point, but you remember that once when you were speaking the electric lights failed, so arbitrarily the electric light globe will help you to remember "failure." Such associations, being unique, tend to stick in the mind. While recently speaking on the six kinds of imagination the present writer formed them into an acrostic—*visual, auditory, motor, gustatory, olfactory*, and *tactile*, furnished the nonsense word *vamgot*, but the six points were easily remembered.

In the same way that children are taught to remember the spelling of teasing words—*separate* comes from *separ*—and as an automobile driver remembers that two C's and then two H's lead him into Castor Road, Cottman Street, Haynes Street and Henry Street, so important points in your address may be fixed in mind by arbitrary symbols invented by yourself. The very work of devising the scheme is a memory action. The psychological process is simple: it is one of noting intently the steps by which a fact, or a truth, or even a word, has come to you. Take advantage of this tendency of the mind to remember by association.

*Repetition* is a powerful aid to memory. Thurlow Weed, the journalist and political leader, was troubled because he so easily forgot the names of persons he met from day to day. He corrected the weakness, relates Professor William James, by forming the habit of attending carefully to names he had heard during the day and then repeating them to his wife every evening. Doubtless Mrs. Weed was heroically longsuffering, but the device worked admirably.

After reading a passage you would remember, close the book, reflect, and repeat the contents—aloud, if possible.

*Reading thoughtfully aloud* has been found by many to be a helpful memory practise.

*Write what you wish to remember.* This is simply one more way of increasing the number and the strength of your mental impressions by utilizing *all* your avenues of impression. It will help to fix a speech in your mind if you speak it aloud, listen to it, write it out, and look at it intently. You have then impressed it on your mind by means of vocal, auditory, muscular and visual impressions.

Some folk have peculiarly distinct auditory memories; they are able to recall things heard much better than things seen. Others have the visual memory; they are best able to recall sight-impressions. As you recall a walk you have taken, are you able to remember better the sights or the sounds? Find out what kinds of impressions your memory retains best, and use them the most. To fix an idea in mind, use *every* possible kind of impression.

*Daily habit* is a great memory cultivator. Learn a lesson from the Marathon runner. Regular exercise, though never so little daily, will strengthen your memory in a surprising measure. Try to describe in detail the dress, looks and manner of the people you pass on the street. Observe the room you are in, close your eyes, and describe its contents. View closely the landscape, and write out a detailed description of it. How much did you miss? Notice the contents of the show windows on the street; how many features are you able to recall? Continual practise in this feat may develop in you as remarkable proficiency as it did in Robert Houdin and his son.

The daily memorizing of a beautiful passage in literature will not only lend strength to the memory, but will store the mind with gems for quotation. But whether by little or much add daily to your memory power by practise.

*Memorize out of doors.* The buoyancy of the wood, the shore, or the stormy night on deserted streets may freshen your mind as it does the minds of countless others.

Lastly, *cast out fear.* Tell yourself that you *can* and *will* and *do* remember. By pure exercise of selfism assert your mastery. Be obsessed with the fear of forgetting and you cannot remember. Practise the reverse. Throw aside your manuscript crutches—you may tumble once or twice, but what matters that, for you are going to learn to walk and leap and run.

## Memorizing a Speech

Now let us try to put into practise the foregoing suggestions. First, reread this chapter, noting the nine ways by which memorizing may be helped.

Then read over the following selection from Beecher, applying so many of the suggestions as are practicable. Get the spirit of the selection firmly in your mind. Make mental note of—write down, if you must—the *succession* of ideas. Now memorize the thought. Then memorize the outline, the order in which the different ideas are expressed. Finally, memorize the exact wording.

No, when you have done all this, with the most faithful attention to directions, you will not find memorizing easy, unless you have previously trained your memory, or it is naturally retentive. Only by constant practise will memory become strong and only by continually observing these same principles will it remain strong. You will, however, have made a beginning, and that is no mean matter.

## The Reign of the Common People

I do not suppose that if you were to go and look upon the experiment of self-government in America you would have a very high opinion of it. I have not either, if I just look upon the surface of things. Why, men will say: "It stands to reason that 60,000,000 ignorant of law, ignorant of constitutional history, ignorant of jurisprudence, of finance, and taxes and tariffs and forms of currency—60,000,000 people that never studied these things—are not fit to rule." Your diplomacy is as complicated as ours, and it is the most complicated on earth, for all things grow in complexity as they develop toward a higher condition. What fitness is there in these people? Well, it is not democracy merely; it is a representative democracy. Our people do not vote in mass for anything; they pick out captains of thought, they pick out the men that do know, and they send them to the Legislature to think for them, and then the people afterward ratify or disallow them.

But when you come to the Legislature I am bound to confess that the thing does not look very much more cheering on the outside. Do they really select the best men? Yes; in times of danger they do very generally, but in ordinary time, "kissing goes by favor." You know what the duty of a regular Republican-Democratic legislator is. It is to get back again next winter. His second duty is what? His second duty is to put himself under that extraordinary providence that takes care of legislators' salaries. The old miracle of the prophet and the meal and the oil is outdone immeasurably in our days, for they go there poor one year, and go home rich; in four years they become moneylenders, all by a trust in that gracious providence that takes care of legislators' salaries. Their next duty after that is to serve the party that sent them up, and then, if there is anything left of them, it belongs to the commonwealth. Someone has said very wisely, that if a man traveling wishes to relish his dinner he had better not go into the kitchen to see where it is cooked; if a man wishes to respect and obey the law, he had better not go to the Legislature to see where that is cooked.

—HENRY WARD BEECHER. *From a lecture delivered in Exeter Hall,*
*London, 1886, when making his last tour of Great Britain*

## In Case of Trouble

But what are you to do if, notwithstanding all your efforts, you should forget your points, and your mind, for the minute, becomes blank? This is a deplorable condition that sometimes arises and must be dealt with. Obviously, you can sit down and admit defeat. Such a consummation is devoutly to be shunned.

Walking slowly across the platform may give you time to grip yourself, compose your thoughts, and stave off disaster. Perhaps the surest and most practical method is to begin a new sentence with your last important word. This is not advocated as a method of composing a speech—it is merely an extreme measure which may save you in tight circumstances. It is like the fire department—the less you must use it the better. If this method is followed very long you are likely to find yourself talking about plum pudding or Chinese Gordon in the most unexpected manner, so of course you will get back to your lines the earliest moment that your feet have hit the platform.

Let us see how this plan works—obviously, your extemporized words will lack somewhat of polish, but in such a pass crudity is better than failure.

Now you have come to a dead wall after saying: "Joan of Arc fought for liberty." By this method you might get something like this:

"Liberty is a sacred privilege for which mankind always had to fight. These struggles [Platitude—but push on] fill the pages of history. History records the gradual triumph of the serf over the lord, the slave over the master. The master has continually tried to usurp unlimited powers. Power during the medieval ages accrued to the owner of the land with a spear and a strong castle; but the strong castle and spear were of little avail after the discovery of gunpowder. Gunpowder was the greatest boon that liberty had ever known."

Thus far you have linked one idea with another rather obviously, but you are getting your second wind now and may venture to relax your grip on the too-evident chain; and so you say:

"With gunpowder the humblest serf in all the land could put an end to the life of the tyrannical baron behind the castle walls. The struggle for liberty, with gunpowder as its aid, wrecked empires, and built up a new era for all mankind."

In a moment more you have gotten back to your outline and the day is saved.

Practising exercises like the above will not only fortify you against the death of your speech when your memory misses fire, but it will also provide an excellent training for fluency in speaking. *Stock up with ideas.*

### QUESTIONS AND EXERCISES

1. Pick out and state briefly the nine helps to memorizing suggested in this chapter.

2. Report on whatever success you may have had with any of the plans for memory culture suggested in this chapter. Have any been less successful than others?

3. Freely criticise any of the suggested methods.

4. Give an original example of memory by association of ideas.

5. List in order the chief ideas of any speech in this volume.

6. Repeat them from memory.

7. Expand them into a speech, using your own words.

8. Illustrate practically what would you do, if in the midst of a speech on Progress, your memory failed you and you stopped suddenly on the following sentence: "The last century saw marvelous progress in varied lines of activity."

9. How many quotations that fit well in the speaker's tool chest can you recall from memory?

10. Memorize the poem on page 27. How much time does it require?

# CHAPTER XXIX

## Right Thinking and Personality

Whatever crushes individuality is despotism, by whatever
name it may be called.

—John Stuart Mill, *On Liberty*

Right thinking fits for complete living by developing the
power to appreciate the beautiful in nature and art, power
to think the true and to will the good, power to live the
life of thought, and faith, and hope, and love.

—N. C. Schaeffer, *Thinking and Learning to Think*

THE SPEAKER'S MOST VALUABLE POSSESSION IS PERSONALITY—THAT INDEFINABLE, imponderable something which sums up what we are, and makes us different from others; that distinctive force of self which operates appreciably on those whose lives we touch. It is personality alone that makes us long for higher things. Rob us of our sense of individual life, with its gains and losses, its duties and joys, and we grovel. "Few human creatures," says John Stuart Mill, "would consent to be changed into any of the lower animals for a promise of the fullest allowance of a beast's pleasures; no intelligent human being would consent to be a fool, no instructed person would be an ignoramus, no person of feeling and conscience would be selfish and base, even though he should be persuaded that the fool, or the dunce, or the rascal is better satisfied with his lot than they with theirs. . . . It is better to be a human being dissatisfied than a pig satisfied, better to be a Socrates dissatisfied than a fool satisfied. And if the fool or the pig is of a different opinion, it is only because they know only their own side of the question. The other party to the comparison knows both sides."

Now it is precisely because the Socrates type of person lives on the plan of right thinking and restrained feeling and willing that he prefers his state to that of the animal. All that a man is, all his happiness, his sorrow, his achievements, his failures, his magnetism, his weakness, all are in an amazingly large measure the direct results of his thinking. Thought and heart combine to produce *right* thinking: "As a man thinketh in his heart so is he." As he does not think in his heart so he can never become.

Since this is true, personality can be developed and its latent powers brought out by careful cultivation. We have long since ceased to believe that we are living in a realm of chance. So clear and exact are nature's laws that we forecast, scores of years in advance, the appearance of a certain comet and foretell to the minute an eclipse of the Sun. And we understand this law of cause and effect in all our material realms. We do not plant potatoes and expect to pluck hyacinths. The law is universal: it applies to our mental powers, to morality, to personality, quite as much as to the heavenly bodies and the grain of the fields. "Whatsoever a man soweth that shall he also reap," and nothing else.

Character has always been regarded as one of the chief factors of the speaker's power. Cato defined the orator as *vir bonus dicendi peritus*—a good man skilled in speaking. Phillips Brooks says: "Nobody can truly stand as a utterer before the world, unless he be profoundly living and earnestly thinking." "Character," says Emerson, "is a natural power, like light and heat, and all nature cooperates with it. The reason why we feel one man's presence, and do not feel another's is as simple as gravity. Truth is the summit of being: justice is the application of it to affairs. All individual natures stand in a scale, according to the purity of this element in them. The will of the pure runs down into other natures, as water runs down from a higher into a lower vessel. This natural force is no more to be withstood than any other natural force. . . . Character is nature in the highest form."

It is absolutely impossible for impure, bestial and selfish thoughts to blossom into loving and altruistic habits. Thistle seeds bring forth only the thistle. Contrariwise, it is entirely impossible for continual altruistic, sympathetic, and serviceful thoughts to bring forth a low and vicious character. Either thoughts or feelings precede and determine all our actions. Actions develop into habits, habits constitute character, and character determines destiny. Therefore to guard our thoughts and control our feelings is to shape our destinies. The syllogism is complete, and old as it is it is still true.

Since "character is nature in the highest form," the development of character must proceed on natural lines. The garden left to itself will bring forth weeds and scrawny plants, but the flower-beds nurtured carefully will blossom into fragrance and beauty.

As the student entering college largely determines his vocation by choosing from the different courses of the curriculum, so do we choose our characters by choosing our thoughts. We are steadily going up toward that which we most wish for, or steadily sinking to the level of our low desires. What we secretly cherish in our hearts is a symbol of what we shall receive. Our trains of thoughts are hurrying us on to our destiny. When you see the flag fluttering to the South, you know the wind is coming from the North. When you see the straws and papers being carried to the Northward you realize the wind is blowing out of the South. It is just as easy to ascertain a man's thoughts by observing the tendency of his character.

Let it not be suspected for one moment that all this is merely a preachment on the question of morals. It is that, but much more, for it touches the whole man—his imaginative nature, his ability to control his feelings, the mastery of his thinking faculties, and—perhaps most largely—his power to will and to carry his volitions into effective action.

Right thinking constantly assumes that the will sits enthroned to execute the dictates of mind, conscience and heart. *Never tolerate for an instant the suggestion that your will is not absolutely efficient.* The way to will is to will—and the very first time you are tempted to break a worthy resolution—and you will be, you may be certain of that—*make your fight then and there.* You cannot afford to lose that fight. You *must* win it—don't swerve for an instant, but keep that resolution if it kills you. It will not, but you must fight just as though life depended on the victory; and indeed your personality may actually lie in the balances!

Your success or failure as a speaker will be determined very largely by your thoughts and your mental attitude. The present writer had a student of limited education enter one of his classes in public speaking. He proved to be a very poor speaker; and the instructor could conscientiously do little but point out faults. However, the young man was warned not to be discouraged. With sorrow in his voice and the essence of earnestness beaming from his eyes, he replied: "I will not be discouraged! I want so badly to know how to speak!" It was warm, human, and from the very heart. And he did keep on trying—and developed into a creditable speaker.

There is no power under the stars that can defeat a man with that attitude. He who down in the deeps of his heart earnestly longs to get facility in speaking, and is willing to make the sacrifices necessary, will reach his goal. "Ask and ye shall receive; seek and ye shall find; knock and it shall be opened unto you," is indeed applicable to those who would acquire speech-power. You will not realize the prize that you wish for languidly, but the goal that you start out to attain with the spirit of the old guard that dies but never surrenders, you will surely reach.

Your belief in your ability and your willingness to make sacrifices for that belief, are the double index to your future achievements. Lincoln had a dream of his possibilities as a speaker. He transmuted that dream into life solely because he walked many miles to borrow books which he read by the log-fire glow at night. He sacrificed much to realize his vision. Livingstone had a great faith in his ability to serve the benighted races of Africa. To actualize that faith he gave up all. Leaving England for the interior of the Dark Continent he struck the death blow to Europe's profits from the slave trade. Joan of Arc had great self-confidence, glorified by an infinite capacity for sacrifice. She drove the English beyond the Loire, and stood beside Charles while he was crowned.

These all realized their strongest desires. The law is universal. Desire greatly, and you shall achieve; sacrifice much, and you shall obtain.

Stanton Davis Kirkham has beautifully expressed this thought: "You may be keeping accounts, and presently you shall walk out of the door that has for so long seemed to you the barrier of your ideals, and shall find yourself before an audience—the pen still behind your ear, the ink stains on your fingers—and then and there shall pour out the torrent of your inspiration. You may be driving sheep, and you shall wander to the city—bucolic and open-mouthed; shall wander under the intrepid guidance of the spirit into the studio of the master, and after a time he shall say, 'I have nothing more to teach you.' And now you have become the master, who did so recently dream of great things while driving sheep. You shall lay down the saw and the plane to take upon yourself the regeneration of the world."

## QUESTIONS AND EXERCISES

1. What, in your own words, is personality?

2. How does personality in a speaker affect you as a listener?

3. In what ways does personality show itself in a speaker?

4. Deliver a short speech on "The Power of Will in the Public Speaker."

5. Deliver a short address based on any sentence you choose from this chapter.

CHAPTER XXX

# After-Dinner and Other Occasional Speaking

The perception of the ludicrous is a pledge of sanity.

—RALPH WALDO EMERSON, *Essays*

And let him be sure to leave other men their turns to speak.

—FRANCIS BACON, *Essay on Civil and Moral Discourse*

PERHAPS THE MOST BRILLIANT, AND CERTAINLY THE MOST ENTERTAINING, OF ALL speeches are those delivered on after-dinner and other special occasions. The air of well-fed content in the former, and of expectancy well primed in the latter, furnishes an audience which, though not readily won, is prepared for the best, while the speaker himself is pretty sure to have been chosen for his gifts of oratory.

The first essential of good occasional speaking is to study the occasion. Precisely what is the object of the meeting? How important is the occasion to the audience? How large will the audience be? What sort of people are they? How large is the auditorium? Who selects the speakers' themes? Who else is to speak? What are they to speak about? Precisely how long am I to speak? Who speaks before I do and who follows?

If you want to hit the nail on the head ask such questions as these.[32] No occasional address can succeed unless it fits the occasion to a T. Many prominent men have lost prestige because they were too careless or too busy or too self-confident to respect the occasion and the audience by learning the exact conditions under which they were to speak. Leaving *too* much to the moment is taking a long chance and generally means a less effective speech, if not a failure.

Suitability is the big thing in an occasional speech. When Mark Twain addressed the Army of the Tennessee in reunion at Chicago, in 1877, he responded to the toast, "The Babies." Two things in that after-dinner speech are remarkable: the bright introduction, by which he subtly *claimed* the interest of all, and the humorous use of military terms throughout:

---

**32** See also page 123.

Mr. Chairman and Gentlemen: "The Babies." Now, that's something like. We
haven't all had the good fortune to be ladies; we have not all been generals, or poets,
or statesmen; but when the toast works down to the babies, we stand on common
ground—for we've all been babies. It is a shame that for a thousand years the
world's banquets have utterly ignored the baby, as if he didn't amount to anything!
If you, gentlemen, will stop and think a minute—if you will go back fifty or a
hundred years, to your early married life, and recontemplate your first baby—you
will remember that he amounted to a good deal—and even something over.

"As a vessel is known by the sound, whether it be cracked or not," said Demosthenes,
"so men are proved by their speeches whether they be wise or foolish." Surely the occasional address furnishes a severe test of a speaker's wisdom. To be trivial on a serious
occasion, to be funereal at a banquet, to be long-winded ever—these are the marks of nonsense. Some imprudent souls seem to select the most friendly of after-dinner occasions
for the explosion of a bomb-shell of dispute. Around the dinner table it is the custom of
even political enemies to bury their hatchets anywhere rather than in some convenient
skull. It is the height of bad taste to raise questions that in hours consecrated to good-will
can only irritate.

Occasional speeches offer good chances for humor, particularly the funny story, for
humor with a genuine point is not trivial. But do not spin a whole skein of humorous
yarns with no more connection than the inane and threadbare "And that reminds me." An
anecdote without bearing may be funny but one less funny that fits theme and occasion is
far preferable. There is no way, short of sheer power of speech, that so surely leads to the
heart of an audience as rich, appropriate humor. The scattered diners in a great banquet-
ing hall, the after-dinner lethargy, the anxiety over approaching last-train time, the over-
full list of over-full speakers—all throw out a challenge to the speaker to do his best to win
an interested hearing. And when success does come it is usually due to a happy mixture
of seriousness and humor, for humor alone rarely scores so heavily as the two combined,
while the utterly grave speech *never* does on such occasions.

If there is one place more than another where second-hand opinions and platitudes
are unwelcome it is in the after-dinner speech. Whether you are toast-master or the last
speaker to try to hold the waning crowd at midnight, be as original as you can. How is
it possible to summarize the qualities that go to make up the good after-dinner speech,
when we remember the inimitable serious-drollery of Mark Twain, the sweet southern eloquence of Henry W. Grady, the funereal gravity of the humorous Charles Battell
Loomis, the charm of Henry Van Dyke, the geniality of F. Hopkinson Smith, and the all-
round delightfulness of Chauncey M. Depew? America is literally rich in such gladsome
speakers, who punctuate real sense with nonsense, and so make both effective.

Commemorative occasions, unveilings, commencements, dedications, eulogies, and
all the train of special public gatherings, offer rare opportunities for the display of tact and
good sense in handling occasion, theme, and audience. When to be dignified and when
colloquial, when to soar and when to ramble arm in arm with your hearers, when to flame

and when to soothe, when to instruct and when to amuse—in a word, the whole matter of APPROPRIATENESS must constantly be in mind lest you write your speech on water.

Finally, remember the beatitude: Blessed is the man that maketh short speeches, for he shall be invited to speak again.

## SELECTIONS FOR STUDY

## Last Days of the Confederacy
### (Extract)

The Rapidan suggests another scene to which allusion has often been made since the war, but which, as illustrative also of the spirit of both armies, I may be permitted to recall in this connection. In the mellow twilight of an April day the two armies were holding their dress parades on the opposite hills bordering the river. At the close of the parade a magnificent brass band of the Union army played with great spirit the patriotic airs, "Hail Columbia," and "Yankee Doodle." Whereupon the Federal troops responded with a patriotic shout. The same band then played the soul-stirring strains of "Dixie," to which a mighty response came from ten thousand Southern troops. A few moments later, when the stars had come out as witnesses and when all nature was in harmony, there came from the same band the old melody, "Home, Sweet Home." As its familiar and pathetic notes rolled over the water and thrilled through the spirits of the soldiers, the hills reverberated with a thundering response from the united voices of both armies. What was there in this old, old music, to so touch the chords of sympathy, so thrill the spirits and cause the frames of brave men to tremble with emotion? It was the thought of home. To thousands, doubtless, it was the thought of that Eternal Home to which the next battle might be the gateway. To thousands of others it was the thought of their dear earthly homes, where loved ones at that twilight hour were bowing round the family altar, and asking God's care over the absent soldier boy.

—GENERAL J. B. GORDON, C. S. A.

## Welcome to Kossuth
### (Extract)

Let me ask you to imagine that the contest, in which the United States asserted their independence of Great Britain, had been unsuccessful; that our armies, through treason or a league of tyrants against us, had been broken and scattered; that the great men who led them, and who swayed our councils—our Washington, our Franklin, and the venerable president of the American Congress—had been driven forth as exiles. If there had existed at that day, in any part of the civilized world, a powerful Republic, with institutions resting on the same foundations of liberty which our own countrymen sought to establish, would there have been in that Republic any hospitality too cordial, any sympathy too deep, any zeal for their glorious but unfortunate cause, too fervent or too active to be shown toward these illustrious fugitives? Gentlemen, the case I have supposed is before you. The Washingtons, the Franklins, the Hancocks of Hungary, driven out by a far worse tyranny than was ever endured here, are wanderers in foreign lands. Some of them have sought a refuge in our country—one sits with this company our guest to-night—and we must measure the duty we owe them by the same standard which we would have had history apply, if our ancestors had met with a fate like theirs.

—WILLIAM CULLEN BRYANT

## The Influence of Universities
### (Extract)

When the excitement of party warfare presses dangerously near our national safeguards, I would have the intelligent conservatism of our universities and colleges warn the contestants in impressive tones against the perils of a breach impossible to repair.

When popular discontent and passion are stimulated by the arts of designing partisans to a pitch perilously near to class hatred or sectional anger, I would have our universities and colleges sound the alarm in the name of American brotherhood and fraternal dependence.

When the attempt is made to delude the people into the belief that their suffrages can change the operation of national laws, I would have our universities and colleges proclaim that those laws are inexorable and far removed from political control.

When selfish interest seeks undue private benefits through governmental aid, and public places are claimed as rewards of party service, I would have our universities and colleges persuade the people to a relinquishment of the demand for party spoils and exhort them to a disinterested and patriotic love of their government, whose unperverted operation secures to every citizen his just share of the safety and prosperity it holds in store for all.

I would have the influence of these institutions on the side of religion and morality. I would have those they send out among the people not ashamed to acknowledge God, and to proclaim His interposition in the affairs of men, enjoining such obedience to His laws as makes manifest the path of national perpetuity and prosperity.

—GROVER CLEVELAND, *delivered at the Princeton Sesqui-Centennial, 1896*

# Eulogy of Garfield
*(Extract)*

Great in life, he was surpassingly great in death. For no cause, in the very frenzy of wantonness and wickedness, by the red hand of murder, he was thrust from the full tide of this world's interest, from its hopes, its aspirations, its victories, into the visible presence of death—and he did not quail. Not alone for the one short moment in which, stunned and dazed, he could give up life, hardly aware of its relinquishment, but through days of deadly languor, through weeks of agony, that was not less agony because silently borne, with clear sight and calm courage, he looked into his open grave. What blight and ruin met his anguished eyes, whose lips may tell—what brilliant, broken plans, what baffled, high ambitions, what sundering of strong, warm, manhood's friendships, what bitter rending of sweet household ties! Behind him a proud, expectant nation, a great host of sustaining friends, a cherished and happy mother, wearing the full rich honors of her early toil and tears; the wife of his youth, whose whole life lay in his; the little boys not yet emerged from childhood's day of frolic; the fair young daughter; the sturdy sons just springing into closest companionship, claiming every day and every day rewarding a father's love and care; and in his heart the eager, rejoicing power to meet all demand. Before him, desolation and great darkness! And his soul was not shaken. His countrymen were thrilled with instant, profound and universal sympathy. Masterful in his mortal weakness, he became the centre of a nation's love, enshrined in the prayers of a world. But all the love and all the sympathy could not share with him his suffering. He trod the wine press alone. With unfaltering front he faced death. With unfailing tenderness he took leave of life. Above the demoniac hiss of the assassin's bullet he heard the voice of God. With simple resignation he bowed to the Divine decree.

—James G. Blaine, *delivered at the memorial service held by the U.S. Senate and House of Representatives*

# Eulogy of Lee
*(Extract)*

At the bottom of all true heroism is unselfishness. Its crowning expression is sacrifice. The world is suspicious of vaunted heroes. But when the true hero has come, and we know that here he is in verity, ah! how the hearts of men leap forth to greet him! how worshipfully we welcome God's noblest work—the strong, honest, fearless, upright man. In Robert Lee was such a hero vouchsafed to us and to mankind, and whether we behold him declining command of the federal army to fight the battles and share the miseries of his own people; proclaiming on the heights in front of Gettysburg that the fault of the disaster was his own; leading charges in the crisis of combat; walking under the yoke of conquest without a murmur of complaint; or refusing fortune to come here and train the youth of his country in the paths of duty,—he is ever the same meek, grand, self-sacrificing spirit. Here he exhibited qualities not less worthy and heroic than those displayed on the broad and open theater of conflict, when the eyes of nations watched his every action. Here in the calm repose of civil and domestic duties, and in the trying routine of incessant tasks, he lived a life as high as when, day by day, he marshalled and led his thin and wasting lines, and slept by night upon the field that was to be drenched again in blood upon the morrow. And now he has vanished from us forever. And is this all that is left of him—this handful of dust beneath the marble stone? No! the ages answer as they rise from the gulfs of time, where lie the wrecks of kingdoms and estates, holding up in their hands as their only trophies, the names of those who have wrought for man in the love and fear of God, and in love—unfearing for their fellow-men. No! the present answers, bending by his tomb. No! the future answers as the breath of the morning fans its radiant brow, and its soul drinks in sweet inspirations from the lovely life of Lee. No! methinks the very heavens echo, as melt into their depths the words of reverent love that voice the hearts of men to the tingling stars.

Come we then to-day in loyal love to sanctify our memories, to purify our hopes, to make strong all good intent by communion with the spirit of him who, being dead yet speaketh. Come, child, in thy spotless innocence; come, woman, in thy purity; come, youth, in thy prime; come, manhood, in thy strength; come, age, in thy ripe wisdom; come, citizen; come, soldier; let us strew the roses and lilies of June around his tomb, for he, like them, exhaled in his life Nature's beneficence, and the grave has consecrated that life and given it to us all; let us crown his tomb with the oak, the emblem of his strength, and with the laurel the emblem of his glory, and let these guns, whose voices he knew of old, awake the echoes of the mountains, that nature herself may join in his solemn requiem. Come, for here he rests, and

> On this green bank, by this fair stream,
> We set to-day a votive stone,
> That memory may his deeds redeem?
> When, like our sires, our sons are gone.

—JOHN WARWICK DANIEL, *on the unveiling of Lee's statue at*
*Washington and Lee University, Lexington, Virginia, 1883*

## QUESTIONS AND EXERCISES

1. Why should humor find a place in after-dinner speaking?

2. Briefly give your impressions of any notable after-dinner address that you have heard.

3. Briefly outline an imaginary occasion of any sort and give three subjects appropriate for addresses.

4. Deliver one such address, not to exceed ten minutes in length.

5. What proportion of emotional ideas do you find in the extracts given in this chapter?

6. Humor was used in some of the foregoing addresses—in which others would it have been inappropriate?

7. Prepare and deliver an after-dinner speech suited to one of the following occasions, and be sure to use humor:

   - A lodge banquet.
   - A political party dinner.
   - A church men's club dinner.
   - A civic association banquet.
   - A banquet in honor of a celebrity.
   - A woman's club annual dinner.
   - A business men's association dinner.
   - A manufacturers' club dinner.
   - An alumni banquet.
   - An old home week barbecue.

# CHAPTER XXXI

# *Making Conversation Effective*

In conversation avoid the extremes of forwardness and reserve.

—CATO

Conversation is the laboratory and workshop of the student.

—EMERSON, *Essays: Circles*

T HE FATHER OF W. E. GLADSTONE CONSIDERED CONVERSATION TO BE BOTH AN ART and an accomplishment. Around the dinner table in his home some topic of local or national interest, or some debated question, was constantly being discussed. In this way a friendly rivalry for supremacy in conversation arose among the family, and an incident observed in the street, an idea gleaned from a book, a deduction from personal experience, was carefully stored as material for the family exchange. Thus his early years of practise in elegant conversation prepared the younger Gladstone for his career as a leader and speaker.

There is a sense in which the ability to converse effectively is efficient public speaking, for our conversation is often heard by many, and occasionally decisions of great moment hinge upon the tone and quality of what we say in private.

Indeed, conversation in the aggregate probably wields more power than press and platform combined. Socrates taught his great truths, not from public rostrums, but in personal converse. Men made pilgrimages to Goethe's library and Coleridge's home to be charmed and instructed by their speech, and the culture of many nations was immeasurably influenced by the thoughts that streamed out from those rich well-springs.

Most of the world-moving speeches are made in the course of conversation. Conferences of diplomats, business-getting arguments, decisions by boards of directors, considerations of corporate policy, all of which influence the political, mercantile and economic maps of the world, are usually the results of careful though informal conversation, and the man whose opinions weigh in such crises is he who has first carefully pondered the words of both antagonist and protagonist.

However important it may be to attain self-control in light social converse, or about the family table, it is undeniably vital to have oneself perfectly in hand while taking part in a momentous conference. Then the hints that we have given on poise, alertness, precision of word, clearness of statement, and force of utterance, with respect to public speech, are equally applicable to conversation.

The form of nervous egotism—for it is both—that suddenly ends in flusters just when the vital words need to be uttered, is the sign of coming defeat, for a conversation is often a contest. If you feel this tendency embarrassing you, be sure to listen to Holmes's advice:

> And when you stick on conversational burs,
> Don't strew your pathway with those dreadful *urs*.

Here bring your will into action, for your trouble is a wandering attention. You must *force* your mind to persist along the chosen line of conversation and resolutely refuse to be diverted by *any* subject or happening that may unexpectedly pop up to distract you. To fail here is to lose effectiveness utterly.

Concentration is the keynote of conversational charm and efficiency. The haphazard habit of expression that uses bird-shot when a bullet is needed insures missing the game, for diplomacy of all sorts rests upon the precise application of precise words, particularly—if one may paraphrase Tallyrand—in those crises when language is no longer used to conceal thought.

We may frequently gain new light on old subjects by looking at word-derivations. Conversation signifies in the original a turn-about exchange of ideas, yet most people seem to regard it as a monologue. Bronson Alcott used to say that many could argue, but few converse. The first thing to remember in conversation, then, is that listening—respectful, sympathetic, alert listening—is not only due to our fellow converser but due to ourselves. Many a reply loses its point because the speaker is so much interested in what he is about to say that it is really no reply at all but merely an irritating and humiliating irrelevancy.

Self-expression is exhilarating. This explains the eternal impulse to decorate totem poles and paint pictures, write poetry and expound philosophy. One of the chief delights of conversation is the opportunity it affords for self-expression. A good conversationalist who monopolizes all the conversation, will be voted a bore because he denies others the enjoyment of self-expression, while a mediocre talker who listens interestedly may be considered a good conversationalist because he permits his companions to please themselves through self-expression. They are praised who please: they please who listen well.

The first step in remedying habits of confusion in manner, awkward bearing, vagueness in thought, and lack of precision in utterance, is to recognize your faults. If you are serenely unconscious of them, no one—least of all yourself—can help you. But once diagnose your own weaknesses, and you can overcome them by doing four things:

1. *WILL* to overcome them, and keep on willing.
2. Hold yourself in hand by assuring yourself that you know precisely what you ought to say. If you cannot do that, be quiet until you are clear on this vital point.
3. Having thus assured yourself, cast out the fear of those who listen to you—they are only human and will respect your words if you really have something to say and say it briefly, simply, and clearly.
4. Have the courage to study the English language until you are master of at least its simpler forms.

## Conversational Hints

Choose some subject that will prove of general interest to the whole group. Do not explain the mechanism of a gas engine at an afternoon tea or the culture of hollyhocks at a stag party.

It is not considered good taste for a man to bare his arm in public and show scars or deformities. It is equally bad form for him to flaunt his own woes, or the deformity of some one else's character. The public demands plays and stories that end happily. All the world is seeking happiness. They cannot long be interested in your ills and troubles. George Cohan made himself a millionaire before he was thirty by writing cheerful plays. One of his rules is generally applicable to conversation: "Always leave them laughing when you say good bye."

Dynamite the "I" out of your conversation. Not one man in nine hundred and seven can talk about himself without being a bore. The man who can perform that feat can achieve marvels without talking about himself, so the eternal "I" is not permissible even in his talk.

If you habitually build your conversation around your own interests it may prove very tiresome to your listener. He may be thinking of bird dogs or dry fly fishing while you are discussing the fourth dimension, or the merits of a cucumber lotion. The charming conversationalist is prepared to talk in terms of his listener's interest. If his listener spends his spare time investigating Guernsey cattle or agitating social reforms, the discriminating conversationalist shapes his remarks accordingly. Richard Washburn Child says he knows a man of mediocre ability who can charm men much abler than himself when he discusses electric lighting. This same man probably would bore, and be bored, if he were forced to converse about music or Madagascar.

Avoid platitudes and hackneyed phrases. If you meet a friend from Keokuk on State Street or on Pike's Peak, it is not necessary to observe: "How small this world is after all!" This observation was doubtless made prior to the formation of Pike's Peak. "This old world is getting better every day." "Farmers' wives do not have to work as hard as formerly." "It is not so much the high cost of living as the cost of high living." Such observations as these excite about the same degree of admiration as is drawn out by the appearance of a 1903-model touring car. If you have nothing fresh or interesting you can always remain silent. How would you like to read a newspaper that flashed out in bold headlines "Nice Weather We Are Having," or daily gave columns to the same old material you had been reading week after week?

## QUESTIONS AND EXERCISES

**1.** Give a short speech describing the conversational bore.

**2.** In a few words give your idea of a charming converser.

**3.** What qualities of the orator should *not* be used in conversation.

**4.** Give a short humorous delineation of the conversational "oracle."

**5.** Give an account of your first day at observing conversation around you.

**6.** Give an account of one day's effort to improve your own conversation.

**7.** Give a list of subjects you heard discussed during any recent period you may select.

**8.** What is meant by "elastic touch" in conversation?

**9.** Make a list of "Bromides," as Gellett Burgess calls those threadbare expressions which "bore us to extinction"—itself a Bromide.

**10.** What causes a phrase to become hackneyed?

**11.** Define the words, (*a*) trite; (*b*) solecism; (*c*) colloquialism; (*d*) slang; (*e*) vulgarism; (*f*) neologism.

**12.** What constitutes pretentious talk?

# *Appendices*

## APPENDIX A
### FIFTY QUESTIONS FOR DEBATE[33]

1. Has Labor Unionism justified its existence?

2. Should all church printing be brought out under the Union Label?

3. Is the Open Shop a benefit to the community?

4. Should arbitration of industrial disputes be made compulsory?

5. Is Profit-Sharing a solution of the wage problem?

6. Is a minimum wage law desirable?

7. Should the eight-hour day be made universal in America?

8. Should the state compensate those who sustain irreparable business loss because of the enactment of laws prohibiting the manufacture and sale of intoxicating drinks?

9. Should public utilities be owned by the municipality?

10. Should marginal trading in stocks be prohibited?

11. Should the national government establish a compulsory system of old-age insurance by taxing the incomes of those to be benefited?

12. Would the triumph of socialistic principles result in deadening personal ambition?

13. Is the Presidential System a better form of government for the United States than the Parliamental System?

14. Should our legislation be shaped toward the gradual abandonment of the protective tariff?

15. Should the government of the larger cities be vested solely in a commission of not more than nine men elected by the voters at large?

16. Should national banks be permitted to issue, subject to tax and government supervision, notes based on their general assets?

17. Should woman be given the ballot on the present basis of suffrage for men?

18. Should the present basis of suffrage be restricted?

---

33 The publishers of this volume will on receipt of request enclosing stamped self-addressed envelope, forward a descriptive list of volumes containing discussions of the art of debate, debatable questions, arguments pro and con, complete briefs and reference sources for debates.

**19.** Is the hope of permanent world-peace a delusion?

**20.** Should the United States send a diplomatic representative to the Vatican?

**21.** Should the Powers of the world substitute an international police for national standing armies?

**22.** Should the United States maintain the Monroe Doctrine?

**23.** Should the Recall of Judges be adopted?

**24.** Should the Initiative and Referendum be adopted as a national principle?

**25.** Is it desirable that the national government should own all railroads operating in interstate territory?

**26.** Is it desirable that the national government should own interstate telegraph and telephone systems?

**27.** Is the national prohibition of the liquor traffic an economic necessity?

**28.** Should the United States army and navy be greatly strengthened?

**29.** Should the same standards of altruism obtain in the relations of nations as in those of individuals?

**30.** Should our government be more highly centralized?

**31.** Should the United States continue its policy of opposing the combination of railroads?

**32.** In case of personal injury to a workman arising out of his employment, should his employer be liable for adequate compensation and be forbidden to set up as a defence a plea of contributory negligence on the part of the workman, or the negligence of a fellow workman?

**33.** Should all corporations doing an interstate business be required to take out a Federal license?

**34.** Should the amount of property that can be transferred by inheritance be limited by law?

**35.** Should equal compensation for equal labor, between women and men, universally prevail?

**36.** Does equal suffrage tend to lessen the interest of woman in her home?

**37.** Should the United States take advantage of the commercial and industrial weakness of foreign nations, brought about by the war, by trying to wrest from them their markets in Central and South America?

**38.** Should teachers of small children in the public schools be selected from among mothers?

**39.** Should football be restricted to colleges, for the sake of physical safety?

40. Should college students who receive compensation for playing summer baseball be debarred from amateur standing?

41. Should daily school-hours and school vacations both be shortened?

42. Should home-study for pupils in grade schools be abolished and longer school-hours substituted?

43. Should the honor system in examinations be adopted in public high-schools?

44. Should all colleges adopt the self-government system for its students?

45. Should colleges be classified by national law and supervision, and uniform entrance and graduation requirements maintained by each college in a particular class?

46. Should ministers be required to spend a term of years in some trade, business, or profession, before becoming pastors?

47. Is the Y.M.C.A. losing its spiritual power?

48. Is the church losing its hold on thinking people?

49. Are the people of the United States more devoted to religion than ever?

50. Does the reading of magazines contribute to intellectual shallowness?

# APPENDIX B

## THIRTY THEMES FOR SPEECHES

*with Source References for Material.*

**1.** KINSHIP, A FOUNDATION STONE OF CIVILIZATION.
"The State," Woodrow Wilson.

**2.** INITIATIVE AND REFERENDUM.
"The Popular Initiative and Referendum," O. M. Barnes.

**3.** RECIPROCITY WITH CANADA.
Article in *Independent*, 53: 2874; article in *North American Review*, 178: 205.

**4.** IS MANKIND PROGRESSING?
Book of same title, M. M. Ballou.

**5.** MOSES THE PEERLESS LEADER.
Lecture by John Lord, in "Beacon Lights of History." [NOTE: This set of books contains a vast store of material for speeches.]

**6.** THE SPOILS SYSTEM.
Sermon by the Rev. Dr. Henry van Dyke, reported in the *New York Tribune*, February 25, 1895.

**7.** THE NEGRO IN BUSINESS.
Part III, Annual Report of the Secretary of Internal Affairs, Pennsylvania, 1912.

**8.** IMMIGRATION AND DEGRADATION.
"Americans or Aliens?" Howard B. Grose.

**9.** WHAT IS THE THEATRE DOING FOR AMERICA?
"The Drama Today," Charlton Andrews.

**10.** SUPERSTITION.
"Curiosities of Popular Custom," William S. Walsh.

**11.** THE PROBLEM OF OLD AGE.
"Old Age Deferred," Arnold Lorand.

**12.** WHO IS THE TRAMP?
Article in *Century*, 28: 41.

**13.** TWO MEN INSIDE.
"Dr. Jekyll and Mr. Hyde," R. L. Stevenson.

**14.** THE OVERTHROW OF POVERTY.
"The Panacea for Poverty," Madison Peters.

**15.** MORALS AND MANNERS.
"A Christian's Habits," Robert E. Speer.

**16.** JEW AND CHRISTIAN.
"Jesus the Jew," Harold Weinstock.

**17.** EDUCATION AND THE MOVING PICTURE.
Article by J. Berg Esenwein in "The Theatre of Science," Robert Grau.

**18.** BOOKS AS FOOD.
"Books and Reading," R. C. Gage and Alfred Harcourt.

**19.** WHAT IS A NOVEL?
"The Technique of the Novel," Charles F. Home.

**20.** MODERN FICTION AND MODERN LIFE.
Article in *Lippincott's*, October, 1907.

**21.** OUR PROBLEM IN MEXICO.
"The Real Mexico," Hamilton Fyfe.

**22.** THE JOY OF RECEIVING.
Article in *Woman's Home Companion*, December, 1914.

**23.** PHYSICAL TRAINING VS. COLLEGE ATHLETICS.
Article in *Literary Digest*, November 28, 1914.

**24.** CHEER UP.
"The Science of Happiness," Jean Finot.

**25.** THE SQUARE PEG IN THE ROUND HOLE.
"The Job, the Man, and the Boss," Katherine Blackford and Arthur Newcomb.

**26.** THE DECAY OF ACTING.
Article in *Current Opinion*, November, 1914.

**27.** THE YOUNG MAN AND THE CHURCH.
"A Young Man's Religion," N. McGee Waters.

**28.** INHERITING SUCCESS.
Article in *Current Opinion*, November, 1914.

**29.** THE INDIAN IN OKLAHOMA.
Article in *Literary Digest*, November 28, 1914.

**30.** HATE AND THE NATION.
Article in *Literary Digest*, November 14, 1914.

# APPENDIX C

## Suggestive Subjects for Speeches[34]
### with Occasional Hints on Treatment

1. **Movies and Morals.**

2. **The Truth About Lying.**
   The essence of truth-telling and lying. Lies that are not so considered. The subtleties of distinctions required. Examples of implied and acted lies.

3. **Benefits That Follow Disasters.**
   Benefits that have arisen out of floods, fires, earthquakes, wars, etc.

4. **Haste for Leisure.**
   How the speed mania is born of a vain desire to enjoy a leisure that never comes or, on the contrary, how the seeming haste of the world has given men shorter hours off labor and more time for rest, study, and pleasure.

5. **St. Paul's Message to New York.**
   Truths from the Epistles pertinent to the great cities of today.

6. **Education and Crime.**

7. **Loss Is the Mother of Gain.**
   How many men have been content until, losing all, they exerted their best efforts to regain success, and succeeded more largely than before.

8. **Egoism vs. Egotism.**

9. **Blunders of Young Fogyism.**

10. **The Waste of Middle-Men in Charity Systems.**
    The cost of collecting funds for, and administering help to, the needy. The weakness of organized philanthropy as compared with the giving that gives itself.

11. **The Economy of Organized Charity.**
    The other side of the picture.

12. **Freedom of the Press.**
    The true forces that hurtfully control too many newspapers are not those of arbitrary governments but the corrupting influences of moneyed and political interests, fear of the liquor power, and the desire to please sensation-loving readers.

13. **Helen Keller: Optimist.**

14. **Back to the Farm.**
    A study of the reasons underlying the movement.

15. **It Was Ever Thus.**
    In ridicule of the pessimist who is never surprised at seeing failure.

---

34 It must be remembered that the phrasing of the subject will not necessarily serve for the title.

**16.** THE VOCATIONAL HIGH SCHOOL.

Value of direct training compared with the policy of laying broader foundations for later building. How the two theories work out in practise. Each plan can be especially applied in cases that seem to need special treatment.

**17.** ALL KINDS OF TURNING DONE HERE.

A humorous, yet serious, discussion of the flopping, wind-mill character.

**18.** THE EGOISTIC ALTRUIST.

Herbert Spencer's theory as discussed in "The Data of Ethics."

**19.** HOW THE CITY MENACES THE NATION.

Economic perils in massed population. Show also the other side. Signs of the problem's being solved.

**20.** THE ROBUST NOTE IN MODERN POETRY.

A comparison of the work of Galsworthy, Masefield and Kipling with that of some earlier poets.

**21.** THE IDEALS OF SOCIALISM.

**22.** THE FUTURE OF THE SMALL CITY.

How men are coming to see the economic advantages of smaller municipalities.

**23.** CENSORSHIP FOR THE THEATRE.

Its relation to morals and art. Its difficulties and its benefits.

**24.** FOR SUCH A TIME AS THIS.

Mordecai's expression and its application to opportunities in modern woman's life.

**25.** IS THE PRESS VENAL?

**26.** SAFETY FIRST.

**27.** MENES AND EXTREMES.

**28.** RUBICONS AND PONTOONS.

How great men not only made momentous decisions but created means to carry them out. A speech full of historical examples.

**29.** ECONOMY A REVENUE.

**30.** THE PATRIOTISM OF PROTEST AGAINST POPULAR IDOLS.

**31.** SAVONAROLA, THE DIVINE OUTCAST.

**32.** THE TRUE POLITICIAN.

Revert to the original meaning of the word. Build the speech around one man as the chief example.

**33.** COLONELS AND SHELLS.

Leadership and "cannon fodder"—a protest against war in its effect on the common people.

34. **WHY IS A MILITANT?**
A dispassionate examination of the claims of the British militant suffragette.

35. **ART AND MORALS.**
The difference between the nude and the naked in art.

36. **CAN MY COUNTRY BE WRONG?**
False patriotism and true, with examples of popularly-hated patriots.

37. **GOVERNMENT BY PARTY.**
An analysis of our present political system and the movement toward reform.

38. **THE EFFECTS OF FICTION ON HISTORY.**

39. **THE EFFECTS OF HISTORY ON FICTION.**

40. **THE INFLUENCE OF WAR ON LITERATURE.**

41. **CHINESE GORDON.**
A eulogy.

42. **TAXES AND HIGHER EDUCATION.**
Should all men be compelled to contribute to the support of universities and professional schools?

43. **PRIZE CATTLE VS. PRIZE BABIES.**
Is Eugenics a science? And is it practicable?

44. **BENEVOLENT AUTOCRACY.**
Is a strongly paternal government better for the masses than a much larger freedom for the individual?

45. **SECOND-HAND OPINIONS.**
The tendency to swallow reviews instead of forming one's own views.

46. **PARENTAGE OR POWER?**
A study of which form of aristocracy must eventually prevail, that of blood or that of talent.

47. **THE BLESSING OF DISCONTENT.**
Based on many examples of what has been accomplished by those who have not "let well-enough alone."

48. **"CORRUPT AND CONTENTED."**
A study of the relation of the apathetic voter to vicious government.

49. **THE MOLOCH OF CHILD-LABOR.**

50. **EVERY MAN HAS A RIGHT TO WORK.**

51. **CHARITY THAT FOSTERS PAUPERISM.**

52. **"NOT IN OUR STARS BUT IN OURSELVES."**
Destiny vs. choice.

53. **ENVIRONMENT VS. HEREDITY.**

**54. THE BRAVERY OF DOUBT.**

Doubt not mere unbelief. True grounds for doubt. What doubt has led to. Examples. The weakness of mere doubt. The attitude of the wholesome doubter *versus* that of the wholesale doubter.

**55. THE SPIRIT OF MONTICELLO.**

A message from the life of Thomas Jefferson.

**56. NARROWNESS IN SPECIALISM.**

The dangers of specializing without first possessing broad knowledge. The eye too close to one object. Balance is a vital prerequisite for specialization.

**57. RESPONSIBILITY OF LABOR UNIONS TO THE LAW**

**58. THE FUTURE OF SOUTHERN LITERATURE.**

What conditions in the history, temperament and environment of our Southern people indicate a bright literary future.

**59. WOMAN THE HOPE OF IDEALISM IN AMERICA.**

**60. THE VALUE OF DEBATING CLUBS.**

**61. AN ARMY OF THIRTY MILLIONS.**

In praise of the Sunday-school.

**62. THE BABY.**

How the ever-new baby holds mankind in unselfish courses and saves us all from going lastingly wrong.

**63. LO, THE POOR CAPITALIST.**

His trials and problems.

**64. HONEY AND STING.**

A lesson from the bee.

**65. UNGRATEFUL REPUBLICS.**

Examples from history.

**66. "EVERY MAN HAS HIS PRICE."**

Horace Walpole's cynical remark is not true now, nor was it true even in his own corrupt era. Of what sort are the men who cannot be bought? Examples.

**67. THE SCHOLAR IN DIPLOMACY.**

Examples in American life.

**68. LOCKS AND KEYS.**

There is a key for every lock. No difficulty so great, no truth so obscure, no problem so involved, but that there is a key to fit the lock. The search for the right key, the struggle to adjust it, the vigilance to retain it—these are some of the problems of success.

**69. RIGHT MAKES MIGHT.**

70. ROOMING WITH A GHOST.
Influence of the woman graduate of fifty years before on the college girl who lives in the room once occupied by the distinguished "old grad."

71. NO FACT IS A SINGLE FACT.
The importance of weighing facts relatively.

72. IS CLASSICAL EDUCATION DEAD TO RISE NO MORE?

73. INVECTIVE AGAINST NIETSCHE'S PHILOSOPHY.

74. WHY HAVE WE BOSSES?
A fair-minded examination of the uses and abuses of the political "leader."

75. A PLEA FOR SETTLEMENT WORK.

76. CREDULITY VS. FAITH.

77. WHAT IS HUMOR?

78. USE AND ABUSE OF THE CARTOON.

79. THE PULPIT IN POLITICS.

80. ARE COLLEGES GROWING TOO LARGE?

81. THE DOOM OF ABSOLUTISM.

82. SHALL WOMAN HELP KEEP HOUSE FOR TOWN, CITY, STATE, AND NATION?

83. THE EDUCATIONAL TEST FOR SUFFRAGE.

84. THE PROPERTY TEST FOR SUFFRAGE.

85. THE MENACE OF THE PLUTOCRAT.

86. THE COST OF HIGH LIVING.

87. THE COST OF CONVENIENCES.

88. WASTE IN AMERICAN LIFE.

89. THE EFFECT OF THE PHOTOPLAY ON THE "LEGITIMATE" THEATRE.

90. ROOM FOR THE KICKER.

91. THE NEED FOR TRAINED DIPLOMATS.

92. THE SHADOW OF THE IRON CHANCELLOR.

93. THE TYRANNY OF THE CROWD.

94. IS OUR TRIAL BY JURY SATISFACTORY?

95. THE HIGH COST OF SECURING JUSTICE.

96. THE NEED FOR SPEEDIER COURT TRIALS.

97. TRIUMPHS OF THE AMERICAN ENGINEER.

98. GOETHALS AND GORGAS.

99. PUBLIC EDUCATION MAKES SERVICE TO THE PUBLIC A DUTY.

100. MAN OWES HIS LIFE TO THE COMMON GOOD.

# APPENDIX D
## SPEECHES FOR STUDY AND PRACTISE


## Brave Little Belgium
### NEWELL DWIGHT HILLIS
*Delivered in Plymouth Church, Brooklyn, N.Y., October 18, 1914.*
*Used by permission.*

Long ago Plato made a distinction between the occasions of war and the causes of war. The occasions of war lie upon the surface, and are known and read of all men, while the causes of war are embedded in racial antagonisms, in political and economic controversies. Narrative historians portray the occasions of war; philosophic historians, the secret and hidden causes. Thus the spark of fire that falls is the occasion of an explosion, but the cause of the havoc is the relation between charcoal, niter and saltpeter. The occasion of the Civil War was the firing upon Fort Sumter. The cause was the collision between the ideals of the Union presented by Daniel Webster and the secession taught by Calhoun. The occasion of the American Revolution was the Stamp Tax; the cause was the conviction on the part of our forefathers that men who had freedom in worship carried also the capacity for self-government. The occasion of the French Revolution was the purchase of a diamond necklace for Queen Marie Antoinette at a time when the treasury was exhausted; the cause of the revolution was feudalism. Not otherwise, the occasion of the great conflict that is now shaking our earth was the assassination of an Austrian boy and girl, but the cause is embedded in racial antagonisms and economic competition.

As for Russia, the cause of the war was her desire to obtain the Bosphorus—and an open seaport, which is the prize offered for her attack upon Germany. As for Austria, the cause of the war is her fear of the growing power of the Balkan States, and the progressive slicing away of her territory. As for France, the cause of the war is the instinct of self-preservation, that resists an invading host. As for Germany, the cause is her deep-seated conviction that every country has a moral right to the mouth of its greatest river; unable to compete with England, by roundabout sea routes and a Kiel Canal, she wants to use the route that nature digged for her through the mouth of the Rhine. As for England, the motherland is fighting to recover her sense of security. During the Napoleonic wars the second William Pitt explained the quadrupling of the taxes, the increase of the navy, and the sending of an English army against France, by the statement that justification of this proposed war is the "Preservation of England's sense of security." Ten years ago England lost her sense of security. Today she is not seeking to preserve, but to recover, the lost sense of security. She proposes to do this by destroying Germany's ironclads, demobilizing her army, wiping out her forts, and the partition of her provinces. The occasions of the war vary, with the color of the paper—"white" and "gray" and "blue"—but the causes of this war are embedded in racial antagonisms and economic and political differences.

## Why Little Belgium Has the Center of the Stage

Tonight our study concerns little Belgium, her people, and their part in this conflict. Be the reasons what they may, this little land stands in the center of the stage and holds the limelight. Once more David, armed with a sling, has gone up against ten Goliaths. It is an amazing spectacle, this, one of the smallest of the States, battling with the largest of the giants! Belgium has a standing army of 42,000 men, and Germany, with three reserves, perhaps 7,000,000 or 8,000,000. Without waiting for any assistance, this little Belgium band went up against 2,000,000. It is as if a honey bee had decided to attack an eagle come to loot its honeycomb. It is as if an antelope had turned against a lion. Belgium has but 11,000 square miles of land, less than the States of Massachusetts, Rhode Island and Connecticut. Her population is 7,500,000, less than the single State of New York. You could put twenty-two Belgiums in our single State of Texas. Much of her soil is thin; her handicaps are heavy, but the industry of her people has turned the whole land into one vast flower and vegetable garden. The soil of Minnesota and the Dakotas is new soil, and yet our farmers there average but fifteen bushels of wheat to the acre. Belgium's soil has been used for centuries, but it averages thirty-seven bushels of wheat to the acre. If we grow twenty-four bushels of barley on an acre of ground, Belgium grows fifty; she produces 300 bushels of potatoes, where the Maine farmer harvests 90 bushels. Belgium's average population per square mile has risen to 645 people. If Americans practised intensive farming; if the population of Texas were as dense as it is in Belgium—100,000,000 of the United States, Canada and Central America could all move to Texas, while if our entire country was as densely populated as Belgium's, everybody in the world could live comfortably within the limits of our country.

## The Life of the People

And yet, little Belgium has no gold or silver mines, and all the treasures of copper and zinc and lead and anthracite and oil have been denied her. The gold is in the heart of her people. No other land holds a race more prudent, industrious and thrifty! It is a land where everybody works. In the winter when the sun does not rise until half past seven, the Belgian cottages have lights in their windows at five, and the people are ready for an eleven-hour day. As a rule all children work after 12 years of age. The exquisite pointed lace that has made Belgium famous, is wrought by women who fulfill the tasks of the household fulfilled by American women, and then begins their task upon the exquisite laces that have sent their name and fame throughout the world. Their wages are low, their work hard, but their life is so peaceful and prosperous that few Belgians ever emigrate to foreign countries. Of late they have made their education compulsory, their schools free. It is doubtful whether any other country has made a greater success of their system of transportation. You will pay 50 cents to journey some twenty odd miles out to Roslyn, on our Long Island railroad, but in Belgium a commuter journeys twenty miles in to the factory and back again every night and makes the six double daily journeys at an entire cost of 37½ cents per week, less than the amount that you pay for the journey one way for a like distance in this country. Out of this has come Belgium's prosperity. She has the money to buy goods from other countries, and she has the property to export to foreign lands. Last year the United States, with its hundred millions of people, imported less than $2,000,000,000, and exported $2,500,000,000. If our people had been as prosperous per capita as Belgium, we would have purchased from other countries $12,000,000,000 worth of goods and exported $10,000,000,000.

So largely have we been dependent upon Belgium that many of the engines used in digging the Panama Canal came from the Cockerill works that produce two thousands of these engines every year in Liege. It is often said that the Belgians have the best courts in existence. The Supreme Court of Little Belgium has but one Justice. Without waiting for an appeal, just as soon as a decision has been reached by a lower Court, while the matters are still fresh in mind and all the witnesses and facts readily obtainable, this Supreme Justice reviews all the objections raised on either side and without a motion from anyone passes on the decision of the inferior court. On the other hand, the lower courts are open to an immediate settlement of disputes between the wage earners, and newsboys and fishermen are almost daily seen going to the judge for a decision regarding a dispute over five or ten cents. When the judge has cross-questioned both sides, without the presence of attorneys, or the necessity of serving a process, or raising a dollar and a quarter, as here, the poorest of the poor have their wrongs righted. It is said that not one decision out of one hundred is appealed, thus calling for the existence of an attorney.

To all other institutions organized in the interest of the wage earner has been added the national savings bank system, that makes loans to men of small means, that enables the farmer and the working man to buy a little garden and build a house, while at the same time insuring the working man against accident and sickness. Belgium is a poor man's country, it has been said, because institutions have been administered in the interest of the men of small affairs.

## The Great Belgium Plain in History

But the institutions of Belgium and the industrial prosperity of her people alone are not equal to the explanation of her unique heroism. Long ago, in his Commentaries, Julius Cæsar said that Gaul was inhabited by three tribes, the Belgæ, the Aquitani, the Celts, "of whom the Belgæ were the bravest." History will show that Belgians have courage as their native right, for only the brave could have survived. The southeastern part of Belgium is a series of rock plains, and if these plains have been her good fortune in times of peace, they have furnished the battlefields of Western Europe for two thousand years. Northern France and Western Germany are rough, jagged and wooded, but the Belgian plains were ideal battlefields. For this reason the generals of Germany and of France have usually met and struggled for the mastery on these wide Belgian plains. On one of these grounds Julius Cæsar won the first battle that is recorded. Then came King Clovis and the French, with their campaigns; toward these plains also the Saracens were hurrying when assaulted by Charles Martel. On the Belgian plains the Dutch burghers and the Spanish armies, led by Bloody Alva, fought out their battle. Hither, too, came Napoleon, and the great mound of Waterloo is the monument to the Duke of Wellington's victory. It was to the Belgian plains, also, that the German general, last August, rushed his troops. Every college and every city searches for some level spot of land where the contest between opposing teams may be held, and for more than two thousand years the Belgian plain has been the scene of the great battles between the warring nations of Western Europe.

Now, out of all these collisions there has come a hardy race, inured to peril, rich in fortitude, loyalty, patience, thrift, self-reliance and persevering faith. For five hundred years the Belgian children and youth have been brought up upon the deeds of noble renown, achieved by their ancestors. If Julius Cæsar were here today he would wear Belgium's bravery like a bright sword, girded to his thigh. And when this brave little people, with a standing army of forty-two thousand men, single-handed defied two millions of Germans, it tells us that Ajax has come back once more to defy the god of lightnings.

### A Thrilling Chapter from Belgium's History

Perhaps one or two chapters torn from the pages of Belgium history will enable us to understand her present-day heroism, just as one golden bough plucked from the forest will explain the richness of the autumn. You remember that Venice was once the financial center of the world. Then when the bankers lost confidence in the navy of Venice they put their jewels and gold into saddle bags and moved the financial center of the world to Nuremburg, because its walls were seven feet thick and twenty feet high. Later, about 1500 A.D., the discovery of the New World turned all the peoples into races of sea-going folk, and the English and Dutch captains vied with the sailors of Spain and Portugal. No captains were more prosperous than the mariners of Antwerp. In 1568 there were 500 marble mansions in this city on the Meuse. Belgium became a casket filled with jewels. Then it was that Spain turned covetous eyes northward. Sated with his pleasures, broken by indulgence and passion, the Emperor Charles the Fifth resigned his gold and throne to his son, King Philip. Finding his coffers depleted, Philip sent the Duke of Alva, with 10,000 Spanish soldiers, out on a looting expedition. Their approach filled Antwerp with consternation, for her merchants were busy with commerce and not with war. The sack of Antwerp by the Spaniards makes up a revolting page in history. Within three days 8,000 men, women and children were massacred, and the Spanish soldiers, drunk with wine and blood, hacked, drowned and burned like fiends that they were. The Belgian historian tells us that 500 marble residences were reduced to blackened ruins. One incident will make the event stand out. When the Spaniards approached the city a wealthy burgher hastened the day of his son's marriage. During the ceremony the soldiers broke down the gate of the city and crossed the threshold of the rich man's house. When they had stripped the guests of their purses and gems, unsatisfied, they killed the bridegroom, slew the men, and carried the bride out into the night. The next morning a young woman, crazed and half clad, was found in the street, searching among the dead bodies. At last she found a youth, whose head she lifted upon her knees, over which she crooned her songs, as a young mother soothes her babe. A Spanish officer passing by, humiliated by the spectacle, ordered a soldier to use his dagger and put the girl out of her misery.

## The Horrors of the Inquisition

Having looted Antwerp, the treasure chest of Belgium, the Spaniards set up the Inquisition as an organized means of securing property. It is a strange fact that the Spaniard has excelled in cruelty as other nations have excelled in art or science or invention. Spain's cruelty to the Moors and the rich Jews forms one of the blackest chapters in history. Inquisitors became fiends. Moors were starved, tortured, burned, flung in wells, Jewish bankers had their tongues thrust through little iron rings; then the end of the tongue was seared that it might swell, and the banker was led by a string in the ring through the streets of the city. The women and the children were put on rafts that were pushed out into the Mediterranean Sea. When the swollen corpses drifted ashore, the plague broke out, and when that black plague spread over Spain it seemed like the justice of outraged nature. The expulsion of the Moors was one of the deadliest blows ever struck at science, commerce, art and literature. The historian tracks Spain across the continents by a trail of blood. Wherever Spain's hand has fallen it has paralyzed. From the days of Cortez, wherever her captains have given a pledge, the tongue that spake has been mildewed with lies and treachery. The wildest beasts are not in the jungle; man is the lion that rends, man is the leopard that tears, man's hate is the serpent that poisons, and the Spaniard entered Belgium to turn a garden into a wilderness. Within one year, 1568, Antwerp, that began with 125,000 people, ended it with 50,000. Many multitudes were put to death by the sword and stake, but many, many thousands fled to England, to begin anew their lives as manufacturers and mariners; and for years Belgium was one quaking peril, an inferno, whose torturers were Spaniards. The visitor in Antwerp is still shown the rack upon which they stretched the merchants that they might yield up their hidden gold. The Painted Lady may be seen. Opening her arms, she embraces the victim. The Spaniard, with his spear, forced the merchant into the deadly embrace. As the iron arms concealed in velvet folded together, one spike passed through each eye, another through the mouth, another through the heart. The Painted Lady's lips were poisoned, so that a kiss was fatal. The dungeon whose sides were forced together by screws, so that each day the victim saw his cell growing less and less, and knew that soon he would be crushed to death, was another instrument of torture. Literally thousands of innocent men and women were burned alive in the market place.

There is no more piteous tragedy in history than the story of the decline and ruin of this superbly prosperous, literary and artistic country, and yet out of the ashes came new courage. Burned, broken, the Belgians and the Dutch were not beaten. Pushed at last into Holland, where they united their fortunes with the Dutch, they cut the dykes of Holland, and let in the ocean, and clinging to the dykes with their finger tips, fought their way back to the land; but no sooner had the last of the Spaniards gone than out of their rags and poverty they founded a university as a monument to the providence of God in delivering them out of the hands of their enemies. For, the Sixteenth Century, in the form of a brave knight, wears little Belgium and Holland like a red rose upon his heart.

## The Death of Egmont

But some of you will say that the Belgian people must have been rebels and guilty of some excess, and that had they remained quiescent, and not fomented treason, that no such fate could have overtaken them at the hands of Spain. Very well. I will take a youth who, at the beginning, believed in Charles the Fifth, a man who was as true to his ideals as the needle to the pole. One day the "Bloody Council" decreed the death of Egmont and Horn. Immediately afterward, the Duke of Alva sent an invitation to Egmont to be the guest of honor at a banquet in his own house. A servant from the palace that night delivered to the Count a slip of paper, containing a warning to take the fleetest horse and flee the city, and from that moment not to eat or sleep without pistols at his hand. To all this Egmont responded that no monster ever lived who could, with an invitation of hospitality, trick a patriot. Like a brave man, the Count went to the Duke's palace. He found the guests assembled, but when he had handed his hat and cloak to the servant, Alva gave a sign, and from behind the curtains came Spanish musqueteers, who demanded his sword. For instead of a banquet hall, the Count was taken to a cellar, fitted up as a dungeon. Already Egmont had all but died for his country. He had used his ships, his trade, his gold, for righting the people's wrongs. He was a man of a large family—a wife and eleven children—and people loved him as to idolatry. But Alva was inexorable. He had made up his mind that the merchants and burghers had still much hidden gold, and if he killed their bravest and best, terror would fall upon all alike, and that the gold he needed would be forthcoming. That all the people might witness the scene, he took his prisoners to Brussels and decided to behead them in the public square. In the evening Egmont received the notice that his head would be chopped off the next day. A scaffold was erected in the public square. That evening he wrote a letter that is a marvel of restraint.

"Sire—I have learned this evening the sentence which your majesty has been pleased to pronounce upon me. Although I have never had a thought, and believe myself never to have done a deed, which would tend to the prejudice of your service, or to the detriment of true religion, nevertheless I take patience to bear that which it has pleased the good God to permit. Therefore, I pray your majesty to have compassion on my poor wife, my children and my servants, having regard to my past service. In which hope I now commend myself to the mercy of God. From Brussels, ready to die, this 5th of June, 1568.

"Lamoral D' Egmont"

Thus died a man who did as much probably for Holland as John Eliot for England, or Lafayette for France, or Samuel Adams for this young republic.

## The Woe of Belgium

And now out of all this glorious past comes the woe of Belgium. Desolation has come like the whirlwind, and destruction like a tornado. But ninety days ago and Belgium was a hive of industry, and in the fields were heard the harvest songs. Suddenly, Germany struck Belgium. The whole world has but one voice, "Belgium has innocent hands." She was led like a lamb to the slaughter. When the lover of Germany is asked to explain Germany's breaking of her solemn treaty upon the neutrality of Belgium, the German stands dumb and speechless. Merchants honor their written obligations. True citizens consider their word as good as their bond; Germany gave treaty, and in the presence of God and the civilized world, entered into a solemn covenant with Belgium. To the end of time, the German must expect this taunt, "as worthless as a German treaty." Scarcely less black the two or three known examples of cruelty wrought upon nonresisting Belgians. In Brooklyn lives a Belgian woman. She planned to return home in late July to visit a father who had suffered paralysis, an aged mother and a sister who nursed both. When the Germans decided to burn that village in Eastern Belgium, they did not wish to burn alive this old and helpless man, so they bayonetted to death the old man and woman, and the daughter that nursed them.

Let us judge not, that we be not judged. This is the one example of atrocity that you and I might be able personally to prove. But every loyal German in the country can make answer: "These soldiers were drunk with wine and blood. Such an atrocity misrepresents Germany and her soldiers. The breaking of Germany's treaty with Belgium represents the dishonor of a military ring, and not the perfidy of 68,000,000 of people. We ask that judgment be postponed until all the facts are in." But, meanwhile, the man who loves his fellows, at midnight in his dreams walks across the fields of broken Belgium. All through the night air there comes the sob of Rachel, weeping for her children, because they are not. In moods of bitterness, of doubt and despair the heart cries out, "How could a just God permit such cruelty upon innocent Belgium?" No man knows. "Clouds and darkness are round about God's throne." The spirit of evil caused this war, but the Spirit of God may bring good out of it, just as the summer can repair the ravages of winter. Meanwhile the heart bleeds for Belgium. For Brussels, the third most beautiful city in Europe! For Louvain, once rich with its libraries, cathedrals, statues, paintings, missals, manuscripts— now a ruin. Alas! for the ruined harvests and the smoking villages! Alas, for the Cathedral that is a heap, and the library that is a ruin. Where the angel of happiness was there stalk Famine and Death. Gone, the Land of Grotius! Perished the paintings of Rubens! Ruined is Louvain. Where the wheat waved, now the hillsides are billowy with graves. But let us believe that God reigns. Perchance Belgium is slain like the Saviour, that militarism may die like Satan. Without shedding of innocent blood there is no remission of sins through tyranny and greed. There is no wine without the crushing of the grapes from the tree of life. Soon Liberty, God's dear child, will stand within the scene and comfort the desolate. Falling upon the great world's altar stairs, in this hour when wisdom is ignorance, and the strongest man clutches at dust and straw, let us believe with faith victorious over tears, that some time God will gather broken-hearted little Belgium into His arms and comfort her as a Father comforteth his well-beloved child.

# The New Americanism

HENRY WATTERSON

*(Abridged)*

Eight years ago tonight, there stood where I am standing now a young Georgian, who, not without reason, recognized the "significance" of his presence here, and, in words whose eloquence I cannot hope to recall, appealed from the New South to New England for a united country.

He is gone now. But, short as his life was, its heaven-born mission was fulfilled; the dream of his childhood was realized; for he had been appointed by God to carry a message of peace on earth, good will to men, and, this done, he vanished from the sight of mortal eyes, even as the dove from the ark.

Grady told us, and told us truly, of that typical American who, in Dr. Talmage's mind's eye, was coming, but who, in Abraham Lincoln's actuality, had already come. In some recent studies into the career of that man, I have encountered many startling confirmations of this judgment; and from that rugged trunk, drawing its sustenance from gnarled roots, interlocked with Cavalier sprays and Puritan branches deep beneath the soil, shall spring, is springing, a shapely tree—symmetric in all its parts—under whose sheltering boughs this nation shall have the new birth of freedom Lincoln promised it, and mankind the refuge which was sought by the forefathers when they fled from oppression. Thank God, the ax, the gibbet, and the stake have had their day. They have gone, let us hope, to keep company with the lost arts. It has been demonstrated that great wrongs may be redressed and great reforms be achieved without the shedding of one drop of human blood; that vengeance does not purify, but brutalizes; and that tolerance, which in private transactions is reckoned a virtue, becomes in public affairs a dogma of the most far-seeing statesmanship.

So I appeal from the men in silken hose who danced to music made by slaves—and called it freedom—from the men in bell-crowned hats, who led *Hester Prynne* to her shame—and called it religion—to that Americanism which reaches forth its arms to smite wrong with reason and truth, secure in the power of both. I appeal from the patriarchs of New England to the poets of New England; from Endicott to Lowell; from Winthrop to Longfellow; from Norton to Holmes; and I appeal in the name and by the rights of that common citizenship—of that common origin—back of both the Puritan and the Cavalier—to which all of us owe our being. Let the dead past, consecrated by the blood of its martyrs, not by its savage hatreds—darkened alike by kingcraft and priestcraft— let the dead past bury its dead. Let the present and the future ring with the song of the singers. Blessed be the lessons they teach, the laws they make. Blessed be the eye to see, the light to reveal. Blessed be Tolerance, sitting ever on the right hand of God to guide the way with loving word, as blessed be all that brings us nearer the goal of true religion, true Republicanism, and true patriotism, distrust of watchwords and labels, shams and heroes, belief in our country and ourselves. It was not Cotton Mather, but John Greenleaf Whittier, who cried:—

"Dear God and Father of us all,
Forgive our faith in cruel lies,
Forgive the blindness that denies.

"Cast down our idols—overturn
Our bloody altars—make us see
Thyself in Thy humanity!"

## Founder's Day Address
### JOHN MORLEY
*(Abridged)*
*Carnegie Institute, Pittsburgh, Pa., November 3, 1904.*

What is so hard as a just estimate of the events of our own time? It is only now, a century and a half later, that we really perceive that a writer has something to say for himself when he calls Wolfe's exploit at Quebec the turning point in modern history. And to-day it is hard to imagine any rational standard that would not make the American Revolution—an insurrection of thirteen little colonies, with a population of 3,000,000 scattered in a distant wilderness among savages—a mightier event in many of its aspects than the volcanic convulsion in France. Again, the upbuilding of your great West on this continent is reckoned by some the most important world movement of the last hundred years. But is it more important than the amazing, imposing and perhaps disquieting apparition of Japan? One authority insists that when Russia descended into the Far East and pushed her frontier on the Pacific to the forty-third degree of latitude that was one of the most far-reaching facts of modern history, tho it almost escaped the eyes of Europe—all her perceptions then monopolized by affairs in the Levant. Who can say? Many courses of the sun were needed before men could take the full historic measures of Luther, Calvin, Knox; the measure of Loyola, the Council of Trent, and all the counter-reformation. The center of gravity is forever shifting, the political axis of the world perpetually changing. But we are now far enough off to discern how stupendous a thing was done when, after two cycles of bitter war, one foreign, the other civil and intestine, Pitt and Washington, within a span of less than a score of years, planted the foundations of the American Republic.

What Forbes's stockade at Fort Pitt has grown to be you know better than I. The huge triumphs of Pittsburg in material production—iron, steel, coke, glass, and all the rest of it—can only be told in colossal figures that are almost as hard to realize in our minds as the figures of astronomical distance or geologic time. It is not quite clear that all the founders of the Commonwealth would have surveyed the wonderful scene with the same exultation as their descendants. Some of them would have denied that these great centers of industrial democracy either in the Old World or in the New always stand for progress. Jefferson said, "I view great cities as pestilential to the morals, the health, and the liberties of man. I consider the class of artificers," he went on, "as the panders of vice, and the instrument by which the liberties of a country are generally overthrown." In England they reckon 70 per cent. of our population as dwellers in towns. With you, I read that only 25 per cent. of the population live in groups so large as 4,000 persons. If Jefferson was right our outlook would be dark. Let us hope that he was wrong, and in fact toward the end of his time qualified his early view. Franklin, at any rate, would, I feel sure, have reveled in it all.

That great man—a name in the forefront among the practical intelligences of human history—once told a friend that when he dwelt upon the rapid progress that mankind was making in politics, morals, and the arts of living, and when he considered that each one improvement always begets another, he felt assured that the future progress of the race was likely to be quicker than it had ever been. He was never wearied of foretelling inventions yet to come, and he wished he could revisit the earth at the end of a century to see how mankind was getting on. With all my heart I share his wish. Of all the men who have built up great States, I do believe there is not one whose alacrity of sound sense and single-eyed beneficence of aim could be more safely trusted than Franklin to draw light from the clouds and pierce the economic and political confusions of our time. We can imagine the amazement and complacency of that shrewd benignant mind if he could watch all the giant marvels of your mills and furnaces, and all the apparatus devised by the wondrous inventive faculties of man; if he could have foreseen that his experiments with the kite in his garden at Philadelphia, his tubes, his Leyden jars would end in the electric appliances of to-day—the largest electric plant in all the world on the site of Fort Duquesne; if he could have heard of 5,000,000,000 of passengers carried in the United States by electric motor power in a year; if he could have realized all the rest of the magician's tale of our time.

Still more would he have been astounded and elated could he have foreseen, beyond all advances in material production, the unbroken strength of that political structure which he had so grand a share in rearing. Into this very region where we are this afternoon, swept wave after wave of immigration; English from Virginia flowed over the border, bringing English traits, literature, habits of mind; Scots, or Scots-Irish, originally from Ulster, flowed in from Central Pennsylvania; Catholics from Southern Ireland; new hosts from Southern and East Central Europe. This is not the Fourth of July. But people of every school would agree that it is no exuberance of rhetoric, it is only sober truth to say that the persevering absorption and incorporation of all this ceaseless torrent of heterogenous elements into one united, stable, industrious, and pacific State is an achievement that neither the Roman Empire nor the Roman Church, neither Byzantine Empire nor Russian, not Charles the Great nor Charles the Fifth nor Napoleon ever rivaled or approached.

We are usually apt to excuse the slower rate of liberal progress in our Old World by contrasting the obstructive barriers of prejudice, survival, solecism, anachronism, convention, institution, all so obstinately rooted, even when the branches seem bare and broken, in an old world, with the open and disengaged ground of the new. Yet in fact your difficulties were at least as formidable as those of the older civilizations into whose fruitful heritage you have entered. Unique was the necessity of this gigantic task of incorporation, the assimilation of people of divers faiths and race. A second difficulty was more formidable still—how to erect and work a powerful and wealthy State on such a system as to combine the centralized concert of a federal system with local independence, and to unite collective energy with the encouragement of individual freedom.

This last difficulty that you have so successfully up to now surmounted, at the present hour confronts the mother country and deeply perplexes her statesmen. Liberty and union have been called the twin ideas of America. So, too, they are the twin ideals of all responsible men in Great Britain; altho responsible men differ among themselves as to the safest path on which to travel toward the common goal, and tho the dividing ocean, in other ways so much our friend, interposes, for our case of an island State, or rather for a group of island States, obstacles from which a continental State like yours is happily altogether free.

Nobody believes that no difficulties remain. Some of them are obvious. But the common-sense, the mixture of patience and determination that has conquered risks and mischiefs in the past, may be trusted with the future.

Strange and devious are the paths of history. Broad and shining channels get mysteriously silted up. How many a time what seemed a glorious high road proves no more than a mule track or mere cul-de-sac. Think of Canning's flashing boast, when he insisted on the recognition of the Spanish republics in South America—that he had called a new world into existence to redress the balance of the old. This is one of the sayings—of which sort many another might be found—that make the fortune of a rhetorician, yet stand ill the wear and tear of time and circumstance. The new world that Canning called into existence has so far turned out a scene of singular disenchantment.

Tho not without glimpses on occasion of that heroism and courage and even wisdom that are the attributes of man almost at the worst, the tale has been too much a tale of anarchy and disaster, still leaving a host of perplexities for statesmen both in America and Europe. It has left also to students of a philosophic turn of mind one of the most interesting of all the problems to be found in the whole field of social, ecclesiastical, religious, and racial movement. Why is it that we do not find in the south as we find in the north of this hemisphere a powerful federation—a great Spanish-American people stretching from the Rio Grande to Cape Horn? To answer that question would be to shed a flood of light upon many deep historic forces in the Old World, of which, after all, these movements of the New are but a prolongation and more manifest extension.

What more imposing phenomenon does history present to us than the rise of Spanish power to the pinnacle of greatness and glory in the sixteenth century? The Mohammedans, after centuries of fierce and stubborn war, driven back; the whole peninsula brought under a single rule with a single creed; enormous acquisitions from the Netherlands of Naples, Sicily, the Canaries; France humbled, England menaced, settlements made in Asia and Northern Africa—Spain in America become possessed of a vast continent and of more than one archipelago of splendid islands. Yet before a century was over the sovereign majesty of Spain underwent a huge declension, the territory under her sway was contracted, the fabulous wealth of the mines of the New World had been wasted, agriculture and industry were ruined, her commerce passed into the hands of her rivals.

Let me digress one further moment. We have a very sensible habit in the island whence I come, when our country misses fire, to say as little as we can, and sink the thing in patriotic oblivion. It is rather startling to recall that less than a century ago England twice sent a military force to seize what is now Argentina. Pride of race and hostile creed vehemently resisting, proved too much for us. The two expeditions ended in failure, and nothing remains for the historian of to-day but to wonder what a difference it might have made to the temperate region of South America if the fortune of war had gone the other way, if the region of the Plata had become British, and a large British immigration had followed. Do not think me guilty of the heinous crime of forgetting the Monroe Doctrine. That momentous declaration was not made for a good many years after our Gen. Whitelocke was repulsed at Buenos Ayres, tho Mr. Sumner and other people have always held that it was Canning who really first started the Monroe Doctrine, when he invited the United States to join him against European intervention in South American affairs.

The day is at hand, we are told, when four-fifths of the human race will trace their pedigree to English forefathers, as four-fifths of the white people in the United States trace their pedigree to-day. By the end of this century, they say, such nations as France and Germany, assuming that they stand apart from fresh consolidations, will only be able to claim the same relative position in the political world as Holland and Switzerland. These musings of the moon do not take us far. The important thing, as we all know, is not the exact fraction of the human race that will speak English. The important thing is that those who speak English, whether in old lands or new, shall strive in lofty, generous and never-ceasing emulation with peoples of other tongues and other stock for the political, social, and intellectual primacy among mankind. In this noble strife for the service of our race we need never fear that claimants for the prize will be too large a multitude.

As an able scholar of your own has said, Jefferson was here using the old vernacular of English aspirations after a free, manly, and well-ordered political life—a vernacular rich in stately tradition and noble phrase, to be found in a score of a thousand of champions in many camps—in Buchanan, Milton, Hooker, Locke, Jeremy Taylor, Roger Williams, and many another humbler but not less strenuous pioneer and confessor of freedom. Ah, do not fail to count up, and count up often, what a different world it would have been but for that island in the distant northern sea! These were the tributary fountains, that, as time went on, swelled into the broad confluence of modern time. What was new in 1776 was the transformation of thought into actual polity.

What is progress? It is best to be slow in the complex arts of politics in their widest sense, and not to hurry to define. If you want a platitude, there is nothing for supplying it like a definition. Or shall we say that most definitions hang between platitude and paradox? There are said, tho I have never counted, to be 10,000 definitions of religion. There must be about as many of poetry. There can hardly be fewer of liberty, or even of happiness.

I am not bold enough to try a definition. I will not try to gauge how far the advance of moral forces has kept pace with that extension of material forces in the world of which this continent, conspicuous before all others, bears such astounding evidence. This, of course, is the question of questions, because as an illustrious English writer—to whom, by the way, I owe my friendship with your founder many long years ago—as Matthew Arnold said in America here, it is moral ideas that at bottom decide the standing or falling of states and nations. Without opening this vast discussion at large, many a sign of progress is beyond mistake. The practise of associated action—one of the master keys of progress—is a new force in a hundred fields, and with immeasurable diversity of forms. There is less acquiescence in triumphant wrong. Toleration in religion has been called the best fruit of the last four centuries, and in spite of a few bigoted survivals, even in our United Kingdom, and some savage outbreaks of hatred, half religious, half racial, on the Continent of Europe, this glorious gain of time may now be taken as secured. Perhaps of all the contributions of America to human civilization this is greatest. The reign of force is not yet over, and at intervals it has its triumphant hours, but reason, justice, humanity fight with success their long and steady battle for a wider sway.

Of all the points of social advance, in my country at least, during the last generation none is more marked than the change in the position of women, in respect of rights of property, of education, of access to new callings. As for the improvement of material well-being, and its diffusion among those whose labor is a prime factor in its creation, we might grow sated with the jubilant monotony of its figures, if we did not take good care to remember, in the excellent words of the President of Harvard, that those gains, like the prosperous working of your institutions and the principles by which they are sustained, are in essence moral contributions, "being principles of reason, enterprise, courage, faith, and justice, over passion, selfishness, inertness, timidity, and distrust." It is the moral impulses that matter. Where they are safe, all is safe.

When this and the like is said, nobody supposes that the last word has been spoken as to the condition of the people either in America or Europe. Republicanism is not itself a panacea for economic difficulties. Of self it can neither stifle nor appease the accents of social discontent. So long as it has no root in surveyed envy, this discontent itself is a token of progress.

What, cries the skeptic, what has become of all the hopes of the time when France stood upon the top of golden hours? Do not let us fear the challenge. Much has come of them. And over the old hopes time has brought a stratum of new.

Liberalism is sometimes suspected of being cold to these new hopes, and you may often hear it said that Liberalism is already superseded by Socialism. That a change is passing over party names in Europe is plain, but you may be sure that no change in name will extinguish these principles of society which are rooted in the nature of things, and are accredited by their success. Twice America has saved liberalism in Great Britain. The War for Independence in the eighteenth century was the defeat of usurping power no less in England than here. The War for Union in the nineteenth century gave the decisive impulse to a critical extension of suffrage, and an era of popular reform in the mother country. Any miscarriage of democracy here reacts against progress in Great Britain.

If you seek the real meaning of most modern disparagement of popular or parliamentary government, it is no more than this, that no politics will suffice of themselves to make a nation's soul. What could be more true? Who says it will? But we may depend upon it that the soul will be best kept alive in a nation where there is the highest proportion of those who, in the phrase of an old worthy of the seventeenth century, think it a part of a man's religion to see to it that his country be well governed.

Democracy, they tell us, is afflicted by mediocrity and by sterility. But has not democracy in my country, as in yours, shown before now that it well knows how to choose rulers neither mediocre nor sterile; men more than the equals in unselfishness, in rectitude, in clear sight, in force, of any absolutist statesman, that ever in times past bore the scepter? If I live a few months, or it may be even a few weeks longer, I hope to have seen something of three elections—one in Canada, one in the United Kingdom, and the other here. With us, in respect of leadership, and apart from height of social prestige, the personage corresponding to the president is, as you know, the prime minister. Our general election this time, owing to personal accident of the passing hour, may not determine quite exactly who shall be the prime minister, but it will determine the party from which the prime minister shall be taken. On normal occasions our election of a prime minister is as direct and personal as yours, and in choosing a member of Parliament people were really for a whole generation choosing whether Disraeli or Gladstone or Salisbury should be head of the government.

The one central difference between your system and ours is that the American president is in for a fixed time, whereas the British prime minister depends upon the support of the House of Commons. If he loses that, his power may not endure a twelvemonth; if on the other hand, he keeps it, he may hold office for a dozen years. There are not many more interesting or important questions in political discussion than the question whether our cabinet government or your presidential system of government is the better. This is not the place to argue it.

Between 1868 and now—a period of thirty-six years—we have had eight ministries. This would give an average life of four and a half years. Of these eight governments five lasted over five years. Broadly speaking, then, our executive governments have lasted about the length of your fixed term. As for ministers swept away by a gust of passion, I can only recall the overthrow of Lord Palmerston in 1858 for being thought too subservient to France. For my own part, I have always thought that by its free play, its comparative fluidity, its rapid flexibility of adaptation, our cabinet system has most to say for itself.

Whether democracy will make for peace, we all have yet to see. So far democracy has done little in Europe to protect us against the turbid whirlpools of a military age. When the evils of rival states, antagonistic races, territorial claims, and all the other formulas of international conflict are felt to be unbearable and the curse becomes too great to be any longer borne, a school of teachers will perhaps arise to pick up again the thread of the best writers and wisest rulers on the eve of the revolution. Movement in this region of human things has not all been progressive. If we survey the European courts from the end of the Seven Years' War down to the French Revolution, we note the marked growth of a distinctly international and pacific spirit. At no era in the world's history can we find so many European statesmen after peace and the good government of which peace is the best ally. That sentiment came to violent end when Napoleon arose to scourge the world.

# On Resigning from the Senate, 1861

ROBERT TOOMBS

*(Abridged)*

The success of the Abolitionists and their allies, under the name of the Republican party, has produced its logical results already. They have for long years been sowing dragons' teeth and have finally got a crop of armed men. The Union, sir, is dissolved. That is an accomplished fact in the path of this discussion that men may as well heed. One of your confederates has already wisely, bravely, boldly confronted public danger, and she is only ahead of many of her sisters because of her greater facility for speedy action. The greater majority of those sister States, under like circumstances, consider her cause as their cause; and I charge you in their name to-day: "Touch not Saguntum."[35] It is not only their cause, but it is a cause which receives the sympathy and will receive the support of tens and hundreds of honest patriot men in the nonslaveholding States, who have hitherto maintained constitutional rights, and who respect their oaths, abide by compacts, and love justice.

And while this Congress, this Senate, and this House of Representatives are debating the constitutionality and the expediency of seceding from the Union, and while the perfidious authors of this mischief are showering down denunciations upon a large portion of the patriotic men of this country, those brave men are coolly and calmly voting what you call revolution—aye, sir, doing better than that: arming to defend it. They appealed to the Constitution, they appealed to justice, they appealed to fraternity, until the Constitution, justice, and fraternity were no longer listened to in the legislative halls of their country, and then, sir, they prepared for the arbitrament of the sword; and now you see the glittering bayonet, and you hear the tramp of armed men from your capitol to the Rio Grande. It is a sight that gladdens the eyes and cheers the hearts of other millions ready to second them. Inasmuch, sir, as I have labored earnestly, honestly, sincerely, with these men to avert this necessity so long as I deemed it possible, and inasmuch as I heartily approve their present conduct of resistance, I deem it my duty to state their case to the Senate, to the country, and to the civilized world.

Senators, my countrymen have demanded no new government; they have demanded no new Constitution. Look to their records at home and here from the beginning of this national strife until its consummation in the disruption of the empire, and they have not demanded a single thing except that you shall abide by the Constitution of the United States; that constitutional rights shall be respected, and that justice shall be done. Sirs, they have stood by your Constitution; they have stood by all its requirements, they have performed all its duties unselfishly, uncalculatingly, disinterestedly, until a party sprang up in this country which endangered their social system—a party which they arraign, and

---

35 Saguntum was a city of Iberia (Spain) in alliance with Rome. Hannibal, in spite of Rome's warnings in 219 B.C., laid siege to and captured it. This became the immediate cause of the war which Rome declared against Carthage.

which they charge before the American people and all mankind with having made proclamation of outlawry against four thousand millions of their property in the Territories of the United States; with having put them under the ban of the empire in all the States in which their institutions exist outside the protection of federal laws; with having aided and abetted insurrection from within and invasion from without with the view of subverting those institutions, and desolating their homes and their firesides. For these causes they have taken up arms.

I have stated that the discontented States of this Union have demanded nothing but clear, distinct, unequivocal, well-acknowledged constitutional rights—rights affirmed by the highest judicial tribunals of their country; rights older than the Constitution; rights which are planted upon the immutable principles of natural justice; rights which have been affirmed by the good and the wise of all countries, and of all centuries. We demand no power to injure any man. We demand no right to injure our confederate States. We demand no right to interfere with their institutions, either by word or deed. We have no right to disturb their peace, their tranquillity, their security. We have demanded of them simply, solely—nothing else—to give us *equality, security* and *tranquillity*. Give us these, and peace restores itself. Refuse them, and take what you can get.

What do the rebels demand? First, "that the people of the United States shall have an equal right to emigrate and settle in the present or any future acquired Territories, with whatever property they may possess (including slaves), and be securely protected in its peaceable enjoyment until such Territory may be admitted as a State into the Union, with or without slavery, as she may determine, on an equality with all existing States." That is our Territorial demand. We have fought for this Territory when blood was its price. We have paid for it when gold was its price. We have not proposed to exclude you, tho you have contributed very little of blood or money. I refer especially to New England. We demand only to go into those Territories upon terms of equality with you, as equals in this great Confederacy, to enjoy the common property of the whole Union, and receive the protection of the common government, until the Territory is capable of coming into the Union as a sovereign State, when it may fix its own institutions to suit itself.

The second proposition is, "that property in slaves shall be entitled to the same protection from the government of the United States, in all of its departments, everywhere, which the Constitution confers the power upon it to extend to any other property, provided nothing herein contained shall be construed to limit or restrain the right now belonging to every State to prohibit, abolish, or establish and protect slavery within its limits." We demand of the common government to use its granted powers to protect our property as well as yours. For this protection we pay as much as you do. This very property is subject to taxation. It has been taxed by you and sold by you for taxes.

The title to thousands and tens of thousands of slaves is derived from the United States. We claim that the government, while the Constitution recognizes our property for the purposes of taxation, shall give it the same protection that it gives yours.

Ought it not to be so? You say no. Every one of you upon the committee said no. Your senators say no. Your House of Representatives says no. Throughout the length and breadth of your conspiracy against the Constitution there is but one shout of no! This recognition of this right is the price of my allegiance. Withhold it, and you do not get my obedience. This is the philosophy of the armed men who have sprung up in this country. Do you ask me to support a government that will tax my property: that will plunder me; that will demand my blood, and will not protect me? I would rather see the population of my native State laid six feet beneath her sod than they should support for one hour such a government. Protection is the price of obedience everywhere, in all countries. It is the only thing that makes government respectable. Deny it and you can not have free subjects or citizens; you may have slaves.

We demand, in the next place, "that persons committing crimes against slave property in one State, and fleeing to another, shall be delivered up in the same manner as persons committing crimes against other property, and that the laws of the State from which such persons flee shall be the test of criminality." That is another one of the demands of an extremist and a rebel.

But the nonslaveholding States, treacherous to their oaths and compacts, have steadily refused, if the criminal only stole a negro and that negro was a slave, to deliver him up. It was refused twice on the requisition of my own State as long as twenty-two years ago. It was refused by Kent and by Fairfield, governors of Maine, and representing, I believe, each of the then federal parties. We appealed then to fraternity, but we submitted; and this constitutional right has been practically a dead letter from that day to this. The next case came up between us and the State of New York, when the present senior senator [Mr. Seward] was the governor of that State; and he refused it. Why? He said it was not against the laws of New York to steal a negro, and therefore he would not comply with the demand. He made a similar refusal to Virginia. Yet these are our confederates; these are our sister States! There is the bargain; there is the compact. You have sworn to it. Both these governors swore to it. The senator from New York swore to it. The governor of Ohio swore to it when he was inaugurated. You can not bind them by oaths. Yet they talk to us of treason; and I suppose they expect to whip freemen into loving such brethren! They will have a good time in doing it!

It is natural we should want this provision of the Constitution carried out. The Constitution says slaves are property; the Supreme Court says so; the Constitution says so. The theft of slaves is a crime; they are a subject-matter of felonious asportation. By the text and letter of the Constitution you agreed to give them up. You have sworn to do it, and you have broken your oaths. Of course, those who have done so look out for pretexts. Nobody expected them to do otherwise. I do not think I ever saw a perjurer, however bald and naked, who could not invent some pretext to palliate his crime, or who could not, for fifteen shillings, hire an Old Bailey lawyer to invent some for him. Yet this requirement of the Constitution is another one of the extreme demands of an extremist and a rebel.

The next stipulation is that fugitive slaves shall be surrendered under the provisions of the Fugitive Slave Act of 1850, without being entitled either to a writ of habeas corpus, or trial by jury, or other similar obstructions of legislation, in the State to which he may flee. Here is the Constitution:

No person held to service or labor in one State, under the laws thereof, escaping into another, shall, in consequence of any law or regulation therein, be discharged from such service or labor, but shall be delivered up on claim of the party to whom such service or labor may be due.

This language is plain, and everybody understood it the same way for the first forty years of your government. In 1793, in Washington's time, an act was passed to carry out this provision. It was adopted unanimously in the Senate of the United States, and nearly so in the House of Representatives. Nobody then had invented pretexts to show that the Constitution did not mean a negro slave. It was clear; it was plain. Not only the federal courts, but all the local courts in all the States, decided that this was a constitutional obligation. How is it now? The North sought to evade it; following the instincts of their natural character, they commenced with the fraudulent fiction that fugitives were entitled to habeas corpus, entitled to trial by jury in the State to which they fled. They pretended to believe that our fugitive slaves were entitled to more rights than their white citizens; perhaps they were right, they know one another better than I do. You may charge a white man with treason, or felony, or other crime, and you do not require any trial by jury before he is given up; there is nothing to determine but that he is legally charged with a crime and that he fled, and then he is to be delivered up upon demand. White people are delivered up every day in this way; but not slaves. Slaves, black people, you say, are entitled to trial by jury; and in this way schemes have been invented to defeat your plain constitutional obligations.

Senators, the Constitution is a compact. It contains all our obligations and the duties of the federal government. I am content and have ever been content to sustain it. While I doubt its perfection, while I do not believe it was a good compact, and while I never saw the day that I would have voted for it as a proposition *de novo*, yet I am bound to it by oath and by that common prudence which would induce men to abide by established forms rather than to rush into unknown dangers. I have given to it, and intend to give to it, unfaltering support and allegiance, but I choose to put that allegiance on the true ground, not on the false idea that anybody's blood was shed for it. I say that the Constitution is the whole compact. All the obligations, all the chains that fetter the limbs of my people, are nominated in the bond, and they wisely excluded any conclusion against them, by declaring that "the powers not granted by the Constitution to the United States, or forbidden by it to the States, belonged to the States respectively or the people."

Now I will try it by that standard; I will subject it to that test. The law of nature, the law of justice, would say—and it is so expounded by the publicists—that equal rights in the common property shall be enjoyed. Even in a monarchy the king can not prevent the subjects from enjoying equality in the disposition of the public property. Even in a despotic government this principle is recognized. It was the blood and the money of the whole people (says the learned Grotius, and say all the publicists) which acquired the public property, and therefore it is not the property of the sovereign. This right of equality being, then, according to justice and natural equity, a right belonging to all States, when did we give it up? You say Congress has a right to pass rules and regulations concerning the Territory and other property of the United States. Very well. Does that exclude those whose blood and money paid for it? Does "dispose of" mean to rob the rightful owners? You must show a better title than that, or a better sword than we have.

What, then, will you take? You will take nothing but your own judgment; that is, you will not only judge for yourselves, not only discard the court, discard our construction, discard the practise of the government, but you will drive us out, simply because you will it. Come and do it! You have sapped the foundations of society; you have destroyed almost all hope of peace. In a compact where there is no common arbiter, where the parties finally decide for themselves, the sword alone at last becomes the real, if not the constitutional, arbiter. Your party says that you will not take the decision of the Supreme Court. You said so at Chicago; you said so in committee; every man of you in both Houses says so. What are you going to do? You say we shall submit to your construction. We shall do it, if you can make us; but not otherwise, or in any other manner. That is settled. You may call it secession, or you may call it revolution; but there is a big fact standing before you, ready to oppose you—that fact is, freemen with arms in their hands.

## Inaugural Address
### Theodore Roosevelt
### (1905)

My Fellow Citizens:—No people on earth have more cause to be thankful than ours, and this is said reverently, in no spirit of boastfulness in our own strength, but with gratitude to the Giver of Good, Who has blessed us with the conditions which have enabled us to achieve so large a measure of well-being and happiness.

To us as a people it has been granted to lay the foundations of our national life in a new continent. We are the heirs of the ages, and yet we have had to pay few of the penalties which in old countries are exacted by the dead hand of a bygone civilization. We have not been obliged to fight for our existence against any alien race; and yet our life has called for the vigor and effort without which the manlier and hardier virtues wither away.

Under such conditions it would be our own fault if we failed, and the success which we have had in the past, the success which we confidently believe the future will bring, should cause in us no feeling of vainglory, but rather a deep and abiding realization of all that life has offered us; a full acknowledgment of the responsibility which is ours; and a fixed determination to show that under a free government a mighty people can thrive best, alike as regard the things of the body and the things of the soul.

Much has been given to us, and much will rightfully be expected from us. We have duties to others and duties to ourselves—and we can shirk neither. We have become a great nation, forced by the fact of its greatness into relation to the other nations of the earth, and we must behave as beseems a people with such responsibilities.

Toward all other nations, large and small, our attitude must be one of cordial and sincere friendship. We must show not only in our words but in our deeds that we are earnestly desirous of securing their good will by acting toward them in a spirit of just and generous recognition of all their rights.

But justice and generosity in a nation, as in an individual, count most when shown not by the weak but by the strong. While ever careful to refrain from wronging others, we must be no less insistent that we are not wronged ourselves. We wish peace; but we wish the peace of justice, the peace of righteousness. We wish it because we think it is right, and not because we are afraid. No weak nation that acts rightly and justly should ever have cause to fear, and no strong power should ever be able to single us out as a subject for insolent aggression.

Our relations with the other powers of the world are important; but still more important are our relations among ourselves. Such growth in wealth, in population, and in power, as a nation has seen during a century and a quarter of its national life, is inevitably accompanied by a like growth in the problems which are ever before every nation that rises to greatness. Power invariably means both responsibility and danger. Our forefathers faced certain perils which we have outgrown. We now face other perils the very existence of which it was impossible that they should foresee.

Modern life is both complex and intense, and the tremendous changes wrought by the extraordinary industrial development of the half century are felt in every fiber of our social and political being. Never before have men tried so vast and formidable an experiment as that of administering the affairs of a continent under the forms of a democratic republic. The conditions which have told for our marvelous material well-being, which have developed to a very high degree our energy, self-reliance, and individual initiative, also have brought the care and anxiety inseparable from the accumulation of great wealth in industrial centers.

Upon the success of our experiment much depends—not only as regards our own welfare, but as regards the welfare of mankind. If we fail, the cause of free self-government throughout the world will rock to its foundations, and therefore our responsibility is heavy, to ourselves, to the world as it is to-day, and to the generations yet unborn.

There is no good reason why we should fear the future, but there is every reason why we should face it seriously, neither hiding from ourselves the gravity of the problems before us, nor fearing to approach these problems with the unbending, unflinching purpose to solve them aright.

Yet after all, tho the problems are new, tho the tasks set before us differ from the tasks set before our fathers, who founded and preserved this Republic, the spirit in which these tasks must be undertaken and these problems faced, if our duty is to be well done, remains essentially unchanged. We know that self-government is difficult. We know that no people needs such high traits of character as that people which seeks to govern its affairs aright through the freely expressed will of the free men who compose it.

But we have faith that we shall not prove false to memories of the men of the mighty past. They did their work; they left us the splendid heritage we now enjoy. We in our turn have an assured confidence that we shall be able to leave this heritage unwasted and enlarged to our children's children.

To do so, we must show, not merely in great crises, but in the everyday affairs of life, the qualities of practical intelligence, of courage, of hardihood, and endurance, and, above all, the power of devotion to a lofty ideal, which made great the men who founded this Republic in the days of Washington; which made great the men who preserved this Republic in the days of Abraham Lincoln.

# On American Motherhood[36]

### THEODORE ROOSEVELT

### (1905)

In our modern industrial civilization there are many and grave dangers to counterbalance the splendors and the triumphs. It is not a good thing to see cities grow at disproportionate speed relatively to the country; for the small land owners, the men who own their little homes, and therefore to a very large extent the men who till farms, the men of the soil, have hitherto made the foundation of lasting national life in every State; and, if the foundation becomes either too weak or too narrow, the superstructure, no matter how attractive, is in imminent danger of falling.

But far more important than the question of the occupation of our citizens is the question of how their family life is conducted. No matter what that occupation may be, as long as there is a real home and as long as those who make up that home do their duty to one another, to their neighbors and to the State, it is of minor consequence whether the man's trade is plied in the country or in the city, whether it calls for the work of the hands or for the work of the head.

No piled-up wealth, no splendor of material growth, no brilliance of artistic development, will permanently avail any people unless its home life is healthy, unless the average man possesses honesty, courage, common sense, and decency, unless he works hard and is willing at need to fight hard; and unless the average woman is a good wife, a good mother, able and willing to perform the first and greatest duty of womanhood, able and willing to bear, and to bring up as they should be brought up, healthy children, sound in body, mind, and character, and numerous enough so that the race shall increase and not decrease.

There are certain old truths which will be true as long as this world endures, and which no amount of progress can alter. One of these is the truth that the primary duty of the husband is to be the home-maker, the breadwinner for his wife and children, and that the primary duty of the woman is to be the helpmate, the housewife, and mother. The woman should have ample educational advantages; but save in exceptional cases the man must be, and she need not be, and generally ought not to be, trained for a lifelong career as the family breadwinner; and, therefore, after a certain point, the training of the two must normally be different because the duties of the two are normally different. This does not mean inequality of function, but it does mean that normally there must be dissimilarity

---

**36** From his speech in Washington on March 13, 1905, before the National Congress of Mothers. Printed from a copy furnished by the president for this collection, in response to a request.

of function. On the whole, I think the duty of the woman the more important, the more difficult, and the more honorable of the two; on the whole I respect the woman who does her duty even more than I respect the man who does his.

No ordinary work done by a man is either as hard or as responsible as the work of a woman who is bringing up a family of small children; for upon her time and strength demands are made not only every hour of the day but often every hour of the night. She may have to get up night after night to take care of a sick child, and yet must by day continue to do all her household duties as well; and if the family means are scant she must usually enjoy even her rare holidays taking her whole brood of children with her. The birth pangs make all men the debtors of all women. Above all our sympathy and regard are due to the struggling wives among those whom Abraham Lincoln called the plain people, and whom he so loved and trusted; for the lives of these women are often led on the lonely heights of quiet, self-sacrificing heroism.

Just as the happiest and most honorable and most useful task that can be set any man is to earn enough for the support of his wife and family, for the bringing up and starting in life of his children, so the most important, the most honorable and desirable task which can be set any woman is to be a good and wise mother in a home marked by self-respect and mutual forbearance, by willingness to perform duty, and by refusal to sink into self-indulgence or avoid that which entails effort and self-sacrifice. Of course there are exceptional men and exceptional women who can do and ought to do much more than this, who can lead and ought to lead great careers of outside usefulness in addition to—not as substitutes for—their home work; but I am not speaking of exceptions; I am speaking of the primary duties, I am speaking of the average citizens, the average men and women who make up the nation.

Inasmuch as I am speaking to an assemblage of mothers, I shall have nothing whatever to say in praise of an easy life. Yours is the work which is never ended. No mother has an easy time, the most mothers have very hard times; and yet what true mother would barter her experience of joy and sorrow in exchange for a life of cold selfishness, which insists upon perpetual amusement and the avoidance of care, and which often finds its fit dwelling place in some flat designed to furnish with the least possible expenditure of effort the maximum of comfort and of luxury, but in which there is literally no place for children?

The woman who is a good wife, a good mother, is entitled to our respect as is no one else; but she is entitled to it only because, and so long as, she is worthy of it. Effort and self-sacrifice are the law of worthy life for the man as for the woman; tho neither the effort nor the self-sacrifice may be the same for the one as for the other. I do not in the least believe in the patient Griselda type of woman, in the woman who submits to gross and long continued ill treatment, any more than I believe in a man who tamely submits to wrongful aggression. No wrong-doing is so abhorrent as wrong-doing by a man toward the wife and the children who should arouse every tender feeling in his nature. Selfishness toward them, lack of tenderness toward them, lack of consideration for them, above all, brutality in any form toward them, should arouse the heartiest scorn and indignation in every upright soul.

I believe in the woman keeping her self-respect just as I believe in the man doing so. I believe in her rights just as much as I believe in the man's, and indeed a little more; and I regard marriage as a partnership, in which each partner is in honor bound to think of the rights of the other as well as of his or her own. But I think that the duties are even more important than the rights; and in the long run I think that the reward is ampler and greater for duty well done, than for the insistence upon individual rights, necessary tho this, too, must often be. Your duty is hard, your responsibility great; but greatest of all is your reward. I do not pity you in the least. On the contrary, I feel respect and admiration for you.

Into the woman's keeping is committed the destiny of the generations to come after us. In bringing up your children you mothers must remember that while it is essential to be loving and tender it is no less essential to be wise and firm. Foolishness and affection must not be treated as interchangeable terms; and besides training your sons and daughters in the softer and milder virtues, you must seek to give them those stern and hardy qualities which in after life they will surely need. Some children will go wrong in spite of the best training; and some will go right even when their surroundings are most unfortunate; nevertheless an immense amount depends upon the family training. If you mothers through weakness bring up your sons to be selfish and to think only of themselves, you will be responsible for much sadness among the women who are to be their wives in the future. If you let your daughters grow up idle, perhaps under the mistaken impression that as you yourselves have had to work hard they shall know only enjoyment, you are preparing them to be useless to others and burdens to themselves. Teach boys and girls alike that they are not to look forward to lives spent in avoiding difficulties, but to lives spent in overcoming difficulties. Teach them that work, for themselves and also for others, is not curse but a blessing; seek to make them happy, to make them enjoy life, but seek also to make them face life with the steadfast resolution to wrest success from labor and adversity, and to do their whole duty before God and to man. Surely she who can thus train her sons and her daughters is thrice fortunate among women.

There are many good people who are denied the supreme blessing of children, and for these we have the respect and sympathy always due to those who, from no fault of their own, are denied any of the other great blessings of life. But the man or woman who deliberately foregoes these blessings, whether from viciousness, coldness, shallowheartedness, self-indulgence, or mere failure to appreciate aright the difference between the all-important and the unimportant,—why, such a creature merits contempt as hearty as any visited upon the soldier who runs away in battle, or upon the man who refuses to work for the support of those dependent upon him, and who tho able-bodied is yet content to eat in idleness the bread which others provide.

The existence of women of this type forms one of the most unpleasant and unwholesome features of modern life. If any one is so dim of vision as to fail to see what a thoroughly unlovely creature such a woman is I wish they would read Judge Robert Grant's novel "Unleavened Bread," ponder seriously the character of Selma, and think of the fate that would surely overcome any nation which developed its average and typical woman along such lines. Unfortunately it would be untrue to say that this type exists only in American novels. That it also exists in American life is made unpleasantly evident by the statistics as to the dwindling families in some localities. It is made evident in equally sinister fashion by the census statistics as to divorce, which are fairly appalling; for easy divorce is now as it ever has been, a bane to any nation, a curse to society, a menace to the home, an incitement to married unhappiness and to immorality, an evil thing for men and a still more hideous evil for women. These unpleasant tendencies in our American life are made evident by articles such as those which I actually read not long ago in a certain paper, where a clergyman was quoted, seemingly with approval, as expressing the general American attitude when he said that the ambition of any save a very rich man should be to rear two children only, so as to give his children an opportunity "to taste a few of the good things of life."

This man, whose profession and calling should have made him a moral teacher, actually set before others the ideal, not of training children to do their duty, not of sending them forth with stout hearts and ready minds to win triumphs for themselves and their country, not of allowing them the opportunity, and giving them the privilege of making their own place in the world, but, forsooth, of keeping the number of children so limited that they might "taste a few good things!" The way to give a child a fair chance in life is not to bring it up in luxury, but to see that it has the kind of training that will give it strength of character. Even apart from the vital question of national life, and regarding only the individual interest of the children themselves, happiness in the true sense is a hundredfold more apt to come to any given member of a healthy family of healthy-minded children, well brought up, well educated, but taught that they must shift for themselves, must win their own way, and by their own exertions make their own positions of usefulness, than it is apt to come to those whose parents themselves have acted on and have trained their children to act on, the selfish and sordid theory that the whole end of life is to "taste a few good things."

The intelligence of the remark is on a par with its morality; for the most rudimentary mental process would have shown the speaker that if the average family in which there are children contained but two children the nation as a whole would decrease in population so rapidly that in two or three generations it would very deservedly be on the point of extinction, so that the people who had acted on this base and selfish doctrine would be giving place to others with braver and more robust ideals. Nor would such a result be in any way regrettable; for a race that practised such doctrine—that is, a race that practised race suicide—would thereby conclusively show that it was unfit to exist, and that it had better give place to people who had not forgotten the primary laws of their being.

To sum up, then, the whole matter is simple enough. If either a race or an individual prefers the pleasure of more effortless ease, of self-indulgence, to the infinitely deeper, the infinitely higher pleasures that come to those who know the toil and the weariness, but also the joy, of hard duty well done, why, that race or that individual must inevitably in the end pay the penalty of leading a life both vapid and ignoble. No man and no woman really worthy of the name can care for the life spent solely or chiefly in the avoidance of risk and trouble and labor. Save in exceptional cases the prizes worth having in life must be paid for, and the life worth living must be a life of work for a worthy end, and ordinarily of work more for others than for one's self.

The woman's task is not easy—no task worth doing is easy—but in doing it, and when she has done it, there shall come to her the highest and holiest joy known to mankind; and having done it, she shall have the reward prophesied in Scripture; for her husband and her children, yes, and all people who realize that her work lies at the foundation of all national happiness and greatness, shall rise up and call her blessed.

# The Call to Democrats

ALTON B. PARKER

*—From a speech opening the National Democratic*
*Convention at Baltimore, Md., June, 1912.*

It is not the wild and cruel methods of revolution and violence that are needed to correct the abuses incident to our Government as to all things human. Neither material nor moral progress lies that way. We have made our Government and our complicated institutions by appeals to reason, seeking to educate all our people that, day after day, year after year, century after century, they may see more clearly, act more justly, become more and more attached to the fundamental ideas that underlie our society. If we are to preserve undiminished the heritage bequeathed us, and add to it those accretions without which society would perish, we shall need all the powers that the school, the church, the court, the deliberative assembly, and the quiet thought of our people can bring to bear.

We are called upon to do battle against the unfaithful guardians of our Constitution and liberties and the hordes of ignorance which are pushing forward only to the ruin of our social and governmental fabric.

Too long has the country endured the offenses of the leaders of a party which once knew greatness. Too long have we been blind to the bacchanal of corruption. Too long have we listlessly watched the assembling of the forces that threaten our country and our firesides.

The time has come when the salvation of the country demands the restoration to place and power of men of high ideals who will wage unceasing war against corruption in politics, who will enforce the law against both rich and poor, and who will treat guilt as personal and punish it accordingly.

What is our duty? To think alike as to men and measures? Impossible! Even for our great party! There is not a reactionary among us. All Democrats are Progressives. But it is inevitably human that we shall not all agree that in a single highway is found the only road to progress, or each make the same man of all our worthy candidates his first choice.

It is impossible, however, and it is our duty to put aside all selfishness, to consent cheerfully that the majority shall speak for each of us, and to march out of this convention shoulder to shoulder, intoning the praises of our chosen leader—and that will be his due, whichever of the honorable and able men now claiming our attention shall be chosen.

# Nominating Woodrow Wilson

## JOHN W. WESCOTT

*—At the National Democratic Convention, Baltimore, Md., June, 1912.*

The New Jersey delegation is commissioned to represent the great cause of Democracy and to offer you as its militant and triumphant leader a scholar, not a charlatan; a statesman, not a doctrinaire; a profound lawyer, not a splitter of legal hairs; a political economist, not an egotistical theorist; a practical politician, who constructs, modifies, restrains, without disturbance and destruction; a resistless debater and consummate master of statement, not a mere sophist; a humanitarian, not a defamer of characters and lives; a man whose mind is at once cosmopolitan and composite of America; a gentleman of unpretentious habits, with the fear of God in his heart and the love of mankind exhibited in every act of his life; above all a public servant who has been tried to the uttermost and never found wanting—matchless, unconquerable, the ultimate Democrat, Woodrow Wilson.

New Jersey has reasons for her course. Let us not be deceived in our premises. Campaigns of vilification, corruption and false pretence have lost their usefulness. The evolution of national energy is towards a more intelligent morality in politics and in all other relations. The situation admits of no compromise. The temper and purpose of the American public will tolerate no other view. The indifference of the American people to politics has disappeared. Any platform and any candidate not conforming to this vast social and commercial behest will go down to ignominious defeat at the polls.

Men are known by what they say and do. They are known by those who hate and oppose them. Many years ago Woodrow Wilson said, "No man is great who thinks himself so, and no man is good who does not try to secure the happiness and comfort of others." This is the secret of his life. The deeds of this moral and intellectual giant are known to all men. They accord, not with the shams and false pretences of politics, but make national harmony with the millions of patriots determined to correct the wrongs of plutocracy and reestablish the maxims of American liberty in all their regnant beauty and practical effectiveness. New Jersey loves Woodrow Wilson not for the enemies he has made. New Jersey loves him for what he is. New Jersey argues that Woodrow Wilson is the only candidate who can not only make Democratic success a certainty, but secure the electoral vote of almost every State in the Union.

New Jersey will indorse his nomination by a majority of 100,000 of her liberated citizens. We are not building for a day, or even a generation, but for all time. New Jersey believes that there is an omniscience in national instinct. That instinct centers in Woodrow Wilson. He has been in political life less than two years. He has had no organization; only a practical ideal—the reestablishment of equal opportunity. Not his deeds alone, not his immortal words alone, not his personality alone, not his matchless powers alone, but all combined compel national faith and confidence in him. Every crisis evolves its master. Time and circumstance have evolved Woodrow Wilson. The North, the South, the East, and the West unite in him. New Jersey appeals to this convention to give the nation

Woodrow Wilson, that he may open the gates of opportunity to every man, woman, and child under our flag, by reforming abuses, and thereby teaching them, in his matchless words, "to release their energies intelligently, that peace, justice and prosperity may reign." New Jersey rejoices, through her freely chosen representatives, to name for the presidency of the United States the Princeton schoolmaster, Woodrow Wilson.

## The Race Problem

HENRY W. GRADY

—*Delivered at the annual banquet of the Boston Merchants'*
*Association, at Boston, Mass., December 12, 1889.*

MR. PRESIDENT:—Bidden by your invitation to a discussion of the race problem—forbidden by occasion to make a political speech—I appreciate, in trying to reconcile orders with propriety, the perplexity of the little maid, who, bidden to learn to swim, was yet adjured, "Now, go, my darling; hang your clothes on a hickory limb, and don't go near the water."

The stoutest apostle of the Church, they say, is the missionary, and the missionary, wherever he unfurls his flag, will never find himself in deeper need of unction and address than I, bidden to-night to plant the standard of a Southern Democrat in Boston's banquet hall, and to discuss the problem of the races in the home of Phillips and of Sumner. But, Mr. President, if a purpose to speak in perfect frankness and sincerity; if earnest understanding of the vast interests involved; if a consecrating sense of what disaster may follow further misunderstanding and estrangement; if these may be counted upon to steady undisciplined speech and to strengthen an untried arm—then, sir, I shall find the courage to proceed.

Happy am I that this mission has brought my feet at last to press New England's historic soil and my eyes to the knowledge of her beauty and her thrift. Here within touch of Plymouth Rock and Bunker Hill—where Webster thundered and Longfellow sang, Emerson thought and Channing preached—here, in the cradle of American letters and almost of American liberty, I hasten to make the obeisance that every American owes New England when first he stands uncovered in her mighty presence. Strange apparition! This stern and unique figure—carved from the ocean and the wilderness—its majesty kindling and growing amid the storms of winter and of wars—until at last the gloom was broken, its beauty disclosed in the sunshine, and the heroic workers rested at its base—while startled kings and emperors gazed and marveled that from the rude touch of this handful cast on a bleak and unknown shore should have come the embodied genius of human government and the perfected model of human liberty! God bless the memory of those immortal workers, and prosper the fortunes of their living sons—and perpetuate the inspiration of their handiwork.

Two years ago, sir, I spoke some words in New York that caught the attention of the North. As I stand here to reiterate, as I have done everywhere, every word I then uttered—to declare that the sentiments I then avowed were universally approved in the South—I realize that the confidence begotten by that speech is largely responsible for my presence here to-night. I should dishonor myself if I betrayed that confidence by uttering one insincere word, or by withholding one essential element of the truth. Apropos of this last, let me confess, Mr. President, before the praise of New England has died on my lips, that I believe the best product of her present life is the procession of seventeen thousand Vermont Democrats that for twenty-two years, undiminished by death, unrecruited by birth or conversion, have marched over their rugged hills, cast their Democratic ballots and gone back home to pray for their unregenerate neighbors, and awake to read the record of twenty-six thousand Republican majority. May the God of the helpless and the heroic help them, and may their sturdy tribe increase.

Far to the South, Mr. President, separated from this section by a line—once defined in irrepressible difference, once traced in fratricidal blood, and now, thank God, but a vanishing shadow—lies the fairest and richest domain of this earth. It is the home of a brave and hospitable people. There is centered all that can please or prosper humankind. A perfect climate above a fertile soil yields to the husbandman every product of the temperate zone. There, by night the cotton whitens beneath the stars, and by day the wheat locks the sunshine in its bearded sheaf. In the same field the clover steals the fragrance of the wind, and tobacco catches the quick aroma of the rains. There are mountains stored with exhaustless treasures; forests—vast and primeval; and rivers that, tumbling or loitering, run wanton to the sea. Of the three essential items of all industries—cotton, iron and wood—that region has easy control. In cotton, a fixed monopoly—in iron, proven supremacy—in timber, the reserve supply of the Republic. From this assured and permanent advantage, against which artificial conditions cannot much longer prevail, has grown an amazing system of industries. Not maintained by human contrivance of tariff or capital, afar off from the fullest and cheapest source of supply, but resting in divine assurance, within touch of field and mine and forest—not set amid costly farms from which competition has driven the farmer in despair, but amid cheap and sunny lands, rich with agriculture, to which neither season nor soil has set a limit—this system of industries is mounting to a splendor that shall dazzle and illumine the world. That, sir, is the picture and the promise of my home—a land better and fairer than I have told you, and yet but fit setting in its material excellence for the loyal and gentle quality of its citizenship. Against that, sir, we have New England, recruiting the Republic from its sturdy loins, shaking from its overcrowded hives new swarms of workers, and touching this land all over with its energy and its courage. And yet—while in the Eldorado of which I have told you but fifteen per cent of its lands are cultivated, its mines scarcely touched, and its population so scant that, were it set equidistant, the sound of the human voice could not be heard from Virginia to Texas—while on the threshold of nearly every house in New England stands a son, seeking, with troubled eyes, some new land in which to carry his modest patrimony, the strange fact remains that in 1880 the South had fewer northern-born citizens than she had in 1870—fewer in '70 than in '60. Why is this? Why is it, sir, though the section line be now but a mist that the breath may dispel, fewer men of the North have crossed it over to the South, than when it was crimson with the best blood of the Republic, or even when the slaveholder stood guard every inch of its way?

There can be but one answer. It is the very problem we are now to consider. The key that opens that problem will unlock to the world the fairest half of this Republic, and free the halted feet of thousands whose eyes are already kindling with its beauty. Better than this, it will open the hearts of brothers for thirty years estranged, and clasp in lasting comradeship a million hands now withheld in doubt. Nothing, sir, but this problem and the suspicions it breeds, hinders a clear understanding and a perfect union. Nothing else stands between us and such love as bound Georgia and Massachusetts at Valley Forge and Yorktown, chastened by the sacrifices of Manassas and Gettysburg, and illumined with the coming of better work and a nobler destiny than was ever wrought with the sword or sought at the cannon's mouth.

If this does not invite your patient hearing to-night—hear one thing more. My people, your brothers in the South—brothers in blood, in destiny, in all that is best in our past and future—are so beset with this problem that their very existence depends on its right solution. Nor are they wholly to blame for its presence. The slave-ships of the Republic sailed from your ports, the slaves worked in our fields. You will not defend the traffic, nor I the institution. But I do here declare that in its wise and humane administration in lifting the slave to heights of which he had not dreamed in his savage home, and giving him a happiness he has not yet found in freedom, our fathers left their sons a saving and excellent heritage. In the storm of war this institution was lost. I thank God as heartily as you do that human slavery is gone forever from American soil. But the freedman remains. With him, a problem without precedent or parallel. Note its appalling conditions. Two utterly dissimilar races on the same soil—with equal political and civil rights—almost equal in numbers, but terribly unequal in intelligence and responsibility—each pledged against fusion—one for a century in servitude to the other, and freed at last by a desolating war, the experiment sought by neither but approached by both with doubt—these are the conditions. Under these, adverse at every point, we are required to carry these two races in peace and honor to the end.

Never, sir, has such a task been given to mortal stewardship. Never before in this Republic has the white race divided on the rights of an alien race. The red man was cut down as a weed because he hindered the way of the American citizen. The yellow man was shut out of this Republic because he is an alien, and inferior. The red man was owner of the land—the yellow man was highly civilized and assimilable—but they hindered both sections and are gone! But the black man, affecting but one section, is clothed with every privilege of government and pinned to the soil, and my people commanded to make good at any hazard, and at any cost, his full and equal heirship of American privilege and prosperity. It matters not that every other race has been routed or excluded without rhyme or reason. It matters not that wherever the whites and the blacks have touched, in any era or in any clime, there has been an irreconcilable violence. It matters not that no two races, however similar, have lived anywhere, at any time, on the same soil with equal rights in peace! In spite of these things we are commanded to make good this change of American policy which has not perhaps changed American prejudice—to make certain here what has elsewhere been impossible between whites and blacks—and to reverse, under the very worst conditions, the universal verdict of racial history. And driven, sir, to this superhuman task with an impatience that brooks no delay—a rigor that accepts no excuse—and a suspicion that discourages frankness and sincerity. We do not shrink from this trial. It is so interwoven with our industrial fabric that we cannot disentangle it if we would—so bound up in our honorable obligation to the world, that we would not if we could. Can we solve it? The God who gave it into our hands, He alone can know. But this the weakest and wisest of us do know: we cannot solve it with less than your tolerant and patient sympathy—with less than the knowledge that the blood that runs in your veins is our blood—and that, when we have done our best, whether the issue be lost or won, we shall feel your strong arms about us and hear the beating of your approving hearts!

The resolute, clear-headed, broad-minded men of the South—the men whose genius made glorious every page of the first seventy years of American history—whose courage and fortitude you tested in five years of the fiercest war—whose energy has made bricks without straw and spread splendor amid the ashes of their war-wasted homes—these men wear this problem in their hearts and brains, by day and by night. They realize, as you cannot, what this problem means—what they owe to this kindly and dependent race—the measure of their debt to the world in whose despite they defended and maintained slavery. And though their feet are hindered in its undergrowth, and their march cumbered with its burdens, they have lost neither the patience from which comes clearness, nor the faith from which comes courage. Nor, sir, when in passionate moments is disclosed to them that vague and awful shadow, with its lurid abysses and its crimson stains, into which I pray God they may never go, are they struck with more of apprehension than is needed to complete their consecration!

Such is the temper of my people. But what of the problem itself? Mr. President, we need not go one step further unless you concede right here that the people I speak for are as honest, as sensible and as just as your people, seeking as earnestly as you would in their place to rightly solve the problem that touches them at every vital point. If you insist that they are ruffians, blindly striving with bludgeon and shotgun to plunder and oppress a race, then I shall sacrifice my self-respect and tax your patience in vain. But admit that they are men of common sense and common honesty, wisely modifying an environment they cannot wholly disregard—guiding and controlling as best they can the vicious and irresponsible of either race—compensating error with frankness, and retrieving in patience what they lost in passion—and conscious all the time that wrong means ruin—admit this, and we may reach an understanding to-night.

The President of the United States, in his late message to Congress, discussing the plea that the South should be left to solve this problem, asks: "Are they at work upon it? What solution do they offer? When will the black man cast a free ballot? When will he have the civil rights that are his?" I shall not here protest against a partisanry that, for the first time in our history, in time of peace, has stamped with the great seal of our government a stigma upon the people of a great and loyal section; though I gratefully remember that the great dead soldier, who held the helm of State for the eight stormiest years of reconstruction, never found need for such a step; and though there is no personal sacrifice

I would not make to remove this cruel and unjust imputation on my people from the archives of my country! But, sir, backed by a record, on every page of which is progress, I venture to make earnest and respectful answer to the questions that are asked. We give to the world this year a crop of 7,500,000 bales of cotton, worth $450,000,000, and its cash equivalent in grain, grasses and fruit. This enormous crop could not have come from the hands of sullen and discontented labor. It comes from peaceful fields, in which laughter and gossip rise above the hum of industry, and contentment runs with the singing plough. It is claimed that this ignorant labor is defrauded of its just hire, I present the tax books of Georgia, which show that the negro twenty-five years ago a slave, has in Georgia alone $10,000,000 of assessed property, worth twice that much. Does not that record honor him and vindicate his neighbors?

What people, penniless, illiterate, has done so well? For every Afro-American agitator, stirring the strife in which alone he prospers, I can show you a thousand negroes, happy in their cabin homes, tilling their own land by day, and at night taking from the lips of their children the helpful message their State sends them from the schoolhouse door. And the schoolhouse itself bears testimony. In Georgia we added last year $250,000 to the school fund, making a total of more than $1,000,000—and this in the face of prejudice not yet conquered—of the fact that the whites are assessed for $368,000,000, the blacks for $10,000,000, and yet forty-nine per cent of the beneficiaries are black children; and in the doubt of many wise men if education helps, or can help, our problem. Charleston, with her taxable values cut half in two since 1860, pays more in proportion for public schools than Boston. Although it is easier to give much out of much than little out of little, the South, with one-seventh of the taxable property of the country, with relatively larger debt, having received only one-twelfth as much of public lands, and having back of its tax books none of the $500,000,000 of bonds that enrich the North—and though it pays annually $26,000,000 to your section as pensions—yet gives nearly one-sixth to the public school fund. The South since 1865 has spent $1,000,000 in education, and this year is pledged to $32,000,000 more for State and city schools, although the blacks, paying one-thirtieth of the taxes, get nearly one-half of the fund. Go into our fields and see whites and blacks working side by side. On our buildings in the same squad. In our shops at the same forge. Often the blacks crowd the whites from work, or lower wages by their greater need and simpler habits, and yet are permitted, because we want to bar them from no avenue in which their feet are fitted to tread. They could not there be elected orators of white universities, as they have been here, but they do enter there a hundred useful trades that are closed against them here. We hold it better and wiser to tend the weeds in the garden than to water the exotic in the window.

In the South there are negro lawyers, teachers, editors, dentists, doctors, preachers, multiplying with the increasing ability of their race to support them. In villages and towns they have their military companies equipped from the armories of the State, their churches and societies built and supported largely by their neighbors. What is the testimony of the courts? In penal legislation we have steadily reduced felonies to misdemeanors, and have led the world in mitigating punishment for crime, that we might save, as far as possible, this dependent race from its own weakness. In our penitentiary record sixty per cent of the prosecutors are negroes, and in every court the negro criminal strikes the colored juror, that white men may judge his case.

In the North, one negro in every 185 is in jail—in the South, only one in 446. In the North the percentage of negro prisoners is six times as great as that of native whites; in the South, only four times as great. If prejudice wrongs him in Southern courts, the record shows it to be deeper in Northern courts. I assert here, and a bar as intelligent and upright as the bar of Massachusetts will solemnly indorse my assertion, that in the Southern courts, from highest to lowest, pleading for life, liberty or property, the negro has distinct advantage because he is a negro, apt to be overreached, oppressed—and that this advantage reaches from the juror in making his verdict to the judge in measuring his sentence.

Now, Mr. President, can it be seriously maintained that we are terrorizing the people from whose willing hands comes every year $1,000,000,000 of farm crops? Or have robbed a people who, twenty-five years from unrewarded slavery, have amassed in one State $20,000,000 of property? Or that we intend to oppress the people we are arming every day? Or deceive them, when we are educating them to the utmost limit of our ability? Or outlaw them, when we work side by side with them? Or re-enslave them under legal forms, when for their benefit we have even imprudently narrowed the limit of felonies and mitigated the severity of law? My fellow-countrymen, as you yourselves may sometimes have to appeal at the bar of human judgment for justice and for right, give to my people to-night the fair and unanswerable conclusion of these incontestable facts.

But it is claimed that under this fair seeming there is disorder and violence. This I admit. And there will be until there is one ideal community on earth after which we may pattern. But how widely is it misjudged! It is hard to measure with exactness whatever touches the negro. His helplessness, his isolation, his century of servitude,—these dispose us to emphasize and magnify his wrongs. This disposition, inflamed by prejudice and partisanry, has led to injustice and delusion. Lawless men may ravage a county in Iowa and it is accepted as an incident—in the South, a drunken row is declared to be the fixed habit of the community. Regulators may whip vagabonds in Indiana by platoons and it scarcely arrests attention—a chance collision in the South among relatively the same classes is gravely accepted as evidence that one race is destroying the other. We might as well claim that the Union was ungrateful to the colored soldier who followed its flag because a Grand Army post in Connecticut closed its doors to a negro veteran as for you to give racial significance to every incident in the South, or to accept exceptional grounds as the rule of our society. I am not one of those who becloud American honor with the parade of the outrages of either section, and belie American character by declaring them to be significant and representative. I prefer to maintain that they are neither, and stand for nothing but the passion and sin of our poor fallen humanity. If society, like a machine, were no stronger than its weakest part, I should despair of both sections. But, knowing that society, sentient and responsible in every fiber, can mend and repair until the whole has the strength of the best, I despair of neither. These gentlemen who come with me here, knit into Georgia's busy life as they are, never saw, I dare assert, an outrage committed on a negro! And if they did, no one of you would be swifter to prevent or punish. It is through them, and the men and women who think with them—making nine-tenths of every Southern community—that these two races have been carried thus far with less of violence than would have been possible anywhere else on earth. And in their fairness and courage and steadfastness—more than in all the laws that can be passed, or all the bayonets that can be mustered—is the hope of our future.

When will the blacks cast a free ballot? When ignorance anywhere is not dominated by the will of the intelligent; when the laborer anywhere casts a vote unhindered by his boss; when the vote of the poor anywhere is not influenced by the power of the rich; when the strong and the steadfast do not everywhere control the suffrage of the weak and shiftless—then, and not till then, will the ballot of the negro be free. The white people of the South are banded, Mr. President, not in prejudice against the blacks—not in sectional estrangement—not in the hope of political dominion—but in a deep and abiding necessity. Here is this vast ignorant and purchasable vote—clannish, credulous, impulsive, and passionate—tempting every art of the demagogue, but insensible to the appeal of the stateman. Wrongly started, in that it was led into alienation from its neighbor and taught to rely on the protection of an outside force, it cannot be merged and lost in the two great parties through logical currents, for it lacks political conviction and even that information on which conviction must be based. It must remain a faction—strong enough in every community to control on the slightest division of the whites. Under that division it becomes the prey of the cunning and unscrupulous of both parties. Its credulity is imposed upon, its patience inflamed, its cupidity tempted, its impulses misdirected— and even its superstition made to play its part in a campaign in which every interest of society is jeopardized and every approach to the ballot-box debauched. It is against such campaigns as this—the folly and the bitterness and the danger of which every Southern community has drunk deeply—that the white people of the South are banded together. Just as you in Massachusetts would be banded if 300,000 men, not one in a hundred able to read his ballot—banded in race instinct, holding against you the memory of a century of slavery, taught by your late conquerors to distrust and oppose you, had already travestied legislation from your State House, and in every species of folly or villainy had wasted your substance and exhausted your credit.

But admitting the right of the whites to unite against this tremendous menace, we are challenged with the smallness of our vote. This has long been flippantly charged to be evidence and has now been solemnly and officially declared to be proof of political turpitude and baseness on our part. Let us see. Virginia—a state now under fierce assault for this alleged crime—cast in 1888 seventy-five per cent of her vote; Massachusetts, the State in which I speak, sixty per cent of her vote. Was it suppression in Virginia and natural causes in Massachusetts? Last month Virginia cast sixty-nine per cent of her vote; and Massachusetts, fighting in every district, cast only forty-nine per cent of hers. If Virginia is condemned because thirty-one per cent of her vote was silent, how shall this State escape, in which fifty-one per cent was dumb? Let us enlarge this comparison. The sixteen Southern States in '88 cast sixty-seven per cent of their total vote—the six New England

States but sixty-three per cent of theirs. By what fair rule shall the stigma be put upon one section while the other escapes? A Congressional election in New York last week, with the polling place in touch of every voter, brought out only 6,000 votes of 28,000—and the lack of opposition is assigned as the natural cause. In a district in my State, in which an opposition speech has not been heard in ten years and the polling places are miles apart—under the unfair reasoning of which my section has been a constant victim—the small vote is charged to be proof of forcible suppression. In Virginia an average majority of 12,000, unless hopeless division of the minority, was raised to 42,000; in Iowa, in the same election, a majority of 32,000 was wiped out and an opposition majority of 8,000 was established. The change of 40,000 votes in Iowa is accepted as political revolution—in Virginia an increase of 30,000 on a safe majority is declared to be proof of political fraud.

It is deplorable, sir, that in both sections a larger percentage of the vote is not regularly cast, but more inexplicable that this should be so in New England than in the South. What invites the negro to the ballot-box? He knows that of all men it has promised him most and yielded him least. His first appeal to suffrage was the promise of "forty acres and a mule;" his second, the threat that Democratic success meant his re-enslavement. Both have been proved false in his experience. He looked for a home, and he got the Freedman's Bank. He fought under promise of the loaf, and in victory was denied the crumbs. Discouraged and deceived, he has realized at last that his best friends are his neighbors with whom his lot is cast, and whose prosperity is bound up in his—and that he has gained nothing in politics to compensate the loss of their confidence and sympathy, that is at last his best and enduring hope. And so, without leaders or organization—and lacking the resolute heroism of my party friends in Vermont that make their hopeless march over the hills a high and inspiring pilgrimage—he shrewdly measures the occasional agitator, balances his little account with politics, touches up his mule, and jogs down the furrow, letting the mad world wag as it will!

The negro voter can never control in the South, and it would be well if partisans at the North would understand this. I have seen the white people of a State set about by black hosts until their fate seemed sealed. But, sir, some brave men, banding them together, would rise as Elisha rose in beleaguered Samaria, and, touching their eyes with faith, bid them look abroad to see the very air "filled with the chariots of Israel and the horsemen thereof." If there is any human force that cannot be withstood, it is the power of the banded intelligence and responsibility of a free community. Against it, numbers and corruption cannot prevail. It cannot be forbidden in the law, or divorced in force. It is the inalienable right of every free community—the just and righteous safeguard against an ignorant or corrupt suffrage. It is on this, sir, that we rely in the South. Not the cowardly menace of mask or shotgun, but the peaceful majesty of intelligence and responsibility, massed and unified for the protection of its homes and the preservation of its liberty. That, sir, is our reliance and our hope, and against it all the powers of earth shall not prevail. It is just as certain that Virginia would come back to the unchallenged control of her white race—that before the moral and material power of her people once more unified, opposition would crumble until its last desperate leader was left alone, vainly striving to rally his disordered hosts—as that night should fade in the kindling glory of the sun. You may pass force bills, but they will not avail. You may surrender your own liberties to federal election law; you may submit, in fear of a necessity that does not exist, that the very form of this government may be changed; you may invite federal interference with the New England town meeting, that has been for a hundred years the guarantee of local government in America; this old State—which holds in its charter the boast that it "is a free and independent commonwealth"—may deliver its election machinery into the hands of the government it helped to create—but never, sir, will a single State of this Union, North or South, be delivered again to the control of an ignorant and inferior race. We wrested our state governments from negro supremacy when the Federal drumbeat rolled closer to the ballot-box, and Federal bayonets hedged it deeper about than will ever again be permitted in this free government. But, sir, though the cannon of this Republic thundered in every voting district in the South, we still should find in the mercy of God the means and the courage to prevent its reestablishment.

I regret, sir, that my section, hindered with this problem, stands in seeming estrangement to the North. If, sir, any man will point out to me a path down which the white people of the South, divided, may walk in peace and honor, I will take that path, though I take it alone—for at its end, and nowhere else, I fear, is to be found the full prosperity of my section and the full restoration of this Union. But, sir, if the negro had not been enfranchised the South would have been divided and the Republic united. His enfranchisement— against which I enter no protest—holds the South united and compact. What solution, then, can we offer for the problem? Time alone can disclose it to us. We simply report progress, and ask your patience. If the problem be solved at all—and I firmly believe it will, though nowhere else has it been—it will be solved by the people most deeply bound in interest, most deeply pledged in honor to its solution. I had rather see my people render back this question rightly solved than to see them gather all the spoils over which faction has contended since Cataline conspired and Cæsar fought. Meantime we treat the negro fairly, measuring to him justice in the fulness the strong should give to the weak, and leading him in the steadfast ways of citizenship, that he may no longer be the prey of the unscrupulous and the sport of the thoughtless. We open to him every pursuit in which he can prosper, and seek to broaden his training and capacity. We seek to hold his confidence and friendship—and to pin him to the soil with ownership, that he may catch in the fire of his own hearthstone that sense of responsibility the shiftless can never know. And we gather him into that alliance of intelligence and responsibility that, though it now runs close to racial lines, welcomes the responsible and intelligent of any race. By this course, confirmed in our judgment, and justified in the progress already made, we hope to progress slowly but surely to the end.

The love we feel for that race, you cannot measure nor comprehend. As I attest it here, the spirit of my old black mammy, from her home up there, looks down to bless, and through the tumult of this night steals the sweet music of her croonings as thirty years ago she held me in her black arms and led me smiling to sleep. This scene vanishes as I speak, and I catch a vision of an old Southern home with its lofty pillars and its white pigeons fluttering down through the golden air. I see women with strained and anxious faces, and children alert yet helpless. I see night come down with its dangers and its apprehensions, and in a big homely room I feel on my tired head the touch of loving hands—now worn and wrinkled, but fairer to me yet than the hands of mortal woman, and stronger yet to lead me than the hands of mortal man—as they lay a mother's blessing there, while at her knees—the truest altar I yet have found—I thank God that she is safe in her sanctuary, because her slaves, sentinel in the silent cabin, or guard at her chamber door, put a black man's loyalty between her and danger.

I catch another vision. The crisis of battle—a soldier, struck, staggering, fallen. I see a slave, scuffing through the smoke, winding his black arms about the fallen form, reckless of hurtling death—bending his trusty face to catch the words that tremble on the stricken lips, so wrestling meantime with agony that he would lay down his life in his master's stead. I see him by the weary bedside, ministering with uncomplaining patience, praying with all his humble heart that God will lift his master up, until death comes in mercy and in honor to still the soldier's agony and seal the soldier's life. I see him by the open grave—mute, motionless, uncovered, suffering for the death of him who in life fought against his freedom. I see him, when the mold is heaped and the great drama of his life is closed, turn away and with downcast eyes and uncertain step start out into new and strange fields, faltering, struggling, but moving on, until his shambling figure is lost in the light of this better and brighter day. And from the grave comes a voice, saying, "Follow him! put your arms about him in his need, even as he put his about me. Be his friend as he was mine." And out into this new world—strange to me as to him, dazzling, bewildering both—I follow! And may God forget my people—when they forget these!

Whatever the future may hold for them, whether they plod along in the servitude from which they have never been lifted since the Cyrenian was laid hold upon by the Roman soldiers, and made to bear the cross of the fainting Christ—whether they find homes again in Africa, and thus hasten the prophecy of the psalmist, who said, "And suddenly Ethiopia shall hold out her hands unto God"—whether forever dislocated and separate, they remain a weak people, beset by stronger, and exist, as the Turk, who lives in the jealousy rather than in the conscience of Europe—or whether in this miraculous Republic they break through the caste of twenty centuries and, belying universal history, reach the full stature of citizenship, and in peace maintain it—we shall give them uttermost justice and abiding friendship. And whatever we do, into whatever seeming estrangement we may be driven, nothing shall disturb the love we bear this Republic, or mitigate our consecration to its service. I stand here, Mr. President, to profess no new loyalty. When General Lee, whose heart was the temple of our hopes, and whose arm was clothed with our strength, renewed his allegiance to this Government at Appomattox, he spoke from a heart too great to be false, and he spoke for every honest man from Maryland to Texas. From that day to this Hamilcar has nowhere in the South sworn young Hannibal to hatred and vengeance, but everywhere to loyalty and to love. Witness the veteran standing at the base of a Confederate monument, above the graves of his comrades, his empty sleeve tossing in the April wind, adjuring the young men about him to serve as earnest and loyal citizens the Government against which their fathers fought. This message, delivered from that sacred presence, has gone home to the hearts of my fellows! And, sir, I declare here, if physical courage be always equal to human aspiration, that they would die, sir, if need be, to restore this Republic their fathers fought to dissolve.

Such, Mr. President, is this problem as we see it, such is the temper in which we approach it, such the progress made. What do we ask of you? First, patience; out of this alone can come perfect work. Second, confidence; in this alone can you judge fairly. Third, sympathy; in this you can help us best. Fourth, give us your sons as hostages. When you plant your capital in millions, send your sons that they may know how true are our hearts and may help to swell the Caucasian current until it can carry without danger this black infusion. Fifth, loyalty to the Republic—for there is sectionalism in loyalty as in estrangement. This hour little needs the loyalty that is loyal to one section and yet holds the other in enduring suspicion and estrangement. Give us the broad and perfect loyalty that loves and trusts Georgia alike with Massachusetts—that knows no South, no North, no East, no West, but endears with equal and patriotic love every foot of our soil, every State of our Union.

A mighty duty, sir, and a mighty inspiration impels every one of us to-night to lose in patriotic consecration whatever estranges, whatever divides. We, sir, are Americans—and we stand for human liberty! The uplifting force of the American idea is under every throne on earth. France, Brazil—these are our victories. To redeem the earth from kingcraft and oppression—this is our mission! And we shall not fail. God has sown in our soil the seed of His millennial harvest, and He will not lay the sickle to the ripening crop until His full and perfect day has come. Our history, sir, has been a constant and expanding miracle, from Plymouth Rock and Jamestown, all the way—aye, even from the hour when from the voiceless and traceless ocean a new world rose to the sight of the inspired sailor. As we approach the fourth centennial of that stupendous day—when the old world will come to marvel and to learn amid our gathered treasures—let us resolve to crown the miracles of our past with the spectacle of a Republic, compact, united, indissoluble in the bonds of love—loving from the Lakes to the Gulf—the wounds of war healed in every heart as on every hill, serene and resplendent at the summit of human achievement and earthly glory, blazing out the path and making clear the way up which all the nations of the earth must come in God's appointed time!

## Last Speech

WILLIAM McKINLEY

*—Delivered at the World's Fair, Buffalo, N.Y., on September 5, 1901,*
*the day before he was assassinated*

I am glad again to be in the city of Buffalo and exchange greetings with her people, to whose generous hospitality I am not a stranger, and with whose good will I have been repeatedly and signally honored. To-day I have additional satisfaction in meeting and giving welcome to the foreign representatives assembled here, whose presence and participation in this Exposition have contributed in so marked a degree to its interest and success.

To the commissioners of the Dominion of Canada and the British Colonies, the French Colonies, the Republics of Mexico and of Central and South America, and the commissioners of Cuba and Porto Rico, who share with us in this undertaking, we give the hand of fellowship and felicitate with them upon the triumphs of art, science, education and manufacture which the old has bequeathed to the new century.

Expositions are the timekeepers of progress. They record the world's advancement. They stimulate the energy, enterprise and intellect of the people, and quicken human genius. They go into the home. They broaden and brighten the daily life of the people. They open mighty storehouses of information to the student. Every exposition, great or small, has helped to some onward step.

Comparison of ideas is always educational and, as such, instructs the brain and hand of man. Friendly rivalry follows, which is the spur to industrial improvement, the inspiration to useful invention and to high endeavor in all departments of human activity. It exacts a study of the wants, comforts, and even the whims of the people, and recognizes the efficacy of high quality and low prices to win their favor. The quest for trade is an incentive to men of business to devise, invent, improve and economize in the cost of production. Business life, whether among ourselves, or with other peoples, is ever a sharp struggle for success. It will be none the less in the future.

Without competition we would be clinging to the clumsy and antiquated process of farming and manufacture and the methods of business of long ago, and the twentieth would be no further advanced than the eighteenth century. But tho commercial competitors we are, commercial enemies we must not be. The Pan-American Exposition has done its work thoroughly, presenting in its exhibits evidences of the highest skill and illustrating the progress of the human family in the Western Hemisphere. This portion of the earth has no cause for humiliation for the part it has performed in the march of civilization. It has not accomplished everything; far from it. It has simply done its best, and without vanity or boastfulness, and recognizing the manifold achievements of others it invites the friendly rivalry of all the powers in the peaceful pursuits of trade and commerce, and will cooperate with all in advancing the highest and best interests of humanity. The wisdom and energy of all the nations are none too great for the world work. The success of art, science, industry and invention is an international asset and a common glory.

After all, how near one to the other is every part of the world. Modern inventions have brought into close relation widely separated peoples and make them better acquainted. Geographic and political divisions will continue to exist, but distances have been effaced. Swift ships and fast trains are becoming cosmopolitan. They invade fields which a few years ago were impenetrable. The world's products are exchanged as never before and with increasing transportation facilities come increasing knowledge and larger trade. Prices are fixed with mathematical precision by supply and demand. The world's selling prices are regulated by market and crop reports. We travel greater distances in a shorter space of time and with more ease than was ever dreamed of by the fathers. Isolation is no longer possible or desirable. The same important news is read, tho in different languages, the same day in all Christendom.

The telegraph keeps us advised of what is occurring everywhere, and the Press fore-shadows, with more or less accuracy, the plans and purposes of the nations. Market prices of products and of securities are hourly known in every commercial mart, and the invest-ments of the people extend beyond their own national boundaries into the remotest parts of the earth. Vast transactions are conducted and international exchanges are made by the tick of the cable. Every event of interest is immediately bulletined. The quick gather-ing and transmission of news, like rapid transit, are of recent origin, and are only made possible by the genius of the inventor and the courage of the investor. It took a special messenger of the government, with every facility known at the time for rapid travel, nine-teen days to go from the City of Washington to New Orleans with a message to General Jackson that the war with England had ceased and a treaty of peace had been signed. How different now! We reached General Miles, in Porto Rico, and he was able through the military telegraph to stop his army on the firing line with the message that the United States and Spain had signed a protocol suspending hostilities. We knew almost instanter of the first shots fired at Santiago, and the subsequent surrender of the Spanish forces was known at Washington within less than an hour of its consummation. The first ship of Cervera's fleet had hardly emerged from that historic harbor when the fact was flashed to our Capitol, and the swift destruction that followed was announced immediately through the wonderful medium of telegraphy.

So accustomed are we to safe and easy communication with distant lands that its temporary interruption, even in ordinary times, results in loss and inconvenience. We shall never forget the days of anxious waiting and suspense when no information was per-mitted to be sent from Pekin, and the diplomatic representatives of the nations in China, cut off from all communication, inside and outside of the walled capital, were surrounded by an angry and misguided mob that threatened their lives; nor the joy that thrilled the world when a single message from the government of the United States brought through our minister the first news of the safety of the besieged diplomats.

At the beginning of the nineteenth century there was not a mile of steam railroad on the globe; now there are enough miles to make its circuit many times. Then there was not a line of electric telegraph; now we have a vast mileage traversing all lands and seas. God and man have linked the nations together. No nation can longer be indifferent to any other. And as we are brought more and more in touch with each other, the less occasion is there for misunderstandings, and the stronger the disposition, when we have differences, to adjust them in the court of arbitration, which is the noblest forum for the settlement of international disputes.

My fellow citizens, trade statistics indicate that this country is in a state of unexampled prosperity. The figures are almost appalling. They show that we are utilizing our fields and forests and mines, and that we are furnishing profitable employment to the millions of workingmen throughout the United States, bringing comfort and happiness to their homes, and making it possible to lay by savings for old age and disability. That all the people are participating in this great prosperity is seen in every American community and shown by the enormous and unprecedented deposits in our savings banks. Our duty in the care and security of these deposits and their safe investment demands the highest integrity and the best business capacity of those in charge of these depositories of the people's earnings.

We have a vast and intricate business, built up through years of toil and struggle in which every part of the country has its stake, which will not permit of either neglect or of undue selfishness. No narrow, sordid policy will subserve it. The greatest skill and wisdom on the part of manufacturers and producers will be required to hold and increase it. Our industrial enterprises, which have grown to such great proportions, affect the homes and occupations of the people and the welfare of the country. Our capacity to produce has developed so enormously and our products have so multiplied that the problem of more markets requires our urgent and immediate attention. Only a broad and enlightened policy will keep what we have. No other policy will get more. In these times of marvelous business energy and gain we ought to be looking to the future, strengthening the weak places in our industrial and commercial systems, that we may be ready for any storm or strain.

By sensible trade arrangements which will not interrupt our home production we shall extend the outlets for our increasing surplus. A system which provides a mutual exchange of commodities is manifestly essential to the continued and healthful growth of our export trade. We must not repose in the fancied security that we can forever sell everything and buy little or nothing. If such a thing were possible it would not be best for us or for those with whom we deal. We should take from our customers such of their products as we can use without harm to our industries and labor. Reciprocity is the natural outgrowth of our wonderful industrial development under the domestic policy now firmly established.

What we produce beyond our domestic consumption must have a vent abroad. The excess must be relieved through a foreign outlet, and we should sell everywhere we can and buy wherever the buying will enlarge our sales and productions, and thereby make a greater demand for home labor.

The period of exclusiveness is past. The expansion of our trade and commerce is the pressing problem. Commercial wars are unprofitable. A policy of good will and friendly trade relations will prevent reprisals. Reciprocity treaties are in harmony with the spirit of the times; measures of retaliation are not. If, perchance, some of our tariffs are no longer needed for revenue or to encourage and protect our industries at home, why should they not be employed to extend and promote our markets abroad? Then, too, we have inadequate steamship service. New lines of steamships have already been put in commission between the Pacific coast ports of the United States and those on the western coasts of Mexico and Central and South America. These should be followed up with direct steamship lines between the western coast of the United States and South American ports. One of the needs of the times is direct commercial lines from our vast fields of production to the fields of consumption that we have but barely touched. Next in advantage to having the thing to sell is to have the conveyance to carry it to the buyer. We must encourage our merchant marine. We must have more ships. They must be under the American flag; built and manned and owned by Americans. These will not only be profitable in a commercial sense; they will be messengers of peace and amity wherever they go.

We must build the Isthmian canal, which will unite the two oceans and give a straight line of water communication with the western coasts of Central and South America and Mexico. The construction of a Pacific cable can not be longer postponed. In the furtherance of these objects of national interest and concern you are performing an important part. This Exposition would have touched the heart of that American statesman whose mind was ever alert and thought ever constant for a larger commerce and a truer fraternity of the republics of the New World. His broad American spirit is felt and manifested here. He needs no identification to an assemblage of Americans anywhere, for the name of Blaine is inseparably associated with the Pan-American movement which finds here practical and substantial expression, and which we all hope will be firmly advanced by the Pan-American Congress that assembles this autumn in the capital of Mexico. The good work will go on. It can not be stopped. Those buildings will disappear; this creation of art and beauty and industry will perish from sight, but their influence will remain to "make it live beyond its too short living with praises and thanksgiving." Who can tell the new thoughts that have been awakened, the ambitions fired and the high achievements that will be wrought through this Exposition?

Gentlemen, let us ever remember that our interest is in concord, not conflict; and that our real eminence rests in the victories of peace, not those of war. We hope that all who are represented here may be moved to higher and nobler efforts for their own and the world's good, and that out of this city may come not only greater commerce and trade for us all, but, more essential than these, relations of mutual respect, confidence and friendship which will deepen and endure. Our earnest prayer is that God will graciously vouchsafe prosperity, happiness and peace to all our neighbors, and like blessings to all the peoples and powers of earth.

## Tribute to McKinley

JOHN HAY

*—From his memorial address at a joint session of the Senate*
*and House of Representatives on February 27, 1903.*

For the third time the Congress of the United States are assembled to commemorate the life and the death of a president slain by the hand of an assassin. The attention of the future historian will be attracted to the features which reappear with startling sameness in all three of these awful crimes: the uselessness, the utter lack of consequence of the act; the obscurity, the insignificance of the criminal; the blamelessness—so far as in our sphere of existence the best of men may be held blameless—of the victim. Not one of our murdered presidents had an enemy in the world; they were all of such preeminent purity of life that no pretext could be given for the attack of passional crime; they were all men of democratic instincts, who could never have offended the most jealous advocates of equity;

they were of kindly and generous nature, to whom wrong or injustice was impossible; of moderate fortune, whose slender means nobody could envy. They were men of austere virtue, of tender heart, of eminent abilities, which they had devoted with single minds to the good of the Republic. If ever men walked before God and man without blame, it was these three rulers of our people. The only temptation to attack their lives offered was their gentle radiance—to eyes hating the light, that was offense enough.

The stupid uselessness of such an infamy affronts the common sense of the world. One can conceive how the death of a dictator may change the political conditions of an empire; how the extinction of a narrowing line of kings may bring in an alien dynasty. But in a well-ordered Republic like ours the ruler may fall, but the State feels no tremor. Our beloved and revered leader is gone—but the natural process of our laws provides us a successor, identical in purpose and ideals, nourished by the same teachings, inspired by the same principles, pledged by tender affection as well as by high loyalty to carry to completion the immense task committed to his hands, and to smite with iron severity every manifestation of that hideous crime which his mild predecessor, with his dying breath, forgave. The sayings of celestial wisdom have no date; the words that reach us, over two thousand years, out of the darkest hour of gloom the world has ever known, are true to life to-day: "They know not what they do." The blow struck at our dear friend and ruler was as deadly as blind hate could make it; but the blow struck at anarchy was deadlier still.

How many countries can join with us in the community of a kindred sorrow! I will not speak of those distant regions where assassination enters into the daily life of government. But among the nations bound to us by the ties of familiar intercourse—who can forget that wise and mild autocrat who had earned the proud title of the liberator? that enlightened and magnanimous citizen whom France still mourns? that brave and chivalrous king of Italy who only lived for his people? and, saddest of all, that lovely and sorrowing empress, whose harmless life could hardly have excited the animosity of a demon? Against that devilish spirit nothing avails,—neither virtue nor patriotism, nor age nor youth, nor conscience nor pity. We can not even say that education is a sufficient safeguard against this baleful evil,—for most of the wretches whose crimes have so shocked humanity in recent years were men not unlettered, who have gone from the common schools, through murder to the scaffold.

The life of William McKinley was, from his birth to his death, typically American. There is no environment, I should say, anywhere else in the world which could produce just such a character. He was born into that way of life which elsewhere is called the middle class, but which in this country is so nearly universal as to make of other classes an almost negligible quantity. He was neither rich nor poor, neither proud nor humble; he knew no hunger he was not sure of satisfying, no luxury which could enervate mind or body. His parents were sober, God-fearing people; intelligent and upright, without pretension and without humility. He grew up in the company of boys like himself, wholesome, honest, self-respecting. They looked down on nobody; they never felt it possible they could be looked down upon. Their houses were the homes of probity, piety, patriotism. They learned in the admirable school readers of fifty years ago the lessons of heroic and splendid life which have come down from the past. They read in their weekly newspapers the story of the world's progress, in which they were eager to take part, and of the sins and wrongs of civilization with which they burned to do battle. It was a serious and thoughtful time. The boys of that day felt dimly, but deeply, that days of sharp struggle and high achievement were before them. They looked at life with the wondering yet resolute eyes of a young esquire in his vigil of arms. They felt a time was coming when to them should be addressed the stern admonition of the Apostle, "Quit you like men; be strong."

The men who are living to-day and were young in 1860 will never forget the glory and glamour that filled the earth and the sky when the long twilight of doubt and uncertainty was ending and the time for action had come. A speech by Abraham Lincoln was an event not only of high moral significance, but of far-reaching importance; the drilling of a militia company by Ellsworth attracted national attention; the fluttering of the flag in the clear sky drew tears from the eyes of young men. Patriotism, which had been a rhetorical expression, became a passionate emotion, in which instinct, logic and feeling were fused. The country was worth saving; it could be saved only by fire; no sacrifice was too great; the young men of the country were ready for the sacrifice; come weal, come woe, they were ready.

At seventeen years of age William McKinley heard this summons of his country. He was the sort of youth to whom a military life in ordinary times would possess no attractions. His nature was far different from that of the ordinary soldier. He had other dreams of life, its prizes and pleasures, than that of marches and battles. But to his mind there was no choice or question. The banner floating in the morning breeze was the beckoning gesture of his country. The thrilling notes of the trumpet called him—him and none other—into the ranks. His portrait in his first uniform is familiar to you all—the short, stocky figure; the quiet, thoughtful face; the deep, dark eyes. It is the face of a lad who could not stay at home when he thought he was needed in the field. He was of the stuff of which good soldiers are made. Had he been ten years older he would have entered at the head of a company and come out at the head of a division. But he did what he could. He enlisted as a private; he learned to obey. His serious, sensible ways, his prompt, alert efficiency soon attracted the attention of his superiors. He was so faithful in little things that they gave him more and more to do. He was untiring in camp and on the march; swift, cool and fearless in fight. He left the army with field rank when the war ended, brevetted by President Lincoln for gallantry in battle.

In coming years when men seek to draw the moral of our great Civil War, nothing will seem to them so admirable in all the history of our two magnificent armies as the way in which the war came to a close. When the Confederate army saw the time had come, they acknowledged the pitiless logic of facts and ceased fighting. When the army of the Union saw it was no longer needed, without a murmur or question, making no terms, asking no return, in the flush of victory and fulness of might, it laid down its arms and melted back into the mass of peaceful citizens. There is no event since the nation was born which has so proved its solid capacity for self-government. Both sections share equally in that crown of glory. They had held a debate of incomparable importance and had fought it out with equal energy. A conclusion had been reached—and it is to the everlasting honor of both sides that they each knew when the war was over and the hour of a lasting peace had struck. We may admire the desperate daring of others who prefer annihilation to compromise, but the palm of common sense, and, I will say, of enlightened patriotism, belongs to the men like Grant and Lee, who knew when they had fought enough for honor and for country.

So it came naturally about that in 1876—the beginning of the second century of the Republic—he began, by an election to Congress, his political career. Thereafter for fourteen years this chamber was his home. I use the word advisedly. Nowhere in the world was he so in harmony with his environment as here; nowhere else did his mind work with such full consciousness of its powers. The air of debate was native to him; here he drank delight of battle with his peers. In after days, when he drove by this stately pile, or when on rare occasions his duty called him here, he greeted his old haunts with the affectionate zest of a child of the house; during all the last ten years of his life, filled as they were with activity and glory, he never ceased to be homesick for this hall. When he came to the presidency, there was not a day when his Congressional service was not of use to him. Probably no other president has been in such full and cordial communion with Congress, if we may except Lincoln alone. McKinley knew the legislative body thoroughly, its composition, its methods, its habit of thought. He had the profoundest respect for its authority and an inflexible belief in the ultimate rectitude of its purposes. Our history shows how surely an executive courts disaster and ruin by assuming an attitude of hostility or distrust to the Legislature; and, on the other hand, McKinley's frank and sincere trust and confidence in Congress were repaid by prompt and loyal support and coöperation. During his entire term of office this mutual trust and regard—so essential to the public welfare—was never shadowed by a single cloud.

When he came to the presidency he confronted a situation of the utmost difficulty, which might well have appalled a man of less serene and tranquil self-confidence. There had been a state of profound commercial and industrial depression from which his friends had said his election would relieve the country. Our relations with the outside world left much to be desired. The feeling between the Northern and Southern sections of the Union was lacking in the cordiality which was necessary to the welfare of both. Hawaii had asked for annexation and had been rejected by the preceding administration. There was a state of things in the Caribbean which could not permanently endure. Our neighbor's house was on fire, and there were grave doubts as to our rights and duties in the premises. A man either weak or rash, either irresolute or headstrong, might have brought ruin on himself and incalculable harm to the country.

The least desirable form of glory to a man of his habitual mood and temper—that of successful war—was nevertheless conferred upon him by uncontrollable events. He felt it must come; he deplored its necessity; he strained almost to breaking his relations with his friends, in order, first to prevent and then to postpone it to the latest possible moment.

But when the die was cast, he labored with the utmost energy and ardor, and with an intelligence in military matters which showed how much of the soldier still survived in the mature statesman, to push forward the war to a decisive close. War was an anguish to him; he wanted it short and conclusive. His merciful zeal communicated itself to his subordinates, and the war, so long dreaded, whose consequences were so momentous, ended in a hundred days.

Mr. McKinley was reelected by an overwhelming majority. There had been little doubt of the result among well-informed people, but when it was known, a profound feeling of relief and renewal of trust were evident among the leaders of capital and industry, not only in this country, but everywhere. They felt that the immediate future was secure, and that trade and commerce might safely push forward in every field of effort and enterprise.

He felt that the harvest time was come, to garner in the fruits of so much planting and culture, and he was determined that nothing he might do or say should be liable to the reproach of a personal interest. Let us say frankly he was a party man; he believed the policies advocated by him and his friends counted for much in the country's progress and prosperity. He hoped in his second term to accomplish substantial results in the development and affirmation of those policies. I spent a day with him shortly before he started on his fateful journey to Buffalo. Never had I seen him higher in hope and patriotic confidence. He was gratified to the heart that we had arranged a treaty which gave us a free hand in the Isthmus. In fancy he saw the canal already built and the argosies of the world passing through it in peace and amity. He saw in the immense evolution of American trade the fulfilment of all his dreams, the reward of all his labors. He was, I need not say, an ardent protectionist, never more sincere and devoted than during those last days of his life. He regarded reciprocity as the bulwark of protection—not a breach, but a fulfilment of the law. The treaties which for four years had been preparing under his personal supervision he regarded as ancillary to the general scheme. He was opposed to any revolutionary plan of change in the existing legislation; he was careful to point out that everything he had done was in faithful compliance with the law itself.

In that mood of high hope, of generous expectation, he went to Buffalo, and there, on the threshold of eternity, he delivered that memorable speech, worthy for its loftiness of tone, its blameless morality, its breadth of view, to be regarded as his testament to the nation. Through all his pride of country and his joy of its success runs the note of solemn warning, as in Kipling's noble hymn, "Lest We Forget."

The next day sped the bolt of doom, and for a week after—in an agony of dread, broken by illusive glimpses of hope that our prayers might be answered—the nation waited for the end. Nothing in the glorious life we saw gradually waning was more admirable and exemplary than its close. The gentle humanity of his words when he saw his assailant in danger of summary vengeance, "Do not let them hurt him;" his chivalrous care that the news should be broken gently to his wife; the fine courtesy with which he apologized for the damage which his death would bring to the great Exhibition; and the heroic resignation of his final words, "It is God's way; His will, not ours, be done," were all the instinctive expressions of a nature so lofty and so pure that pride in its nobility at once softened and enhanced the nation's sense of loss. The Republic grieved over such a son,—but is proud forever of having produced him. After all, in spite of its tragic ending, his life was extraordinarily happy. He had, all his days, troops of friends, the cheer of fame and fruitful labor; and he became at last,

> "On fortune's crowning slope,
> The pillar of a people's hope,
> The center of a world's desire."

## The Prince of Peace[37]

### WILLIAM JENNINGS BRYAN

*(1894)*

I offer no apology for speaking upon a religious theme, for it is the most universal of all themes. I am interested in the science of government, but I am interested more in religion than in government. I enjoy making a political speech—I have made a good many and shall make more—but I would rather speak on religion than on politics. I commenced speaking on the stump when I was only twenty, but I commenced speaking in the church six years earlier—and I shall be in the church even after I am put of politics. I feel sure of my ground when I make a political speech, but I feel even more certain of my ground when I make a religious speech. If I addrest you upon the subject of law I might interest the lawyers; if I discuss the science of medicine I might interest the physicians; in like manner merchants might be interested in comments on commerce, and farmers in matters pertaining to agriculture; but no one of these subjects appeals to all. Even the science of government, tho broader than any profession or occupation, does not embrace the whole sum of life, and those who think upon it differ so among themselves that I could not speak upon the subject so as to please a part of the audience without displeasing others. While to me the science of government is intensely absorbing, I recognize that the most important things in life lie outside of the realm of government and that more depends upon what the individual does for himself than upon what the government does or can do for him. Men can be miserable under the best government and they can be happy under the worst government.

Government affects but a part of the life which we live here and does not deal at all with the life beyond, while religion touches the infinite circle of existence as well as the small arc of that circle which we spend on earth. No greater theme, therefore, can engage our attention. If I discuss questions of government I must secure the coöperation of a majority before I can put my ideas into practise, but if, in speaking on religion, I can touch one human heart for good, I have not spoken in vain no matter how large the majority may be against me.

---

**37** Used by permission.

Man is a religious being; the heart instinctively seeks for a God. Whether he worships on the banks of the Ganges, prays with his face upturned to the sun, kneels toward Mecca or, regarding all space as a temple, communes with the Heavenly Father according to the Christian creed, man is essentially devout.

There are honest doubters whose sincerity we recognize and respect, but occasionally I find young men who think it smart to be skeptical; they talk as if it were an evidence of larger intelligence to scoff at creeds and to refuse to connect themselves with churches. They call themselves "Liberal," as if a Christian were narrow minded. Some go so far as to assert that the "advanced thought of the world" has discarded the idea that there is a God. To these young men I desire to address myself.

Even some older people profess to regard religion as a superstition, pardonable in the ignorant but unworthy of the educated. Those who hold this view look down with mild contempt upon such as give to religion a definite place in their thoughts and lives. They assume an intellectual superiority and often take little pains to conceal the assumption. Tolstoy administers to the "cultured crowd" (the words quoted are his) a severe rebuke when he declares that the religious sentiment rests not upon a superstitious fear of the invisible forces of nature, but upon man's consciousness of his finiteness amid an infinite universe and of his sinfulness; and this consciousness, the great philosopher adds, man can never outgrow. Tolstoy is right; man recognizes how limited are his own powers and how vast is the universe, and he leans upon the arm that is stronger than his. Man feels the weight of his sins and looks for One who is sinless.

Religion has been defined by Tolstoy as the relation which man fixes between himself and his God, and morality as the outward manifestation of this inward relation. Every one, by the time he reaches maturity, has fixt some relation between himself and God and no material change in this relation can take place without a revolution in the man, for this relation is the most potent influence that acts upon a human life.

Religion is the foundation of morality in the individual and in the group of individuals. Materialists have attempted to build up a system of morality upon the basis of enlightened self-interest. They would have man figure out by mathematics that it pays him to abstain from wrong-doing; they would even inject an element of selfishness into altruism, but the moral system elaborated by the materialists has several defects. First, its virtues are borrowed from moral systems based upon religion. All those who are intelligent enough to discuss a system of morality are so saturated with the morals derived from systems resting upon religion that they cannot frame a system resting upon reason alone. Second, as it rests upon argument rather than upon authority, the young are not in a position to accept or reject. Our laws do not permit a young man to dispose of real estate until he is twenty-one. Why this restraint? Because his reason is not mature; and yet a man's life is largely moulded by the environment of his youth. Third, one never knows just how much of his decision is due to reason and how much is due to passion or to selfish interest. Passion can dethrone the reason—we recognize this in our criminal laws. We also recognize the bias of self-interest when we exclude from the jury every man, no matter how reasonable or upright he may be, who has a pecuniary interest in the result of the trial. And, fourth, one whose morality rests upon a nice calculation of benefits to be secured spends time figuring that he should spend in action. Those who keep a book account of their good deeds seldom do enough good to justify keeping books. A noble life cannot be built upon an arithmetic; it must be rather like the spring that pours forth constantly of that which refreshes and invigorates.

Morality is the power of endurance in man; and a religion which teaches personal responsibility to God gives strength to morality. There is a powerful restraining influence in the belief that an all-seeing eye scrutinizes every thought and word and act of the individual.

There is wide difference between the man who is trying to conform his life to a standard of morality about him and the man who seeks to make his life approximate to a divine standard. The former attempts to live up to the standard, if it is above him, and down to it, if it is below him—and if he is doing right only when others are looking he is sure to find a time when he thinks he is unobserved, and then he takes a vacation and falls. One needs the inner strength which comes with the conscious presence of a personal God. If those who are thus fortified sometimes yield to temptation, how helpless and hopeless must those be who rely upon their own strength alone!

There are difficulties to be encountered in religion, but there are difficulties to be encountered everywhere. If Christians sometimes have doubts and fears, unbelievers have more doubts and greater fears. I passed through a period of skepticism when I was in college and I have been glad ever since that I became a member of the church before I left home for college, for it helped me during those trying days. And the college days cover the dangerous period in the young man's life; he is just coming into possession of his powers, and feels stronger than he ever feels afterward—and he thinks he knows more than he ever does know.

It was at this period that I became confused by the different theories of creation. But I examined these theories and found that they all assumed something to begin with. You can test this for yourselves. The nebular hypothesis, for instance, assumes that matter and force existed—matter in particles infinitely fine and each particle separated from every other particle by space infinitely great. Beginning with this assumption, force working on matter—according to this hypothesis—created a universe. Well, I have a right to assume, and I prefer to assume, a Designer back of the design—a Creator back of the creation; and no matter how long you draw out the process of creation, so long as God stands back of it you cannot shake my faith in Jehovah. In Genesis it is written that, in the beginning, God created the heavens and the earth, and I can stand on that proposition until I find some theory of creation that goes farther back than "the beginning." We must begin with something—we must start somewhere—and the Christian begins with God.

I do not carry the doctrine of evolution as far as some do; I am not yet convinced that man is a lineal descendant of the lower animals. I do not mean to find fault with you if you want to accept the theory; all I mean to say is that while you may trace your ancestry back to the monkey if you find pleasure or pride in doing so, you shall not connect me with your family tree without more evidence than has yet been produced. I object to the theory for several reasons. First, it is a dangerous theory. If a man links himself in generations with the monkey, it then becomes an important question whether he is going toward him or coming from him—and I have seen them going in both directions. I do not know of any argument that can be used to prove that man is an improved monkey that may not be used just as well to prove that the monkey is a degenerate man, and the latter theory is more plausible than the former.

It is true that man, in some physical characteristics resembles the beast, but man has a mind as well as a body, and a soul as well as a mind. The mind is greater than the body and the soul is greater than the mind, and I object to having man's pedigree traced on one-third of him only—and that the lowest third. Fairbairn, in his "Philosophy of Christianity," lays down a sound proposition when he says that it is not sufficient to explain man as an animal; that it is necessary to explain man in history—and the Darwinian theory does not do this. The ape, according to this theory, is older than man and yet the ape is still an ape while man is the author of the marvelous civilization which we see about us.

One does not escape from mystery, however, by accepting this theory, for it does not explain the origin of life. When the follower of Darwin has traced the germ of life back to the lowest form in which it appears—and to follow him one must exercise more faith than religion calls for—he finds that scientists differ. Those who reject the idea of creation are divided into two schools, some believing that the first germ of life came from another planet and others holding that it was the result of spontaneous generation. Each school answers the arguments advanced by the other, and as they cannot agree with each other, I am not compelled to agree with either.

If I were compelled to accept one of these theories I would prefer the first, for if we can chase the germ of life off this planet and get it out into space we can guess the rest of the way and no one can contradict us, but if we accept the doctrine of spontaneous generation we cannot explain why spontaneous generation ceased to act after the first germ was created.

Go back as far as we may, we cannot escape from the creative act, and it is just as easy for me to believe that God created man *as he is* as to believe that, millions of years ago, He created a germ of life and endowed it with power to develop into all that we see to-day. I object to the Darwinian theory, until more conclusive proof is produced, because I fear we shall lose the consciousness of God's presence in our daily life, if we must accept the theory that through all the ages no spiritual force has touched the life of man or shaped the destiny of nations.

But there is another objection. The Darwinian theory represents man as reaching his present perfection by the operation of the law of hate—the merciless law by which the strong crowd out and kill off the weak. If this is the law of our development then, if there is any logic that can bind the human mind, we shall turn backward toward the beast in proportion as we substitute the law of love. I prefer to believe that love rather than hatred is the law of development. How can hatred be the law of development when nations have advanced in proportion as they have departed from that law and adopted the law of love?

But, I repeat, while I do not accept the Darwinian theory I shall not quarrel with you about it; I only refer to it to remind you that it does not solve the mystery of life or explain human progress. I fear that some have accepted it in the hope of escaping from the miracle, but why should the miracle frighten us? And yet I am inclined to think that it is one of the test questions with the Christian.

Christ cannot be separated from the miraculous; His birth, His ministrations, and His resurrection, all involve the miraculous, and the change which His religion works in the human heart is a continuing miracle. Eliminate the miracles and Christ becomes merely a human being and His gospel is stript of divine authority.

The miracle raises two questions: "Can God perform a miracle?" and, "Would He want to?" The first is easy to answer. A God who can make a world can do anything He wants to do with it. The power to perform miracles is necessarily implied in the power to create. But would God *want* to perform a miracle?—this is the question which has given most of the trouble. The more I have considered it the less inclined I am to answer in the negative. To say that God *would not* perform a miracle is to assume a more intimate knowledge of God's plans and purposes than I can claim to have. I will not deny that God does perform a miracle or may perform one merely because I do not know how or why He does it. I find it so difficult to decide each day what God wants done now that I am not presumptuous enough to attempt to declare what God might have wanted to do thousands of years ago. The fact that we are constantly learning of the existence of new forces suggests the possibility that God may operate through forces yet unknown to us, and the mysteries with which we deal every day warn me that faith is as necessary as sight. Who would have credited a century ago the stories that are now told of the wonder-working electricity? For ages man had known the lightning, but only to fear it; now, this invisible current is generated by a man-made machine, imprisoned in a man-made wire and made to do the bidding of man. We are even able to dispense with the wire and hurl words through space, and the X-ray has enabled us to look through substances which were supposed, until recently, to exclude all light. The miracle is not more mysterious than many of the things with which man now deals—it is simply different. The miraculous birth of Christ is not more mysterious than any other conception—it is simply unlike it; nor is the resurrection of Christ more mysterious than the myriad resurrections which mark each annual seed-time.

It is sometimes said that God could not suspend one of His laws without stopping the universe, but do we not suspend or overcome the law of gravitation every day? Every time we move a foot or lift a weight we temporarily overcome one of the most universal of natural laws and yet the world is not disturbed.

Science has taught us so many things that we are tempted to conclude that we know everything, but there is really a great unknown which is still unexplored and that which we have learned ought to increase our reverence rather than our egotism. Science has disclosed some of the machinery of the universe, but science has not yet revealed to us the great secret—the secret of life. It is to be found in every blade of grass, in every insect, in every bird and in every animal, as well as in man. Six thousand years of recorded history and yet we know no more about the secret of life than they knew in the beginning. We live, we plan; we have our hopes, our fears; and yet in a moment a change may come over anyone of us and this body will become a mass of lifeless clay. What is it that, having, we live, and having not, we are as the clod? The progress of the race and the civilization which we now behold are the work of men and women who have not yet solved the mystery of their own lives.

And our food, must we understand it before we eat it? If we refused to eat anything until we could understand the mystery of its growth, we would die of starvation. But mystery does not bother us in the dining-room; it is only in the church that it is a stumbling block.

I was eating a piece of watermelon some months ago and was struck with its beauty. I took some of the seeds and dried them and weighed them, and found that it would require some five thousand seeds to weigh a pound; and then I applied mathematics to that forty-pound melon. One of these seeds, put into the ground, when warmed by the sun and moistened by the rain, takes off its coat and goes to work; it gathers from somewhere two hundred thousand times its own weight, and forcing this raw material through a tiny stem, constructs a watermelon. It ornaments the outside with a covering of green; inside the green it puts a layer of white, and within the white a core of red, and all through the red it scatters seeds, each one capable of continuing the work of reproduction. Where does that little seed get its tremendous power? Where does it find its coloring matter? How does it collect its flavoring extract? How does it build a watermelon? Until you can explain a watermelon, do not be too sure that you can set limits to the power of the Almighty and say just what He would do or how He would do it. I cannot explain the watermelon, but I eat it and enjoy it.

The egg is the most universal of foods and its use dates from the beginning, but what is more mysterious than an egg? When an egg is fresh it is an important article of merchandise; a hen can destroy its market value in a week's time, but in two weeks more she can bring forth from it what man could not find in it. We eat eggs, but we cannot explain an egg.

Water has been used from the birth of man; we learned after it had been used for ages that it is merely a mixture of gases, but it is far more important that we have water to drink than that we know that it is not water.

Everything that grows tells a like story of infinite power. Why should I deny that a divine hand fed a multitude with a few loaves and fishes when I see hundreds of millions fed every year by a hand which converts the seeds scattered over the field into an abundant harvest? We know that food can be multiplied in a few months' time; shall we deny the power of the Creator to eliminate the element of time, when we have gone so far in eliminating the element of space? Who am I that I should attempt to measure the arm of the Almighty with my puny arm, or to measure the brain of the Infinite with my finite mind? Who am I that I should attempt to put metes and bounds to the power of the Creator?

But there is something even more wonderful still—the mysterious change that takes place in the human heart when the man begins to hate the things he loved and to love the things he hated—the marvelous transformation that takes place in the man who, before the change, would have sacrificed a world for his own advancement but who, after the change, would give his life for a principle and esteem it a privilege to make sacrifice for his convictions! What greater miracle than this, that converts a selfish, self-centered human being into a center from which good influences flow out in every direction! And yet this miracle has been wrought in the heart of each one of us—or may be wrought—and we have seen it wrought in the hearts and lives of those about us. No, living a life that is a mystery, and living in the midst of mystery and miracles, I shall not allow either to deprive me of the benefits of the Christian religion. If you ask me if I understand everything in the Bible, I answer, no, but if we will try to live up to what we do understand, we will be kept so busy doing good that we will not have time to worry about the passages which we do not understand.

Some of those who question the miracle also question the theory of atonement; they assert that it does not accord with their idea of justice for one to die for all. Let each one bear his own sins and the punishments due for them, they say. The doctrine of vicarious suffering is not a new one; it is as old as the race. That one should suffer for others is one of the most familiar of principles and we see the principle illustrated every day of our lives. Take the family, for instance; from the day the mother's first child is born, for twenty or thirty years her children are scarcely out of her waking thoughts. Her life trembles in the balance at each child's birth; she sacrifices for them, she surrenders herself to them. Is it because she expects them to pay her back? Fortunate for the parent and fortunate for the child if the latter has an opportunity to repay in part the debt it owes. But no child can compensate a parent for a parent's care. In the course of nature the debt is paid, not to the parent, but to the next generation, and the next—each generation suffering, sacrificing for and surrendering itself to the generation that follows. This is the law of our lives.

Nor is this confined to the family. Every step in civilization has been made possible by those who have been willing to sacrifice for posterity. Freedom of speech, freedom of the press, freedom of conscience and free government have all been won for the world by those who were willing to labor unselfishly for their fellows. So well established is this doctrine that we do not regard anyone as great unless he recognizes how unimportant his life is in comparison with the problems with which he deals.

I find proof that man was made in the image of his Creator in the fact that, throughout the centuries, man has been willing to die, if necessary, that blessings denied to him might be enjoyed by his children, his children's children and the world.

The seeming paradox: "He that saveth his life shall lose it and he that loseth his life for my sake shall find it," has an application wider than that usually given to it; it is an epitome of history. Those who live only for themselves live little lives, but those who stand ready to give themselves for the advancement of things greater than themselves find a larger life than the one they would have surrendered. Wendell Phillips gave expression to the same idea when he said, "What imprudent men the benefactors of the race have been. How prudently most men sink into nameless graves, while now and then a few *forget* themselves into immortality." We win immortality, not by remembering ourselves, but by forgetting ourselves in devotion to things larger than ourselves.

Instead of being an unnatural plan, the plan of salvation is in perfect harmony with human nature as we understand it. Sacrifice is the language of love, and Christ, in suffering for the world, adopted the only means of reaching the heart. This can be demonstrated not only by theory but by experience, for the story of His life, His teachings, His sufferings and His death has been translated into every language and everywhere it has touched the heart.

But if I were going to present an argument in favor of the divinity of Christ, I would not begin with miracles or mystery or with the theory of atonement. I would begin as Carnegie Simpson does in his book entitled, "The Fact of Christ." Commencing with the undisputed fact that Christ lived, he points out that one cannot contemplate this fact without feeling that in some way it is related to those now living. He says that one can read of Alexander, of Cæsar or of Napoleon, and not feel that it is a matter of personal concern; but that when one reads that Christ lived, and how He lived and how He died, he feels that somehow there is a cord that stretches from that life to his. As he studies the character of Christ he becomes conscious of certain virtues which stand out in bold relief—His purity, His forgiving spirit, and His unfathomable love. The author is correct, Christ presents an example of purity in thought and life, and man, conscious of his own imperfections and grieved over his shortcomings, finds inspiration in the fact that He was tempted in all points like as we are, and yet without sin. I am not sure but that each can find just here a way of determining for himself whether he possesses the true spirit of a Christian. If the sinlessness of Christ inspires within him an earnest desire to conform his life more nearly to the perfect example, he is indeed a follower; if, on the other hand, he resents the reproof which the purity of Christ offers, and refuses to mend his ways, he has yet to be born again.

The most difficult of all the virtues to cultivate is the forgiving spirit. Revenge seems to be natural with man; it is human to want to get even with an enemy. It has even been popular to boast of vindictiveness; it was once inscribed on a man's monument that he had repaid both friends and enemies more than he had received. This was not the spirit of Christ. He taught forgiveness and in that incomparable prayer which He left as model for our petitions, He made our willingness to forgive the measure by which we may claim forgiveness. He not only taught forgiveness but He exemplified His teachings in His life. When those who persecuted Him brought Him to the most disgraceful of all deaths, His spirit of forgiveness rose above His sufferings and He prayed, "Father, forgive them, for they know not what they do!"

But love is the foundation of Christ's creed. The world had known love before; parents had loved their children, and children their parents; husbands had loved their wives, and wives their husbands; and friend had loved friend; but Jesus gave a new definition of love. His love was as wide as the sea; its limits were so far-flung that even an enemy could not travel beyond its bounds. Other teachers sought to regulate the lives of their followers by rule and formula, but Christ's plan was to purify the heart and then to leave love to direct the footsteps.

What conclusion is to be drawn from the life, the teachings and the death of this historic figure? Reared in a carpenter shop; with no knowledge of literature, save Bible literature; with no acquaintance with philosophers living or with the writings of sages dead, when only about thirty years old He gathered disciples about Him, promulgated a higher code of morals than the world had ever known before, and proclaimed Himself the Messiah. He taught and performed miracles for a few brief months and then was crucified; His disciples were scattered and many of them put to death; His claims were disputed, His resurrection denied and His followers persecuted; and yet from this beginning His religion spread until hundreds of millions have taken His name with reverence upon their lips and millions have been willing to die rather than surrender the faith which He put into their hearts. How shall we account for Him? Here is the greatest fact of history; here is One who has with increasing power, for nineteen hundred years, moulded the hearts, the thoughts and the lives of men, and He exerts more influence to-day than ever before. "What think ye of Christ?" It is easier to believe Him divine than to explain in any other way what he said and did and was. And I have greater faith, even than before, since I have visited the Orient and witnessed the successful contest which Christianity is waging against the religions and philosophies of the East.

I was thinking a few years ago of the Christmas which was then approaching and of Him in whose honor the day is celebrated. I recalled the message, "Peace on earth, good will to men," and then my thoughts ran back to the prophecy uttered centuries before His birth, in which He was described as the Prince of Peace. To reinforce my memory I re-read the prophecy and I found immediately following a verse which I had forgotten—a verse which declares that of the increase of His peace and government there shall be no end, And, Isaiah adds, that He shall judge His people with justice and with judgment. I had been reading of the rise and fall of nations, and occasionally I had met a gloomy philosopher who preached the doctrine that nations, like individuals, must of necessity have their birth, their infancy, their maturity and finally their decay and death. But here I read of a government that is to be perpetual—a government of increasing peace and blessedness—the government of the Prince of Peace—and it is to rest on justice. I have thought of this prophecy many times during the last few years, and I have selected this theme that I might present some of the reasons which lead me to believe that Christ has fully earned the right to be called The Prince of Peace—a title that will in the years to come be more and more applied to Him. If he can bring peace to each individual heart, and if His creed when applied will bring peace throughout the earth, who will deny His right to be called the Prince of Peace?

All the world is in search of peace; every heart that ever beat has sought for peace, and many have been the methods employed to secure it. Some have thought to purchase it with riches and have labored to secure wealth, hoping to find peace when they were able to go where they pleased and buy what they liked. Of those who have endeavored to purchase peace with money, the large majority have failed to secure the money. But what has been the experience of those who have been eminently successful in finance? They all tell the same story, viz., that they spent the first half of their lives trying to get money from others and the last half trying to keep others from getting their money, and that they found peace in neither half. Some have even reached the point where they find difficulty in getting people to accept their money; and I know of no better indication of the ethical awakening in this country than the increasing tendency to scrutinize the methods of money-making. I am sanguine enough to believe that the time will yet come when respectability will no longer be sold to great criminals by helping them to spend their ill-gotten gains. A long step in advance will have been taken when religious, educational and charitable institutions refuse to condone conscienceless methods in business and leave the possessor of illegitimate accumulations to learn how lonely life is when one prefers money to morals.

Some have sought peace in social distinction, but whether they have been within the charmed circle and fearful lest they might fall out, or outside, and hopeful that they might get in, they have not found peace. Some have thought, vain thought, to find peace in political prominence; but whether office comes by birth, as in monarchies, or by election, as in republics, it does not bring peace. An office is not considered a high one if all can occupy it. Only when few in a generation can hope to enjoy an honor do we call it a great honor. I am glad that our Heavenly Father did not make the peace of the human heart to depend upon our ability to buy it with money, secure it in society, or win it at the polls, for in either case but few could have obtained it, but when He made peace the reward of a conscience void of offense toward God and man, He put it within the reach of all. The poor can secure it as easily as the rich, the social outcasts as freely as the leader of society, and the humblest citizen equally with those who wield political power.

To those who have grown gray in the Church, I need not speak of the peace to be found in faith in God and trust in an overruling Providence. Christ taught that our lives are precious in the sight of God, and poets have taken up the thought and woven it into immortal verse. No uninspired writer has exprest it more beautifully than William Cullen Bryant in his Ode to a Waterfowl. After following the wanderings of the bird of passage as it seeks first its southern and then its northern home, he concludes:

> Thou art gone; the abyss of heaven
> > Hath swallowed up thy form, but on my heart
> Deeply hath sunk the lesson thou hast given,
> > And shall not soon depart.
>
> He who, from zone to zone,
> > Guides through the boundless sky thy certain flight,
> In the long way that I must tread alone,
> > Will lead my steps aright.

Christ promoted peace by giving us assurance that a line of communication can be established between the Father above and the child below. And who will measure the consolations of the hour of prayer?

And immortality! Who will estimate the peace which a belief in a future life has brought to the sorrowing hearts of the sons of men? You may talk to the young about death ending all, for life is full and hope is strong, but preach not this doctrine to the mother who stands by the death-bed of her babe or to one who is within the shadow of a great affliction. When I was a young man I wrote to Colonel Ingersoll and asked him for his views on God and immortality. His secretary answered that the great infidel was not at home, but enclosed a copy of a speech of Col. Ingersoll's which covered my question. I scanned it with eagerness and found that he had exprest himself about as follows: "I do not say that there is no God, I simply say I do not know. I do not say that there is no life beyond the grave, I simply say I do not know." And from that day to this I have asked myself the question and have been unable to answer it to my own satisfaction, how could anyone find pleasure in taking from a human heart a living faith and substituting therefor the cold and cheerless doctrine, "I do not know."

Christ gave us proof of immortality and it was a welcome assurance, altho it would hardly seem necessary that one should rise from the dead to convince us that the grave is not the end. To every created thing God has given a tongue that proclaims a future life.

If the Father deigns to touch with divine power the cold and pulseless heart of the buried acorn and to make it burst forth from its prison walls, will he leave neglected in the earth the soul of man, made in the image of his Creator? If he stoops to give to the rose bush, whose withered blossoms float upon the autumn breeze, the sweet assurance of another springtime, will He refuse the words of hope to the sons of men when the frosts of winter come? If matter, mute and inanimate, tho changed by the forces of nature into a multitude of forms, can never die, will the imperial spirit of man suffer annihilation when it has paid a brief visit like a royal guest to this tenement of clay? No, I am sure that He who, notwithstanding his apparent prodigality, created nothing without a purpose, and wasted not a single atom in all his creation, has made provision for a future life in which man's universal longing for immortality will find its realization. I am as sure that we live again as I am sure that we live to-day.

In Cairo I secured a few grains of wheat that had slumbered for more than thirty centuries in an Egyptian tomb. As I looked at them this thought came into my mind: If one of those grains had been planted on the banks of the Nile the year after it grew, and all its lineal descendants had been planted and replanted from that time until now, its progeny would to-day be sufficiently numerous to feed the teeming millions of the world. An unbroken chain of life connects the earliest grains of wheat with the grains that we sow and reap. There is in the grain of wheat an invisible something which has power to discard the body that we see, and from earth and air fashion a new body so much like the old one that we cannot tell the one from the other. If this invisible germ of life in the grain of wheat can thus pass unimpaired through three thousand resurrections, I shall not doubt that my soul has power to clothe itself with a body suited to its new existence when this earthly frame has crumbled into dust.

A belief in immortality not only consoles the individual, but it exerts a powerful influence in bringing peace between individuals. If one actually thinks that man dies as the brute dies, he will yield more easily to the temptation to do injustice to his neighbor when the circumstances are such as to promise security from detection. But if one really expects to meet again, and live eternally with, those whom he knows to-day, he is restrained from evil deeds by the fear of endless remorse. We do not know what rewards are in store for us or what punishments may be reserved, but if there were no other it would be some punishment for one who deliberately and consciously wrongs another to have to live forever in the company of the person wronged and have his littleness and selfishness laid bare. I repeat, a belief in immortality must exert a powerful influence in establishing justice between men and thus laying the foundation for peace.

Again, Christ deserves to be called The Prince of Peace because He has given us a measure of greatness which promotes peace. When His disciples quarreled among themselves as to which should be greatest in the Kingdom of Heaven, He rebuked them and said: "Let him who would be chiefest among you be the servant of all." Service is the measure of greatness; it always has been true; it is true to-day, and it always will be true, that he is greatest who does the most of good. And how this old world will be transformed when this standard of greatness becomes the standard of every life! Nearly all of our controversies and combats grow out of the fact that we are trying to get something from each other—there will be peace when our aim is to do something for each other. Our enmities and animosities arise largely from our efforts to get as much as possible out of the world— there will be peace when our endeavor is to put as much as possible into the world. The human measure of a human life is its income; the divine measure of a life is its outgo, its overflow—its contribution to the welfare of all.

Christ also led the way to peace by giving us a formula for the propagation of truth. Not all of those who have really desired to do good have employed the Christian method— not all Christians even. In the history of the human race but two methods have been used. The first is the forcible method, and it has been employed most frequently. A man has an idea which he thinks is good; he tells his neighbors about it and they do not like it. This makes him angry; he thinks it would be so much better for them if they would like it, and, seizing a club, he attempts to make them like it. But one trouble about this rule is that it works both ways; when a man starts out to compel his neighbors to think as he does, he generally finds them willing to accept the challenge and they spend so much time in trying to coerce each other that they have no time left to do each other good.

The other is the Bible plan—"Be not overcome of evil but overcome evil with good." And there is no other way of overcoming evil. I am not much of a farmer—I get more credit for my farming than I deserve, and my little farm receives more advertising than it is entitled to. But I am farmer enough to know that if I cut down weeds they will spring up again; and farmer enough to know that if I plant something there which has more vitality than the weeds I shall not only get rid of the constant cutting, but have the benefit of the crop besides.

In order that there might be no mistake in His plan of propagating the truth, Christ went into detail and laid emphasis upon the value of example—"So live that others seeing your good works may be constrained to glorify your Father which is in Heaven." There is no human influence so potent for good as that which goes out from an upright life. A sermon may be answered; the arguments presented in a speech may be disputed, but no one can answer a Christian life—it is the unanswerable argument in favor of our religion.

It may be a slow process—this conversion of the world by the silent influence of a noble example—but it is the only sure one, and the doctrine applies to nations as well as to individuals. The Gospel of the Prince of Peace gives us the only hope that the world has—and it is an increasing hope—of the substitution of reason for the arbitrament of force in the settlement of international disputes. And our nation ought not to wait for other nations—it ought to take the lead and prove its faith in the omnipotence of truth.

But Christ has given us a platform so fundamental that it can be applied successfully to all controversies. We are interested in platforms; we attend conventions, sometimes traveling long distances; we have wordy wars over the phraseology of various planks, and then we wage earnest campaigns to secure the endorsement of these platforms at the polls. The platform given to the world by The Prince of Peace is more far-reaching and more comprehensive than any platform ever written by the convention of any party in any country. When He condensed into one commandment those of the ten which relate to man's duty toward his fellows and enjoined upon us the rule, "Thou shalt love thy neighbor as thyself," He presented a plan for the solution of all the problems that now vex society or may hereafter arise. Other remedies may palliate or postpone the day of settlement, but this is all-sufficient and the reconciliation which it effects is a permanent one.

My faith in the future—and I have faith—and my optimism—for I am an optimist—my faith and my optimism rest upon the belief that Christ's teachings are being more studied to-day than ever before, and that with this larger study will come a larger application of those teachings to the everyday life of the world, and to the questions with which we deal. In former times when men read that Christ came "to bring life and immortality to light," they placed the emphasis upon immortality; now they are studying Christ's relation to human life. People used to read the Bible to find out what it said of Heaven; now they read it more to find what light it throws upon the pathway of to-day. In former years many thought to prepare themselves for future bliss by a life of seclusion here; we are learning that to follow in the footsteps of the Master we must go about doing good. Christ declared that He came that we might have life and have it more abundantly. The world is learning that Christ came not to narrow life, but to enlarge it—not to rob it of its joy, but to fill it to overflowing with purpose, earnestness and happiness.

But this Prince of Peace promises not only peace but strength. Some have thought His teachings fit only for the weak and the timid and unsuited to men of vigor, energy and ambition. Nothing could be farther from the truth. Only the man of faith can be courageous. Confident that he fights on the side of Jehovah, he doubts not the success of his cause. What matters it whether he shares in the shouts of triumph? If every word spoken in behalf of truth has its influence and every deed done for the right weighs in the final account, it is immaterial to the Christian whether his eyes behold victory or whether he dies in the midst of the conflict.

"Yea, tho thou lie upon the dust,
  When they who helped thee flee in fear,
Die full of hope and manly trust,
  Like those who fell in battle here.

Another hand thy sword shall wield,
  Another hand the standard wave,
Till from the trumpet's mouth is pealed,
  The blast of triumph o'er thy grave."

Only those who *believe* attempt the seemingly impossible, and, by attempting, prove that one, with God, can chase a thousand and that two can put ten thousand to flight. I can imagine that the early Christians who were carried into the coliseum to make a spectacle for those more savage than the beasts, were entreated by their doubting companions not to endanger their lives. But, kneeling in the center of the arena, they prayed and sang until they were devoured. How helpless they seemed, and, measured by every human rule, how hopeless was their cause! And yet within a few decades the power which they invoked proved mightier than the legions of the emperor and the faith in which they died was triumphant o'er all the land. It is said that those who went to mock at their sufferings returned asking themselves, "What is it that can enter into the heart of man and make him die as these die?" They were greater conquerors in their death than they could have been had they purchased life by a surrender of their faith.

What would have been the fate of the church if the early Christians had had as little faith as many of our Christians of to-day? And if the Christians of to-day had the faith of the martyrs, how long would it be before the fulfilment of the prophecy that "every knee shall bow and every tongue confess?"

I am glad that He, who is called the Prince of Peace—who can bring peace to every troubled heart and whose teachings, exemplified in life, will bring peace between man and man, between community and community, between State and State, between nation and nation throughout the world—I am glad that He brings courage as well as peace so that those who follow Him may take up and each day bravely do the duties that to that day fall.

As the Christian grows older he appreciates more and more the completeness with which Christ satisfies the longings of the heart, and, grateful for the peace which he enjoys and for the strength which he has received, he repeats the words of the great scholar, Sir William Jones:

"Before thy mystic altar, heavenly truth,
  I kneel in manhood, as I knelt in youth,
Thus let me kneel, till this dull form decay,
  And life's last shade be brightened by thy ray."

# Eulogy of Webster

RUFUS CHOATE

*—Delivered at Dartmouth College, July 27, 1853.*

Webster possessed the element of an impressive character, inspiring regard, trust and admiration, not unmingled with love. It had, I think, intrinsically a charm such as belongs only to a good, noble, and beautiful nature. In its combination with so much fame, so much force of will, and so much intellect, it filled and fascinated the imagination and heart. It was affectionate in childhood and youth, and it was more than ever so in the few last months of his long life. It is the universal testimony that he gave to his parents, in largest measure, honor, love, obedience; that he eagerly appropriated the first means which he could command to relieve the father from the debts contracted to educate his brother and himself; that he selected his first place of professional practice that he might soothe the coming on of his old age.

Equally beautiful was his love of all his kindred and of all his friends. When I hear him accused of selfishness, and a cold, bad nature, I recall him lying sleepless all night, not without tears of boyhood, conferring with Ezekiel how the darling desire of both hearts should be compassed, and he, too, admitted to the precious privileges of education; courageously pleading the cause of both brothers in the morning; prevailing by the wise and discerning affection of the mother; suspending his studies of the law, and registering deeds and teaching school to earn the means, for both, of availing themselves of the opportunity which the parental self-sacrifice had placed within their reach; loving him through life, mourning him when dead, with a love and a sorrow very wonderful, passing the sorrow of woman; I recall the husband, the father of the living and of the early departed, the friend, the counselor of many years, and my heart grows too full and liquid for the refutation of words.

His affectionate nature, craving ever friendship, as well as the presence of kindred blood, diffused itself through all his private life, gave sincerity to all his hospitalities, kindness to his eye, warmth to the pressure of his hand, made his greatness and genius unbend themselves to the playfulness of childhood, flowed out in graceful memories indulged of the past or the dead, of incidents when life was young and promised to be happy,— gave generous sketches of his rivals,—the high contention now hidden by the handful of earth,—hours passed fifty years ago with great authors, recalled for the vernal emotions which then they made to live and revel in the soul. And from these conversations of friendship, no man—no man, old or young—went away to remember one word of profaneness, one allusion of indelicacy, one impure thought, one unbelieving suggestion, one doubt cast on the reality of virtue, of patriotism, of enthusiasm, of the progress of man,—one doubt cast on righteousness, or temperance, or judgment to come.

I have learned by evidence the most direct and satisfactory that in the last months of his life, the whole affectionateness of his nature—his consideration of others, his gentleness, his desire to make them happy and to see them happy—seemed to come out in more and more beautiful and habitual expressions than ever before. The long day's public tasks were felt to be done; the cares, the uncertainties, the mental conflicts of high place, were ended; and he came home to recover himself for the few years which he might still expect would be his before he should go hence to be here no more. And there, I am assured and duly believe, no unbecoming regrets pursued him; no discontent, as for injustice suffered or expectations unfulfilled; no self-reproach for anything done or anything omitted by himself; no irritation, no peevishness unworthy of his noble nature; but instead, love and hope for his country, when she became the subject of conversation, and for all around him, the dearest and most indifferent, for all breathing things about him, the overflow of the kindest heart growing in gentleness and benevolence—paternal, patriarchal affections, seeming to become more natural, warm, and communicative every hour. Softer and yet brighter grew the tints on the sky of parting day; and the last lingering rays, more even than the glories of noon, announced how divine was the source from which they proceeded; how incapable to be quenched; how certain to rise on a morning which no night should follow.

Such a character was made to be loved. It was loved. Those who knew and saw it in its hour of calm—those who could repose on that soft green—loved him. His plain neighbors loved him; and one said, when he was laid in his grave, "How lonesome the world seems!" Educated young men loved him. The ministers of the gospel, the general intelligence of the country, the masses afar oft, loved him. True, they had not found in his speeches, read by millions, so much adulation of the people; so much of the music which robs the public reason of itself; so many phrases of humanity and philanthropy; and some had told them he was lofty and cold—solitary in his greatness; but every year they came nearer and nearer to him, and as they came nearer, they loved him better; they heard how tender the son had been, the husband, the brother, the father, the friend, and neighbor; that he was plain, simple, natural, generous, hospitable—the heart larger than the brain; that he loved little children and reverenced God, the Scriptures, the Sabbath-day, the Constitution, and the law—and their hearts clave unto him. More truly of him than even of the great naval darling of England might it be said that "his presence would set the church bells ringing, and give schoolboys a holiday, would bring children from school and old men from the chimney-corner, to gaze on him ere he died." The great and unavailing lamentations first revealed the deep place he had in the hearts of his countrymen.

You are now to add to this his extraordinary power of influencing the convictions of others by speech, and you have completed the survey of the means of his greatness. And here, again I begin by admiring an aggregate made up of excellences and triumphs, ordinarily deemed incompatible. He spoke with consummate ability to the bench, and yet exactly as, according to every sound canon of taste and ethics, the bench ought to be addressed. He spoke with consummate ability to the jury, and yet exactly as, according to every sound canon, that totally different tribunal ought to be addressed. In the halls of Congress, before the people assembled for political discussion in masses, before audiences smaller and more select, assembled for some solemn commemoration of the past or of the dead—in each of these, again, his speech, of the first form of ability, was exactly adapted, also, to the critical properties of the place; each achieved, when delivered, the most instant and specific success of eloquence—some of them in a splendid and remarkable degree; and yet, stranger still, when reduced to writing, as they fell from his lips, they compose a body of reading in many volumes—solid, clear, rich, and full of harmony—a classical and permanent political literature.

And yet all these modes of his eloquence, exactly adapted each to its stage and its end, were stamped with his image and superscription, identified by characteristics incapable to be counterfeited and impossible to be mistaken. The same high power of reason, intent in every one to explore and display some truth; some truth of judicial, or historical, or biographical fact; some truth of law, deduced by construction, perhaps, or by illation; some truth of policy, for want whereof a nation, generations, may be the worse—reason seeking and unfolding truth; the same tone, in all, of deep earnestness, expressive of strong desire that what he felt to be important should be accepted as true, and spring up to action; the same transparent, plain, forcible, and direct speech, conveying his exact thought to the mind—not something less or more; the same sovereignty of form, of brow, and eye, and tone, and manner—everywhere the intellectual king of men, standing before you—that same marvelousness of qualities and results, residing, I know not where, in words, in pictures, in the ordering of ideas, infelicities indescribable, by means whereof, coming from his tongue, all things seemed mended—truth seemed more true, probability more plausible, greatness more grand, goodness more awful, every affection more tender than when coming from other tongues—these are, in all, his eloquence.

But sometimes it became individualized and discriminated even from itself; sometimes place and circumstances, great interests at stake, a stage, an audience fitted for the highest historic action, a crisis, personal or national, upon him, stirred the depths of that emotional nature, as the anger of the goddess stirs the sea on which the great epic is beginning; strong passions themselves kindled to intensity, quickened every faculty to a new life; the stimulated associations of ideas brought all treasures of thought and knowledge within command; the spell, which often held his imagination fast, dissolved, and she arose and gave him to choose of her urn of gold; earnestness became vehemence, the simple, perspicuous, measured and direct language became a headlong, full, and burning tide of speech; the discourse of reason, wisdom, gravity, and beauty changed to that superhuman, that rarest consummate eloquence—grand, rapid, pathetic, terrible; the *aliquid immensum infinitumque* that Cicero might have recognized; the master triumph of man in the rarest opportunity of his noble power.

Such elevation above himself, in Congressional debate, was most uncommon. Some such there were in the great discussions of executive power following the removal of the deposits, which they who heard them will never forget, and some which rest in the tradition of hearers only. But there were other fields of oratory on which, under the influence of more uncommon springs of inspiration, he exemplified, in still other forms, an eloquence in which I do not know that he has had a superior among men. Addressing masses by tens of thousands in the open air, on the urgent political questions of the day, or designed to lead the meditations of an hour devoted to the remembrance of some national era, or of some incident marking the progress of the nation, and lifting him up to a view of what is, and what is past, and some indistinct revelation of the glory that lies in the future, or of some great historical name, just borne by the nation to his tomb—we have learned that then and there, at the base of Bunker Hill, before the corner-stone was laid, and again when from the finished column the centuries looked on him; in Faneuil Hall, mourning for those with whose spoken or written eloquence of freedom its arches had so often resounded; on the Rock of Plymouth; before the Capitol, of which there shall not be one stone left on another before his memory shall have ceased to live—in such scenes, unfettered by the laws of forensic or parliamentary debate, multitudes uncounted lifting up their eyes to him; some great historical scenes of America around; all symbols of her glory and art and power and fortune there; voices of the past, not unheard; shapes beckoning from the future, not unseen—sometimes that mighty intellect, borne upward to a height and kindled to an illumination which we shall see no more, wrought out, as it were, in an instant a picture of vision, warning, prediction; the progress of the nation; the contrasts of its eras; the heroic deaths; the motives to patriotism; the maxims and arts imperial by which the glory has been gathered and may be heightened—wrought out, in an instant, a picture to fade only when all record of our mind shall die.

In looking over the public remains of his oratory, it is striking to remark how, even in that most sober and massive understanding and nature, you see gathered and expressed the characteristic sentiments and the passing time of our America. It is the strong old oak which ascends before you; yet our soil, our heaven, are attested in it as perfectly as if it were a flower that could grow in no other climate and in no other hour of the year or day. Let me instance in one thing only. It is a peculiarity of some schools of eloquence that they embody and utter, not merely the individual genius and character of the speaker, but a national consciousness—a national era, a mood, a hope, a dread, a despair—in which you listen to the spoken history of the time. There is an eloquence of an expiring nation, such as seems to sadden the glorious speech of Demosthenes; such as breathes grand and gloomy from visions of the prophets of the last days of Israel and Judah; such as gave a spell to the expression of Grattan and of Kossuth—the sweetest, most mournful, most awful of the words which man may utter, or which man may hear—the eloquence of a perishing nation.

There is another eloquence, in which the national consciousness of a young or renewed and vast strength, of trust in a dazzling certain and limitless future, an inward glorying in victories yet to be won, sounds out as by voice of clarion, challenging to contest for the highest prize of earth; such as that in which the leader of Israel in its first days holds up to the new nation the Land of Promise; such as that which in the well-imagined speeches scattered by Livy over the history of the "majestic series of victories" speaks the Roman consciousness of growing aggrandizement which should subject the world; such as that through which, at the tribunes of her revolution, in the bulletins of her rising soldiers, France told to the world her dream of glory.

And of this kind somewhat is ours—cheerful, hopeful, trusting, as befits youth and spring; the eloquence of a state beginning to ascend to the first class of power, eminence, and consideration, and conscious of itself. It is to no purpose that they tell you it is in bad taste; that it partakes of arrogance and vanity; that a true national good breeding would not know, or seem to know, whether the nation is old or young; whether the tides of being are in their flow or ebb; whether these coursers of the sun are sinking slowly to rest, wearied with a journey of a thousand years, or just bounding from the Orient unbreathed. Higher laws than those of taste determine the consciousness of nations. Higher laws than those of taste determine the general forms of the expression of that consciousness. Let the downward age of America find its orators and poets and artists to erect its spirit, or grace and soothe its dying; be it ours to go up with Webster to the Rock, the Monument, the Capitol, and bid "the distant generations hail!"

Until the seventh day of March, 1850, I think it would have been accorded to him by an almost universal acclaim, as general and as expressive of profound and intelligent conviction and of enthusiasm, love, and trust, as ever saluted conspicuous statesmanship, tried by many crises of affairs in a great nation, agitated ever by parties, and wholly free.

## Pass Prosperity Around

ALBERT J. BEVERIDGE

*—Delivered as Temporary Chairman of Progressive*
*National Convention, Chicago, Ill., June, 1911.*

We stand for a nobler America. We stand for an undivided Nation. We stand for a broader liberty, a fuller justice. We stand for a social brotherhood as against savage individualism. We stand for an intelligent coöperation instead of a reckless competition. We stand for mutual helpfulness instead of mutual hatred. We stand for equal rights as a fact of life instead of a catch-word of politics. We stand for the rule of the people as a practical truth instead of a meaningless pretense. We stand for a representative government that represents the people. We battle for the actual rights of man.

To carry out our principles we have a plain program of constructive reform. We mean to tear down only that which is wrong and out of date; and where we tear down we mean to build what is right and fitted to the times. We harken to the call of the present. We mean to make laws fit conditions as they are and meet the needs of the people who are on earth to-day. That we may do this we found a party through which all who believe with us can work with us; or, rather, we declare our allegiance to the party which the people themselves have founded.

For this party comes from the grass roots. It has grown from the soil of the people's hard necessities. It has the vitality of the people's strong convictions. The people have work to be done and our party is here to do that work. Abuse will only strengthen it, ridicule only hasten its growth, falsehood only speed its victory. For years this party has been forming. Parties exist for the people; not the people for parties. Yet for years the politicians have made the people do the work of the parties instead of the parties doing the work of the people—and the politicians own the parties. The people vote for one party and find their hopes turned to ashes on their lips; and then to punish that party, they vote for the other party. So it is that partisan victories have come to be merely the people's vengeance; and always the secret powers have played their game.

Like other free people, most of us Americans are progressive or reactionary, liberal or conservative. The neutrals do not count. Yet to-day neither of the old parties is either wholly progressive or wholly reactionary. Democratic politicians and office seekers say to reactionary Democratic voters that the Democratic party is reactionary enough to express reactionary views; and they say to progressive Democrats that the Democratic party is progressive enough to express progressive views. At the same time, Republican politicians and office seekers say the same thing about the Republican party to progressive and reactionary Republican voters.

Sometimes in both Democratic and Republican States the progressives get control of the party locally and then the reactionaries recapture the same party in the same State; or this process is reversed. So there is no nation-wide unity of principle in either party, no stability of purpose, no clear-cut and sincere program of one party at frank and open war with an equally clear-cut and sincere program of an opposing party.

This unintelligent tangle is seen in Congress. Republican and Democratic Senators and Representatives, believing alike on broad measures affecting the whole Republic, find it hard to vote together because of the nominal difference of their party membership. When, sometimes, under resistless conviction, they do vote together, we have this foolish spectacle: legislators calling themselves Republicans and Democrats support the same policy, the Democratic legislators declaring that that policy is Democratic and Republican legislators declaring that it is Republican; and at the very same time other Democratic and Republican legislators oppose that very same policy, each of them declaring that it is not Democratic or not Republican.

The condition makes it impossible most of the time, and hard at any time, for the people's legislators who believe in the same broad policies to enact them into logical, comprehensive laws. It confuses the public mind. It breeds suspicion and distrust. It enables such special interests as seek unjust gain at the public expense to get what they want. It creates and fosters the degrading boss system in American politics through which these special interests work.

This boss system is unknown and impossible under any other free government in the world. In its very nature it is hostile to general welfare. Yet it has grown until it now is a controlling influence in American public affairs. At the present moment notorious bosses are in the saddle of both old parties in various important States which must be carried to elect a President. This Black Horse Cavalry is the most important force in the practical work of the Democratic and Republican parties in the present campaign. Neither of the old parties' nominees for President can escape obligation to these old-party bosses or shake their practical hold on many and powerful members of the National Legislature.

Under this boss system, no matter which party wins, the people seldom win; but the bosses almost always win. And they never work for the people. They do not even work for the party to which they belong. They work only for those anti-public interests whose political employees they are. It is these interests that are the real victors in the end.

These special interests which suck the people's substance are bi-partisan. They use both parties. They are the invisible government behind our visible government. Democratic and Republican bosses alike are brother officers of this hidden power. No matter how fiercely they pretend to fight one another before election, they work together after election. And, acting so, this political conspiracy is able to delay, mutilate or defeat sound and needed laws for the people's welfare and the prosperity of honest business and even to enact bad laws, hurtful to the people's welfare and oppressive to honest business.

It is this invisible government which is the real danger to American institutions. Its crude work at Chicago in June, which the people were able to see, was no more wicked than its skillful work everywhere and always which the people are not able to see.

But an even more serious condition results from the unnatural alignment of the old parties. To-day we Americans are politically shattered by sectionalism. Through the two old parties the tragedy of our history is continued; and one great geographical part of the Republic is separated from other parts of the Republic by an illogical partisan solidarity.

The South has men and women as genuinely progressive and others as genuinely reactionary as those in other parts of our country. Yet, for well-known reasons, these sincere and honest southern progressives and reactionaries vote together in a single party, which is neither progressive nor reactionary. They vote a dead tradition and a local fear, not a living conviction and a national faith. They vote not for the Democratic party, but against the Republican party. They want to be free from this condition; they can be free from it through the National Progressive party.

For the problems which America faces to-day are economic and national. They have to do with a more just distribution of prosperity. They concern the living of the people; and therefore the more direct government of the people by themselves.

They affect the South exactly as they affect the North, the East or the West. It is an artificial and dangerous condition that prevents the southern man and woman from acting with the northern man and woman who believe the same thing. Yet just that is what the old parties do prevent.

Not only does this out-of-date partisanship cut our Nation into two geographical sections; it also robs the Nation of a priceless asset of thought in working out our national destiny. The South once was famous for brilliant and constructive thinking on national problems, and to-day the South has minds as brilliant and constructive as of old. But southern intellect cannot freely and fully aid, in terms of politics, the solving of the Nation's problems. This is so because of a partisan sectionalism which has nothing to do with those problems. Yet these problems can be solved only in terms of politics.

The root of the wrongs which hurt the people is the fact that the people's government has been taken away from them—the invisible government has usurped the people's government. Their government must be given back to the people. And so the first purpose of the Progressive party is to make sure the rule of the people. The rule of the people means that the people themselves shall nominate, as well as elect, all candidates for office, including Senators and Presidents of the United States. What profiteth it the people if they do only the electing while the invisible government does the nominating?

The rule of the people means that when the people's legislators make a law which hurts the people, the people themselves may reject it. The rule of the people means that when the people's legislators refuse to pass a law which the people need, the people themselves may pass it. The rule of the people means that when the people's employees do not do the people's work well and honestly, the people may discharge them exactly as a business man discharges employees who do not do their work well and honestly. The people's officials are the people's servants, not the people's masters.

We progressives believe in this rule of the people that the people themselves may deal with their own destiny. Who knows the people's needs so well as the people themselves? Who so patient as the people? Who so long suffering, who so just? Who so wise to solve their own problems?

Today these problems concern the living of the people. Yet in the present stage of American development these problems should not exist in this country. For, in all the world there is no land so rich as ours. Our fields can feed hundreds of millions. We have more minerals than the whole of Europe. Invention has made easy the turning of this vast natural wealth into supplies for all the needs of man. One worker today can produce more than twenty workers could produce a century ago.

The people living in this land of gold are the most daring and resourceful on the globe. Coming from the hardiest stock of every nation of the old world their very history in the new world has made Americans a peculiar people in courage, initiative, love of justice and all the elements of independent character.

And, compared with other peoples, we are very few in numbers. There are only ninety millions of us, scattered over a continent. Germany has sixty-five millions packed in a country very much smaller than Texas. The population of Great Britain and Ireland could be set down in California and still have more than enough room for the population of Holland. If this country were as thickly peopled as Belgium there would be more than twelve hundred million instead of only ninety million persons within our borders.

So we have more than enough to supply every human being beneath the flag. There ought not to be in this Republic a single day of bad business, a single unemployed work-ingman, a single unfed child. American business men should never know an hour of uncertainty, discouragement or fear; American workingmen never a day of low wages, idleness or want. Hunger should never walk in these thinly peopled gardens of plenty.

And yet in spite of all these favors which providence has showered upon us, the living of the people is the problem of the hour. Hundreds of thousands of hard-working Americans find it difficult to get enough to live on. The average income of an American laborer is less than $500 a year. With this he must furnish food, shelter and clothing for a family.

Women, whose nourishing and protection should be the first care of the State, not only are driven into the mighty army of wage-earners, but are forced to work under unfair and degrading conditions. The right of a child to grow into a normal human being is sacred; and yet, while small and poor countries, packed with people, have abolished child labor, American mills, mines, factories and sweat-shops are destroying hundreds of thousands of American children in body, mind and soul.

At the same time men have grasped fortunes in this country so great that the human mind cannot comprehend their magnitude. These mountains of wealth are far larger than even that lavish reward which no one would deny to business risk or genius.

On the other hand, American business is uncertain and unsteady compared with the business of other nations. American business men are the best and bravest in the world, and yet our business conditions hamper their energies and chill their courage. We have no permanency in business affairs, no sure outlook upon the business future. This unsettled state of American business prevents it from realizing for the people that great and continuous prosperity which our country's location, vast wealth and small population justifies.

We mean to remedy these conditions. We mean not only to make prosperity steady, but to give to the many who earn it a just share of that prosperity instead of helping the few who do not earn it to take an unjust share. The progressive motto is "Pass prosperity around." To make human living easier, to free the hands of honest business, to make trade and commerce sound and steady, to protect womanhood, save childhood and restore the dignity of manhood—these are the tasks we must do.

What, then, is the progressive answer to these questions? We are able to give it specifically and concretely. The first work before us is the revival of honest business. For business is nothing but the industrial and trade activities of all the people. Men grow the products of the field, cut ripe timber from the forest, dig metal from the mine, fashion all for human use, carry them to the market place and exchange them according to their mutual needs—and this is business.

With our vast advantages, contrasted with the vast disadvantages of other nations, American business all the time should be the best and steadiest in the world. But it is not. Germany, with shallow soil, no mines, only a window on the seas and a population more than ten times as dense as ours, yet has a sounder business, a steadier prosperity, a more contented because better cared for people.

What, then, must we do to make American business better? We must do what poorer nations have done. We must end the abuses of business by striking down those abuses instead of striking down business itself. We must try to make little business big and all business honest instead of striving to make big business little and yet letting it remain dishonest.

Present-day business is as unlike old-time business as the old-time ox-cart is unlike the present-day locomotive. Invention has made the whole world over again. The railroad, telegraph, telephone have bound the people of modern nations into families. To do the business of these closely knit millions in every modern country great business concerns came into being. What we call big business is the child of the economic progress of mankind. So warfare to destroy big business is foolish because it can not succeed and wicked because it ought not to succeed. Warfare to destroy big business does not hurt big business, which always comes out on top, so much as it hurts all other business which, in such a warfare, never comes out on top.

With the growth of big business came business evils just as great. It is these evils of big business that hurt the people and injure all other business. One of these wrongs is over capitalization which taxes the people's very living. Another is the manipulation of prices to the unsettlement of all normal business and to the people's damage. Another is interference in the making of the people's laws and the running of the people's government in the unjust interest of evil business. Getting laws that enable particular interests to rob the people, and even to gather criminal riches from human health and life is still another.

An example of such laws is the infamous tobacco legislation of 1902, which authorized the Tobacco Trust to continue to collect from the people the Spanish War tax, amounting to a score of millions of dollars, but to keep that tax instead of turning it over to the government, as it had been doing. Another example is the shameful meat legislation, by which the Beef Trust had the meat it sent abroad inspected by the government so that foreign countries would take its product and yet was permitted to sell diseased meat to our own people. It is incredible that laws like these could ever get on the Nation's statute books. The invisible government put them there; and only the universal wrath of an enraged people corrected them when, after years, the people discovered the outrages.

It is to get just such laws as these and to prevent the passage of laws to correct them, as well as to keep off the statute books general laws which will end the general abuses of big business that these few criminal interests corrupt our politics, invest in public officials and keep in power in both parties that type of politicians and party managers who debase American politics.

Behind rotten laws and preventing sound laws, stands the corrupt boss; behind the corrupt boss stands the robber interest; and commanding these powers of pillage stands bloated human greed. It is this conspiracy of evil we must overthrow if we would get the honest laws we need. It is this invisible government we must destroy if we would save American institutions.

Other nations have ended the very same business evils from which we suffer by clearly defining business wrong-doing and then making it a criminal offense, punishable by imprisonment. Yet these foreign nations encourage big business itself and foster all honest business. But they do not tolerate dishonest business, little or big.

What, then, shall we Americans do? Common sense and the experience of the world says that we ought to keep the good big business does for us and stop the wrongs that big business does to us. Yet we have done just the other thing. We have struck at big business itself and have not even aimed to strike at the evils of big business. Nearly twenty-five years ago Congress passed a law to govern American business in the present time which Parliament passed in the reign of King James to govern English business in that time.

For a quarter of a century the courts have tried to make this law work. Yet during this very time trusts grew greater in number and power than in the whole history of the world before; and their evils flourished unhindered and unchecked. These great business concerns grew because natural laws made them grow and artificial law at war with natural law could not stop their growth. But their evils grew faster than the trusts themselves because avarice nourished those evils and no law of any kind stopped avarice from nourishing them.

Nor is this the worst. Under the shifting interpretation of the Sherman law, uncertainty and fear is chilling the energies of the great body of honest American business men. As the Sherman law now stands, no two business men can arrange their mutual affairs and be sure that they are not law-breakers. This is the main hindrance to the immediate and permanent revival of American business. If German or English business men, with all their disadvantages compared with our advantages, were manacled by our Sherman law, as it stands, they soon would be bankrupt. Indeed, foreign business men declare that, if their countries had such a law, so administered, they could not do business at all.

Even this is not all. By the decrees of our courts, under the Sherman law, the two mightiest trusts on earth have actually been licensed, in the practical outcome, to go on doing every wrong they ever committed. Under the decrees of the courts the Oil and Tobacco Trusts still can raise prices unjustly and already have done so. They still can issue watered stock and surely will do so. They still can throttle other business men and the United Cigar Stores Company now is doing so. They still can corrupt our politics and this moment are indulging in that practice.

The people are tired of this mock battle with criminal capital. They do not want to hurt business, but they do want to get something done about the trust question that amounts to something. What good does it do any man to read in his morning paper that the courts have "dissolved" the Oil Trust, and then read in his evening paper that he must thereafter pay a higher price for his oil than ever before? What good does it do the laborer who smokes his pipe to be told that the courts have "dissolved" the Tobacco Trust and yet find that he must pay the same or a higher price for the same short-weight package of tobacco? Yet all this is the practical result of the suits against these two greatest trusts in the world.

Such business chaos and legal paradoxes as American business suffers from can be found nowhere else in the world. Rival nations do not fasten legal ball and chain upon their business—no, they put wings on its flying feet. Rival nations do not tell their business men that if they go forward with legitimate enterprise the penitentiary may be their goal. No! Rival nations tell their business men that so long as they do honest business their governments will not hinder but will help them.

But these rival nations do tell their business men that if they do any evil that our business men do, prison bars await them. These rival nations do tell their business men that if they issue watered stock or cheat the people in any way, prison cells will be their homes.

Just this is what all honest American business wants; just this is what dishonest American business does not want; just this is what the American people propose to have; just this the national Republican platform of 1908 pledged the people that we would give them; and just this important pledge the administration, elected on that platform, repudiated as it repudiated the more immediate tariff pledge.

Both these reforms, so vital to honest American business, the Progressive party will accomplish. Neither evil interests nor reckless demagogues can swerve us from our purpose; for we are free from both and fear neither.

We mean to put new business laws on our statute books which will tell American business men what they can do and what they cannot do. We mean to make our business laws clear instead of foggy—to make them plainly state just what things are criminal and what are lawful. And we mean that the penalty for things criminal shall be prison sentences that actually punish the real offender, instead of money fines that hurt nobody but the people, who must pay them in the end.

And then we mean to send the message forth to hundreds of thousands of brilliant minds and brave hearts engaged in honest business, that they are not criminals but honorable men in their work to make good business in this Republic. Sure of victory, we even now say, "Go forward, American business men, and know that behind you, supporting you, encouraging you, are the power and approval of the greatest people under the sun. Go forward, American business men, and feed full the fires beneath American furnaces; and give employment to every American laborer who asks for work. Go forward, American business men, and capture the markets of the world for American trade; and know that on the wings of your commerce you carry liberty throughout the world and to every inhabitant thereof. Go forward, American business men, and realize that in the time to come it shall be said of you, as it is said of the hand that rounded Peter's Dome, 'he builded better than he knew.'"

The next great business reform we must have to steadily increase American prosperity is to change the method of building our tariffs. The tariff must be taken out of politics and treated as a business question instead of as a political question. Heretofore, we have done just the other thing. That is why American business is upset every few years by unnecessary tariff upheavals and is weakened by uncertainty in the periods between. The greatest need of business is certainty; but the only thing certain about our tariff is uncertainty.

What, then, shall we do to make our tariff changes strengthen business instead of weakening business? Rival protective tariff nations have answered that question. Common sense has answered it. Next to our need to make the Sherman law modern, understandable and just, our greatest fiscal need is a genuine, permanent, non-partisan tariff commission.

Five years ago, when the fight for this great business measure was begun in the Senate the bosses of both parties were against it. So, when the last revision of the tariff was on and a tariff commission might have been written into the tariff law, the administration would not aid this reform. When two years later the administration supported it weakly, the bi-partisan boss system killed it. There has not been and will not be any sincere and honest effort by the old parties to get a tariff commission. There has not been and will not be any sincere and honest purpose by those parties to take the tariff out of politics.

For the tariff in politics is the excuse for those sham political battles which give the spoilers their opportunity. The tariff in politics is one of the invisible government's methods of wringing tribute from the people. Through the tariff in politics the beneficiaries of tariff excesses are cared for, no matter which party is "revising."

Who has forgotten the tariff scandals that made President Cleveland denounce the Wilson-Gorman bill as "a perfidy and a dishonor?" Who ever can forget the brazen robberies forced into the Payne-Aldrich bill which Mr. Taft defended as "the best ever made?" If everyone else forgets these things the interests that profited by them never will forget them. The bosses and lobbyists that grew rich by putting them through never will forget them. That is why the invisible government and its agents want to keep the old method of tariff building. For, though such tariff "revisions" may make lean years for the people, they make fat years for the powers of pillage and their agents.

So neither of the old parties can honestly carry out any tariff policies which they pledge the people to carry out. But even if they could and even if they were sincere, the old party platforms are in error on tariff policy. The Democratic platform declares for free trade; but free trade is wrong and ruinous. The Republican platform permits extortion; but tariff extortion is robbery by law. The Progressive party is for honest protection; and honest protection is right and a condition of American prosperity.

A tariff high enough to give American producers the American market when they make honest goods and sell them at honest prices but low enough that when they sell dishonest goods at dishonest prices, foreign competition can correct both evils; a tariff high enough to enable American producers to pay our workingmen American wages and so arranged that the workingmen will get such wages; a business tariff whose changes will be so made as to reassure business instead of disturbing it—this is the tariff and the method of its making in which the Progressive party believes, for which it does battle and which it proposes to write into the laws of the land.

The Payne-Aldrich tariff law must be revised immediately in accordance to these principles. At the same time a genuine, permanent, non-partisan tariff commission must be fixed in the law as firmly as the Interstate Commerce Commission. Neither of the old parties can do this work. For neither of the old parties believes in such a tariff; and, what is more serious, special privilege is too thoroughly woven into the fiber of both old parties to allow them to make such a tariff. The Progressive party only is free from these influences. The Progressive party only believes in the sincere enactment of a sound tariff policy. The Progressive party only can change the tariff as it must be changed.

These are samples of the reforms in the laws of business that we intend to put on the Nation's statute books. But there are other questions as important and pressing that we mean to answer by sound and humane laws. Child labor in factories, mills, mines and sweat-shops must be ended throughout the Republic. Such labor is a crime against childhood because it prevents the growth of normal manhood and womanhood. It is a crime against the Nation because it prevents the growth of a host of children into strong, patriotic and intelligent citizens.

Only the Nation can stop this industrial vice. The States cannot stop it. The States never stopped any national wrong—and child labor is a national wrong. To leave it to the State alone is unjust to business; for if some States stop it and other States do not, business men of the former are at a disadvantage with the business men of the latter, because they must sell in the same market goods made by manhood labor at manhood wages in competition with goods made by childhood labor at childhood wages. To leave it to the States is unjust to manhood labor; for childhood labor in any State lowers manhood labor in every State, because the product of childhood labor in any State competes with the product of manhood labor in every State. Children workers at the looms in South Carolina means bayonets at the breasts of men and women workers in Massachusetts who strike for living wages. Let the States do what they can, and more power to their arm; but let the Nation do what it should and cleanse our flag from this stain.

Modern industrialism has changed the status of women. Women now are wage earners in factories, stores and other places of toil. In hours of labor and all the physical conditions of industrial effort they must compete with men. And they must do it at lower wages than men receive—wages which, in most cases, are not enough for these women workers to live on.

This is inhuman and indecent. It is unsocial and uneconomic. It is immoral and unpatriotic. Toward women the Progressive party proclaims the chivalry of the State. We propose to protect women wage-earners by suitable laws, an example of which is the minimum wage for women workers—a wage which shall be high enough to at least buy clothing, food and shelter for the woman toiler.

The care of the aged is one of the most perplexing problems of modern life. How is the workingman with less than five hundred dollars a year, and with earning power waning as his own years advance, to provide for aged parents or other relatives in addition to furnishing food, shelter and clothing for his wife and children? What is to become of the family of the laboring man whose strength has been sapped by excessive toil and who has been thrown upon the industrial scrap heap? It is questions like these we must answer if we are to justify free institutions. They are questions to which the masses of people are chained as to a body of death. And they are questions which other and poorer nations are answering.

We progressives mean that America shall answer them. The Progressive party is the helping hand to those whom a vicious industrialism has maimed and crippled. We are for the conservation of our natural resources; but even more we are for the conservation of human life. Our forests, water power and minerals are valuable and must be saved from the spoilers; but men, women and children are more valuable and they, too, must be saved from the spoilers.

Because women, as much as men, are a part of our economic and social life, women, as much as men, should have the voting power to solve all economic and social problems. Votes for women are theirs as a matter of natural right alone; votes for women should be theirs as a matter of political wisdom also. As wage-earners, they should help to solve the labor problem; as property owners they should help to solve the tax problem; as wives and mothers they should help to solve all the problems that concern the home. And that means all national problems; for the Nation abides at the fireside.

If it is said that women cannot help defend the Nation in time of war and therefore that they should not help to determine the Nation's destinies in time of peace, the answer is that women suffer and serve in time of conflict as much as men who carry muskets. And the deeper answer is that those who bear the Nation's soldiers are as much the Nation's defenders as their sons.

Public spokesmen for the invisible government say that many of our reforms are unconstitutional. The same kind of men said the same thing of every effort the Nation has made to end national abuses. But in every case, whether in the courts, at the ballot box, or on the battlefield, the vitality of the Constitution was vindicated.

The Progressive party believes that the Constitution is a living thing, growing with the people's growth, strengthening with the people's strength, aiding the people in their struggle for life, liberty and the pursuit of happiness, permitting the people to meet all their needs as conditions change. The opposition believes that the Constitution is a dead form, holding back the people's growth, shackling the people's strength but giving a free hand to malign powers that prey upon the people. The first words of the Constitution are "We the people," and they declare that the Constitution's purpose is "to form a perfect Union and to promote the general welfare." To do just that is the very heart of the progressive cause.

The Progressive party asserts anew the vitality of the Constitution. We believe in the true doctrine of states' rights, which forbids the Nation from interfering with states' affairs, and also forbids the states from interfering with national affairs. The combined intelligence and composite conscience of the American people is as irresistible as it is righteous; and the Constitution does not prevent that force from working out the general welfare.

From certain sources we hear preachments about the danger of our reforms to American institutions. What is the purpose of American institutions? Why was this Republic established? What does the flag stand for? What do these things mean?

They mean that the people shall be free to correct human abuses.

They mean that men, women and children shall not be denied the opportunity to grow stronger and nobler.

They mean that the people shall have the power to make our land each day a better place to live in.

They mean the realities of liberty and not the academics of theory.

They mean the actual progress of the race in tangible items of daily living and not the theoretics of barren disputation.

If they do not mean these things they are as sounding brass and tinkling cymbals.

A Nation of strong, upright men and women; a Nation of wholesome homes, realizing the best ideals; a Nation whose power is glorified by its justice and whose justice is the conscience of scores of millions of God-fearing people—that is the Nation the people need and want. And that is the Nation they shall have.

For never doubt that we Americans will make good the real meaning of our institutions. Never doubt that we will solve, in righteousness and wisdom, every vexing problem. Never doubt that in the end, the hand from above that leads us upward will prevail over the hand from below that drags us downward. Never doubt that we are indeed a Nation whose God is the Lord.

And, so, never doubt that a braver, fairer, cleaner America surely will come; that a better and brighter life for all beneath the flag surely will be achieved. Those who now scoff soon will pray. Those who now doubt soon will believe.

Soon the night will pass; and when, to the Sentinel on the ramparts of Liberty the anxious ask: "Watchman, what of the night?" his answer will be "Lo, the morn appeareth."

Knowing the price we must pay, the sacrifice we must make, the burdens we must carry, the assaults we must endure—knowing full well the cost—yet we enlist, and we enlist for the war. For we know the justice of our cause, and we know, too, its certain triumph.

Not reluctantly then, but eagerly, not with faint hearts but strong, do we now advance upon the enemies of the people. For the call that comes to us is the call that came to our fathers. As they responded so shall we.

> "He hath sounded forth a trumpet that shall never call retreat,
> He is sifting out the hearts of men before His judgment seat.
> Oh, be swift our souls to answer Him, be jubilant our feet,
> Our God is marching on."

## Acres of Diamonds[38]

### RUSSELL CONWELL

I am astonished that so many people should care to hear this story over again. Indeed, this lecture has become a study in psychology; it often breaks all rules of oratory, departs from the precepts of rhetoric, and yet remains the most popular of any lecture I have delivered in the forty-four years of my public life. I have sometimes studied for a year upon a lecture and made careful research, and then presented the lecture just once—never delivered it again. I put too much work on it. But this had no work on it—thrown together perfectly at random, spoken offhand without any special preparation, and it succeeds when the thing we study, work over, adjust to a plan, is an entire failure.

The "Acres of Diamonds" which I have mentioned through so many years are to be found in Philadelphia, and you are to find them. Many have found them. And what man has done, man can do. I could not find anything better to illustrate my thought than a story I have told over and over again, and which is now found in books in nearly every library.

In 1870 we went down the Tigris River. We hired a guide at Bagdad to show us Persepolis, Nineveh and Babylon, and the ancient countries of Assyria as far as the Arabian Gulf. He was well acquainted with the land, but he was one of those guides who love to entertain their patrons; he was like a barber that tells you many stories in order to keep your mind off the scratching and the scraping. He told me so many stories that I grew tired of his telling them and I refused to listen—looked away whenever he commenced; that made the guide quite angry. I remember that toward evening he took his Turkish cap off his head and swung it around in the air. The gesture I did not understand and I did not dare look at him for fear I should become the victim of another story. But, although I am not a woman, I did look, and the instant I turned my eyes upon that worthy guide he was off again. Said he, "I will tell you a story now which I reserve for my particular friends!" So then, counting myself a particular friend, I listened, and I have always been glad I did.

---

38 Reported by A. Russell Smith and Harry E. Greager. Used by permission.
On May 21, 1914, when Dr. Conwell delivered this lecture for the five thousandth time, Mr. John Wanamaker said that if the proceeds had been put out at compound interest the sum would aggregate eight millions of dollars. Dr. Conwell has uniformly devoted his lecturing income to works of benevolence.

He said there once lived not far from the River Indus an ancient Persian by the name of Al Hafed. He said that Al Hafed owned a very large farm with orchards, grain fields and gardens. He was a contented and wealthy man—contented because he was wealthy, and wealthy because he was contented. One day there visited this old farmer one of those ancient Buddhist priests, and he sat down by Al Hafed's fire and told that old farmer how this world of ours was made. He said that this world was once a mere bank of fog, which is scientifically true, and he said that the Almighty thrust his finger into the bank of fog and then began slowly to move his finger around and gradually to increase the speed of his finger until at last he whirled that bank of fog into a solid ball of fire, and it went rolling through the universe, burning its way through other cosmic banks of fog, until it condensed the moisture without, and fell in floods of rain upon the heated surface and cooled the outward crust. Then the internal flames burst through the cooling crust and threw up the mountains and made the hills of the valley of this wonderful world of ours. If this internal melted mass burst out and copied very quickly it became granite; that which cooled less quickly became silver; and less quickly, gold; and after gold diamonds were made. Said the old priest, "A diamond is a congealed drop of sunlight."

This is a scientific truth also. You all know that a diamond is pure carbon, actually deposited sunlight—and he said another thing I would not forget: he declared that a diamond is the last and highest of God's mineral creations, as a woman is the last and highest of God's animal creations. I suppose that is the reason why the two have such a liking for each other. And the old priest told Al Hafed that if he had a handful of diamonds he could purchase a whole country, and with a mine of diamonds he could place his children upon thrones through the influence of their great wealth. Al Hafed heard all about diamonds and how much they were worth, and went to his bed that night a poor man—not that he had lost anything, but poor because he was discontented and discontented because he thought he was poor. He said: "I want a mine of diamonds!" So he lay awake all night, and early in the morning sought out the priest. Now I know from experience that a priest when awakened early in the morning is cross. He awoke that priest out of his dreams and said to him, "Will you tell me where I can find diamonds?" The priest said, "Diamonds? What do you want with diamonds?" "I want to be immensely rich," said Al Hafed, "but I don't know where to go." "Well," said the priest, "if you will find a river that runs over white sand between high mountains, in those sands you will always see diamonds." "Do you really believe that there is such a river?" "Plenty of them, plenty of them; all you have to do is just go and find them, then you have them." Al Hafed said, "I will go." So he sold his farm, collected his money at interest, left his family in charge of a neighbor, and away he went in search of diamonds. He began very properly, to my mind, at the Mountains of the Moon. Afterwards he went around into Palestine, then wandered on into Europe, and at last when his money was all spent, and he was in rags, wretchedness and poverty, he stood on the shore of that bay in Barcelona, Spain, when a tidal wave came rolling through the Pillars of Hercules and the poor afflicted, suffering man could not resist the awful temptation to cast himself into that incoming tide, and he sank beneath its foaming crest, never to rise in this life again.

When that old guide had told me that very sad story, he stopped the camel I was riding and went back to fix the baggage on one of the other camels, and I remember thinking to myself, "Why did he reserve that for his *particular friends?*" There seemed to be no beginning, middle or end—nothing to it. That was the first story I ever heard told or read in which the hero was killed in the first chapter. I had but one chapter of that story and the hero was dead. When the guide came back and took up the halter of my camel again, he went right on with the same story. He said that Al Hafed's successor led his camel out into the garden to drink, and as that camel put its nose down into the clear water of the garden brook Al Hafed's successor noticed a curious flash of light from the sands of the shallow stream, and reaching in he pulled out a black stone having an eye of light that reflected all the colors of the rainbow, and he took that curious pebble into the house and left it on the mantel, then went on his way and forgot all about it. A few days after that, this same old priest who told Al Hafed how diamonds were made, came in to visit his successor, when he saw that flash of light from the mantel. He rushed up and said, "Here is a diamond— here is a diamond! Has Al Hafed returned?" "No, no; Al Hafed has not returned and that is not a diamond; that is nothing but a stone; we found it right out here in our garden." "But I know a diamond when I see it," said he; "that is a diamond!"

Then together they rushed to the garden and stirred up the white sands with their fingers and found others more beautiful, more valuable diamonds than the first, and thus, said the guide to me, were discovered the diamond mines of Golconda, the most magnificent diamond mines in all the history of mankind, exceeding the Kimberley in its value. The great Kohinoor diamond in England's crown jewels and the largest crown diamond on earth in Russia's crown jewels, which I had often hoped she would have to sell before they had peace with Japan, came from that mine, and when the old guide had called my attention to that wonderful discovery he took his Turkish cap off his head again and swung it around in the air to call my attention to the moral. Those Arab guides have a moral to each story, though the stories are not always moral. He said, had Al Hafed remained at home and dug in his own cellar or in his own garden, instead of wretchedness, starvation, poverty and death in a strange land, he would have had "acres of diamonds"—for every acre, yes, every shovelful of that old farm afterwards revealed the gems which since have decorated the crowns of monarchs. When he had given the moral to his story, I saw why he had reserved this story for his "particular friends." I didn't tell him I could see it; I was not going to tell that old Arab that I could see it. For it was that mean old Arab's way of going around a thing, like a lawyer, and saying indirectly what he did not dare say directly, that there was a certain young man that day traveling down the Tigris River that might better be at home in America. I didn't tell him I could see it.

I told him his story reminded me of one, and I told it to him quick. I told him about that man out in California, who, in 1847, owned a ranch out there. He read that gold had been discovered in Southern California, and he sold his ranch to Colonel Sutter and started off to hunt for gold. Colonel Sutter put a mill on the little stream in that farm and one day his little girl brought some wet sand from the raceway of the mill into the house and placed it before the fire to dry, and as that sand was falling through the little girl's fingers a visitor saw the first shining scales of real gold that were ever discovered in California; and the man who wanted the gold had sold this ranch and gone away, never to return. I delivered this lecture two years ago in California, in the city that stands near that farm, and they told me that the mine is not exhausted yet, and that a one-third owner of that farm has been getting during these recent years twenty dollars of gold every fifteen minutes of his life, sleeping or waking. Why, you and I would enjoy an income like that!

But the best illustration that I have now of this thought was found here in Pennsylvania. There was a man living in Pennsylvania who owned a farm here and he did what I should do if I had a farm in Pennsylvania—he sold it. But before he sold it he concluded to secure employment collecting coal oil for his cousin in Canada. They first discovered coal oil there. So this farmer in Pennsylvania decided that he would apply for a position with his cousin in Canada. Now, you see, this farmer was not altogether a foolish man. He did not leave his farm until he had something else to do. Of all the simpletons the stars shine on there is none more foolish than a man who leaves one job before he has obtained another. And that has especial reference to gentlemen of my profession, and has no reference to a man seeking a divorce. So I say this old farmer did not leave one job until he had obtained another. He wrote to Canada, but his cousin replied that he could not engage him because he did not know anything about the oil business. "Well, then," said he, "I will understand it." So he set himself at the study of the whole subject. He began at the second day of the creation, he studied the subject from the primitive vegetation to the coal oil stage, until he knew all about it. Then he wrote to his cousin and said, "Now I understand the oil business." And his cousin replied to him, "All right, then, come on."

That man, by the record of the county, sold his farm for eight hundred and thirty-three dollars—even money, "no cents." He had scarcely gone from that farm before the man who purchased it went out to arrange for the watering the cattle and he found that the previous owner had arranged the matter very nicely. There is a stream running down the hillside there, and the previous owner had gone out and put a plank across that stream at an angle, extending across the brook and down edgewise a few inches under the surface of the water. The purpose of the plank across that brook was to throw over to the other bank a dreadful-looking scum through which the cattle would not put their noses to drink above the plank, although they would drink the water on one side below it. Thus that man who had gone to Canada had been himself damming back for twenty-three years a flow of coal oil which the State Geologist of Pennsylvania declared officially, as early as 1870, was then worth to our State a hundred millions of dollars. The city of Titusville now stands on that farm and those Pleasantville wells flow on, and that farmer who had studied all about the formation of oil since the second day of God's creation clear down to the present time, sold that farm for $833, no cents—again I say, "no sense."

But I need another illustration, and I found that in Massachusetts, and I am sorry I did, because that is my old State. This young man I mention went out of the State to study—went down to Yale College and studied Mines and Mining. They paid him fifteen dollars a week during his last year for training students who were behind their classes in mineralogy, out of hours, of course, while pursuing his own studies. But when he graduated they raised his pay from fifteen dollars to forty-five dollars and offered him a professorship. Then he went straight home to his mother and said, "Mother, I won't work for forty-five dollars a week. What is forty-five dollars a week for a man with a brain like mine! Mother, let's go out to California and stake out gold claims and be immensely rich." "Now," said his mother, "it is just as well to be happy as it is to be rich."

But as he was the only son he had his way—they always do; and they sold out in Massachusetts and went to Wisconsin, where he went into the employ of the Superior Copper Mining Company, and he was lost from sight in the employ of that company at fifteen dollars a week again. He was also to have an interest in any mines that he should discover for that company. But I do not believe that he has ever discovered a mine—I do not know anything about it, but I do not believe he has. I know he had scarcely gone from the old homestead before the farmer who had bought the homestead went out to dig potatoes, and as he was bringing them in in a large basket through the front gateway, the ends of the stone wall came so near together at the gate that the basket hugged very tight. So he set the basket on the ground and pulled, first on one side and then on the other side. Our farms in Massachusetts are mostly stone walls, and the farmers have to be economical with their gateways in order to have some place to put the stones. That basket hugged so tight there that as he was hauling it through he noticed in the upper stone next the gate a block of native silver, eight inches square; and this professor of mines and mining and mineralogy, who would not work for forty-five dollars a week, when he sold that homestead in Massachusetts, sat right on that stone to make the bargain. He was brought up there; he had gone back and forth by that piece of silver, rubbed it with his sleeve, and it seemed to say, "Come now, now, now, here is a hundred thousand dollars. Why not take me?" But he would not take it. There was no silver in Newburyport; it was all away off—well, I don't know where; he didn't, but somewhere else—and he was a professor of mineralogy.

I do not know of anything I would enjoy better than to take the whole time to-night telling of blunders like that I have heard professors make. Yet I wish I knew what that man is doing out there in Wisconsin. I can imagine him out there, as he sits by his fireside, and he is saying to his friends, "Do you know that man Conwell that lives in Philadelphia?" "Oh, yes, I have heard of him." "And do you know that man Jones that lives in that city?" "Yes, I have heard of him." And then he begins to laugh and laugh and says to his friends, "They have done the same thing I did, precisely." And that spoils the whole joke, because you and I have done it.

Ninety out of every hundred people here have made that mistake this very day. I say you ought to be rich; you have no right to be poor. To live in Philadelphia and not be rich is a misfortune, and it is doubly a misfortune, because you could have been rich just as well as be poor. Philadelphia furnishes so many opportunities. You ought to be rich. But persons with certain religious prejudice will ask, "How can you spend your time advising the rising generation to give their time to getting money—dollars and cents—the commercial spirit?"

Yet I must say that you ought to spend time getting rich. You and I know there are some things more valuable than money; of course, we do. Ah, yes! By a heart made unspeakably sad by a grave on which the autumn leaves now fall, I know there are some things higher and grander and sublimer than money. Well does the man know, who has suffered, that there are some things sweeter and holier and more sacred than gold. Nevertheless, the man of common sense also knows that there is not any one of those things that is not greatly enhanced by the use of money. Money is power. Love is the grandest thing on God's earth, but fortunate the lover who has plenty of money. Money is power; money has powers; and for a man to say, "I do not want money," is to say, "I do not wish to do any good to my fellowmen." It is absurd thus to talk. It is absurd to disconnect them. This is a wonderfully great life, and you ought to spend your time getting money, because of the power there is in money. And yet this religious prejudice is so great that some people think it is a great honor to be one of God's poor. I am looking in the faces of people who think just that way. I heard a man once say in a prayer meeting that he was thankful that he was one of God's poor, and then I silently wondered what his wife would say to that speech, as she took in washing to support the man while he sat and smoked on the veranda. I don't want to see any more of that land of God's poor. Now, when a man could have been rich just as well, and he is now weak because he is poor, he has done some great wrong; he has been untruthful to himself; he has been unkind to his fellowmen. We ought to get rich if we can by honorable and Christian methods, and these are the only methods that sweep us quickly toward the goal of riches.

I remember, not many years ago a young theological student who came into my office and said to me that he thought it was his duty to come in and "labor with me." I asked him what had happened, and he said: "I feel it is my duty to come in and speak to you, sir, and say that the Holy Scriptures declare that money is the root of all evil." I asked him where he found that saying, and he said he found it in the Bible. I asked him whether he had made a new Bible, and he said, no, he had not gotten a new Bible, that it was in the old Bible. "Well," I said, "if it is in my Bible, I never saw it. Will you please get the text-book and let me see it?" He left the room and soon came stalking in with his Bible open, with all the bigoted pride of the narrow sectarian, who founds his creed on some misinterpretation of Scripture, and he put the Bible down on the table before me and fairly squealed into my ear, "There it is. You can read it for yourself." I said to him, "Young man, you will learn, when you get a little older, that you cannot trust another denomination to read the Bible for you." I said, "Now, you belong to another denomination. Please read it to me, and remember that you are taught in a school where emphasis is exegesis." So he took the Bible and read it: "The *love* of money is the root of all evil." Then he had it right. The Great Book has come back into the esteem and love of the people, and into the respect of the greatest minds of earth, and now you can quote it and rest your life and your death on it without more fear. So, when he quoted right from the Scriptures he quoted the truth. "The love of money is the root of all evil." Oh, that is it. It is the worship of the means instead of the end, though you cannot reach the end without the means. When a man makes an idol of the money instead of the purposes for which it may be used, when he squeezes the dollar until the eagle squeals, then it is made the root of all evil. Think, if you only had the money, what you could do for your wife, your child, and for your home and your city. Think how soon you could endow the Temple College yonder if you only had the money and the disposition to give it; and yet, my friend, people say you and I should not spend the time getting rich. How inconsistent the whole thing is. We ought to be rich, because money has power. I think the best thing for me to do is to illustrate this, for if I say you ought to get rich, I ought, at least, to suggest how it is done. We get a prejudice against rich men because of the lies that are told about them. The lies that are told about Mr. Rockefeller because he has two hundred million dollars—so many believe them; yet how false is the representation of that man to the world. How little we can tell what is true nowadays when newspapers try to sell their papers entirely on some sensation! The way they lie about the rich men is something terrible, and I do not know that there is anything to illustrate this better than what the newspapers now say about the city of Philadelphia. A young man came to me the other day and said, "If Mr. Rockefeller, as you think, is a good man, why is it that everybody says so much against him?" It is because he has gotten ahead of us; that is the whole of it—just gotten ahead of us. Why is it Mr. Carnegie is criticised so sharply by an envious world? Because he has gotten more than we have. If a man knows more than I know, don't I incline to criticise somewhat his learning? Let a man stand in a pulpit and preach to thousands, and if I have fifteen people in my church, and they're all asleep, don't I criticise him? We always do that to the man who gets ahead of us. Why, the man you are criticising has one hundred millions, and you have fifty cents, and both of you have just what you are worth. One of the richest men in this country came into my home and sat down in my parlor and said: "Did you see all those lies about my family in the paper?" "Certainly I did; I knew they were lies when I saw them." "Why do they lie about me the way they do?" "Well," I said to him, "if you will give me your check for one hundred millions, I will take all the lies along with it." "Well," said he, "I don't see any sense in their thus talking about my family and myself. Conwell, tell me frankly, what do you think the American people think of me?" "Well," said I, "they think you are the blackest-hearted villain that ever trod the soil!" "But what can I do about it?" There is nothing he can do about it, and yet he is one of the sweetest Christian men I ever knew. If you get a hundred millions you will have the lies; you will be lied about, and you can judge your success in any line by the lies that are told about you. I say that you ought to be rich. But there are ever coming to me young men who say, "I would like to go into business, but I cannot." "Why not?" "Because I have no capital to begin on." Capital, capital to begin on! What! young man! Living in Philadelphia and looking at this wealthy generation, all of whom began as poor boys, and you want capital to begin on? It is fortunate for you that you have no capital. I am glad you have no money. I pity a rich man's son. A rich man's son in these days of ours occupies a very difficult position. They are to be pitied. A rich man's son cannot know the very best things in human life. He cannot. The statistics of Massachusetts show us that not one out of seventeen rich men's sons ever die rich. They are raised in luxury, they die in poverty. Even if a rich man's son retains his father's money even then he cannot know the best things of life.

A young man in our college yonder asked me to formulate for him what I thought was the happiest hour in a man's history, and I studied it long and came back convinced that the happiest hour that any man ever sees in any earthly matter is when a young man takes his bride over the threshold of the door, for the first time, of the house he himself has earned and built, when he turns to his bride and with an eloquence greater than any language of mine, he sayeth to his wife, "My loved one, I earned this home myself; I earned it all. It is all mine, and I divide it with thee." That is the grandest moment a human heart may ever see. But a rich man's son cannot know that. He goes into a finer mansion, it may be, but he is obliged to go through the house and say, "Mother gave me this, mother gave me that, my mother gave me that, my mother gave me that," until his wife wishes she had married his mother. Oh, I pity a rich man's son. I do. Until he gets so far along in his dudeism that he gets his arms up like that and can't get them down. Didn't you ever see any of them astray at Atlantic City? I saw one of these scarecrows once and I never tire thinking about it. I was at Niagara Falls lecturing, and after the lecture I went to the hotel, and when I went up to the desk there stood there a millionaire's son from New York. He was an indescribable specimen of anthropologic potency. He carried a gold-headed cane under his arm—more in its head than he had in his. I do not believe I could describe the young man if I should try. But still I must say that he wore an eye-glass he could not see through; patent leather shoes he could not walk in, and pants he could not sit down in—dressed like a grasshopper! Well, this human cricket came up to the clerk's desk just as I came in. He adjusted his unseeing eye-glass in this wise and lisped to the clerk, because it's "Hinglish, you know," to lisp: "Thir, thir, will you have the kindness to fuhnish me with thome papah and thome envelopehs!" The clerk measured that man quick, and he pulled out a drawer and took some envelopes and paper and cast them across the counter and turned away to his books. You should have seen that specimen of humanity when the paper and envelopes came across the counter—he whose wants had always been anticipated by servants. He adjusted his unseeing eye-glass and he yelled after that clerk: "Come back here, thir, come right back here. Now, thir, will you order a thervant to take that papah and thothe envelopes and carry them to yondah dethk." Oh, the poor miserable, contemptible American monkey! He couldn't carry paper and envelopes twenty feet. I suppose he could not get his arms down. I have no pity for such travesties of human nature. If you have no capital, I am glad of it. You don't need capital; you need common sense, not copper cents.

A. T. Stewart, the great princely merchant of New York, the richest man in America in his time, was a poor boy; he had a dollar and a half and went into the mercantile business. But he lost eighty-seven and a half cents of his first dollar and a half because he bought some needles and thread and buttons to sell, which people didn't want.

Are you poor? It is because you are not wanted and are left on your own hands. There was the great lesson. Apply it whichever way you will it comes to every single person's life, young or old. He did not know what people needed, and consequently bought something they didn't want and had the goods left on his hands a dead loss. A. T. Stewart learned there the great lesson of his mercantile life and said, "I will never buy anything more until I first learn what the people want; then I'll make the purchase." He went around to the doors and asked them what they did want, and when he found out what they wanted, he invested his sixty-two and a half cents and began to supply "a known demand." I care not what your profession or occupation in life may be; I care not whether you are a lawyer, a doctor, a housekeeper, teacher or whatever else, the principle is precisely the same. We must know what the world needs first and then invest ourselves to supply that need, and success is almost certain. A. T. Stewart went on until he was worth forty millions. "Well," you will say, "a man can do that in New York, but cannot do it here in Philadelphia." The statistics very carefully gathered in New York in 1889 showed one hundred and seven millionaires in the city worth over ten millions apiece. It was remarkable and people think they must go there to get rich. Out of that one hundred and seven millionaires only seven of them made their money in New York, and the others moved to New York after their fortunes were made, and sixty-seven out of the remaining hundred made their fortunes in towns of less than six thousand people, and the richest man in the country at that time lived in a town of thirty-five hundred inhabitants, and always lived there and never moved away. It is not so much where you are as what you are. But at the same time if the largeness of the city comes into the problem, then remember it is the smaller city that furnishes the great opportunity to make the millions of money. The best illustration that I can give is in reference to John Jacob Astor, who was a poor boy and who made all the money of the Astor family. He made more than his successors have ever earned, and yet he once held a mortgage on a millinery store in New York, and because the people could not make enough money to pay the interest and the rent, he foreclosed the mortgage and took possession of the store and went into partnership with the man who had failed. He kept the same stock, did not give them a dollar capital, and he left them alone and went out and sat down upon a bench in the park. Out there on that bench in the park he had the most important, and to my mind, the pleasantest part of that partnership business. He was watching the ladies as they went by; and where is the man that wouldn't get rich at that business? But when John Jacob Astor saw a lady pass, with her shoulders back and her head up, as if she did not care if the whole world looked on her, he studied her bonnet; and before that bonnet was out of sight he knew the shape of the frame and the color of the trimmings, the curl of the—something on a bonnet. Sometimes I try to describe a woman's bonnet, but it is of little use, for it would be out of style to-morrow night. So John Jacob Astor went to the store and said: "Now, put in the show window just such a bonnet as I describe to you because," said he, "I have just seen a lady who likes just such a bonnet. Do not make up any more till I come back." And he went out again and sat on that bench in the park, and another lady of a different form and complexion passed him with a bonnet of different shape and color, of course. "Now," said he, "put such a bonnet as that in the show window." He didn't fill his show window with hats and bonnets which drive people away and then sit in the back of the store and bawl because the people go somewhere else to trade. He didn't put a hat or bonnet in that show window the like of which he had not seen before it was made up.

In our city especially there are great opportunities for manufacturing, and the time has come when the line is drawn very sharply between the stockholders of the factory and their employés. Now, friends, there has also come a discouraging gloom upon this country and the laboring men are beginning to feel that they are being held down by a crust over their heads through which they find it impossible to break, and the aristocratic money-owner himself is so far above that he will never descend to their assistance. That is the thought that is in the minds of our people. But, friends, never in the history of our country was there an opportunity so great for the poor man to get rich as there is now in the city of Philadelphia. The very fact that they get discouraged is what prevents them from getting rich. That is all there is to it. The road is open, and let us keep it open between the poor and the rich. I know that the labor unions have two great problems to contend with, and there is only one way to solve them. The labor unions are doing as much to prevent its solving as are the capitalists to-day, and there are positively two sides to it. The labor union has two difficulties; the first one is that it began to make a labor scale for all classes on a par, and they scale down a man that can earn five dollars a day to two and a half a day, in order to level up to him an imbecile that cannot earn fifty cents a day. That is one of the most dangerous and discouraging things for the working man. He cannot get the results of his work if he do better work or higher work or work longer; that is a dangerous thing, and in order to get every laboring man free and every American equal to every other American, let the laboring man ask what he is worth and get it—not let any capitalist say to him: "You shall work for me for half of what you are worth;" nor let any labor organization say: "You shall work for the capitalist for half your worth." Be a man, be independent, and then shall the laboring man find the road ever open from poverty to wealth. The other difficulty that the labor union has to consider, and this problem they have to solve themselves, is the kind of orators who come and talk to them about the oppressive rich. I can in my dreams recite the oration I have heard again and again under such circumstances. My life has been with the laboring man. I am a laboring man myself. I have often, in their assemblies, heard the speech of the man who has been invited to address the labor union. The man gets up before the assembled company of honest laboring men and he begins by saying: "Oh, ye honest, industrious laboring men, who have furnished all the capital of the world, who have built all the palaces and constructed all the railroads and covered the ocean with her steamships. Oh, you laboring men! You are nothing but slaves; you are ground down in the dust by the capitalist who is gloating over you as he enjoys his beautiful estates and as he has his banks filled with gold, and every dollar he owns is coined out of the hearts' blood of the honest laboring man." Now, that is a lie, and you know it is a lie; and yet that is the kind of speech that they are all the time hearing, representing the capitalists as wicked and the laboring men so enslaved. Why, how wrong it is! Let the man who loves his flag and believes in American principles endeavor with all his soul to bring the capitalist and the laboring man together until they stand side by side, and arm in arm, and work for the common good of humanity.

He is an enemy to his country who sets capital against labor or labor against capital.

Suppose I were to go down through this audience and ask you to introduce me to the great inventors who live here in Philadelphia. "The inventors of Philadelphia," you would say, "Why we don't have any in Philadelphia. It is too slow to invent anything." But you do have just as great inventors, and they are here in this audience, as ever invented a machine.

But the probability is that the greatest inventor to benefit the world with his discovery is some person, perhaps some lady, who thinks she could not invent anything. Did you ever study the history of invention and see how strange it was that the man who made the greatest discovery did it without any previous idea that he was an inventor? Who are the great inventors? They are persons with plain, straightforward common sense, who saw a need in the world and immediately applied themselves to supply that need. If you want to invent anything, don't try to find it in the wheels in your head nor the wheels in your machine, but first find out what the people need, and then apply yourself to that need, and this leads to invention on the part of the people you would not dream of before. The great inventors are simply great men; the greater the man the more simple the man; and the more simple a machine, the more valuable it is. Did you ever know a really great man? His ways are so simple, so common, so plain, that you think any one could do what he is doing. So it is with the great men the world over. If you know a really great man, a neighbor of yours, you can go right up to him and say, "How are you, Jim, good morning, Sam." Of course you can, for they are always so simple.

When I wrote the life of General Garfield, one of his neighbors took me to his back door, and shouted, "Jim, Jim, Jim!" and very soon "Jim" came to the door and General Garfield let me in—one of the grandest men of our century. The great men of the world are ever so. I was down in Virginia and went up to an educational institution and was directed to a man who was setting out a tree. I approached him and said, "Do you think it would be possible for me to see General Robert E. Lee, the President of the University?" He said, "Sir, I am General Lee." Of course, when you meet such a man, so noble a man as that, you will find him a simple, plain man. Greatness is always just so modest and great inventions are simple.

I asked a class in school once who were the great inventors, and a little girl popped up and said, "Columbus." Well, now, she was not so far wrong. Columbus bought a farm and he carried on that farm just as I carried on my father's farm. He took a hoe and went out and sat down on a rock. But Columbus, as he sat upon that shore and looked out upon the ocean, noticed that the ships, as they sailed away, sank deeper into the sea the farther they went. And since that time some other "Spanish ships" have sunk into the sea. But as Columbus noticed that the tops of the masts dropped down out of sight, he said: "That is the way it is with this hoe handle; if you go around this hoe handle, the farther off you go the farther down you go. I can sail around to the East Indies." How plain it all was. How simple the mind—majestic like the simplicity of a mountain in its greatness. Who are the great inventors? They are ever the simple, plain, everyday people who see the need and set about to supply it.

I was once lecturing in North Carolina, and the cashier of the bank sat directly behind a lady who wore a very large hat. I said to that audience, "Your wealth is too near to you; you are looking right over it." He whispered to his friend, "Well, then, my wealth is in that hat." A little later, as he wrote me, I said, "Wherever there is a human need there is a greater fortune than a mine can furnish." He caught my thought, and he drew up his plan for a better hat pin than was in the hat before him, and the pin is now being manufactured.

He was offered fifty-five thousand dollars for his patent. That man made his fortune before he got out of that hall. This is the whole question: Do you see a need?

I remember well a man up in my native hills, a poor man, who for twenty years was helped by the town in his poverty, who owned a wide-spreading maple tree that covered the poor man's cottage like a benediction from on high. I remember that tree, for in the spring—there were some roguish boys around that neighborhood when I was young—in the spring of the year the man would put a bucket there and the spouts to catch the maple sap, and I remember where that bucket was; and when I was young the boys were, oh, so mean, that they went to that tree before that man had gotten out of bed in the morning, and after he had gone to bed at night, and drank up that sweet sap. I could swear they did it. He didn't make a great deal of maple sugar from that tree. But one day he made the sugar so white and crystalline that the visitor did not believe it was maple sugar; thought maple sugar must be red or black. He said to the old man: "Why don't you make it that way and sell it for confectionery?" The old man caught his thought and invented the "rock maple crystal," and before that patent expired he had ninety thousand dollars and had built a beautiful palace on the site of that tree. After forty years owning that tree he awoke to find it had fortunes of money indeed in it. And many of us are right by the tree that has a fortune for us, and we own it, possess it, do what we will with it, but we do not learn its value because we do not see the human need, and in these discoveries and inventions this is one of the most romantic things of life.

I have received letters from all over the country and from England, where I have lectured, saying that they have discovered this and that, and one man out in Ohio took me through his great factories last spring, and said that they cost him $680,000, and said he, "I was not worth a cent in the world when I heard your lecture 'Acres of Diamonds;' but I made up my mind to stop right here and make my fortune here, and here it is." He showed me through his unmortgaged possessions. And this is a continual experience now as I travel through the country, after these many years. I mention this incident, not to boast, but to show you that you can do the same if you will.

Who are the great inventors? I remember a good illustration in a man who used to live in East Brookfield, Mass. He was a shoemaker, and he was out of work, and he sat around the house until his wife told him to "go out doors." And he did what every husband is compelled by law to do—he obeyed his wife. And he went out and sat down on an ash barrel in his back yard. Think of it! Stranded on an ash barrel and the enemy in possession of the house! As he sat on that ash barrel, he looked down into that little brook which ran through that back yard into the meadows, and he saw a little trout go flashing up the stream and hiding under the bank. I do not suppose he thought of Tennyson's beautiful poem:

> "Chatter, chatter, as I flow,
>     To join the brimming river,
> Men may come, and men may go,
>     But I go on forever."

But as this man looked into the brook, he leaped off that ash barrel and managed to catch the trout with his fingers, and sent it to Worcester. They wrote back that they would give him a five dollar bill for another such trout as that, not that it was worth that much, but they wished to help the poor man. So this shoemaker and his wife, now perfectly united, that five dollar bill in prospect, went out to get another trout. They went up the stream to its source and down to the brimming river, but not another trout could they find in the whole stream; and so they came home disconsolate and went to the minister. The minister didn't know how trout grew, but he pointed the way. Said he, "Get Seth Green's book, and that will give you the information you want." They did so, and found all about the culture of trout. They found that a trout lays thirty-six hundred eggs every year and every trout gains a quarter of a pound every year, so that in four years a little trout will furnish four tons per annum to sell to the market at fifty cents a pound. When they found that, they said they didn't believe any such story as that, but if they could get five dollars apiece they could make something. And right in that same back yard with the coal sifter up stream and window screen down the stream, they began the culture of trout. They afterwards moved to the Hudson, and since then he has become the authority in the United States upon the raising of fish, and he has been next to the highest on the United States Fish Commission in Washington. My lesson is that man's wealth was out there in his back yard for twenty years, but he didn't see it until his wife drove him out with a mop stick.

I remember meeting personally a poor carpenter of Hingham, Massachusetts, who was out of work and in poverty. His wife also drove him out of doors. He sat down on the shore and whittled a soaked shingle into a wooden chain. His children quarreled over it in the evening, and while he was whittling a second one, a neighbor came along and said, "Why don't you whittle toys if you can carve like that?" He said, "I don't know what to make!" There is the whole thing. His neighbor said to him: "Why don't you ask your own children?" Said he, "What is the use of doing that? My children are different from other people's children." I used to see people like that when I taught school. The next morning when his boy came down the stairway, he said, "Sam, what do you want for a toy?" "I want a wheelbarrow." When his little girl came down, he asked her what she wanted, and she said, "I want a little doll's washstand, a little doll's carriage, a little doll's umbrella," and went on with a whole lot of things that would have taken his lifetime to supply. He consulted his own children right there in his own house and began to whittle out toys to please them. He began with his jack-knife, and made those unpainted Hingham toys. He is the richest man in the entire New England States, if Mr. Lawson is to be trusted in his statement concerning such things, and yet that man's fortune was made by consulting his own children in his own house. You don't need to go out of your own house to find out what to invent or what to make. I always talk too long on this subject.

I would like to meet the great men who are here to-night. The great men! We don't have any great men in Philadelphia. Great men! You say that they all come from London, or San Francisco, or Rome, or Manayunk, or anywhere else but here—anywhere else but Philadelphia—and yet, in fact, there are just as great men in Philadelphia as in any city of its size. There are great men and women in this audience. Great men, I have said, are very simple men. Just as many great men here as are to be found anywhere. The greatest error in judging great men is that we think that they always hold an office. The world knows nothing of its greatest men. Who are the great men of the world? The young man and young woman may well ask the question. It is not necessary that they should hold an office, and yet that is the popular idea. That is the idea we teach now in our high schools and common schools, that the great men of the world are those who hold some high office, and unless we change that very soon and do away with that prejudice, we are going to change to an empire. There is no question about it. We must teach that men are great only on their intrinsic value, and not on the position that they may incidentally happen to occupy. And yet, don't blame the young men saying that they are going to be great when they get into some official position. I ask this audience again who of you are going to be great? Says a young man: "I am going to be great." "When are you going to be great?" "When I am elected to some political office." Won't you learn the lesson, young man; that it is *prima facie* evidence of littleness to hold public office under our form of government? Think of it. This is a government of the people, and by the people, and for the people, and not for the office-holder, and if the people in this country rule as they always should rule, an office-holder is only the servant of the people, and the Bible says that "the servant cannot be greater than his master." The Bible says that "he that is sent cannot be greater than him who sent him." In this country the people are the masters, and the office-holders can never be greater than the people; they should be honest servants of the people, but they are not our greatest men. Young man, remember that you never heard of a great man holding any political office in this country unless he took that office at an expense to himself. It is a loss to every great man to take a public office in our country. Bear this in mind, young man, that you cannot be made great by a political election.

Another young man says, "I am going to be a great man in Philadelphia some time." "Is that so? When are you going to be great?" "When there comes another war! When we get into difficulty with Mexico, or England, or Russia, or Japan, or with Spain again over Cuba, or with New Jersey, I will march up to the cannon's mouth, and amid the glistening bayonets I will tear down their flag from its staff, and I will come home with stars on my shoulders, and hold every office in the gift of the government, and I will be great." "No, you won't! No, you won't; that is no evidence of true greatness, young man." But don't blame that young man for thinking that way; that is the way he is taught in the high school. That is the way history is taught in college. He is taught that the men who held the office did all the fighting.

I remember we had a Peace Jubilee here in Philadelphia soon after the Spanish war. Perhaps some of these visitors think we should not have had it until now in Philadelphia, and as the great procession was going up Broad street I was told that the tally-ho coach stopped right in front of my house, and on the coach was Hobson, and all the people threw up their hats and swung their handkerchiefs, and shouted "Hurrah for Hobson!" I would have yelled too, because he deserves much more of his country than he has ever received. But suppose I go into the High School to-morrow and ask, "Boys, who sunk the Merrimac?" If they answer me "Hobson," they tell me seven-eighths of a lie—seven-eighths of a lie, because there were eight men who sunk the Merrimac. The other seven men, by virtue of their position, were continually exposed to the Spanish fire, while Hobson, as an officer, might reasonably be behind the smoke-stack. Why, my friends, in this intelligent audience gathered here to-night I do not believe I could find a single person that can name the other seven men who were with Hobson. Why do we teach history in that way? We ought to teach that however humble the station a man may occupy, if he does his full duty in his place, he is just as much entitled to the American people's honor as is a king upon a throne. We do teach it as a mother did her little boy in New York when he said, "Mamma, what great building is that?" "That is General Grant's tomb." "Who was General Grant?" "He was the man who put down the rebellion." Is that the way to teach history?

Do you think we would have gained a victory if it had depended on General Grant alone? Oh, no. Then why is there a tomb on the Hudson at all? Why, not simply because General Grant was personally a great man himself, but that tomb is there because he was a representative man and represented two hundred thousand men who went down to death for their nation and many of them as great as General Grant. That is why that beautiful tomb stands on the heights over the Hudson.

I remember an incident that will illustrate this, the only one that I can give to-night. I am ashamed of it, but I don't dare leave it out. I close my eyes now; I look back through the years to 1863; I can see my native town in the Berkshire Hills, I can see that cattle-show ground filled with people; I can see the church there and the town hall crowded, and hear bands playing, and see flags flying and handkerchiefs streaming—well do I recall at this moment that day. The people had turned out to receive a company of soldiers, and that company came marching up on the Common. They had served out one term in the Civil War and had reënlisted, and they were being received by their native townsmen. I was but a boy, but I was captain of that company, puffed out with pride on that day—why, a cambric needle would have burst me all to pieces. As I marched on the Common at the head of my company, there was not a man more proud than I. We marched into the town hall and then they seated my soldiers down in the center of the house and I took my place down on the front seat, and then the town officers filed through the great throng of people, who stood close and packed in that little hall. They came up on the platform, formed a half circle around it, and the mayor of the town, the "chairman of the Selectmen" in New England, took his seat in the middle of that half circle. He was an old man, his hair was gray; he never held an office before in his life. He thought that an office was all he needed to be a truly great man, and when he came up he adjusted his powerful spectacles and glanced calmly around the audience with amazing dignity. Suddenly his eyes fell upon me, and then the good old man came right forward and invited me to come up on the stand with the town officers. Invited me up on the stand! No town officer ever took notice of me before I went to war. Now, I should not say that. One town officer was there who advised the teacher to "whale" me, but I mean no "honorable mention." So I was invited up on the stand with the town officers. I took my seat and let my sword fall on the floor, and folded my arms across my breast and waited to be received. Napoleon the Fifth! Pride goeth before destruction and a fall. When I had gotten my seat and all became silent through the hall, the chairman of the Selectmen arose and came forward with great dignity to the table, and we all supposed he would introduce the Congregational minister, who was the only orator in the town, and who would give the oration to the returning soldiers. But, friends, you should have seen the surprise that ran over that audience when they discovered that this old farmer was going to deliver that oration himself. He had never made a speech in his life before, but he fell into the same error that others have fallen into, he seemed to think that the office would make him an orator. So he had written out a speech and walked up and down the pasture until he had learned it by heart and frightened the cattle, and he brought that manuscript with him, and taking it from his pocket, he spread it carefully upon the table. Then he adjusted his spectacles to be sure that he might see it, and walked far back on the platform and then stepped forward like this. He must have studied the subject much, for he assumed an elocutionary attitude; he rested heavily upon his left heel, slightly advanced the right foot, threw back his shoulders, opened the organs of speech, and advanced his right hand at an angle of forty-five. As he stood in that elocutionary attitude this is just the way that speech went, this is it precisely. Some of my friends have asked me if I do not exaggerate it, but I could not exaggerate it. Impossible! This is the way it went; although I am not here for the story but the lesson that is back of it:

"Fellow citizens." As soon as he heard his voice, his hand began to shake like that, his knees began to tremble, and then he shook all over. He coughed and choked and finally came around to look at his manuscript. Then he began again: "Fellow citizens: We—are—we are—we are—we are—We are very happy—we are very happy—we are very happy—to welcome back to their native town these soldiers who have fought and bled—and come back again to their native town. We are especially—we are especially—we are especially—we are especially pleased to see with us to-day this young hero (that meant me)—this young hero who in imagination (friends, remember, he said "imagination," for if he had not said that, I would not be egotistical enough to refer to it)—this young hero who, in imagination, we have seen leading his troops—leading—we have seen leading—we have seen leading his troops on to the deadly breach. We have seen his shining—his shining—we have seen his shining—we have seen his shining—his shining sword—flashing in the sunlight as he shouted to his troops, 'Come on!'"

Oh, dear, dear, dear, dear! How little that good, old man knew about war. If he had known anything about war, he ought to have known what any soldier in this audience knows is true, that it is next to a crime for an officer of infantry ever in time of danger to go ahead of his men. I, with my shining sword flashing in the sunlight, shouting to my troops: "Come on." I never did it. Do you suppose I would go ahead of my men to be shot in the front by the enemy and in the back by my own men? That is no place for an officer. The place for the officer is behind the private soldier in actual fighting. How often, as a staff officer, I rode down the line when the Rebel cry and yell was coming out of the woods, sweeping along over the fields, and shouted, "Officers to the rear! Officers to the rear!" and then every officer goes behind the line of battle, and the higher the officer's rank, the farther behind he goes. Not because he is any the less brave, but because the laws of war require that to be done. If the general came up on the front line and were killed you would lose your battle anyhow, because he has the plan of the battle in his brain, and must be kept in comparative safety. I, with my "shining sword flashing in the sunlight." Ah! There sat in the hall that day men who had given that boy their last hard-tack, who had carried him on their backs through deep rivers. But some were not there; they had gone down to death for their country. The speaker mentioned them, but they were but little noticed, and yet they had gone down to death for their country, gone down for a cause they believed was right and still believe was right, though I grant to the other side the same that I ask for myself. Yet these men who had actually died for their country were little noticed, and the hero of the hour was this boy. Why was he the hero? Simply because that man fell into that same foolishness. This boy was an officer, and those were only private soldiers. I learned a lesson that I will never forget. Greatness consists not in holding some office; greatness really consists in doing some great deed with little means, in the accomplishment of vast purposes from the private ranks of life; that is true greatness. He who can give to this people better streets, better homes, better schools, better churches, more religion, more of happiness, more of God, he that can be a blessing to the community in which he lives to-night will be great anywhere, but he who cannot be a blessing where he now lives will never be great anywhere on the face of God's earth. "We live in deeds, not years, in feeling, not in figures on a dial; in thoughts, not breaths; we should count time by heart throbs, in the cause of right." Bailey says: "He most lives who thinks most."

If you forget everything I have said to you, do not forget this, because it contains more in two lines than all I have said. Bailey says: "He most lives who thinks most, who feels the noblest, and who acts the best."

# Honoré de Balzac

VICTOR HUGO

—*Delivered at the Funeral of Balzac, August 20, 1850.*

Gentlemen: The man who now goes down into this tomb is one of those to whom public grief pays homage.

In one day all fictions have vanished. The eye is fixed not only on the heads that reign, but on heads that think, and the whole country is moved when one of those heads disappears. To-day we have a people in black because of the death of the man of talent; a nation in mourning for a man of genius.

Gentlemen, the name of Balzac will be mingled in the luminous trace our epoch will leave across the future.

Balzac was one of that powerful generation of writers of the nineteenth century who came after Napoleon, as the illustrious Pleiad of the seventeenth century came after Richelieu,—as if in the development of civilization there were a law which gives conquerors by the intellect as successors to conquerors by the sword.

Balzac was one of the first among the greatest, one of the highest among the best. This is not the place to tell all that constituted this splendid and sovereign intelligence. All his books form but one book,—a book living, luminous, profound, where one sees coming and going and marching and moving, with I know not what of the formidable and terrible, mixed with the real, all our contemporary civilization;—a marvelous book which the poet entitled "a comedy" and which he could have called history; which takes all forms and all style, which surpasses Tacitus and Suetonius; which traverses Beaumarchais and reaches Rabelais;—a book which realizes observation and imagination, which lavishes the true, the esoteric, the commonplace, the trivial, the material, and which at times through all realities, swiftly and grandly rent away, allows us all at once a glimpse of a most sombre and tragic ideal. Unknown to himself, whether he wished it or not, whether he consented or not, the author of this immense and strange work is one of the strong race of Revolutionist writers. Balzac goes straight to the goal.

Body to body he seizes modern society; from all he wrests something, from these an illusion, from those a hope; from one a catch-word, from another a mask. He ransacked vice, he dissected passion. He searched out and sounded man, soul, heart, entrails, brain,—the abyss that each one has within himself. And by grace of his free and vigorous nature; by a privilege of the intellect of our time, which, having seen revolutions face to face, can see more clearly the destiny of humanity and comprehend Providence better,— Balzac redeemed himself smiling and severe from those formidable studies which produced melancholy in Moliere and misanthropy in Rousseau.

This is what he has accomplished among us, this is the work which he has left us,—a work lofty and solid,—a monument robustly piled in layers of granite, from the height of which hereafter his renown shall shine in splendor. Great men make their own pedestal, the future will be answerable for the statue.

His death stupefied Paris! Only a few months ago he had come back to France. Feeling that he was dying, he wished to see his country again, as one who would embrace his mother on the eve of a distant voyage. His life was short, but full, more filled with deeds than days.

Alas! this powerful worker, never fatigued, this philosopher, this thinker, this poet, this genius, has lived among us that life of storm, of strife, of quarrels and combats, common in all times to all great men. To-day he is at peace. He escapes contention and hatred. On the same day he enters into glory and the tomb. Thereafter beyond the clouds, which are above our heads, he will shine among the stars of his country. All you who are here, are you not tempted to envy him?

Whatever may be our grief in presence of such a loss, let us accept these catastrophes with resignation! Let us accept in it whatever is distressing and severe; it is good perhaps, it is necessary perhaps, in an epoch like ours, that from time to time the great dead shall communicate to spirits devoured with skepticism and doubt, a religious fervor. Providence knows what it does when it puts the people face to face with the supreme mystery and when it gives them death to reflect on,—death which is supreme equality, as it is also supreme liberty. Providence knows what it does, since it is the greatest of all instructors.

There can be but austere and serious thoughts in all hearts when a sublime spirit makes its majestic entrance into another life, when one of those beings who have long soared above the crowd on the visible wings of genius, spreading all at once other wings which we did not see, plunges swiftly into the unknown.

No, it is not the unknown; no, I have said it on another sad occasion and I shall repeat it to-day, it is not night, it is light. It is not the end, it is the beginning! It is not extinction, it is eternity! Is it not true, my hearers, such tombs as this demonstrate immortality? In presence of the illustrious dead, we feel more distinctly the divine destiny of that intelligence which traverses the earth to suffer and to purify itself,—which we call man.